Disruptive Security Technologies with Mobile Code and Peer-to-Peer Networks

Disruptive Security Technologies with Mobile Code and Peer-to-Peer Networks

R. R. Brooks

CRC PRESS

Boca Raton   London   New York   Washington, D.C.

Library of Congress Cataloging-in-Publication Data

Brooks, R. R. (Richard R.)
  Disruptive security technologies with mobile code and peer-to-peer networks / Richard R. Brooks.
    p. cm.
  Includes bibliographical references and index.
  ISBN 0-8493-2272-3 (alk. paper)
  1. Peer-to-peer architecture (Computer networks) 2. Computer networks—Security
measures. 3. Computer viruses. I. Title.

QC611.92.F65 2004
537.6'23--dc22   2004057902

Visit the CRC Press Web site at www.crcpress.com

© 2005 by CRC Press

No claim to original U.S. Government works
International Standard Book Number 0-8493-2272-3
Library of Congress Card Number 2004057902

Dedication

Dedicated to my wife Birgit for her patience and perseverance,

and to all the colleagues who helped in performing the research presented here,

especially Dr. Shashi Phoha and Christopher Griffin

Preface

This book presents results from a Critical Infrastructure Protection University Research Initiative (CIP/URI) basic research project managed by the Office of Naval Research (ONR). The Mobile Ubiquitous Security Environment (MUSE) project was one of several tasked with "understanding mobile code." Mobile code is easily defined as programs that execute on computers other than the ones where they are stored. Once computer connections to the Internet became commonplace, it was natural for mobile code to exist. These programs are only now fully utilizing their networked environment. Probably the most widely recognized (but not necessarily most widely used) instances of mobile code are Java Applets and Mobile Agents. Mobile code was labeled a security risk and understanding the nature of the threat became important.

Mobile code has been labeled as a "disruptive technology." Another disruptive technology is peer-to-peer networking. Both are described in detail in this book. Technologies are considered disruptive when they radically change the way systems are used, disrupting traditional approaches. Revolutionary is a possible synonym for disruptive in this context. There are many similarities between the effect of disruptive technologies on distributed systems and the impact of the Revolution in Military Affairs (RMA) on the defense establishment.

Those familiar with military history are likely to agree that technologies are rarely purely offensive or purely defensive. For example, the "nuclear umbrella" during the cold war was a successful defense policy built using an obviously offensive technology. In the MUSE project, we explore both defensive and offensive aspects of mobile code. I hope that by the end of this book the reader will agree that mobile code and other "disruptive technologies" are not purely a threat. These tools can be abused, but they can also create systems that are more secure than previous approaches.

To the best of my knowledge, unless stated otherwise, the approaches presented in this book are new. The contents of the book are results from collaboration with professors in industrial engineering, computer science, and electrical engineering. This book should be useful at many levels:

- As a research monograph, it presents recent research results in information assurance aspects of mobile code.
- For system implementers, it presents detailed and theoretically sound design guidelines for mobile code and peer-to-peer systems.

- It is appropriate for a graduate advanced-topics course, or an upper-division undergraduate course. The contents presented in this book have been used in a critical infrastructure protection course cross-listed between the Industrial and Manufacturing Engineering and Computer Science and Engineering Departments of the Penn State College of Engineering.
- It will be accessible to readers interested in computer security and new technologies.

This book is self-contained. We assume the reader is technically literate, with the equivalent of two years undergraduate work in computer science or engineering. Knowledge of computer programming, the Internet Protocols, graph theory, probability, statistics, and linear algebra is advisable. Every attempt is made to reference tutorials on challenging subject matter when appropriate. This is done in an attempt to present a text that flows properly for a large set of readers with differing technical backgrounds and needs.

Some of the expertise used in this project originates in the National Information Infrastructure (NII) program of Dr. Phoha. Some of the work is the result of collaborations with Drs. Vijaykrishnan Narayanan and Mahmut Kandemir in the Penn State Computer Science and Engineering Department, as well as Dr. Gautam in the Penn State Industrial and Manufacturing Engineering Department. Outside of Penn State, collaborations with Dr. Suresh Rai of Louisiana State University and Dr. Satish Bukkapatnam of Oklahoma State University deserve mention. The expertise of Christopher Griffin, Eric Grele, John Koch, Art Jones, and Dr. John Zachary has contributed greatly to this work. I also had the privilege of supervising the following students in the course of this program: Jason Schwier, Jamila Moore, Nathan Orr, Eric Swankoski, Glenn Carl, Amit Kapur, Matthew Piretti, Thomas Keiser, Devaki Shah, Mengxia Zhu, Michael Young, and Margaret Aichele. Other students contributing to this work include Saputra Hendra and Greg Link. I will attempt to indicate special contributions of individuals in individual chapters as appropriate.

Special thanks to Karen Heichel for the cover art.

Dr. Bennet Yee and Dr. Michael Franz were principal investigators of other CIP/URI projects tasked with understanding mobile code. They both have greatly advanced the state of the art in this area. I benefited from intellectual exchanges with them. At different times, Mr. Frank Deckelman and Dr. Ralph Wachter of the Office of Naval Research were program managers for this effort. Their support and encouragement is gratefully acknowledged.

ACKNOWLEDGEMENT AND DISCLAIMER

This material is based on work supported by the Office of Naval Research under Award No. N00014-01-1-0859. Any opinions, findings, and conclusions or recommendations expressed in this presentation are those of the author and do not necessarily reflect the views of the Office of Naval Research.

Table of Contents

CHAPTER 1
Overview

The Internet is a complex entity composed of multiple interacting components with minimal, if any, centralized coordination. It is a constantly evolving system. New technologies are introduced, accepted, and become ubiquitous at an astounding pace. Some new technologies have been labeled "disruptive" because of their enormous impact on the Internet. I propose that some "disruption" could improve network security.

The vulnerability to attack of both individual nodes and the Internet as a whole is increasingly obvious. Viruses and worms are common. Old viruses are eradicated slowly, and worms are becoming increasingly disruptive. The parallels between computer virus infections and communicable diseases are well documented [Barabasi 2002]. Biological viruses mutate in response to the drugs taken to counteract them. This makes many antibiotics ineffective over time. Similarly, computer viruses are difficult to eradicate, since they are edited, modified, and reintroduced to the network by hackers on a regular basis. An example of this is the Klez virus, which remained one of the most virulent viruses for over a year. This is primarily due to new variants arising. Variants are difficult for virus scanners to detect. New virus signatures need to be distributed retroactively for each new variant.

In this context, the new "disruptive" technologies of mobile code and peer-to-peer networks have been seen primarily as a major security threat. After all, viruses and worms are mobile code implementations *par excellence*. Peer-to-peer systems have enabled uncontrolled sharing of resources that may surreptitiously provide back doors to thousands, if not millions, of computers. Disruptive technologies are frequently seen as threats, and reactions include banning them entirely from systems.

The research presented in this book has another viewpoint. The network environment has changed. Protecting systems against attacks, like Distributed Denial of Service (DDoS) attacks, by increasing the defenses of individual nodes, is tantamount to building a better Maginot line after World War II. The fortress mentality of current approaches is outdated. As with modern warfare, the environment has changed. From this viewpoint, mobile code, peer-to-peer networks, and other adaptive technologies are tools that may put system builders on an equal footing with attackers.

This book presents initial steps towards creating secure systems that overcome attacks through adaptation. Disruptive technologies are works in progress. Design principles for, and a fundamental understanding of, disruptive technologies are lacking in the current literature. Chapters in this book provide a model explaining mobile code [Brooks 2002] and methods for designing robust peer-to-peer networks [Kapur 2002]. Methods are provided for implementing adaptive systems designed to tolerate many current attacks.

The first three chapters provide background on computer security. Major threats and currently available security tools are discussed in detail. For didactic reasons, they are handled in separate chapters. Particular attention will be paid to issues that are research topics, such as security automata for expressing security policies. This book considers dependability and quality of service as part of systems security. The increasing prevalence of Denial of Service (DoS) attacks illustrates the impact of dependability and quality of service on system security.

Chapters 4 and 5 describe recent advances in technology. Chapter 4 introduces disruptive technologies by describing mobile code, peer-to-peer networks, and complex adaptive systems; basic concepts and current implementations are described. I explain how they are "disruptive" in that they radically change how networks can be used. Chapter 5 provides an overview of the current understanding of networks. In addition to dealing with the Internet, it discusses networks of embedded systems. The topology of the Internet is explained in-depth, as well as the implications its topology has on dependability and virus propagation. Similarly, results from empirical studies of Internet traffic flows are given. Of particular importance is the multifractal model of network flow, which explains the observed self-similarity of Internet traffic at many scales. The chapter also hints at the tools needed to detect suspect behaviors in networks.

Chapters 6 through 13 provide results from our Information Assurance research programs. Chapter 6 gives the model for mobile code paradigms introduced in [Brooks 2002, Brooks 2002a]. Paradigms are described as interacting automata, and a system for simulating paradigms is described. The model describes both existing mobile code paradigms and possible future mobile code implementations. Paradigms include remote procedure calls, code on demand (Java), remote evaluation (CORBA), mobile agents, worms, and viruses. Empirical results of studies using the simulator are given [Griffin 2003, Orr 2002]. These results include example mobile code migration profiles. The profiles indicate network flow bottlenecks inherent in some mobile code paradigms. We also describe a mobile code daemon we have implemented that can emulate existing paradigms, and other new paradigms [Moore 2003, Brooks 2000, Keiser 2003].

The issue of protecting mobile code from a malicious host is introduced in Chapter 7. Code obfuscation techniques are described in detail. This includes inserting variables and modifying the control flow. A new technique uses information theoretic concepts to measure the quality of code obfuscation [Saputra 2003a]. Another technique uses smart cards to verify that a host has not been corrupted [Zachary 2003].

Chapter 8 considers constructing secure computing platforms for mobile code by integrating compiler and hardware design. Power analysis attacks of smart cards and embedded hardware are discussed as an example problem. The method in [Saputra 2002, Saputra 2003b] is discussed in detail. This work integrates compiler and hardware design to protect variables. Variables are tagged with security levels in the source code. The compiler associates a different set of hardware instructions to sensitive variables. The secure hardware instructions in our current implementation mask resource consumption. We show how this has been used to prevent the inference of keys used for Data Encryption Standard (DES) encryption.

Chapter 9 shows how to maintain trust between mobile code and the host executing it in a distributed system [Zachary 2003]. This involves using a minimal trusted computing base, which could be a smartcard or a secure coprocessor. This chapter integrates cryptographic primitives into protocols that allow each entity in the process to verify the trustworthy nature of the other participants. To make this tractable, the approach starts from a given known state that is assumed to be trustworthy.

One advantage of the daemon described in Chapter 6 is that it shares mobile code in a peer-to-peer framework. Chapter 10 takes this concept one step further. Peer-to-peer systems are analyzed as random graph structures [Kapur 2002]. This is appropriate; as the lack of central control makes them act like nondeterministic systems. Use of randomization allows us to study the global behavior of the system using a statistical description of individual participants. This chapter contains a number of new results. Methods for estimating system connectivity, dependability, and quality of service are described in detail [Kapur 2002, Kapur 2003, Brooks 2003, Brooks 2003b, Brooks 2003c]. This allows us to create distributed systems containing stochastic components. System statistics define the global behavior of the system. Attacks on individual elements will not be able to appreciably modify these global attributes of the system. The combination of mobile code and peer-to-peer networks [Keiser 2003] is then explored as the basis for constructing resilient critical infrastructure.

Chapter 11 describes distributed adaptation techniques based on complex adaptive system research [Brooks 2000a, Brooks 2003a, Brooks 2003d, Brooks 2003e]. It starts by providing background on *ad hoc* routing in wireless networks. The new techniques are novel in that logic controlling them contains a significant random component. Empirical results are given, showing the ability of these techniques to overcome internal inconsistencies and external attacks. A detailed analysis of the resources these techniques require is given in the context of an application involving adaptation to malicious attacks in a wireless urban battlefield environment.

Chapter 12 is a detailed study of DoS attacks. Techniques for quickly detecting attacks by monitoring network flow are given [He 2002]. We also explain how these techniques have been validated using simulations, online laboratory tests of DoS attacks, logs of attacks, and online monitoring of Internet traffic [Young 2003]. We finish the chapter by showing how to use combinatorial game theory to find DoS vulnerabilities in networks. Vulnerabilities are essentially bottlenecks in the system structure. This allows network structures to be modified to make attacks more difficult. In addition to this, once DoS attacks are detected, the system overcomes them by adapting and reconfiguring itself.

Chapter 13 concludes the discussion of our disruptive security research by explaining how "disruptive" technologies provide exciting tools for designing secure systems. While disruptive technologies provide significant challenges for network security, they may also have benefits for system implementers.

The book is most effective when read and executed sequentially. Alternatively, it is possible to group it into the following functional groups:

- *Security issues:* Chapters 2 and 3
- *Understanding distributed systems:* Chapters 4, 5, and 6
- *Security implementations:* Chapters 7, 8, 9, 10, 11, 12, 13, and 14.

The first two functional groups are necessary for understanding the rest of the book. If necessary, the chapters in the security implementations group can be visited at will. It would be appropriate to structure an advanced topics course that covers the first two functional groups jointly, and then has individual students, or groups, explore the topics in the security implementations functional group independently. Ideally, group projects could be performed that implement variations on the ideas presented in these chapters. The work presented here is appropriate for many engineering and technical disciplines.

CHAPTER 2

Network Security Problems

Traditionally, security is viewed as maintaining the following services [Stallings 1995]:

- *Confidentiality*: Information should be accessible only to authorized parties.
- *Authentication*: The origin of information is correctly identified.
- *Integrity*: Only authorized parties can modify information.
- *Nonrepudiation*: Neither sender nor receiver can deny the existence of a message.
- *Access control*: Access to information is controlled and limited.
- *Availability:* Computer assets should be available to authorized users as needed.

The viewpoint taken by this book contains these services as a proper subset, but considers security from a slightly larger perspective. In our view security is the ability to maintain a system's correct functionality in response to attacks; this requires understanding the system's behavior. This chapter explains known attacks.

The Internet is a large decentralized system. As of January 2001, it consists of over 100,000,000 hosts [IDS 2001]. Its collective behavior is defined by interactions among these hosts. Interactions include

- *Linear effects* – e.g., the number of packets in a channel is the sum of the packets sent by participating nodes.
- *Nonlinear effects* – e.g., channel throughput increases until a channel's capacity is saturated and then it remains constant or decreases.
- *Positive feedback* – e.g., word of mouth makes popular search engines even more popular.
- *Negative feedback* – e.g., slow response times cause users to switch to alternate equivalent services.

Recent studies show network traffic exhibiting a quasi-fractal nature with self-similarity over a wide range of time scales [Leland 1994, Grossglauer 1999]. These traffic patterns are typical of systems where behavior is defined by nonlinear interactions [Alligood 1996]. Current models do not adequately explain the burstiness of data flows. Network interactions are likely to become more chaotic as the Internet expands to include an increasing number of wireless [Weiss 2000] and embedded [Boriello 2000] devices.

A central tenet of this book is that network behavior can only be understood as an emergent system built of multiple interacting components. The global behavior of a network, like the Internet, is a function of both network configuration and behavior of the individual components.

Distributed systems, such as computer networks, have global properties. Properties of interest include

- *Dependability* – The expected time to system failure [Brooks 1998]. If the Internet is considered operational only when any two end nodes can communicate, dependability decreases exponentially with the number of nodes.
- *Availability* – The percentage of time the system is operational [Brooks 1998]. As with dependability, depending on what is meant by operational, it can decrease exponentially as network size increases.
- *Safety* – When a predefined set of undesirable events never occurs, a system has safety [Gaertner 1999]. This is one aspect of fault tolerance.
- *Liveness* – When a system always eventually returns to a set of desirable states, it has liveness [Gaertner 1999]. This is another aspect of fault tolerance.
- *Self-stabilizability* – A system's ability to recover from any possible fault [Gaertner 1999, Schneider 1993]. It is an extreme form of fault tolerance.

These properties are usually verified using either static or statistical models. Traditionally, system dependability and system security have been looked upon as separate issues. The work described in this book strives toward constructing dynamic systems, which create flexible, secure, dependable infrastructures. To this end, this book will consider security and dependability as being intertwined.

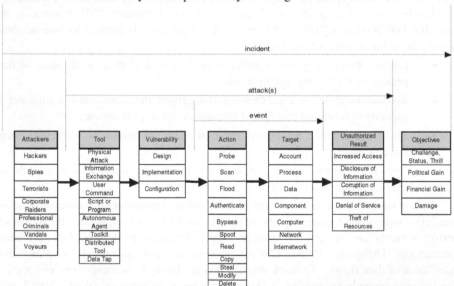

Figure 2.1. Taxonomy of security incidents from [Howard 1998] and used with author's permission. This taxonomy contains the essential elements of any security failure.

The goal of system security is to produce a system that functions properly under as many foreseeable conditions as possible. The qualifier "properly" can refer to the system attributes of authentication, anonymity, privacy, and so forth. Dependability approaches are generally limited to foreseeing conditions that are random and uncorrelated. System security is concerned with malicious attacks. Security foresees conditions issues including intentional, worse case disruptions.

Consider the taxonomy in Figure 2.1 from [Howard 1998]. It is a taxonomy and language for classifying security incidents. In each incident, an attacker abuses the system to achieve an objective. The incident is composed of one or more attacks. For each attack, the perpetrator uses one or more tools to exploit system vulnerabilities and create a result that helps achieve the attacker's objective. Single events represent ways of exploiting vulnerabilities. Each event consists of an aggressive action taken against a target.

The rest of this chapter discusses computer and network security in detail. In Section 1 we describe system vulnerabilities in detail. We then describe the attacks that exploit these vulnerabilities in Section 2. To stop attacks, it is important to start with a model of the threats that need to be contained as discussed in Section 3. Threat models describe the likely intruders and help determine the appropriate level of security. The gamut of threats to be considered runs from script kiddies to national security apparatus. Sections 4 through 17 discuss important security flaws, exploits, and vulnerabilities in detail.

1. VULNERABILITIES

Executive order 130101 established a commission to study critical infrastructure protection on July 15, 1996. The order divided the critical infrastructure of the United States into the following sectors: telecommunications, electric power systems, transportation, gas and oil transportation, banking and finance, water supply systems, emergency services, and continuity of government. This list was eventually aggregated into information and communications, banking and finance, energy, physical distribution, and vital human services [Ware 1996]. The commission was instigated due to concerns of the vulnerability of the United States to attacks on its critical infrastructure. The report concluded that attention and action were critically necessary.

This book discusses security issues of the information and communications sector. Since all infrastructure sectors are strongly interconnected, the vulnerability of one sector represents dangers for the others as well. A failure of the communications infrastructure will quickly have consequences in the finance and physical distribution sectors. They rely on it for coordination. Disruption of finance and transportation would quickly spill over into the energy and human services sectors. The self-evident long-term dependence of communications and information infrastructure on energy and finance completes the cycle. The interconnectedness of our national infrastructure can help faults propagate through complex coupled systems producing unforeseen macroscopic errors. These errors are difficult to prepare for and/or correct, like the failure of the electric infrastructure in the western

United States in the summer of 1996 [CNN 1996, PBS 1996] or the power blackout of August 14, 2003, in the northeastern United States. The second blackout is thought to be partly due to degraded data communications caused by the spread of the Blaster worm [Berghel 2003].

These failures were almost certainly due to random equipment failures. What havoc could be wreaked by intentional disruptions caused by foreign governments, terrorists, or organized criminal groups? Attacks on the information infrastructure are attractive for several reasons, including low cost, high profile, large effect, difficulty to trace, and ease. Information warfare attacks are asymmetric threats. The military dominance of the United States makes direct enemy attacks on the battlefield unlikely. Terrorist attacks, sabotage, information warfare, and other lower-risk avenues of attack are more likely attack vectors.

Note that military and civilian information infrastructures are increasingly intertwined, making the Department of Defense (DoD) dependent on the National Information Infrastructure (NII) for maintaining communications, command and control, and intelligence capabilities [Anderson 1999]. The DISA Commercial Satellite Communications Initiative (CSCI), considering the use of commercial infrastructure for military needs, is a good example of this dependency [Bonds 2000]. In many ways, the civilian infrastructure has become an attractive military target.

The military information infrastructure itself has been the victim of cyberattacks that may have been state sponsored. The February 1998 "Solar Sunrise" incident involved attacks on DoD systems that seemed to prepare for large scale follow on attacks [GS 2003]. Another set of attacks, which started in 1998 and continued for at least two years, is known as "Moonlight Maze." Much of the information about "Moonlight Maze" is classified, but it appears to have been a set of systematic intrusions into the DoD network that partially compromised U.S. national security. Some of the attacks were traced to a mainframe system in the Former Soviet Union. "Solar Sunrise" and "Moonlight Maze" both came after a 1997 internal DoD study called "Eligible Receiver." In "Eligible Receiver," a National Security Agency red team of hackers was able to penetrate network defenses and take control of Pacific command center computers, power grids, and 911 systems in nine major cities in the United States [PBS 2003].

To counteract NII vulnerabilities, it has been suggested that we secure a minimal portion of the NII for defense use to create a Minimal Essential Information Infrastructure (MEII) [Anderson 1999]. The MEII needs to be diverse, redundant, and adaptable to make it more difficult to attack. It should be a dynamic process, riding on top of the existing infrastructure. This book discusses and presents some enabling technologies for creating an MEII-like infrastructure. In addition to guarding individual nodes, we look at creating, from mobile code, complex adaptive structures like those required by the MEII. These structures are suited for both military and civilian applications.

The NII and MEII are vulnerable to a number of disruptive influences. Some disruptions are the result of external influences, including deliberate attacks [Molander 1996]. Other disruptions are manifestations of system design flaws

[Jalote 1994] or the inability to cope with normal errors [Ware 1996]. Threats and vulnerabilities exist at two levels: those affecting individual system components and those targeting the system as a whole. In this section we discuss sources of threats and their operational implications. External threats include hackers, malicious code, information warfare, natural phenomena, carelessness, accidents, and oversights [Ware 1996].

At the lowest level of disruption any system has spurious events that occur daily. Distributed systems need to anticipate and tolerate disruptions of this type with minimal disruption. For example, users mistype passwords when attempting to access computer systems. Natural phenomena (floods, fires, earthquakes, storms, and volcanoes) disrupt networks. Loss of service due to network congestion is also part of this class. Other problems occur due to operator carelessness, accidents, and oversights [Ware 1996]. The infrastructure must handle these minor malfunctions without significant loss of service. This level can be considered noise, random events with no real meaning attached to them that obscure other information [Ware 1996]. Noise is the normal, chaotic environment of network computer operations.

The next highest level of disruption consists of low-level attacks and intrusions. These are intentional and difficult to distinguish from noise. The results of these attacks are generally more severe. Distributed Denial of Service (DDoS) attacks are in this category [Garber 2000]. These attacks may come from isolated hackers, saboteurs, and the like. It may be difficult to distinguish between small-scale attacks and normal network noise [Ware 1996].

The most significant level of destruction consists of high-level attacks like Strategic Information Warfare. These attacks use information warfare tools to advance specific strategic intentions. This asymmetric threat is attractive in part because of its low entry cost, potential propaganda payoff, and the lack of effective tactics for countering the attack [Molander 1996]. Information warfare threats are viable due to the existence of system vulnerabilities. DoD studies compiled the following list of 20 vulnerabilities in 7 categories [Anderson 1999]:

Architecture/Design vulnerabilities are a direct consequence of the system structure. Correcting these vulnerabilities requires major modifications to the system.

- Components unique to this system may not have been thoroughly tested.
- Single points of failure can cause an entire system to fail and singular components that exist in one place can be exploitable.
- Centralization of system control on a single process.
- Network separability can allow components or processes to be isolated from the network and compromised using a "divide and conquer" strategy.
- If all component instances are homogeneous, the same attack can be repeated to disable all of them. They can be attacked one at a time.

Behavioral complexity vulnerabilities are characterized by how the system reacts to its environment.

- A system that is sensitive to variations in use may be vulnerable to attacks that pinpoint a specific aspect of its behavior.
- If a system's reaction is predictable, this can be used to construct attacks.

Adaptability and Manipulation in a system can lead to the system being used to aid an attack.

- It is hard to subvert a rigid system, but neither can the system adapt automatically to attacks.
- On the other hand, a malleable system can be easily modified and subverted.
- Gullible systems that do not verify inputs can easily be used to subvert other applications. The ability to spoof the Internet is an example.

Operation/Configuration changes allow systems to be used in attacks.

- Resource capacity limits can be used in attacks. Denial of Service (DoS) and buffer overflow attacks are examples.
- If a system takes an inordinate amount of effort to reconfigure or recover from failures this can be exploited.
- Systems that lack introspection are unable to detect attacks and correct the situation.
- Systems that are awkward and difficult to configure and administer can more easily be misconfigured.
- Complacency can results in there being a lack of effective administrative procedures.

Nonphysical exposure refers to access to devices that does not involve physical contact.

- Remote system access is a stepping stone to system misuse. Connecting a system to the Internet permits attacks, such as password guessing.
- The more open and transparent a system is, the easier it is to probe for vulnerabilities. Attackers have even subverted the network time protocol and postscript printers to access systems remotely.

Physical exposure refers to vulnerabilities requiring physical access to a device. These vulnerabilities are particularly important for embedded systems. The judicious use of tamperproof hardware can mitigate some of these risks.

- Physical access to a system almost certainly guarantees the possibility of DoS through sabotage or destruction.
- Physical access also extends to attacks on power or communications lines.
- In many cases, the electromagnetic radiation emanating from computer equipment can be captured and used to compromise or steal information. Intrusion or equipment damage may also be possible using electromagnetic radiation. These attacks are often referred to by the codename "tempest."

Dependency on supporting infrastructure is an important vulnerability. Lack of electric power, air conditioning, network connections, and the like causes computer systems to fail.

Note that this list of vulnerabilities is inconsistent. For example, rigidity makes a system vulnerable by making it unable to adapt. Malleability makes it vulnerable by making the system easy to manipulate. It is possible to exploit the system's structure in either case. The conclusions in [Anderson 1999], based on analysis of Computer Emergency Response Team (CERT) incidents during 1989-1995, are that vulnerabilities based on systems being homogeneous and open were the most widely exploited.

Other studies of vulnerabilities have been made. The computer security incident taxonomy in [Howard 1998] classifies vulnerabilities as being design, implementation, or configuration issues. Another taxonomy can be found in [Landwehr 1993], where flaws are categorized using three different criteria:

- *Genesis* – The flaw's origin.
  - o Intentional flaws are either malicious (Trojan horse, trapdoor, and logic bomb) or nonmalicious (ex. covert channel).
  - o Inadvertent flaws of several types exist, including the following errors: validation, domain, aliasing, inadequate authentication, and boundary condition violations.
- *Time of introduction* – When the flaw was created.
  - o During development errors can be made as part of the design, coding, or build processes.
  - o Flaws can be introduced as part of maintenance.
  - o Security flaws can also be created during system operation.
- *Location* – Components containing the flaw.
  - o Software flaws can be in the operating system components, support environment, or application being used.
  - o Hardware security can also be inadequate.

It is often said that security is a process rather than an object to be attained. This discussion of system vulnerabilities illustrates that. Up to now, no methods adequately guarantee the production of error-free software or hardware. The complexity of system design and implementation makes it unlikely that methods will ever be found. The list of vulnerabilities we provided from [Anderson 1999] is rather exhaustive but inconsistent. Systems should neither be rigid nor supple. Uniqueness and homogeneity can both be turned against the system. The taxonomy from [Landwehr 1993] provides a similar lesson. Flaws can be introduced at any point in the system's lifecycle and they can be present in any component. Constant vigilance is required.

2. ATTACKS

Adopting the terminology from [Howard 1998], shown in Figure 2.1, a system attack is the exploitation of a system vulnerability to create an unauthorized result. For the security aspects of confidentiality, authentication, integrity, nonrepudiation, access control, and availability, four general classes of attacks exist [Stallings 1995]:

- *Interruption:* Availability of an asset is disrupted.
- *Interception:* Unauthorized access to an asset.
- *Modification:* Unauthorized tampering with an asset.

- *Fabrication:* Creation of a fictitious asset.

In addition, attacks can be passive or active. Passive attacks monitor systems. Active attacks change a system's state.

Information warfare threats have a larger scope than the traditional security issues [Molander 1996]. DoD studies have found 21 information warfare threats in 5 categories [Anderson 1999]:

- *External passive attack* – Wiretapping, emanations analysis (tempest), signals analysis, traffic analysis.
- *External active attack* – Substitution or insertion, jamming, overload, spoof, malicious logic.
- *Attacks against a running system* – Reverse engineering, cryptanalysis.
- *Internal attack* – Scavenging, theft of service, theft of data.
- *Attacks involving access to and modification of a system* – Violation of permissions, deliberate disclosure, database query analysis, false denial of origin, false denial of receipt, logic tapping, tampering.

These attacks describe the basic arsenal of cyber-warfare. Known attacks on Internet Protocol based networks include:

- *DoS by flooding* – Multiple messages request packets for a particular address cause congestion and hinder delivery of correct packets. "Smurfing" is an example [Anderson 1999].
- *DoS by forging* – The network is sent incorrect routing update messages; intentionally inducing network congestion [Anderson 1999].
- *Packet sniffing* – Unencrypted traffic moving through the network can be intercepted [Anderson 1999].
- *Host intrusion* – Use of the network for unauthorized access to a network node [Anderson 1999].
- *Attacks on lower-level protocols* – IP packets can be delivered using a number of physical and link layer protocols. DoS would be possible by attacking an ATM service [Anderson 1999].
- *Physical attacks* – Destruction of nodes or critical links [Anderson 1999].
- *DDoS* – Triggering a DoS attack from multiple locations simultaneously is an order of magnitude more difficult to identify and correct than attacks from a single location [Garber 2000]. For this reason we list DDoS separately.

Switched networks, like the voice telephone system, have known vulnerabilities similar to those of IP networks [Anderson 1999]:

- *Sabotage* – Destruction of equipment, lines, or offices. These are physical attacks.
- *Line tapping* – The analog equivalent of packet sniffing.
- *Jamming transmissions* – This is indiscriminate tampering with wireless communications to provoke a DoS attack.

- *Intrusion and tampering* – If unauthorized access to a switch is possible, the switch can be improperly reprogrammed. Eavesdropping and forging voicemails is also possible.

Much of this book concentrates on distributed attacks on distributed systems. Attacks based on circumventing authentication extend the security risks faced by individual nodes to the whole system. Other attacks, particularly DoS, exploit the distributed structure of networks and present a different risk. The NII's behavior emerges from node interactions, like DDoS attacks where traffic propagation through coupled systems have macroscopic effects. These behaviors are difficult to foresee and correct. Similar problems exist in the rest of the critical infrastructure, like the failure of the electric grid in the western United States in the summer of 1996 [CNN 1996, PBS 1996].

The ability to tolerate attacks and intrusions is a type of system dependability. Intelligent opponents plan attacks. The appropriate fault model is therefore the Byzantine Generals Problem, which allows for collusion and intelligent behavior among faulty components [Lynch 1996]. The Byzantine Generals Problem refers to a set of commanders who must decide whether to attack or lay siege to a city with the following constraints [Barborak 1993]:

- They know that a subset of the commanders is treacherous and working for the enemy.
- If all loyal commanders make the same decision, they will prevail.

This fault model is attractive for security problems, since it allows for collusion and intelligence among the system's opponents.

It has been proven that Byzantine faults can be tolerated by distributed systems, if the number of faulty components (f = number of faulty components, n = total number of components) and system connectivity fulfill known limits of $f < n/3$ and > $2f$ respectively [Lynch 1996, Brooks 1996, Brooks 1998]. A distributed system fulfilling these criteria is therefore tolerant to attack. It will function correctly as long as the known limits are satisfied. Unfortunately, algorithms for identifying which components are faulty generally require an exponential number of rounds of communications [Barborak 1993]. Later chapters will look at ways of tolerating attacks that do not have to identify the corrupted components.

3. THREAT MODELING

Given infinite resources (money, knowledge, computation, etc.) any security approach can and will be broken. This is a tautology. If the enemy is omniscient and omnipotent, it can circumvent any safeguard. At the same time, there are limitations to the amount of resources that can be used to sustain system security. Even if, as in the case of national security, these limits can be astonishingly high.

Two basic factors always limit the amount of security that can be provided. The first factor is simply that complex systems, especially software systems, contain bugs [Knight 1998]. Errors are made in system design, implementation, testing, and maintenance. Although steps can be taken to mitigate this unfortunate fact, there is no indication that this will change in the foreseeable future. Very often these bugs can be exploited for launching system attacks.

The second factor is economic; even if systems were conceived in an altruistic manner they are rarely implemented that way. In any commercial system, cost of development and profitability are of paramount importance. In particular, for most systems, there is more financial incentive to get a system to market than there is to ensure that it is free of implementation defects. In addition, legitimate system test groups and attackers will discover flaws independently. The odds that the flaws discovered by attackers are fully contained in the set found by system testing are rather small [Anderson 2001].

These factors motivate the need for threat modeling. A system will not be free of flaws. An attacker with an infinite amount of resources will be capable of circumventing security measures. Threat models need to consider the most attractive targets for an attack and the most likely attack vectors. This information can then be used to channel security resources into creating effective countermeasures. The importance of threat modeling is shown by a study of crypto-system effectiveness performed in the UK. The study found most crypto-systems failed, not as expected due to cryptanalysis deciphering the key, but due to implementation errors and management failures [Tipton 2003].

One threat modeling approach is to perform a dataflow analysis of the system. Data stores show where information may easily be accessed. Data transmission paths can be monitored. Data processing tasks can also be subverted. Given the data flow diagram, it should be analyzed to consider the following vulnerabilities [Howard 2003]:

- Identity spoofing
- Data tampering
- Transaction repudiation
- Information disclosure
- Denial of service
- Elevation of privilege

This information can be used to create threat trees, a modification of the fault tree approach to modeling system dependability. This approach complements attack graphs, which are discussed in Chapter 3.

4. PHYSICAL SECURITY

The physical exposure and dependency on supporting infrastructure vulnerabilities in Section 1 illustrate the importance of keeping systems physically secure, when possible. Computer and network security can be expressed as a set of rings surrounding sensitive information; physical security is the first line of defense [Zimmerli 1984]. Specific physical security threats can be grouped into the following categories [Tipton 2003]:

- *Natural threats* – Fire, severe weather, earthquakes, other natural disasters, dry heat, moisture, wind, plants (e.g., mold, fungus), animals (e.g., rats, insects), etc.
- *Man-made threats* – Theft, fraud, espionage, sabotage, workplace violence, civil insurrection, etc.
- *Environmental threats* – Climate problems (e.g., heat, static electricity, dryness, excessive moisture), water damage, electrical interruption, electromagnetic pulse, radiation, etc.

These can be prioritized by their associated risk: product of the probability of an event occurring and its potential damage [Zimmerli 1984].

Strategies for physical security can be fairly straightforward. Determine the sensitivity of the equipment and information. Keep sensitive materials in controlled areas as much as possible. Controlled areas should be built to reduce risk. They should be in safe neighborhoods. Fences, lights, surveillance cameras, and posted warnings may be appropriate. In other cases, a lower profile is advisable. Buildings should withstand likely acts of nature. Pay special attention to the electrical and communications infrastructure. Uninterruptible power supplies and generators are common.

Contingency planning is important. Create a structured plan for crisis situations. Document the actions to be taken and allocate backup equipment for recovery. Data and equipment need to be stored in more than one location to reduce the number of single points of failure [Zimmerli 1984]. The cost of backup installations can be shared among multiple organizations as a form of mutual insurance policy.

Consider the existence of covert communications channels, i.e., mechanisms not intended for communications but that can be used for that purpose [Phoha 2001]. Electromagnetic emanations from computer equipment, such as screens, can be used to recreate computer sessions. These attacks are generally referred to using the codeword "tempest." More recently, attacks using information leakage from LED status indicators have been created [Loughry 2002]. Optical and electrical emanations should therefore be considered as equally sensitive. Differential power analysis is another important covert channel. By analyzing the power consumption of a processor, it is possible to infer the contents of a data stream being processed [Kocher 1999]. In some cases, this can be used to infer the value of cryptographic keys. We discuss differential power analysis in detail in Chapter 8.

It is useful to create zones of varying security levels, control access to sensitive zones, and monitor movements between zones. Security zones should have a clear hierarchy. The use of remote surveillance, security personnel, and access control is often advisable. One or more of the following is typically used for access control: knowledge (e.g., password, key code), token (e.g., key, badge, ATM card), or biometrics (e.g., fingerprint, palm print, retinal scan, voice print). The use of challenge response pairs is particularly useful for knowledge-based access control.

The physical security of servers is fairly straightforward, since direct contact to them is rarely needed. Workstations are more difficult to secure, they must be accessible to their users, which makes them vulnerable. Portable devices, such as laptops and PDAs, are particularly problematic, since they will be transported through uncontrolled areas.

Guaranteeing the security of equipment that is not kept in a controlled environment is problematic. To illustrate this point, researchers have used physical attacks to violate type safety. Exposing a processor to radiation causes soft memory errors. These soft errors can cause pointers for one object type to point to another object type. This violation of type safety circumvents the virtual machine security guarantees provided by Java and .NET [Govindavajhala 2003].

The use of secure coprocessors can add security to machines located in a physically insecure environment. Secure coprocessors are special purpose hardware constructed to be tamperproof. This generally includes a Faraday cage and mechanisms to delete the contents of the processor should tampering be detected. The IBM Citadel processor is one example. We refer the reader to [Yee 1994] for the authoritative work on this subject. In Chapter 9, we discuss using secure coprocessors to maintain trust in a distributed system.

5. SOCIAL ENGINEERING

There are limits to the ability of technology to secure systems. Often people are the weakest link. Social engineering refers to attacks using the human element. Recent e-mail viruses show a number of simple ploys that coerce people into activating e-mail attachments:

- Claiming the attachment contains a picture of an attractive woman
- Claiming the attachment is an update from Microsoft
- Claiming the attachment is a love letter from an anonymous admirer
- Claiming that the attachment a wicked screen saver
- Making various claims that the attachment is a reply to a request, related to a monetary transaction, associated with a promotion at work, etc.

Social engineering attacks get people to disclose information or perform actions that compromise security. The most successful hacker of all time considers social engineering the primary reason for his success [Mitnick 2002]. These attacks use deception and take advantage of human nature, appealing to people's ego, sympathy, or fear [Tipton 2003]. Social engineering includes mundane activities like dumpster diving.

Social engineering countermeasures include creating appropriate policies and educating employees about policies. Employees need to know which information is sensitive and why. Some basic principles should be maintained by the policy [Tipton 2003]:

- The employee's primary loyalty is due to the employer.
- Conflicts of interest should be identified and avoided.
- All people should take due diligence to fulfill their tasks.
- The principle of least privilege should be maintained. Every person should be given the privileges and access needed to perform their tasks and no more.

- Some tasks require the approval of more than one participant.
- Individuals are accountable for their actions.
- Management supports and enforces the policies.

In addition to these principles, it is necessary to integrate control structures, periodic audits, and periodic penetration testing [Zimmerli 1984].

6. PRIVACY

"You already have zero privacy. Get over it."
– Scott McNealy, Chairman, Sun Microsystems, 1999

Privacy means that others cannot examine a user's data without the user's permission. This right is generally not recognized in the United States. U.S. federal law prohibits access of e-mail in transit or temporary storage by federal agencies. Other parties, such as employers, are not restricted from inspecting user data [Microsoft 1997]. Some specific industries in the United States, such as health care and telecommunications, have data privacy obligations. The European Union has much stronger laws concerning privacy guarantees for an individual's data [EU 2003], including a ban on exporting data about individuals to countries that do not guarantee privacy. This difference in legal protections has become an issue in international trade. Important questions under debate include who owns an individual's data and what level of control an individual should have over data derived from personal transactions.

The technical issues involving data privacy, although difficult, are probably more tractable than the social and legal issues. Privacy is linked to confidentiality, which is a security property that can be enforced. The following privacy requirements are part of the Common Criteria security specification standard [CC 1999]:

- *Anonymity* – Users can use resources without disclosing their identity.
- *Pseudonymity* – Users can use resources without disclosing their identity, but they are still accountable for the use.
- *Unlinkability* – Users can make multiple uses of resources without others being able to group these actions.
- *Unobservability* – Users may use resources without others being able to detect that the resource is being used.

Inclusion of privacy attributes in the Common Criteria means that standard specifications and testing procedures exist for systems where they are appropriate. Enforcement of privacy generally relies on user authentication and cryptography, which are discussed in Chapter 3.

7. FRAUD

Fraud is criminal deception [OED 2003]. Since accounting was one of the first applications of computers, it is reasonable to assume that computer fraud started in the late 1950s or early 1960s. The use of communications for deception has been documented back to the days of Sun Tzu, circa 500 B.C. More recently, computer networks have become important for credit card fraud and identity theft. Identity theft is defined as [Com 2003]

> "The co-option of another person's personal information (e.g., name, social security number, credit card number, passport) without that person's knowledge and the fraudulent use of such knowledge"

Online scams and intrusions into commercial information systems have become common vectors for identity theft. Another variation of computer fraud uses scanning; a computer tests various strings until one is accepted. This is used to find credit card numbers, passwords, and telephone numbers with computer access [Tipton 2003].

Fraud is not innately tied to computers or computer networks. Although identity theft is a growing computer crime segment, in the form of credit card fraud it pre-dates the widespread use of computers and the Internet. The availability of e-commerce and the Internet has simply given criminals powerful tools for committing fraudulent transactions.

8.   SCAVENGING

Scavenging is the acquisition of data from residue [Phoha 2001]. The most banal example is searching through rubbish bins [Tipton 2003]. Information in physical residue (i.e., program listings, carbon copies, other waste paper, etc.) can be protected by requiring sensitive information be shredded or burned. Procedures explaining the information considered sensitive and associated training of employees is advisable.

Electronic residue is more difficult to control. Buffer space in memory or cache is not always erased when being freed or allocated. Allocating memory and scanning the contents of the buffer before use can leak information from other tasks. Users can do little to correct these issues in existing commercial systems.

Similarly, in some operating systems deleting files amounts to making their physical storage area available for reuse. Later reallocation of these disk blocks can make the file contents accessible. These issues exist for all magnetic media including floppy disks and tapes. This is often done to avoid performance degradation due to the amount of computer time required. Bad disk blocks can also retain information. Many systems support overwriting deleted files with different bit patterns. Specialized hardware exists that can read overwritten data, but this requires a very invasive procedure. Degaussing media is better than overwriting, but is also not foolproof. Physically destroying the old media is probably the most secure way of avoiding file scavenging.

Keystroke monitoring and packet sniffing are other forms of data scavenging. A keystroke monitor is a background process that records keyboard inputs. These can be transmitted to another node at a later date. This is often used to scavenge sensitive information (i.e., passwords, bank accounts, etc.). Packet sniffing software monitors an Ethernet port and records packet contents. This records all the unencrypted traffic over the network.

The widespread acceptance of wireless Ethernet means that sniffing can be possible for attackers with no physical connection to the network. When wireless Ethernet is used attackers can monitor network activity without entering the building. Initial solutions to this problem, such as the Wireless Applications Protocol, provide only marginal security [Nichols 2002]. This vulnerability has led to the practice of war-driving, searching for unsecured wireless networks while driving a car.

9.   TROJAN HORSES

A Trojan horse is a program that contains functionality that is hidden from the user. The name comes from Ulysses' ploy in Homer's *Iliad*. Trojans can steal or modify data, erase or reformat disks, and so on. Some Trojans are designed to trigger actions after a given point in time or when a specific condition is satisfied (e.g., a specific employee terminated). These Trojans are frequently referred to as logic bombs. As a rule Trojans are almost impossible to detect and only limited countermeasures exist.

Perhaps the best example of how difficult it is to detect a Trojan horse comes from Ken Thompson's 1984 Turing Award Lecture [Thompson 1984]. He wrote a version of the Unix login command that would provide a trapdoor. He then wrote a modified C compiler that recognized the Unix login source code and created object code including the login Trojan. A second modified C compiler detected C compiler source code and produced object code containing his modifications. Users given the final compiler could compile and link perfectly sound C compiler source code. This compiler executable automatically inserts a trapdoor in any Unix distribution it compiled.

10.   TRAPDOORS

A trapdoor, also known as a backdoor, is a code segment inserted into a program to circumvent access controls. Sometimes these hidden entry points are created to aid system debug and test. They are difficult to detect, as illustrated in [Thompson 1984], and compromise system security.

The Clipper Chip is an excellent example of a trapdoor. In the 1990s the U.S. government proposed the Clipper Chip as an encryption standard. Each chip would have unique keys associated with it; these keys would be held in escrow to allow law enforcement to decrypt information encrypted using the chip. Due to public skepticism related to this trapdoor, the approach was never accepted for widespread use [Nichols 2002].

Unfortunately, the term *trapdoor* has an unrelated definition that is used in cryptography. In cryptography, a trapdoor is an easily computed function whose reverse function is difficult to compute [Weisstein 1999]. In this book, trapdoor refers to circumvention of access controls.

11. VIRUSES

Virus refers to a program that reproduces by introducing a copy of itself into another program. When the first virus was developed is debatable. Von Neumann developed a cellular automata model of machine reproduction in the 1940s [von Neumann 1966]. The idea of a "virus" program was mentioned in a 1972 science fiction novel [Gerrold 1972]. It is also defensible that Thompson's trapdoor exploit [Thompson 1984] was an early virus. Other obscure exploits before the mid-1980s existed that resembled viruses. It is, however, clear that the term virus was first used to refer to computer software implementations as part of Fred Cohen's research leading to his Ph.D. dissertation at the University of Southern California [Cohen 1986]. Cohen is the first researcher to specifically consider viruses as a security threat, and potential research topic.

By the end of 1985, viruses started appearing on personal computers. The origin of most viruses is obscure. Many viruses in the late 1980s could be traced to "virus factories" in the Eastern Bloc, notably Bulgaria [Bontchev 1989], leading to suspicions that some viruses were state sponsored or at least tolerated by hostile foreign governments. As Internet use and software sharing became more widespread, the number of virus variants and the number of machines infected increased. Techniques from epidemiology are used to study the spread of viruses in computer networks [Kephart 1993] and discussed in later chapters (notably 5 and 6). Epidemiology is especially useful for tracking the spread of e-mail viruses [Ludwig 2002]. Following the definitions here, the term virus is a misnomer for most e-mail viruses. They are in fact worms and are discussed in that section.

A typical virus has four components:

- *Search routine* – Subroutine looks for uninfected files that are susceptible to infection.
- *Copy routine* – Infection code inserts a copy of the virus into a susceptible file.
- *Payload* – Extra code that can be triggered by the virus. This may be a logic bomb.
- *Profile* – Information in infected files that aids in detecting uninfected files.

When an infected program is run, the following typically occurs:

- The search routine finds one or more files of the type the virus can infect that do not contain the profile. The profile is necessary to keep from infecting the same file repeatedly. Reinfection wastes disk space and processing time. It makes the virus easier to detect.
- The copy routine infects one or more of these susceptible files. Often the virus is appended to the end of the file and the program start address in the header is modified to point to the virus code. On termination, the virus code jumps to the original program start address.
- If the virus contains a payload, the payload can be run before returning control to the host program. If the payload is a logic bomb, this execution may be conditional on other factors.

The first viruses infected primarily executable files or disk boot sectors. Boot sector viruses infect computer disks instead of individual files and run during system initialization. The advent of executable content has made it possible for viruses to be contained in many other file types that previously were thought safe. Microsoft Word macro viruses are an example, but the possibility of postscript viruses exists as well.

The most common defense uses scanners to detect known viruses. The virus can then be extracted from an infected file. The virus profile used to detect the virus and the logic used to extract the virus are both unique to each virus. Reverse engineering of captured viruses is used to derive both. This has been somewhat effective in containing viruses, but is based on reacting to viruses after they have spread. Even then, this approach is of limited use against polymorphic viruses that change their behavior and internal structure with each execution. Another problem is the tendency of some attackers to make minor modifications to existing viruses and reintroduce them into the wild.

Some work has been done on developing heuristics for detecting new viruses before reverse engineering is performed. Similarly, memory resident programs have been developed that block harmful behaviors often associated with viruses. Both approaches have been plagued by a large rate of false positives. When the false positive rate is too high, real detections tend to be ignored [Aesop 2000]. There is a good reason for this high false positive rate. Deciding whether or not an arbitrary computer program contains a virus is undecidable. It has been shown to be equivalent to the halting problem [Cohen 1987]. An in-depth study of the complexity issues inherent in detecting computer viruses base on Goedel numbering techniques can be found in [Adleman 1988].

Some basic defenses against viruses are possible. The first defense against viruses is to only use software from trusted sources [Thompson 1984]. Unfortunately, since viruses have been found in shrink-wrapped software and have been shipped by Microsoft, and Linux distribution sites have been hacked on occasion, this is not a practical defense.

A more promising idea is to avoid embedding computer programs in data and protect programs so that it is difficult to modify them. For example, restrict the ability to modify executables to compilers. This would greatly restrict the ability of viruses to spread. Unfortunately, these ideas go against the current trend of object-oriented programming. It is also worth noting that most operating systems in wide use base access rights on the user and not on the program being used.

A more formal approach is to create a partially ordered set (POset) of domains in a system [Cohen 1988]. Consider a system where each program or user belongs to a domain D_i. Each D_i can execute programs only from domain D_j with $j \geq i$. Elements of D_i can modify data or programs only in D_k with $i \geq k$. This would mean of necessity that a virus introduced in domain D_l can spread only to domains D_m with $l \geq m$. This enforces isolation in the system. Note that in this approach, the users or programs that can access the largest number of domains have the fewest number of actions that they can perform. This is exactly the opposite of privilege structures in widely used operating systems. This concept will be revisited in Chapters 7 and 8.

12. WORMS

"… a self-perpetuating tapeworm, … which would shunt itself from
one nexus to another every time his credit-code was punched into a
keyboard. It could take days to kill a worm like that, and sometimes
weeks."
– John Brunner, *The Shockwave Rider* [Brunner 1975]
First use of "worm" to refer to a malicious network program, predating
widespread Internet use, and computer worm infestations.

"Worm (computer program), in computer science, a program that
propagates itself across computers, usually by spawning copies of itself
in each computer's memory. A worm might duplicate itself in one
computer so often that it causes the computer to crash. Sometimes
written in separate "segments," a worm is introduced surreptitiously
into a host system either for "fun" or with intent to damage or destroy
information. The term comes from a science-fiction novel …"
– Encarta Encyclopedia [Encarta 1998]

A worm is an attack that propagates through the network by creating copies of itself. Unlike viruses, worms do not infect other executables. They are independent processes. The first worm implementations are generally attributed to researchers at Xerox PARC, who in the late 1970s wrote useful worm utilities. The first worm attack was in 1988. A proof of concept written by Robert Tappan Morris, a graduate student at Cornell at the time, infected over 10% of the Internet within a number of hours [Tipton 2003]. The years 2001-2003 saw several major worm incidents, including Nimda, Slammer, Blaster, Code Red I, and Code Red II. Collateral damage from these network attacks was reported to include affecting Automated Teller Machines [SPI 2003], airplane flight schedules [CNN 2003], elections [Moore 2003], and possibly the Northeast power grid [Berghel 2003].

According to our definition the typical e-mail virus is really a worm since it does not modify other programs. It merely mails copies of itself. Another definition differentiates between worms and viruses by saying that viruses require a user action to reproduce and worms do not [Tipton 2003]. E-mail viruses would thus be viruses. This differentiation is rather academic now; hybrid attacks like Nimda fit both categories [Wired 2001].

Worms are particularly interesting because they are intrinsically network processes. The epidemiology-based analysis, used for virus propagation, is even more important for studying worm behavior. The Morris worm spread to IP addresses found on the infected host. This simple logic allowed it to spread within hours to what was then over 10% of the Internet.

The Code Red I worm of July 2001 set up multiple threads. Each thread would attempt to start an exploit on a machine chosen at random from the IP address space. Version 1 (CRv1) had limited success due to an error in the random number generator. Version 2 (CRv2) corrected this error and more than 359,000 out of an estimated 2,000,000 susceptible hosts were infected in less than 14 hours [CAIDA 2001, Zou 2002]. At its height it infected almost 18% of the susceptible machines. This worm was designed to restart its infection cycle periodically and also perform a DDoS attack on the www.whitehouse.gov webpage.

Code Red II was an entirely new worm using new exploits. Its propagation model was similar to CRv2, with a few improvements. It used more threads than CRv2, allowing it to search a larger space. It also used subaddress masking [Stevens 1994] to search for machines within the same local address range. This was very effective since machines in the same local subnetwork are likely to be in the same Autonomous System (AS), most likely running similar software configurations, and thus more likely to be susceptible to infection. Other advantages to attacking nodes in the same subnet are that the latency between machines is probably less and they may even be behind the same firewall. Detailed propagation data for Code Red II is difficult to determine due to its overlap with Code Red I [Staniford 2002]. This worm appears to have been designed primarily to set up a trapdoor allowing access to the infected systems.

The Slammer worm attack started on January 25, 2003 and within 10 minutes it had infected over 90% of the hosts vulnerable to its attack. It exploited a buffer overflow vulnerability in Microsoft SQL products. Its rate of spread was over two orders of magnitude faster than Code Red I. As with Code Red I, it chose hosts to infect by picking them at random [Moore 2003a]. Slammer propagated so quickly by using UDP [Stevens 1994] to send small packets containing the entire exploit. Its propagation rate was thus limited solely by the aggregate network bandwidth on the infected machines. Slammer's code base concentrated entirely on worm propagation and contained no hidden exploits [Moore 2003a]. It caused multiple network outages and was an extremely effective DoS attack.

In addition to random scanning and subnet scanning, other methods have been considered for allowing worms to propagate more quickly. One approach is to construct a list of vulnerable machines in advance. This would allow the worm to selectively target a small number of machines initially, which it is sure to infect. Another approach is to have each machine construct a pseudo-random permutation of the addresses in the network. These permutations could be further subdivided to avoid simultaneous infection attempts on the same machine [Staniford 2002]. This would reduce congestion, speed the worm's propagation, and make it harder to detect. As of this writing, these approaches have been limited to theory. They are sometimes referred to as flash worms or Warhol worms.

It is also worth noting that worms have secondary effects. Both Code Red II and Nimda caused many network outages. These changes in traffic behavior triggered the Internet's Border Gateway Protocol (BGP). BGP is designed to route messages between ASs along the most efficient path. A number of BGP message storms were detected concurrent with the height of Code Red II and Nimda propagation [Cowie 2001]. It is feared that global disruptions caused by worms could lead to routing table instabilities that would perturb traffic more than the network saturation experienced to date. Vestiges of Code Red and Nimda are reported to still be active on the Internet as of this writing.

As should be obvious from the list of exploits, no adequate worm countermeasures exist for the moment. It is a research topic. Many of the technologies in Chapters 7 through 12 are initial steps towards developing countermeasures against this type of attack.

13. REVERSE ENGINEERING

Reverse engineering infers how an object works by inspecting it. For hardware, this usually amounts to the recursive process of dismantling the hardware, determining interactions between components, and dismantling each component to infer its internal function and structure. Exploitation of covert communications channels and blackbox analysis can also be used to reverse engineer systems. Hardware reverse engineering may be thwarted by tamperproofing. Attempts to dismantle tamperproof hardware usually destroy important portions of the hardware. Obfuscation and the removal of covert channels, as discussed in Chapters 3, 7, and 8, can also be used.

An interesting concept for countering reverse engineering is the use of physical unclonable functions: circuits that provide different answers when identical copies are created in silicon. These circuits are at the limits of fabrication technology and utilize transient timing effects that vary due to imperfections in the silicon substrate. This is a research topic with many unanswered important questions [Devadas 2003].

For software, a hex dump of a program extract its object code and assembly instructions. In many cases, a decompiler infers the higher-level language code constructs. Software reverse engineering may be thwarted by encrypting or obfuscating the code. Both approaches are discussed in Chapter 3. Chapters 7 and 8 discuss new technologies to help counter reverse engineering.

14. COVERT COMMUNICATIONS CHANNELS

Covert channels were first mentioned in [Lampson 1973]. They are information transmission channels that were not implemented for this use. The first documented examples of covert channels [Lampson 1973] include writing encoded information and using program control flow to modify system behavior (e.g., intentionally paging to slow a system). Covert communications implies that the transmitter is intentionally cooperating with the receiver. An important illustrative example of a covert channel is in [Simmons 1998]. A system proposed for verifying an arms limitations treaty contained a covert channel capable of compromising the American nuclear deterrent. A related problem is information inferencing, which extracts sensitive information without collusion. Inferencing is related to reverse engineering. This section discusses both.

Identification and removal of covert channels in software systems, such as databases, is particularly challenging. Several types of covert channels exist [Sabelfield 2003]:

- *Implicit flow* – Program control structures are used.
- *Termination channel* – Termination or nontermination of a process provides the signal.

- *Timing channel* – Timing information, such as program execution time, transmits information.

- *Probabilistic channel* – Probability distributions of observable data are modified.

- *Resource exhaustion* – All of a finite shared resource is used.

- *Power channel* – The power consumption of the processor is varied.

Static verification of a program's control flow can remove many covert channels. The entire implementation needs to be checked, since some forms of information leakage will not be contained in the system specifications [Tsai 1990]. Program analysis to identify all variables that may contain leaked information is described in [Sabelfield 2003]. Use of a similar approach to remove covert channels from a dialect of Unix is described in [Tsai 1990]. Even when program verification is done, low-level covert channels, such as disk-head positions, may still leak information [Tsai 1990]. Trade-offs can exist between system performance and its ability to mask covert data transmissions [Son 2000].

One important form of covert channel is steganography, or information hiding. A common steganographic method is modifying the least significant bits in an image file. Changes in the viewed image are almost undetectable, but differencing the modified image with the original provides hidden data. Applications of steganography include image water marking and digital rights management. An application of steganography is given in Chapter 7.

Covert communications and inferencing can be stopped by completely isolating the system from the rest of the world. This is rarely practical. Potential covert channels include file names, resource usage, power consumption, and status diodes. The existence of covert channels is a major enforcement issue for mandatory access controls. Electromagnetic emanations are important sources of information leakage. It is possible to capture electrical signals from keyboards, screens, and processors at a distance. These signals are used to reproduce the system's internal workings. These are also known as tempest or Van Eck attacks. A new variation, called "optical tempest," monitors the flickering lights of router status diodes to reproduce routed data streams [Loughry 2002].

Monitoring resource consumption is another important source of information leakage. There is an urban legend that during government crises (before major military operations) government employees work long hours in the White House (Pentagon) and the number of pizza deliveries increases. By monitoring pizza deliveries, it should be possible to foresee crises (military operations).

Similarly, monitoring the volume of traffic entering or leaving a firewall provides important information about the underlying application. Packet source and destination addresses (or address ranges) provide even more information. Resource consumption masking, i.e., shaping traffic flow to maintain the same volume no matter what the actual needs are, can defeat this attack [Guan 2001]. Traffic transmission rates are uniformly set to the maximum amount needed to maintain Quality of Service (QoS). Dummy packets are used as needed.

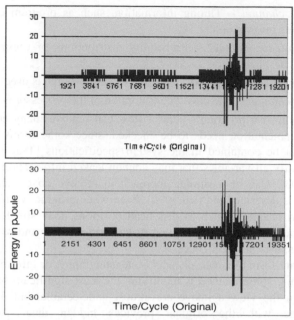

Figure 2.2. Differential power analysis of two Data Encryption Standard (DES) executions, with different keys (top) and different clear text inputs (bottom). Tests run by H. Saputra, V. Narayanan, and M. Kandemir.

System power consumption also leaks information. This is an important weakness of smart cards. Many applications use smart cards to perform encryption and authenticate users. The key is embedded on the smart card to limit the ability to decrypt information to the person possessing the card [Dhem 2001]. Unfortunately, monitoring power consumption lets attackers infer the processor's internal functions. This can be noninvasive; tamperproofing can no longer protect the key. Differential power analysis, comparing power consumption when different keys or clear text are used, is difficult to stop [Kocher 1999]. Figure 2.2 shows examples. The differences between DES runs with different keys and text inputs are significant and predictable. With this data, it is possible to infer the DES key embedded on the card. We discuss how to foil these attacks in Chapter 8.

15. BUFFER OVERFLOW AND STACK SMASHING

Buffer overflow attacks write past the ends of arrays in memory. Figure 2.3 shows simplified subroutine activation records containing four pointers. Activation records are used to support recursion in function calls. Parameter values are stored at the top of the record. A control pointer points to the address of the instruction to be called on function exit. Local variable values are stored after the control pointer. In Figure 2.3 one function has been called twice recursively.

Each local pointer can be used to launch a buffer overflow attack. Here are some simplified examples. Local pointer 1 points to a buffer in static memory. By writing to buffer positions past the buffer end, it is possible to overwrite the program in memory as it executes. At some point, the program executes the binary value instructions written by the attacker at those addresses. This attack is not possible when architectures separate code and data address spaces.

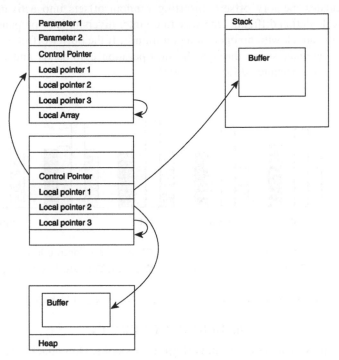

Figure 2.3. Activation records are in the upper left hand corner. Each activation record has three local pointers. Local pointer 1 points to static memory. Local pointer 2 points to a dynamically allocated buffer. Local pointer 3 points to a local array. All three can launch a buffer overflow attack.

Local pointer 3 points to a local array. When the address of this array is passed to the recursive function call, the function may write after the end of the array to overwrite the control pointer in its own activation record. When the function exits, the computer executes the instructions pointed to by the new control pointer value. Local pointer 2 points to a dynamically allocated buffer on the heap. Writing to an invalid offset from this array overwrites the control pointer. These attacks are sometimes referred to as stack smashing.

Why are buffer overflows possible? Many programming languages do not enforce bounds checking to avoid performance overhead. Figure 2.4 illustrates the overhead incurred by array bounds checking on various benchmarks. For each benchmark, execution time is shown for (left to right): no checking, checking for every array access, checking once per loop iteration, and checking once before loop entry. These results show that bounds checking can incur minimal overhead. Unfortunately the final two bounds checking techniques occasionally stop valid array accesses.

You can make buffer overflow attacks more difficult by introducing diversity into systems [Forrest 1997]. Buffer overflow attacks either overwrite a pointer with the address of a buffer or directly overwrite the program in memory. To do this, the attack calculates memory offsets. Inserting random offsets into activation records makes the calculation difficult. One way to counter diversity is to prepend the buffer containing the attack with no operation commands. If the buffer offset is slightly off, the program counter slides through the no-operation commands and executes the attack when it is encountered [Russell 2003].

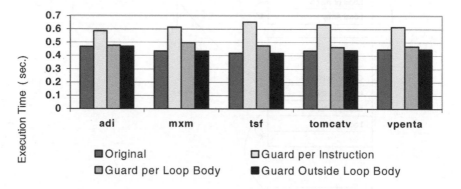

Figure 2.4. Overhead incurred by array bounds checking. Tests courtesy of M. Kandemir.

16. DENIAL OF SERVICE

DoS attacks prevent a system from performing its tasks. DoS attacks are perpetrated either locally or over the network. On a multiuser system, any user consuming an inordinate amount of resources launches a simple DoS attack on other users. This is stopped by attentive system maintenance. Sabotaging equipment is another simple DoS attack, countered by physically protecting devices. Remote DoS attacks using the Internet are of primary interest.

Two main classes of Internet DoS attacks exist: system exploit attacks and network attacks. System exploit attacks use system specific vulnerabilities. The Ping of Death exploit, which used malformed ping packets to crash computers, fits into this category. Applying patches and bug fixes as vulnerabilities are discovered fixes these attacks.

Networking attacks take advantage of vagueness or weakness in protocol specifications. Known Internet DoS exploits include attacks on root Internet nameservers, attacks on merchant and media sites, and the Slammer worm. The network traffic generated by Slammer triggered DoS events for other systems.

Most networking attacks flood the network with spurious traffic to block legitimate traffic. In the case of SYN floods, the attacker fills the buffer that keeps track of Transport Control Protocol (TCP) connections being initiated [Stevens 1994]. This buffer was too small in some operating system versions and it was easy to keep the buffer full, isolating the victim from the network. More brute force attacks are also possible, where a large volume of packets fills all of the available bandwidth. Packet queues fill on intermediate machines and legitimate packets get dropped. Packet dropping forces TCP to retransmit packets while flow control slows the packet throughput rate. The network is then unusable for its intended purpose.

17. DISTRIBUTED DENIAL OF SERVICE

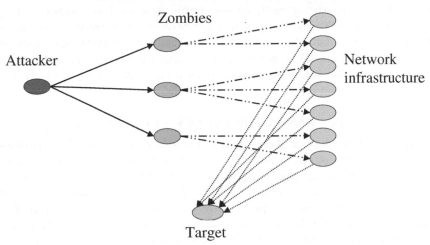

Figure 2.5. Example spoofing ping flood DDoS attack.

A DDoS attack is a networked DoS where nodes work together. Figure 2.5 shows an example of a ping flood DDoS. The attacker gains access to multiple machines over time and plants zombie processes. A zombie is a daemon that performs the actual attack [Garber 2000]. At a predetermined time the zombies, located on different computers, launch the attack on the target. In this case, spoofed ping requests, listing the target as the initiator, are sent to random nodes from the IP address space. The random nodes send replies to the target. Hundreds or thousands of zombies working together swamp the bandwidth of the target's network connections.

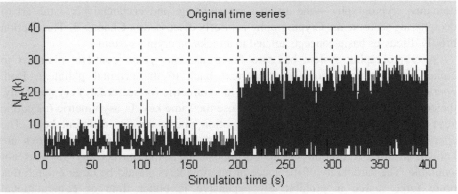

Figure 2.6. DoS attack as viewed by the victim. (ns-2 simulation data from Jason Schwier.) Each point on the graph is the number of packets received by the node during a discrete time interval.

A DDoS attack is difficult to avoid. The attacker does not need to access any machine on the same subnetwork as the target. It is impossible to enforce stringent security on all the Internet ASs. Many systems are not even in the United States. Many IP stack protocols can be used.

The attack in Figure 2.5 is difficult to stop. After it starts, the victim is isolated from the network and has limited ability to act. The victim perceives the attack as shown in Figure 2.6. The normally chaotic traffic flow suddenly increases. Ping responses arrive from nodes strewn across the network infrastructure. This set of nodes may vary over time. The zombie processes need to be stopped. Since they are sending spoofed packets, this is not trivial. Even after the zombies are stopped it is difficult to find the attacker, who may have planted the zombies months in advance. Chapters 5 and 12 revisit DDoS issues.

18.   MAN-IN-THE-MIDDLE ATTACKS

By masquerading as a service, it may be possible to intercept protocol initialization requests and subsequent communications. An attacker thus positioned between a client and server can set up separate secure communications links to both the client and server. The intermediary captures confidential information in clear text. Neither client nor server detects the deception, since they are both using encrypted data channels. This attack may be avoided by requiring responses to challenge queries that unambiguously identify the other party in a transaction.

19.   REPLAY ATTACKS

It is also possible to intercept and store communications for later use. It may not even be necessary to decrypt the messages. Special care should be taken to avoid replay attacks for identification certificates and financial transactions. Retransmitting old packets can commit parties to bogus transactions.

20.   CRYPTANALYSIS

Cryptology is the science of secret communications. It is divided into two sub-domains: cryptography – the art of secret writing, and cryptanalysis – the art of deciphering secret texts. Cryptography is briefly discussed in Chapter 3. This section briefly discusses basic concepts related to attacks on crypto-systems.

A cryptographic system has two functions: *encryption* converts plaintext to ciphertext; *decryption* converts ciphertext back to the original plaintext. Both operations have an associated key value. In symmetric (or secret key) cryptography, the encryption and decryption operations use the same key. In asymmetric (or public key) cryptography, encryption and decryption operations use different keys. The encryption and decryption operations should be straightforward if the keys are known. Ideally, decryption should be impossible if the correct key value is not available. The cardinality of the space of possible keys should be large enough that brute force search is prohibitively expensive in either time or computational resources.

The four basic operations of cryptanalysis are [Friedman 1980]

- Determination of the clear text message language.
- Determination of the cryptographic method used.
- Reconstruction of the key or keys used.
- Reconstruction of the clear text message from the ciphertext.

Attacks on the cryptographic system can be either passive or active. Passive attacks monitor and record transmissions. Active attacks can also modify ciphertext transmissions or transmission channels [Menezes 1997].

General classes of attacks on encryption schemes, usually assuming that the adversary knows the encryption scheme, include [Menezes 1997, Schneier 1996]

- *Ciphertext only attack* – Deduce the key or clear text directly from the ciphertext with no additional information.
- *Known-plaintext attack* – Given examples ciphertext and corresponding plaintext deduce the key or keys.
- *Chosen plaintext attack* – The attacker receives the ciphertext for a given plaintext and uses this information to deduce keys.
- *Adaptive chosen plaintext* – A series of chosen plaintext attacks where the plaintext varies depending on previous results.
- *Chosen ciphertext attack* – The plaintext is made available for a given ciphertext.
- *Adaptive chosen ciphertext* – A series of chosen ciphertexts can be decoded and the choice of ciphertext can depend on earlier results.

Successful encryption algorithm attacks result in the attacker: finding the key, finding an alternate algorithm for decrypting ciphertext without the key, finding the plaintext message, or finding some information about the plaintext message [Schneier 1996]. Mathematical techniques, like those given in [Friedman 1980], may not be needed to break codes. Brute force methods, like those in [EFF 1998], may be more effective, especially when using special purpose hardware.

Other cryptanalytic attacks target protocols using encryption, rather than encryption algorithms. Man-in-the-middle and replay attacks, which we have already discussed, fit into this category. Other protocol attacks include [Menezes 1997]

- *Known key attack* – The current key can be inferred using knowledge of earlier keys.
- *Dictionary attack* – Comparison of the ciphertext with a large collection of encrypted (or hashed) possible plaintexts finds the plaintext corresponding to the ciphertext.

There are several known variations on these basic attacks.

21. DNS AND BGP VULNERABILITIES

There are many protocols in the IP suite. All are vulnerable to implementation errors, such as buffer overflow attacks. Vulnerabilities have been found in most every protocol, including even the time-of-day reporting services. This section discusses security aspects of two IP networking protocols. The Distributed Name Service

(DNS) and Border Gateway Protocol (BGP) are essential parts of the IP networking layer. DNS translates Internet node names into numeric IP addresses. BGP maintains routing tables used to forward packets between AS domains. Many vulnerabilities, similar to protocol attacks on cryptography implementations, have been found in both.

Although TCP is supported, DNS requests are generally sent in a single unencrypted User Datagram Protocol (UDP) packet from a node to its local name server. Local servers have a cache of names. If the resource record for the name requested is not in the cache, the record is routed through a hierarchical tree until a name server is found that can resolve the request. The response is also typically in a single unencrypted UDP packet [Stevens 1994]. Eavesdropping by sniffing DNS request packets is trivial. Man-in-the-middle attacks are easy. Intercepting DNS requests and returning bogus information is not terribly difficult. Cache poisoning is when bogus entries are sent in response to a request. They remain in the local name server's cache, so that future name requests are consistently translated to the wrong IP address. DNS is vulnerable to DoS attacks [Atkins 2003] and packet-flooding attacks have been attempted on the DNS root servers. The attacks we have listed do not even require compromising nodes in the DNS hierarchy, using a buffer overflow attack for example. Methods for securing name servers, including an authentication mechanism, exist and alleviate some of these problems [Householder 2002].

In the BGP protocol, ASs exchange reachability information about Internet domains. Packets are then routed through ASs on what appears to be the most efficient path to the destination. The existing protocol has a number of issues related to scalability, convergence speed, and stability [Farley 2003]. BGP is built on TCP and is vulnerable to TCP based attacks, like packet-flooding DoS attacks [Xiao 2002]. Currently BGP updates are not authenticated, although a public key based authentication is under consideration [Xiao 2002]. BGP messages are thus subject to modification, deletion, forgery, and replay [Farley 2003]. In 1997, a misconfigured router sent incorrect routing information, stating that the router was on the shortest path to everywhere. This information propagated through the BGP causing widespread congestion and packet losses. In addition to accidental, or possibly intentional, configuration errors, route updates propagate through the network unevenly. This lack of synchronization can cause routing instability and packet loss. This instability can result in routes oscillating. Paths can thus remain unstable for extended periods of time. Since spoofing and forging BGP updates is possible, these basic instabilities can easily be aggravated resulting in a large scale DoS. The ability to intentionally lure traffic for a given AS (target) through another AS (man-in-the-middle), by AS (man-in-the-middle) misrepresenting the number of hops between them, can lead to more sinister manipulations. Fixes to these vulnerabilities have been proposed, based on public key information verification and testing the contents of update requests [Xiao 2002, Farley 2003].

22. EXERCISES

Exercise 2.1 Modify the security image in Figure 2.1 by associating the vulnerabilities from Section 1 with columns or elements of columns.

Exercise 2.2 For Sections 8 through 21, list the vulnerabilities in Section 1 used by the exploit.

Exercise 2.3 Research a known worm or virus exploit. List the vulnerabilities it used. Create a diagram like Figure 2.1 that clearly explains the exploit.

Exercise 2.4 Create a graph structure that shows the relationships between classes of exploits.

Exercise 2.5 Create a graph structure that shows the relationships between vulnerabilities in Section 1.

Exercise 2.6 Make a flow chart that explains the process for discovering buffer overflow vulnerabilities in a software package. Estimate the work required to integrate this into a software testing system to guarantee that these faults do not exist. Estimate the work required to discover a buffer overflow vulnerability and associated attack.

Exercise 2.7 Describe a hypothetical hybrid exploit that combines features of at least three separate classes of attacks.

CHAPTER 3
Current Security Solutions

Given the system vulnerabilities and attacks described in Chapter 2, what defenses keep systems secure and dependable? This chapter reviews current art. Most approaches secure isolated machines; few distributed countermeasures exist. We consider distributed countermeasures and global security issues starting in Chapter 7.

This chapter presents security tools in approximate order of acceptance and use. Practical implementations thus appear first and theoretical approaches later. Coincidentally, techniques dealing with global issues are more likely to be found at the end of the chapter.

1. AUDITS

Auditing businesses is common practice. Independent experts verify office finances and business practices. Technical security audits, where independent experts verify system security goals and implementation, can be part of this process. This includes evaluating the risks associated with a system and determining the appropriate resources and measures for minimizing these risks [Tipton 2003, Zimmerli 1984]. A security audit may include penetration testing where a team of experts, called a tiger or red team, tries to circumvent system security. Penetration testing is common in the Department of Defense [Tipton 2003] and the "eligible receiver" study found vulnerabilities in the 911 emergency response systems in many cities [PBS 2003].

Computer systems typically maintain log files as audit trails for discovering and diagnosing security breaches. Before the advent of personal computers, mainframes and minicomputers commonly had teletypes as system consoles, where security violations and the use of privileged commands were printed to provide a paper audit trail. To change the system log, an intruder needed physical access to the system console. Unfortunately, searching for security alarms required manually leafing through reams of paper. Almost all modern systems store log messages in computer files, making detecting and isolating security alarms easier. Unfortunately, if intruders gain access to privileged accounts they can erase or modify log files, ruining evidence and hiding intrusions. One way to counteract this is to store log files on inerasable media, like write once read many tape, to make a permanent audit log that can be used as evidence.

Audit logs are not limited to single machines. Protocols, like the Simple Network Management Protocol (SNMP), allow events to be monitored throughout the network. Management Information Base (MIB) messages, including security alerts, are transmitted to a network management workstation [Leinwand 1996]. MIB logs, like other logs, can be subject to after the fact modification by intruders [Russell 2003].

Unfortunately, the volume of information gathered is often enough to seriously impact network performance. In practice, these monitoring tools are frequently disabled. Network monitoring is a major part of any intrusion detection system (IDS). IDSs monitor network usage in order to infer system misuse. Although many commercial IDS packages exist, they are notoriously plagued by false positives. Not only are actual attacks buried in multiple events of no consequence, the volume of alarms can lead to systems crashing on their own [Newman 2002]. Reliable and effective intrusion detection is an area of active research.

Much of this book covers in detail security issues involving the "disruptive technologies" of mobile code and peer-to-peer networking. Audits can be useful in detecting tampering with mobile code packages by untrustworthy hosts. One approach is to keep itineraries of the nodes visited by a mobile code package. If a code package starts behaving incorrectly, it may be possible to infer the platform that corrupted it. Other packages that the platform has handled would then become suspect [Jansen 1999]. Similarly, mobile code can have an associated audit trail. Partial results can be logged throughout a distributed computation. This can aid computer forensics in determining after the fact which hosts are malicious [Jansen 1999].

2. ENCRYPTION

Cryptology is the science of writing in codes. It consists of two sub-domains: *cryptography* – the science of encrypting information so it cannot be read by unauthorized parties, and *cryptanalysis* – the science of decrypting information to read it without authorization. A message in its original form is said to be in cleartext. Encryption converts cleartext information into ciphertext. Decryption converts ciphertext back to the original cleartext [Schneier 1996].

Numerous algorithms, or ciphers, exist for encrypting cleartext to create ciphertext. Each cipher algorithm has an associated decryption algorithm. A common misconception is that an encryption algorithm is secure when it is secret. This approach has been found woefully inadequate in practice. It is referred to as security through obscurity. On the other hand, some information must be secret to allow authorized parties to retrieve the cleartext and stop unauthorized parties from retrieving the information. In modern approaches, this secret is reduced to a single binary value called the key.

In an ideal cipher, encryption and decryption have low complexity when the key value is known, but retrieving cleartext without the key, or finding the key value, has very high complexity. Current approaches integrate mathematical problems into the encryption process that are known to be computationally intractable. This guarantees the security of the encryption algorithm. An attacker must perform a brute force search of the space of possible keys to decipher the message and/or find the original key. The key length thus determines how secure an encryption implementation is.

An excellent discussion of these issues can be found in [EFF 1998], which highlights weaknesses of the Data Encryption Standard (DES).

We introduce two formalisms for expressing encryption protocols. Let M represent the cleartext message. The formalism in [Schneier 1996] represents the ciphertext C as the result of encrypting M using algorithm $E()$ and key k_1. Its associated decryption algorithm $D()$ uses key k_2. More formally,

$$C = E_{k_1}(M) \quad M = D_{k_2}(C) \tag{1}$$

Another formalism in [Ryan 2001] is derived from Hoare's Communicating Sequential Processes (CSP) and is suited to automatic protocol verification. Variables are concatenated using the "." operator and $\{M\}_k$ represents encryption of M using key k. For example the following statement

$$a \rightarrow b : \{k_{ab}.a\}_{k_b} \tag{2}$$

indicates that a transmits the following message to b: a concatenation of key k_{ab} and the address of a encrypted using key k_b.

As stated in Chapter 2, Section 20, symmetric key approaches use the same key for both encryption and decryption. Public key algorithms use different keys for encryption and decryption. The extra flexibility provided by public key approaches typically has an associated computational cost. Many protocols use public key encryption to establish a temporary symmetric key, which is used for the bulk of the communications. This provides both flexibility and efficient communications.

Cryptography is the tool of choice for enforcing the traditional security goals of confidentiality, authentication, access control, and nonrepudiation [Stallings 1995]. It is an essential element of most security systems. Interested readers are referred to [Schneier 1996] and [Menezes 1997] for details of cryptography theory and practice. Recall that the weak point of most cryptography systems is protocol implementation and support infrastructure (including people), not the underlying algorithm [Tipton 2003]. In this book, we will discuss communications protocols using cryptographic primitives in Chapters 6 through 9.

For mobile code applications where sensitive information needs to be computed on untrusted hardware, traditional cryptography is of limited utility. The remote host will have access to the key and be able to decrypt sensitive data. To alleviate this weakness, interesting work has been initiated toward computing with encrypted functions. It has been shown possible in some cases to execute encrypted functions on data provided by the host [Sander 1998]. The host performing the computation has no way of interpreting data inputs, outputs, or program structure; securing the program from both malicious corruption and reverse engineering. An interesting extension of this performs functions in a domain with redundant representations of data. Random errors corrupt the computation, but those knowing the encoding scheme can retrieve the correct information [Loureiro 2002]. This is an area of continuing research and analysis.

Field Programmable Gate Arrays (FPGAs) are hardware devices designed to support adaptation and reprogramming of their internal logic. A more thorough description of FPGA technology will be given in Chapter 4. At this point, consider an FPGA as a hardware device whose logic can be rewritten and under certain conditions read. An important issue is the protection of product intellectual property from piracy. One protection technique is tamperproofing that erases the FPGA logic when attempts are made to read the internal configuration [Yee 1994]. Another approach is to encrypt and corrupt the FPGA configuration so that special hardware is needed to interpret the FPGA code [Austin 1995]. An interesting extension of this concept encrypts selected portions of the design. Naïve attempts to clone a product will work almost correctly [Yip 2000]. The effort required to detect, isolate, and correct intermittent problems is likely to be more time-consuming and expensive than the effort needed to decrypt a totally encrypted FPGA. This work provides many important lessons:

- Mobile code techniques are migrating into the hardware domain.
- The line between hardware and software is increasingly porous.
- Selective or adaptive encryption may make cryptanalysis more difficult.
- Confusion can be an effective security tool.

3.   STEGANOGRAPHY

Steganography is the security through obscurity concept that is not accepted by the encryption community. It is the science of hiding information. One piece of data is hidden within another. For example, changing the lower order bits of an image or music file is unlikely to noticeably change the original item. Whitespace characters in documents or computer source code can also contain hidden information. Comparing the original and modified data items allows the hidden data to be retrieved easily.

Herodotus documented the use of steganography for covert communications. Recent concerns about the use of steganography for secret communications by terrorist organizations is most likely overstated [Wired 2001a, CW 2002]. In addition to being used for covert communications, steganography is being applied to digital watermarking. Information hidden in images, sound, or other data can be used to verify the origin of the data. This is useful for protection of intellectual property rights.

Note that steganographic information is secure solely because others are unaware of its presence. Once a hiding place is detected, recovery of the information is usually fairly straightforward. Steganalysis refers to discovering and recovering hidden information. Removal of hidden information is often straightforward, once it has been detected.

4.   OBFUSCATION

To obfuscate is to make a concept so "confused and opaque that it is difficult to understand" [AH 1992]. There is a long history of obfuscation in politics and software engineering. Obfuscation in software design is not always intentional. Examples showing effective obfuscation of computer code can be found in the results of the annual obfuscated C code-writing contest [IOCCC 2004]. With obfuscation, object or source code is deliberately scrambled in a manner that keeps it functional but hard to reverse engineer. Sometimes obfuscation is derided as being an inferior form of encryption, trying to hide information without providing the complexity guarantees present in modern encryption techniques.

Table 3.1. Taxonomy of Obfuscation Techniques Presented in [Collberg 1997]

Layout obfuscation - these are simple, straightforward, irreversible, and fairly ineffective	
Replace identifier names in source or intermediate code with arbitrary values.	
Remove formatting information in source or intermediate files.	
Remove comments explaining code.	
Data obfuscation - makes data structures less obvious	
Store and encode data in unusual forms.	
	Create a transformation that maps a variable into a domain requiring multiple inputs.
	Promote scalar values to objects or insert into a larger data structure.
	Convert static data into a procedure that outputs the constant values desired.
	Change variable encodings into an equivalent domain.
	Change variable lifetime and scope.
Change the grouping of data structures.	
	If the range of two variables are restricted they can be joined into one variable with a larger range. (ex. two 32-bit variables can be stored in a 64-bit variable.)
	Modify inheritance relations between objects, including inserting useless classes in the class structure.
	Change the dimensionality of arrays.
Reorder program instructions and data structures in a random manner.	
	Data declarations can be randomized.
	The order of instructions can be randomized, so long as this does not change program meaning.
	Positions of data in arrays can be randomized.
Control obfuscation- changes program flow adding execution overhead.	
Aggregation - combine unrelated computations into one module or separate related computations into multiple modules.	
	Replace a procedure call with an inline copy of the procedure.
	Take two separate code components and insert them into a common procedure.
	Take two separate code components and interleave their statements in a common procedure.
	Make multiple copies of a single subroutine to make calling patterns less obvious.
	Modify loop structures by combining, splitting or unrolling the loop.
Ordering - randomize the order computations are performed.	
	Reorder statements.
	Reorder loops.
	Reorder expressions.
Computations - modify algorithms.	
	Insert dead code that is irrelevant into a program.
	Use native or virtual machine commands that can not be expressed in the higher-level languages.
	Make loop exit conditions needlessly complex without affecting the number of times a loop is executed.
	Replace library calls and standard constructs with nonstandard ones.
	Parallelize the program.
	Include an interpreter in the program that executes code native to that nonstandard interpreter.
Preventive transformations	
Targeted - explore weaknesses in current decompilers.	
Inherent- Explore problems with known deobfuscation techniques.	

In reality, obfuscation differs subtly from encryption. With the exception of computing with encrypted functions (computing with encrypted functions could also be considered a type of obfuscation), an encrypted program needs to be decrypted using the key to run. Once a program has been decrypted it can be reverse engineered or modified. A user that is authorized to execute the program has easy access to the program's internal structure. Obfuscated programs can be executed in their obfuscated form and users do not have a key to reverse the obfuscation process. Thus, users that can execute the program still have barriers hindering their access to the program's internal structure [Collberg 1997].

Many types of obfuscation exist. Table 3.1 summarizes the obfuscation taxonomy presented in [Collberg 1997].

Obfuscation has been suggested as a method of protecting mobile code from attacks by malicious hosts. If code (data) is modified to remain valid only for a short period of time, the time needed for reverse engineering may be longer than the period of time the code (data) is valid. In theory, this approach retains the advantages of code encryption [Hohl 1997] and can be applied to arbitrary functions. Unfortunately, it is difficult to quantify the time needed to reverse engineer obfuscated code and robustly establish the code validity time periods [Jansen 1999].

5.   PUBLIC KEY INFRASTRUCTURE

In public (asymmetric) key cryptography, each party has a public and a private key. Possessors of the private (public) key can read data encrypted using the associated public (private) key. Encryption using the private key verifies the message source to a recipient with the public key. Transmission privacy is assured by encrypting a message with the public key, since only possessors of the private key can decrypt the message.

As long as the encryption method has not been compromised, secure communications protocols can be built from this. Only public keys need to be shared, and they can be widely distributed. Each user maintains the secrecy of their private key, which need not be communicated. In practice, things are more complicated. Public key encryption needs more computational resources than symmetric key approaches. It is also unsuited to hardware implementation. Public key encryption is often used to exchange a symmetric key that is used for the rest of the session.

Public Key Infrastructure (PKI) implementations attempt to fill the following gaps:

- How do you find the public key of the party you want to communicate with?
- How do you know the person sending you a public key is who they say they are?
- What happens when a key is compromised?

Most PKI approaches are built on the X.509 standard described in RFC2459 [Housely 1999]. X standards are data network recommendations from the International Telecommunications Union (www.itu.int). The X.500 series deals with directory systems for networks, and X.509 describes directories for public-key certificates. RFC documents are Internet recommendations maintained by the Internet Engineering Task Force (IETF).

The PKI is a directory for finding public keys associated with users. A Certification Authority (CA) maintains the directory. A certificate is a data structure that binds a public key to its owner. The certificate is valid for a limited period of time and signed (code signing is described in Section 6) by the CA providing a guarantee that the certificate comes from the CA and has not been tampered with. Users register their public key via a Registration Authority (RA). The RA verifies the identity of anyone registering a key before submitting the key to the CA. The RA also tells the CA to revoke certificates as keys or users become invalid.

Certification may or may not be hierarchical. A user may trust a given CA or try to establish a chain of trust from the top-level Internet Policy Registration Authority to the CA. When receiving an encrypted message from a third party, a user verifies certificate authenticity using the CA's public key. The user should also query the CA's Certificate Revocation List (CRL) to verify that the key has not been revoked and is still valid.

PKI is often the basis for distributed authentication systems, as in [Thompson 2003]. An analysis of distributed authentication issues for group collaboration using PKI can be found in [Ellison 2003].

6.   CODE SIGNING

Hash functions take binary data as input and produce a shorter data value. A common application for them is creating look-up tables for database records. Hash functions should be easily computed and greatly compress the input string. Secure hash functions have two additional properties [Menezes 1997]:

- It is difficult to create input that maps to a known hash value.
- It is difficult to find two values that map to the same hash value.

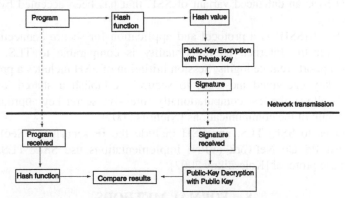

Figure 3.1. Diagram showing the code signing process using public key encryption.

Modification detection codes (MDCs) are secure hash functions used to detect changes to a given data object. Well-known MDC algorithms include MD5 and

SHA-1. An MDC value can be provided to ensure that a program has not been modified. Inputting program binary into SHA-1 produces output that should match the independently provided hash value. If they do not match, the program has been corrupted in some way [Menezes 1997].

Message authentication codes (MACs) use a secret key as part of the hash calculation process. Authorized users will have a copy of the secret key and can use the key in the hashing function to verify, not only that the code has not been tampered with, but also that the MAC was computed by someone possessing the secret key. The use of a shared key is an obvious weakness for this approach, which is also subject to "birthday attacks" (i.e., the probability of finding anther string with the same hash is high within a bounded number of tries) [Menezes 1997].

A digital signature is similar to a MAC, except public key techniques are used to prove the source of the message instead of symmetric key cryptography. The hash is computed and encrypted using the private key to produce a signature. The signature can be decrypted using the public key. The decrypted value is compared with the hash value of the program [Howard 2003]. This guarantees both that the program has not been tampered with and that the signature provider had the associated private key; ensuring that code is from a trusted source. This process is shown in Figure 3.1. Microsoft's ActiveX uses this approach [Rubin 1998]. This assumes that, when the source of software is a reputable supplier, it is relatively risk-free to use the software. The code is as secure as "shrink-wrap" software.

7.   SSL, TLS, AND SSH

Secure Sockets Layer (SSL) is a protocol for establishing an encrypted pipe using a TCP/IP connection. SSL interacts with the OSI application and presentation layers. It contains a handshake protocol that allows nodes to agree on an encryption key, and a record protocol that defines the format for encapsulating encrypted data encapsulated in Transmission Control Protocol (TCP) packets. Transport Layer Security (TLS) is an enhanced variant of SSL that has been accepted by the IETF [Nichols 2002].

Secure Shell (SSH) is a protocol and application for secure connection of two computers over the Internet. Its functionality is comparable to TLS. The SSH application supports remote logins. Session initiation of SSH includes a protocol that uses public key encrypted messages to securely establish a shared key for the session. This allows the less computationally intensive secret key approaches to be used for the bulk of the communications [Nichols 2002].

Alternatives to SSL, TLS, and SSH include the IP security (IPSec) standard. Many Virtual Private Network (VPN) implementations use SSL, TLS, SSH, or IPSec as a base protocol [Kolesnikov 2002].

8.   FORMAL METHODS

The weak link in most cryptography implementations is not the cryptography algorithm. When cryptography systems are broken it is most likely due to implementation errors, other security breaches (including human error), and incorrect protocol design. Formal methods exist for expressing and analyzing distributed protocols. These methods include Hoare's CSP and various computational calculi (including Church's original λ-calculus that formalizes computation using functions, Milner's π-calculus that adds parallelism, and Eberbach's $-calculus that adds introspective consideration of computational resources). There is even the spi-calculus, which is a formal framework designed specifically for verifying cryptographic security protocols [Abadi 1999].

Formal methods exist in four main categories (or combinations thereof) [Ryan 2001]: (*i*) logic-based, (*ii*) model-checking and state enumeration, (*iii*) proof-based, and (*iv*) cryptographic. The first step in using formal methods is to construct an abstract model of the problem using operators like those in Equations (1) and (2). The tools used in cryptographic protocol design are included as atomic elements of the formal language. These include encryption, decryption, nonces (random values), time stamps, hash functions, and PKI certificates.

The approach in [Ryan 2001] is to state the properties the protocol should have as specifications. The properties can include secrecy, authentication, integrity, nonrepudiation, fairness, anonymity, and availability. These specifications are phrased as logic statements in the formal language. Both the protocol to be analyzed and the attacks to be considered are written in the formal language as well. An automated model checker can then enumerate all the reachable states for the system and verify that the specifications hold under all conditions.

These methods are worthwhile extensions to cryptographic primitives. They can verify that the proposed approach will hold as long as the stated assumptions hold against the attacks foreseen. It should be noted that they are not suited to protection against attacks like resource monitoring, which attempt to compromise the system at an entirely different level.

9.   VIRUS SCANNERS

There are a number of antivirus software products on the market. Many products inspect files looking for patterns indicating the presence of a virus. Inspections are commonly periodic scans of an entire hard drive or inspections of files as they arrive at the computer.

Pattern recognition may take many forms. The most common form of pattern recognition is to search for a virus signature in a file. The signature is obtained by reverse engineering multiple instances of the virus. The antivirus program scans files trying to match the contents of the file with records in a database of signatures. The database needs to be updated frequently as new virus implementations are discovered [Tipton 2003]. This approach is inherently reactive. Signatures are derived from instances of existing exploits.

There is no way to correctly decide whether or not an arbitrary program has a virus, since solving this problem would be equivalent to solving the halting problem [Cohen 1986]. (The exact complexity of this problem is established in [Adelmann 1988].) Measures exist for hiding viruses from scanners. Polymorphic viruses modify themselves each time they infect a new file [CVDQ 1992]. One of the earliest implementations of this approach is attributed to the Bulgarian virus writer Dark Avenger who created a mutation engine. Details on how to create a polymorphic virus can be found in [Ludwig 1995]. Interestingly, the explanation in [Ludwig 1995] is in terms of cryptography. Ten years later, the Bagle e-mail virus was very successful at foiling virus detection software by encapsulating itself in encrypted zip archive files [Leyden 2004]. Another approach to avoiding detection is to place portions of the virus in places scanning software cannot locate. For example, some blocks on the hard disk could be marked as bad blocks and the virus stored in those bad blocks. The infected program would still be able to access those blocks using low-level input-output routines and execute the virus code. How to do this is explained in [Ludwig 1991].

Heuristic approaches to detecting viruses, such as looking for programs that open executable files in write mode, have been attempted. This sounds deceptively easy. In operating systems, there are many ways to hide the name of a program being accessed until run-time. Several techniques for defeating heuristics are outlined in [Ludwig 2002]. Many of the techniques are obfuscation techniques. Another problem with heuristics is that many have high false positive rates, which lead eventually to real detections being ignored [Aesop 2000].

The most extreme method for avoiding the spread of e-mail viruses can be found in some e-mail clients and/or servers that no longer allow some types of e-mail attachments (e.g., .vbs, .exe, .com, etc.) to be delivered to users. In many cases, this is overly restrictive and counterproductive. For example, to transfer executables, some users have created zip archives of the files to override this countermeasure. To exploit this practice, one variant of the Bagle e-mail virus transmits itself as an encrypted zip archive [Leyden 2004].

10. ATTACK GRAPHS

In Chapter 2, we introduced the security incident taxonomy from [Howard 1998] that is used by the Computer Emergency Response Team (CERT) to describe and classify security breaches. In the taxonomy, each attack has an objective and unauthorized results that are obtained to advance that objective.

In the auditing section, we described the use of red teams to attack existing systems and find their vulnerabilities. To plan their attacks red teams produce attack graphs. An attack graph culminates in a final state that represents attainment of a final goal. The final goal is a successful breach of system security. The red team probes the system and finds vulnerabilities in order to construct the graph. Each path through the graph from the initial state to the goal represents a potentially successful attack [Jha 2002].

Attack graphs are a type of threat model. Vulnerabilities are generally in one of the following threat categories [Howard 2003]:

- *Spoofing* – Posing as another user.
- *Tampering* – Maliciously modifying data or programs.
- *Repudiation* – Denying actions taken.
- *Information disclosure* – Revealing data to unauthorized users.

- *Denial of service* – Making a service unavailable or unusable.
- *Elevation of privilege* – Attaining administrative status without authorization.

Vulnerabilities can also be ranked by considering the following [Howard 2003]:

- *Damage potential* – How serious is the breach?
- *Reproducibility* – How easy is it to get to work?
- *Exploitability* – How much expertise is required to use the vulnerability?
- *Affected users* – How large is the potential impact?
- *Discoverability* – How likely is it that the exploit will be discovered?

If the attack graphs do not contain loops, they can be considered a tree structure. The root of the tree is a system compromise. Internal nodes of the tree can represent either "or" conditions where any of a number of conditions is sufficient, or "and" conditions where all conditions must be in place. [Moore 2001] describes how to construct an attack tree for a fictitious enterprise. This approach strongly resembles the use of fault trees to analyze system dependability [Limnios 2000]. Unfortunately the quantitative aspects of fault tree formalisms all depend on an assumption of independence, which is not justified in the case of deliberate attacks.

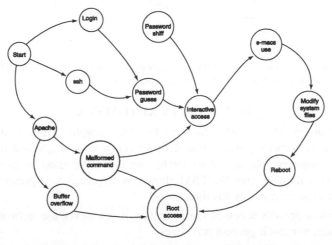

Figure 3.2. Example attack graph that shows paths an attacker can take to get root access.

It is also possible to automatically generate attack graphs using model-checking software [Jha 2002, JhaSW 2002]. An abstract model is created of the system to be attacked as well as the security property to be maintained (this approach can only enforce safety properties, we will discuss them further in the sections on security automata and dependability). Model checking software exhaustively evaluates possible transitions of the system and keeps a list of the set of system states that do not satisfy the security (safety) property. The attack graph is defined by this set of states and their associated transitions. This tree can be analyzed to be certain there are no unnecessary states. Note the similarity between this approach and the formal methods discussed in Section 8.

The attack graph can be analyzed to help secure the system. The minimum cut set of states between the initial and terminal sets of the attack graph provides the smallest set of vulnerabilities that must be addressed to secure the system. Alternatively the graph can be used to express a Markov Decision Process that helps determine the attacks that are most likely to occur, or possibly least costly to counteract [Jha 2002]. As with other model checking based approaches, the results obtained depend on the fidelity of the model used. Vulnerabilities that are not expressed by the model will not be found. An example attack graph is shown in Figure3.2.

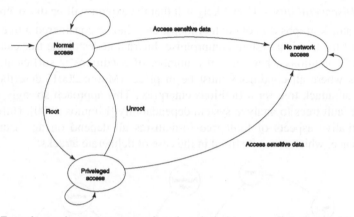

Figure 3.3. Example security automata expressing a hypothetical (and unrealistically simple) security policy designed to prevent sensitive data from network access.

11. SECURITY AUTOMATA

Security automata are complementary to attack graphs. Finite State Machines (FSMs) express security policies that define what a user is allowed to do on the system.   A language like lex [Aho 1986] can easily be used to implement this approach. An automata, like the FSM shown in Figure 3.3, expresses a security policy. In this case, the policy has three rules:

- Once a process accesses sensitive data it can never use network resources again, nor can it get root privileges.
- Processes with root privileges cannot modify executables that do not belong to root.
- Accessing sensitive information automatically revokes root privileges and removes the process' access to network resources.

These policies are enforced using an Inline Reference Monitor (IRM). Each command must be approved by the IRM before execution. The IRM changes the state of the process' associated FSM as execution proceeds. If execution of a command would violate the security policy expressed by the active policy, the process is terminated before the command executes [Schneider 2000].

The policies that an IRM can enforce are clearly defined. Terminating the process before it violates the security policy enforces a prefix closure property on the regular language associated with the FSM [Aho 1986]. The policies are a subset of the set of safety properties [Schneider 2000], which are discussed in the dependability section of this chapter. A safety property prevents an undesirable event from occurring.

This concept has been expanded. [Bauer 2002] proposes a number of approaches with actions other than terminating processes that violate the security policy:

- *Insertion automata* – Add instructions to the execution stream.

- *Suppression automata* – Remove instructions from the execution stream.

- *Edit automata* – Replace offending instructions with other instructions.

The properties these automata can enforce differ from the enforceable set of IRM enforcement policies in [Schneider 2000]. This approach presupposes methods exist for detecting policy violations and changes to the instruction streams are known *a priori* or are computable. It is not clear that these assumptions hold in practice.

12. SANDBOXING

Sandboxing limits the instructions available for use. Java uses this method. Its virtual machine restricts an Applet's ability to read and write on the local disk, as well as communicate with other nodes. In spite of this, malicious Applets can circumvent restrictions [Rubin 1998]. This has been primarily possible due to implementation and design errors on specific virtual machines (VMs) [Knight 1998].

Sandboxing is often used in conjunction with VMs. A VM is a software system that emulates the hardware interfaces [Blunden 2002]. Although Java has the best-known VM, commercial packages exist that successfully emulate Intel systems. Both Windows and Linux operating systems can be installed on these VMs, and the vast majority of software packages execute flawlessly within the virtual environment. The VM intercepts all calls to the hardware from the software it executes. Restricting program access to limited regions on the hard disk (for example) is trivial when using a VM. For example, a VM can limit requests to file access to a limited portion of the file system (e.g., C:\SANDBOX\).

13. FIREWALLS

A firewall limits the machines that can access the Internet. It forces nodes to go through gateways that scan and filter network traffic including mobile code before the code enters a secure zone. This filtering can occur at many different levels in the protocol stack. Usually it occurs at layer 3 (network routing) or above. Filtering can also simultaneously occur at multiple levels. Filtering is often based on

- Source and/or destination IP addresses

- Protocol used

- Source and/or destination port numbers

Filtering at higher levels of the protocol stack requires more sophistication and potentially has a larger impact on network performance [Tipton 2003]. Some firewalls maintain state indicators for network connections. This reduces network overhead, since it is assumed that an active connection does not violate any of the filtering rules.

Most firewalls filter attempts at connections. They do not consider the contents of the communications streams. The halting problem provides a hard limit to the ability of a system to scan and determine the safety of data contents (e.g., mobile code modules) [Cohen 1986]. Many companies now have a Demilitarized Zone (DMZ) on their network, which is located between the router and the firewall. This subset of machines can be allowed network access with the knowledge that they will eventually be compromised.

14. RED/BLACK SEPARATION

Red/black separation means that sensitive and nonsensitive data are handled on different machines that are not colocated. These machines also need to use separate cabling and power sources. This approach is used to guard against covert channel vulnerabilities, such as information leakage due to electromagnetic radiation (tempest). Red and black may signify different levels of information classification, or the difference between ciphertext and plaintext.

15. PROOF CARRYING CODE

Proof Carrying Code (PCC) has been proposed as a technology for securing mobile code. The code producer is obliged to construct an explicit proof that the code is safe. A copy of the site's security policy is provided and a formal proof is constructed showing that the program can under no conditions violate the system's policy. The proof is put into a signature that is transmitted along with the code. Upon receipt, the host verifies the proof before executing the code. Since proof checking software is relatively mature the checking process is relatively efficient. Proof verification does not have to be repeated if the program is rerun. This approach has been implemented with typed assembly language [Crary 1999], a subset of C [Necula 1998] and a subset of Java [Necula 2002].

The literature indicates this approach is used only in research environments by its creators [Rubin 1998]. Many problems exist with the automated generation of proofs. Policies can be generated automatically for type and memory safety [Necula 1998], but it should be noted that many information flow characteristics can never be proven [Rubin 1998]. In addition the proof size can be orders of magnitude larger than the program; it may even grow exponentially [Necula 1998]. In addition to these drawbacks, recent work using physical attacks show that it may be possible to corrupt a correct program during execution to violate type safety [Govindavajhala 2003].

Model carrying code is a similar approach to proof carrying code [Sekar 2001]. In this approach, a higher-level model of the code is automatically extracted. Both the model and code are cryptographically signed and delivered to the consumer. The finite automaton code model is analyzed for conformance to the local security policy. The user can then decide whether or not to execute the code, given any existing security considerations. A runtime monitor ensures that the code conforms to its model. This approach attempts to merge the strong points of security automata and proof carrying code. To some extent it resolves the problem of automatic proof generation, and it is capable of enforcing the same policies as the inline reference monitors of security automata. On the other hand, the guarantees provided do not have the certainty of proof carrying code.

Another extension is to have the compiler create an encoding of the source that guarantees safety properties. Project TransPROSE has been compared with newspeak in the novel *1984*. The compilation process produces an encoding of the parse tree that is unable to express a program that is not type safe, much as in Orwell's fantasy newspeak could not express subversive thoughts [Amme 2001]. The parse tree is compact and easily transmitted. It also presents the program in a form well suited for runtime optimizations to be performed on the remote host. In this approach, they consider the source program to be the proof. To date this approach is used solely to enforce type safety [Haldar 2002].

16. SECURE HARDWARE

Many security techniques, like type safety enforcement, can be circumvented by physical attacks. To prevent physical attacks, devices have to be located in a physically secure area or have some type of secure hardware. Deploying security measures in hardware has many advantages. Software is easier to modify and disable.

The design of hardware for security applications has a long history. One of the earliest electronic computers, Colossus, was created to aid the Allied code breaking effort at Betchley Park in World War II. The groundbreaking Multics operating system, developed jointly by MIT, Bell Labs, and General Electric in the late 1960s, integrated hardware into its security enforcement scheme. A series of n protection rings (for the Multics hardware $n = 8$) was created. At each protection level i, unbridled access was given to all information at all levels $>i$. Access to levels $<i$ required passing through well defined procedure calls. Rings $0 - 3$ were reserved for the operating system [Madnick 1978]. This resembles using a partially ordered set (POset) to contain viruses as proposed in [Cohen 1988] and predates the existence of computer viruses by about a decade.

A common security measure is to make hardware tamperproof. A common external tamperproofing technique is encasing the chip in epoxy, so that any attempt to physically access it will destroy it. Embedding a Faraday cage in the epoxy will capture the chip's electromagnetic radiation, securing it from tempest attacks. IBM citadel processors use these approaches and more to guard against physical attacks [Yee 1994]. These processors include a secure bootstrap mechanism that guarantees that the cryptographic keys enclosed in the system cannot be compromised after system initialization. They are physically accessible only during a part of the initialization process. The concept of a secure bootstrap originated in [Yee 1994].

For many applications the IBM citadel processor is too expensive and bulky. So-called smart cards are often used because of these considerations. Smart cards are usually the size of a normal credit card, containing a small processor. They are often used as a security token [Dhem 2001]. They may include special purpose cryptography circuits with the cryptographic key stored on the card. Smart cards are more vulnerable to invasive attacks than secure coprocessors like the IBM product [Dhem 2001].

Methods for using tamperproof hardware for protecting programs can be found in [Loureiro 2001] and [Zachary 2003]. Viruses, worms, or other software attacks cannot corrupt hardware implementations that are not mutable. In many cases, this means that mobile code packages can execute on these nodes without fear of tampering or corruption [Loureiro 2000].

It may also be possible to create techniques that uniquely identify the physical device being used. Researchers have manufactured systems containing Physical Unclonable Functions (PUFs) or Physical Random Functions (PRFs). Normally, circuits are created so that the signal stabilizes before results are delivered. These functions are circuits whose outcomes depend on transient signals in the processor. The state of manufacturing technology is such that identical copies of the same circuit on different pieces of silicon will give different answers. The results on a given processor, however, tend to converge to the same answer [Gassend 2003]. This approach is still experimental. It is not clear that results from PUFs will not change significantly over time. Practical applications may also require multiple repetitions of a computation to be certain that the transient values converge to a reliably repeatable result.

17. DEPENDABILITY, SAFETY, LIVENESS

Frequently, topics related to system dependability are not considered in security research. Dependability tends to consider system failures due to natural effects, component aging, or stochastic events. Security concentrates on intentional attacks. This is a shortsighted and unnatural division. On the one hand, a system is not dependable if it is easily subverted, and on the other hand, systems are more easily attacked when not running at full capacity.

Dependability is a generic term for either *reliability*, the probability that the system is working at a given mission time, or *availability*, the percentage of time that the system is functional. Reliability is generally used for systems where no human intervention is possible, such as deep space probes and military hardware. Availability, on the other hand, is used to describe systems that can be repaired, such as telecommunications networks.

When a system with strict dependability requirements is being designed, many difficult tradeoffs must be made. A detailed analysis is needed to describe exactly how reliable the system must be. Also you need to consider what assumptions can safely be made in designing the system. No system will ever be 100% dependable. Any number of catastrophic events could occur with a very low probability. A system capable of withstanding all such events would be too expensive to be practical and most likely would be less dependable due to the increased complexity.

Fault masking systems [Krol 1991], also referred to as *N*-modular redundancy [Siewiorek 1982], achieve fault tolerance by duplication of components. This is a standard method for achieving system dependability. Redundancy has also been used as a distributed technique for securing mobile code. Multiple code packages can work in parallel on multiple hosts and compare their results. The aggregate system can thus detect tampering that causes isolated anomalies [Jansen 1999].

For any combination of components, a Markov chain can be constructed that accurately models the state of the system [Alj 1990, Rai 1990, Roseaux 1987, Sahner 1987, Siewiorek 1982]. A Markov chain is a representation of a system that can be characterized as consisting of a number of states, with stochastic rates of transition between the states. Formally, a Markov chain is defined by

- S – A set of states (the set S may be either finite or infinite)
- P – A matrix whose elements p_{ij} are the probability (or rate) of transitions from state i to state j
- Π – A set of initial probabilities of the system being in the given states

The set of states must contain all of the information needed to describe the system. If the system consists of N components, each of which is either functional or faulty, the system is described by a set of 2^N states [Siewiorek 1982]. If some of the components are identical, generally you can combine states to reduce the complexity of the model. Each state then represents the number of components that are operational.

The model assumes that the state of the system is all that is needed to describe the system. It contains neither any information about the amount of time the system has been in a state, nor the path taken through the chain to arrive in that state.

If the matrix P is constant, then the rate of failure and repair of components are also constant. The probability distributions of the states will then be exponential distributions. Also the elements of P can be functions of time. If that case exists, the chain is more difficult to evaluate numerically, and solving the chain analytically may be impossible.

Markov chains are useful tools for studying stochastic systems since a number of tools have been developed for evaluating them. In particular, since a Markov chain is a graph, many algorithms from graph theory [Baase 1988] can be used to evaluate Markov chains. In particular, graph theory can be used to determine whether or not a Markov chain will reach a steady state. If a finite Markov chain is strongly connected and contains a state with a nonzero probability of remaining in the same state, then the Markov chain is guaranteed to eventually reach a steady state [Roseaux 1987].

The probability of the system being in any given state of a Markov chain can be calculated using one of the following approaches:

- Constructing a set of differential equations directly from the chain and solving the equations using Laplace transforms
- Using statistical distributions for each component, and assuming independent failure deducing a direct solution based on probability

- Using Kirchoff's law and the frequency of transition between states, deducing for the steady state the probability of the system being in a set of states
- Evaluating the chain using stochastic Petri networks [David 1989]

In addition to dependability, systems can be characterized by safety and liveness properties [Gaertner 2001]. Safety properties state that an undesirable event will never happen. Formally, a logical predicate is defined and it is shown that the property holds for every reachable system state. This property is very similar to the concept of controllability in Discrete Event Dynamic Systems (DEDS). On the other hand, liveness properties mean that a desirable event will eventually happen. This means that from every possible system state there is a sequence of events that can eventually lead to a state with the desired property. For example, systems that suffer from deadlock will not have liveness. *Self-stabilizability* is a system's ability to recover from any possible fault [Gaertner 1989, Schneider 1993]. It is an extreme form of fault tolerance.

Evaluation of system dependability, safety and/or liveness requires the specification of an error model [Gaertner 2001]. Common models include

- *Fail-stop* – If an error occurs, the system stops working and states that it is not working when asked.
- *Crash* – Includes fail-stop errors, but also does not reply to requests saying that it is not working.
- *Omission* – Includes crash errors, but in addition can simply lose any set of messages without a trace.
- *Crash-recovery* – Systems can crash and spontaneously recover. Some amount of long-term storage is available, so that some (but not all) messages remain after a crash.
- *Byzantine errors* – Byzantine errors are the most challenging error model. Faulty machines are allowed to have arbitrary, even intelligent, behavior. We discuss this error model in more detail.

The Byzantine Generals Problem concerns a mythical siege of an opponent's camp by the Byzantine army. The commander-in-chief of the army has several troops positioned around the city. Each position is under the command of a general. The commander-in-chief knows that many of his generals and messengers are traitors loyal to the opposing army. He must tell all the generals to either attack or retreat. The generals can discuss the decisions among themselves via messengers. If all loyal armies follow the orders of a loyal commander-in-chief, they stand a good chance of success; if one part of the army attacks while another part retreats, they face certain defeat. How can the loyal generals guarantee, by exchanging messages among themselves, that all generals make the same decision, and that this decision is given by a loyal commander-in-chief [Lamport 1982]?

This problem can be rephrased as a system of N independent processing nodes, up to t of which may be faulty. We need to develop a protocol that guarantees that for a broadcast performed by any processor X

- The nonfaulty nodes agree on the contents of the data received from X.
- If X is nonfaulty, the agreement should equal the contents of the message sent from X.

This guarantee can also be termed "general interactive consistency" [Krol 1986].

[Lamport 1982] prove some interesting characteristics of this problem. The problem can be solved only if t, the number of traitors, is less than one-third of N, the total number of nodes. The proof is done by showing that in a graph of only three nodes with one faulty node, a correct processor cannot diagnose which of the other two nodes is faulty.

[Dolev 1982] shows that t must be less than half the connectivity of the graph. This can be seen intuitively. Since a node can change messages passing through it, any part of the graph that receives a majority of messages potentially modified by traitors will be fooled. In other words, to tolerate t faults, the system must have at least $3t + 1$ nodes and every node must be connected directly to at least $2t + 1$ other nodes [Dolev 1982]. An algorithm that solves the Byzantine Generals Problem must execute at least $t + 1$ rounds of broadcasts between the nodes [Fisher 1982].

Systems with high reliability and availability tend to be more robust and more difficult to attack. The security automata discussed earlier enforce safety properties. A system deadlock can be exploited as a Denial of Service (DoS) attack.

18. QUALITY OF SERVICE

Quality of Service (QoS) is another system parameter often mistakenly omitted from security discussions. QoS refers to the ability of a network to guarantee a given level of service. International Organization for Standardization (ISO) specifies 11 QoS parameters [Iren 1999]:

- Connection establishment delay
- Connection establishment failure probability
- Throughput (effective bandwidth)
- Transit delay (latency)
- Residual error rate (percent of packets that are incorrect)
- Transfer failure probability (percent of transfers that are incorrect)
- Connection release delay
- Connection release failure probability
- Protection (against unauthorized access)
- Priority
- Resilience (probability that a connection is terminated due to internal or network problems)

The common QoS factors we will concentrate on are: latency – the expected delay in information delivery; effective bandwidth – the expected volume of information that can be delivered in a time period; and jitter – the expected variance of information latency [Gautam 1997, Kapur 2002].

QoS is important for system security, at the very least, because DoS attacks are designed to disrupt a system's ability to function in a timely manner. A lack of QoS guarantees makes a system vulnerable to DoS. Chapter 10 discusses some QoS modeling issues in more detail. It is interesting to note that while we consider QoS a security issue, others have considered security a network QoS issue [Irvine 2000].

19. ARTIFICIAL IMMUNE SYSTEMS

Network intrusion detection is a difficult problem, which many have attempted to solve. Commercial solutions exist, but they have limited utility. A major issue is finding ways to differentiate between normal and abusive system behavior.

A recent comparison of commercially available IDSs [Newman 2002] states: *"One thing that can be said with certainty about network-based intrusion-detection systems is that they're guaranteed to detect and consume all your available bandwidth ... Because no product distinguished itself, we are not naming a winner."* In addition to false positives obscuring the presence of real intrusions, the volume of false positives was enough to crash almost every IDS package during the test. CPU usage by the IDS packages was over 90% in many cases. One IDS froze the system using it on over 30% of the days it was used.

The taxonomy in [Axelsson 2000] provides an overview of intrusion detection. Many IDSs (and most commercial antivirus software) look for signatures that identify known attacks. These systems are by definition unable to detect and retard new attacks. Other IDSs detect deviations from normal system behavior. [Axelsson 2000] further divides anomaly detectors into self-learning and programmed. [Axelsson 2000] also divides IDSs into centralized and distributed systems.

[Brooks 2002] uses cellular automata models of the network flow dynamics to characterize network pathologies. [Marin 2002] utilizes the concept of changing traffic distribution and predicted the Hurst parameter by tracking the second moment over time to detect the attacks. Their approach relies on two essential notions – (*i*) traffic before the attack remains self-similar, and (*ii*) detecting a DoS attack is an *a posteriori* phenomenon. This describes an offline solution and does not consider the fact that the Hurst parameter is valid only in a limited range of scales.

Other approaches exist that model computer network traffic using techniques from statistical physics. The Therminator project at the Naval Postgraduate School modeled network traffic using entropy equations [Donald 2001]. The end result was a display of network state, which skilled users were able to use to verify that the network was performing normally. [Burgess 2000] models networks as thermal reservoirs where fluctuations represent the exchange of information. [Gudonov 2001] consider information flow as a dynamical system with a phase-space of dimension 10–12.

In 1999 DARPA funded an extensive analysis of intrusion detection technologies using a testbed especially created for this purpose [Haines 2001]. They combined live machines with a simulated network to simulate a larger network in order to derive a realistic system that could be subjected to known attacks. We have used data from this system, ns-2 simulations, and collected from the Penn State network to verify preliminary IDS concepts that are discussed in Chapter 12. Our analysis indicated that the background traffic for [Haines 2001] was more realistic than ns-2 simulated traffic, but was significantly less "bursty" than the traffic collected at Penn State. This indicates that empirical tests on real networks are essential for creating IDS systems.

[Lazarevic 2002] uses datasets like those in [Haines 2001] to compare different intrusion detection approaches. The approaches in [Lazarevic 2002] achieve impressively low false positive rates, but are data mining approaches. They are computationally unsuited for online intrusion detection. Possibly the most interesting aspect of [Lazarevic 2002] is the statistical methods used for evaluating IDS performance.

The basic problem faced by every IDS is differentiating between normal behaviors and the behaviors of intruders. In nature, immune systems face a similar problem. Multi-cellular organisms maintain themselves through complex distributed interactions. Intruders, including viruses, bacteria, and other infections, take advantage of these interactions to reproduce. The task of immune systems is to identify the intruders from their behaviors, isolate them, and remove them from the system. Stephanie Forrest and her student Hofmeyr have studied the internals of immune systems, in the hope that these insights could lead to robust IDSs [Forrest 2000]. They used this approach to perform intrusion detection by monitoring network traffic. The features they use are tuples consisting of source address, destination address, and port number [Hofmeyr 2000]. This approach resembles network sniffers like SNORT [Snort 2003], which capture network packets and use rule bases to infer intrusions from packet contents. This approach requires a significant amount of training, and it is not yet clear how well the artificial immune system design can work in operational networks.

20. EXERCISES

Exercise 3.1 Map the vulnerabilities in Chapter 2 to the countermeasures presented in this chapter.

Exercise 3.2 Use the vulnerabilities from Chapter 2 to create an attack graph that describes how to get root access to a machine. The graph should contain at least three disjoint paths.

Exercise 3.3 Create a security policy that an inline reference monitor can use to foil the attack derived in Exercise 3.2. Create an explicit verification that the security policy will foil the attack.

Exercise 3.4 Create a list of vulnerabilities that are not adequately addressed by current countermeasures. Explain why the current countermeasures are not adequate.

Exercise 3.5 Create a small mathematical model of the economics of computer system implementation. Assume that a given number of errors occur at random and that work required to find and repair errors is constant per error. Consider the work required by an intruder to find a single vulnerability. Show who has the advantage in this competition.

CHAPTER 4
Disruptive Technologies

The term *disruptive technology,* coined by Clayton Christensen, refers to simple, often inexpensive, innovations that radically change a competitive market [Christensen 1997]. These initially inferior innovative products replace existing technologies. Low cost disruptive technologies create economic networks with synergies that encourage further innovation. New products evolve from the inferior initial implementations, and their quality eventually surpasses the technologies that they finally displace. Examples of disruptive technologies include printing presses, automobiles, digital cameras, and personal computers. The erosion of existing markets by disruptive technologies often destroys successful, once dominant, companies.

The personal computer, the Internet, open source software, and wireless communications are disruptive technologies that radically changed both the computing marketplace and how systems are implemented. In this book we discuss four currently disruptive technologies:

- Mobile code
- Peer-to-Peer (P2P) networks
- Field Programmable Gate Arrays (FPGAs)
- Complex adaptive systems

All are simple ideas for making computer systems flexible. Mobile code and P2P are currently seen primarily as security risks. FPGAs are accepted as tools for prototyping hardware-based security solutions, but are likely to fundamentally change hardware design approaches in the near future. Complex adaptive systems are primarily studied by physicists, chemists, and biologists. Unfortunately, this research has had little impact on engineering to date, and even less impact in the design of secure/dependable systems.

These four disruptive technologies are radically changing how computer networks work. Physicists are studying the Internet as a complex adaptive system and acquiring insights on issues like computer virus and worm propagation [Barabasi 2002]. Although mobile code's promise of increased system flexibility, scalability, and reliability has yet to be fully realized, mobile code implementations have been accepted by the marketplace. Java, Jini, Postscript, and .NET are widely accepted mobile code implementations. P2P networks have shown themselves to be efficient, adaptive, and resilient content delivery mechanisms. Despite intensive attempts by large economic interests to suppress P2P file sharing, the technology has continued to spread. FPGAs allow custom hardware implementations to be created economically in small lots. Their user communities accept these technologies, and as with other disruptive technologies, the market will follow.

The rest of this book describes these four disruptive technologies and attempts to further our understanding of their capabilities and networks in general. There is no reason why these technologies cannot be applied to creating secure distributed systems. Disruption will hurt security systems only if we insist on ignoring the advantages of new technologies and dwelling only on the potential threats they pose. Only computers that are never turned on and not attached to a network are truly secure. The question should be how to best maintain security in functioning systems.

1.   MOBILE CODE

Mobile code technology allows programs to move from node to node on the network. The concept is not particularly new. Commercial implementation began at the latest in the early 1970s [Sapaty 1999]. A number of paradigms, which have been proposed as methods for designing mobile code systems, are presented in Chapter 6. These paradigms are unnecessarily restrictive and incapable of expressing many consequences of mobile code use. They look at how an implementation can be constructed, rather than considering the capabilities and limitations of code mobility.

In particular, mobile code effects on the global network behavior have not been addressed. Studies have been made concerning system vulnerabilities to mobile code [Tschudin 1993, Ludwig 1991, Sander 1998, Rubin 1998]. The use of mobile code in a proactive manner to safeguard network dependability and security has hardly been considered.

Von Neumann, a father of computer science, invented flow charts, programming languages, and the serial "von Neumann" computer [von Neumann 1966]. His seminal concept of an automaton controlling another automaton [von Neumann 1966] can be viewed as a form of mobile code. The mobile code concept is evident in the 1960s remote job entry terminals that transfer programs to mainframe computers. Sapaty's wave system, created in the Ukraine [Sapaty 1999] in the 1970s, provided full mobile code functionality. In the 1980s, packet radio enthusiasts in Scandinavia developed a Forth-based approach to remotely transfer and execute programs through a wireless infrastructure [NF 1985]. In the 1990s Java was developed by Sun Microsystems and became the first widely used mobile code implementation. Along the way, mobile code has been viewed from many different perspectives and paradigms.

Given an input data file f on node n_f, a program p on node n_p to be executed, and a user u using node n_u, existing mobile code paradigms would determine the following courses of action [Fugetta 1998]:

- *Client-server* – Data file f is transferred from n_f to n_p. Program p executes on n_p and the results transferred to n_u.
- *Remote evaluation* – Program p is transferred to n_f and executes there. Results are returned to n_u.
- *Code on demand* – Data file f and program p are transferred to n_u and execute there.

- *Mobile agents* – Program p is transferred to n_f and executes there. Program p carries the results to n_u.

In reality both code and programs are mobile. The proper course of action depends on the volume of data, the size of the program, network congestion, and computational loads on the nodes. The course of action should be determined at run-time from locally available information. All approaches listed above are possible. Figure 4.1 shows the relevant abstractions.

Data	**Program**	**Infrastructure**
• Interfaces with programs	• Interfaces with data, other programs, and the infrastructure	• Interfaces with programs and other infrastructures
• Nonexecutable		
• Usually mobile	• Executable	• Executable
• Conversion on demand	• Usually mobile	• Fixed (i.e., not mobile)
• Multiple formats	• Initiates processing	• Tracks resource availability
• Types of compression	• Determines tasks done	
• Data domains	• Registered with broker	• Sets processing location
• Program input and output	• Communicates using infrastructure	• Includes broker tasks
		• Provides resources for programs

Figure 4.1. Three abstractions for mobile code systems: data, programs, and infrastructure.

Consider a mobile code implementation tied with a service broker. A P2P repository of mobile code exists. The repository contains mobile code packages that can be downloaded and executed as needed. This is independent of the operating system or computer language. Figure 4.2 shows typical processing that may be required to run programs written in different computer languages. Packages can be prefetched, made permanently available, or called on demand. By default, code availability is handled in a manner similar to cache memory on computer systems. This encourages implementation of small packages. This approach is particularly suited to integration of legacy systems into mobile code packages. Many security issues are orthogonal to this implementation.

Two concepts that are unique to our work are polymorphism and distributed dynamic linking. Both rely on the fact that multiple implementations of mobile code packages may exist. Polymorphism supports implementations of equivalent processes for different underlying hardware. We implemented the system to run cooperatively on Windows NT, Linux, and Windows CE. When a mobile code package is requested for a particular node, the repository downloads an implementation suited to the execution environment of that particular node.

Distributed dynamic linking [Brooks 2000b] allows the service broker to choose among multiple implementations of a particular service and choose the most appropriate one. When multiple implementations exist, depending on the metric used (speed, accuracy, power, etc.) one implementation is chosen. This is particularly useful for implementing software redundancy [Brooks 1996].

A natural application of mobile code technology is network management. [Halls 1997] describes using the tube system to efficiently manage ATM networks. [Breugst 1998] uses mobile agents to provide advanced telecommunications services, such as call screening and call forwarding.

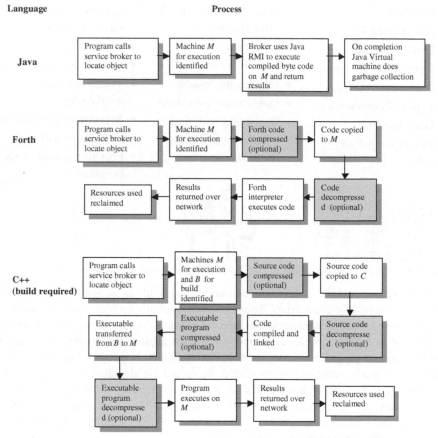

Figure 4.2. Typical processing performed by the service broker to invoke a service. More steps exist when calls are bound to service classes. Forth and Java portions are fairly standard. C++ libraries may consist of source, object, or executable files. C++ processing is shown for the case where the library stores source code.

Some mobile code implementations may be considered adaptive. Java is probably the best-known mobile code implementation. Applets can be downloaded and executed locally. Remote Method Invocation (RMI) allows applets registered with a service to be executed on a remote node. Use of a standardized language allows virtual machines running on different processors to execute the same intermediate code. Java's "write-once run-anywhere" implementation essentially restricts the system to a single standardized language like ANSI C.

Any language that can link to an application programming interface (API) can make mobile code calls. The mobile code modules can be written in any language with a compiler for the host machine, or interpreted language with an interpreter for the host machine. Our use of daemons to run remote invocations resembles RMI to a certain extent.

[Milojicic 1999] describes a number of task migration approaches. They are divided into kernel or user space methods. The V system has a precopying mechanism that copies code to a node before task migration. Tui allows migration of processes among heterogeneous architectures by compiling programs written in a standardized language once for each target machine. Tui does not consider code morphing for efficiency improvement. Most implementations, including MOSIX and Sprite, are designed for distributed computing environments with a high-speed dependable network infrastructure.

Researchers from Berkeley and Oak Ridge National Laboratories have developed a linear algebra and scientific computing software library, PHiPAC, which adapts to its underlying hardware [Science 1999, Bilmes 1998]. The library probes the host's hardware to determine the memory and cache structure. Knowledge of the underlying substrate allows PHiPAC to modify computations and be more efficient. Performance increases of 300% have been reported. Researchers at Duke University have designed real-time task scheduling software that varies processor clock rates for tasks with different priorities and real-time deadlines. Energy consumption has been reduced by up to 70% [Swaminathan 2000]. These examples are evidence that adaptive software and hardware technologies have tremendous potentials for time and energy savings.

2.   PEER-TO-PEER NETWORKS

Mobile code approaches frequently require mobile code to be in specific locations. Either its location is known *a priori* as in Java, or its position is registered with a central name service as in CORBA or Jini. Recent advances in P2P network services provide a more robust and efficient distributed design.

P2P networks are characterized by a lack of central authority. Implementations generally allow nodes to join and leave the infrastructure at will. We characterize the network as a graph consisting of n nodes and a bidirectional arcs connecting them. Each node has an associated degree k, which is the number of arcs incident on the node. The length of each arc is one. We are interested in the general class of P2P networks and not a particular instance. For P2P systems, no central control enforces a specific topology. This supports our analysis of P2P systems using random graph formalisms [Bollobás 2001] in Chapter 10.

As described in [Oram 2001], many technologies can be classified as P2P. Initially, the most widespread P2P networking service was Napster [NYTimes 2000]. Napster is a file-sharing network with only one central index. This index contains a database of users and their files. When a user connects to Napster, a list of files available on the user's machine is added to a central index. When the user requests a specific file, a list of participating machines containing the file is returned. The file can be retrieved from any machine on the list. This is an efficient architecture. File names and machine addresses contain tens of bytes. Files being exchanged typically contain megabytes of data. The large data transfers occur between machines chosen virtually at random. This tends to spread data traffic evenly throughout the Internet. On the other hand, its survivability is poor as a single failure or a court order can stop the entire network by switching off the central index.

GNUtella [GNUtella 2000] is an open source extension of the Napster concept with a radically different approach [Kan 2001]. It is fully distributed with no single point of failure. Each node has an index of its own files. A computer running GNUtella connects with another computer that is part of the distributed GNUtella community. File discovery is performed by flooding the network with request packets. There appears to be serious scalability issues with this approach [Hong 2001, Ritter 2001]. File downloads are handled on a peer-to-peer basis. To disable the GNUtella service, all GNUtella hosts have to be disabled. There is no way of knowing *a priori* of how many hosts are running GNUtella at any given moment.

Freenet [Freenet 2000], which was developed at the University of Edinburgh, resembles GNUtella. File locations are managed by a hashing system, which makes their exact location difficult to determine. Information is stored, cached and retrieved in a transparent manner. If multiple users are interested in data, multiple copies may exist. On the other hand, a single copy may be transferred to a single location, convenient to all the users. This addresses the scalability issues of GNUtella [Langley 2001].

Other P2P decentralized networks with different routing schemes are less widely used. They address the issues of scalability and fault tolerance in different ways. Chord [Dabek 2001] maps the P2P nodes to a circular identifier space. A distributed hashing scheme maps identifiers to network addresses. The system forms a distributed index structure. CAN (Content Addressable Network) [Ratnasamy 2001] is another distributed hashing scheme. In addition to providing a distributed hashing and data storage system, data can be replicated and locally cached. While document retrieval should be efficient, it is unclear how much overhead would be required to maintain the Chord and CAN systems if frequent updates are required due to files changing their location. Pastry [Rowstron 2001] is a distributed routing system. Nodes enter the network and are assigned identifiers. The routing algorithm scales logarithmically. Pastry is based on the questionable assumption that nodes will know the machine containing the information desired.

Other research programs exist that provide insights into P2P systems. [Abelson 1999] describes a novel research agenda for a new class of computational entities. Amorphous computing is computation as carried out by a network of cooperating automata. Each individual computational entity is fallible. It is hypothesized that nanotechnology will support low cost construction of individual low power networked computational devices. Approaches embedding computation into living cells [Coore 1999] have also been explored. Their approach to system design and evaluations uses cellular automata (CA) abstractions and is relevant to the work proposed here. They assume that all nodes have identical software and do not consider mobile code. The standard CA model is modified to assume that the grid is not regular and communications are asynchronous. The use of mobile code and interactions among nonuniform automata are technologies that could significantly advance amorphous computing research.

[Weiser 1991] suggests the concept of ubiquitous computing. Computers as such should become invisible technology. Intelligence should be embedded directly into existing devices. General-purpose computers will no longer be necessary. At Xerox PARC a number of prototypes have been constructed following this general concept. Ubiquitous computing has inspired recent research in smart spaces and commercial products like Jini [Sun 1999]. Ubiquitous computing can best be achieved through cooperating networks of embedded processors. Work in the DARPA Sensor Information Technology Program [Brooks 2000] applies mobile code technology to similar systems.

3.   FIELD PROGRAMMABLE GATE ARRAYS

Initially, computing equipment could be divided into hardware (physical devices and circuits) and software (logic and programs). The creation of firmware, Read Only Memory (ROM) – a physical storage medium for program logic – confused the boundary between the two. ROMs were followed by Programmable Read Only Memory (PROM) and Erasable PROM (EPROM). ROMs, PROMs, and EPROMs could be considered programs, data storage, and/or hardware depending on the context.

In the early 1970s the frontier between hardware and software was made more permeable with the advent of Programmable Logic Arrays (PLAs) [Brown 1996]. PLAs are devices designed to support quick implementation of logic circuits in reusable hardware. A number of improvements (PAL, PLD, SPLD, CPLD, and MPGA) on this initial concept eventually lead to the development of FPGAs [Brown 1996, Mano 1997, Compton 2002].

An FPGA is a very large scale integration (VLSI) device containing a large array of logic blocks that use input output blocks to communicate with the outside world. The internal logic of all of these blocks can be reprogrammed, as can the interconnections between them [Mano 1997]. FPGAs are often coupled with traditional processors, such as the PowerPC. Frequently, an FPGA is a regular array of logic blocks interspersed with routing units.

Usually specifications for the device are written either in a hardware design language, such as Verilog or VHDL, or possibly in a higher-level language like C. A compiler, in conjunction with circuit libraries or circuit generation software, outputs the configuration information that is used by the FPGA. The configuration information is downloaded to the FPGA and placed in the device's configuration registers, at which point the FPGA is a functional hardware prototype [Compton 2002].

Work is being done on supporting runtime reconfiguration of FPGAs. By modifying the context of configuration registers, it becomes possible to change the logic circuits of the device on the fly. This can be done by [Compton 2002]

- Allowing logic blocks to have multiple contexts and dynamically switch between them.
- Supporting reconfiguration of portions of the FPGA, instead of the entire device.
- Integrating the FPGA into a pipeline concept, where portions of the device are reprogrammed in sequence. This allows the device to execute circuits larger than the device could normally physically contain.
- Using the results from partial evaluations to determine which circuits best fit the remaining computational needs.

To support runtime reconfiguration, the following technologies are being explored [Compton 2002]:

- Overlapping of configuration redefinition and code execution
- Compression of configuration data during transfer
- Garbage collection and defragmentation of partial configurations left on the device
- Caching future configurations

In spite of the promises of these ideas, it is not clear that runtime reconfiguration is practical. It reduces the amount of space available for use on the FPGA. Problems with memory protection and coordination among multiple hardware configurations are easy to foresee [Compton 2002].

FPGAs have been accepted within the security community as excellent tools for prototyping hardware based security solutions. They can be used as dedicated network coprocessors, like in the Gigabit Rate IP Security project at USC/ISI East [GRIP 2002]. They have successfully created a network coprocessor implementation of the IPsec protocol that supports gigabit throughput. They are also well suited for use as dedicated processors for use in symmetric encryption [Swankoski 2004], which is discussed further in Chapter 8.

4.   ADAPTATION

The national infrastructure now consists of dynamic systems relying on interactions among multiple semiautonomous entities. The physics of these types of systems has been studied and understood in continuous [Alligood 1996, Haken 1978, Nicolis 1997] and discrete [Wolfram 1994, Delorme 1999, Sarkar 2000, Brooks 2000a] domains. Hybrid systems that integrate both are needed and have been neglected. Traditional dependability models rely on queuing theory and statistical methods [Siewiorek 1982, Rai 1990, Rai 1990a]. Since many system pathologies are caused by dynamic nonlinear interactions between components [Kott 1999], it is essential to create these hybrid mathematical models and update theory to provide a new generation of systems that adapt to chaotic environments.

Among the common characteristics of engineering designs are failure modes and pathologies. [Kott 1999] provides an initial taxonomy of pathologies for complex systems, which lists pathological behaviors and mechanisms that are often responsible. Pathologies are general descriptions of ways the system deviates from its goal states. The taxonomy includes ubiquitous problems such as race conditions, deadlock, livelock, oscillation, and thrashing. Reasons for pathology occurrence include lack of information, inappropriate thresholds, inconsistency, and excessive constraints [Kott 1999].

Pathological behavior is endemic to complex systems like the Internet, which are composed of multiple nontrivial components with nonlinear dynamic interactions. Components may not be homogeneous. Their internal composition may vary over time. Studies of interacting components indicate extremely complex chaotic behavior occurs even in systems consisting of homogeneous, simple automata with static configurations [Wolfram 1994]. System behavior has both local and global aspects. Correct system behavior relies on synergetic effects emerging between local and global regimes.

Advances in computing and mathematics make it possible to study and model interactions and dynamics of large complex systems, which were undecipherable until recently.

Ongoing research in complexity and self-organization has produced some general rules describing adaptation of groups of autonomous entities. The following research has been particularly influential:

- Nobel Prize laureate Ilya Prigogine has discovered dissipative structures in nonequilibrium thermodynamics and chemistry [Nicolis 1977].
- Hermann Haken has founded the research field of synergetics [Haken 1978] on his work in quantum optics and lasers. The same principles have been applied to urban planning [Portugali 2000].
- Multiple researchers at the Santa Fe Institute have published revolutionary concepts in evolution [Kauffman 1993], biological adaptation [Bonabeau 1999], and complexity theory [Cowan 1994].

The concepts developed by these researchers are directly applicable to designing adaptive network services. Although the underlying system dynamics are discrete, the work based on differential equations [Nicolis 1977, Haken 1978] may be applicable for large-scale applications where effects due to discrete packet sizes are negligible. This is supported by successful applications of computer network fluid flow models [Ahuja 1993, Gautam 1997]. Models based on extensions to CAs [Portugali 2000], insect societies [Bonabeau 1999], and evolutionary dynamics [Kauffman 1993] present principles of adaptation that should apply to networks at all levels of resolution.

These systems are best modeled as macroscopic entities made up of a large number of smaller elements [Haken 1978, Portugali 2000]. Self-organization is found when complex macroscopic behaviors occur as a nontrivial consequence of interactions between the individual elements. Self-organization occurs only in systems far from equilibrium [Nicolis 1977]. System behavior ranges from strict order to chaos.

We use the term *emergent* to characterize system behaviors with the following characteristics:

- They arise from interactions between multiple entities.
- All behaviors are based on local information.
- They contain a significant stochastic component.
- Positive feedback is used to encourage desirable behaviors.
- Negative feedback stabilizes the system.
- Global system behaviors contain spontaneous phase changes.
- The global behaviors are not trivial consequences of the local behaviors.

Researchers at the Computer Emergency Response Team (CERT) of Carnegie Mellon's Software Engineering Institute have identified the use of emergent algorithms as one of the most promising approaches to creating truly survivable systems [Fisher 1999].

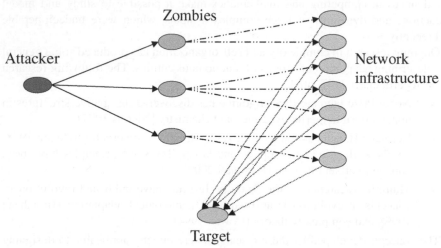

Figure 4.3. An attacker creates a Distributed Denial of Service (DDoS) to disrupt network traffic for the target. Processes are surreptitiously planted on a number of nodes (zombies). At a fixed time, all the zombie processes send network ping messages to a number of nodes on the network. The ping messages are forged so that responses are sent by the network infrastructure to the target. The resulting congestion effectively disables the target.

The concept of emergence can be applied to many existing engineering systems, and others currently being designed. The fact that recent studies of Internet traffic detect self-similarity in traffic flow [Leland 1994, Grossglauer 1999] supports our supposition that the basic tenets of synergetics [Haken 1978] will hold for critical infrastructure like sensor networks. In these engineered systems, a large number of complex individual entities merge to form a larger system. In many ways, the macroscopic behavior of the aggregate system emerges from interactions between individuals. These behaviors limit the ability to control the system from the top down in ways that are not immediately evident. An example of this is fault propagation through complex coupled systems producing unforeseen macroscopic errors. These errors are difficult to foresee and/or correct, like the failure of the electric infrastructure in the western United States in the summer of 1996 [CNN 1996, PBS 1996].

On the negative side, attacks like DDoS attack the network as a distributed entity [Garber 2000]. Network traffic pathologies [Kott 1999] can be instigated that violate safety, liveness, and stabilizability [Gaertner 1999] constraints for the distributed system. Figure 4.3 illustrates how a DDoS attack exploits the distributed network structure to exploit a number of vulnerabilities into a very effective attack on a network service. Multiple layers of separation exist between the attacker and the target, which makes the attack difficult to trace and neutralize. The possibility of delays between planting zombie processes and triggering the attack can further blur the connection between attacker and target.

Emergent behaviors could be the proper tool for negating these types of attacks [Fisher 199]. Emergent behaviors are group behaviors that result from the nontrivial aggregation of actions taken by multiple individuals. Ideally, the individual behaviors use locally available information and require little or no central coordination. Since the logic is distributed throughout a number of nodes, emergent algorithms are very robust to component failures. The lack of central coordination is especially desirable, since the resulting system has minimal timing requirements. The design of emergent algorithms is an open question [Fisher 1999]. CA models, like the one given in Chapter 6, are common for studies of emergent phenomena [Wolfram 1994, Portugali 2000, Sole 2000]. An example of the use of CA for designing emergent behavior can be found in [Hordijk 1999]. Chapter 6 presents an initial step in that direction.

A. CONTINUOUS MODELS

For emergent behavior to arise, the systems must be complex and have a large number of degrees of freedom. Their behavior depends on a large number of system variables and has many modes of behavior. The effects of any given variable may be controllable or unstable, depending on the mode of operation [Haken 1978]. The change from one mode of system behavior to another occurs abruptly at a critical value of a single system variable [Jensen 1998].

Variables may be continuous or discrete. For continuous variables, a Singular Value Decomposition (SVD) can be performed to decouple interactions and find those variables with the strongest influence on system behavior. The effects of some variables are controllable, while nonlinear interactions make the effects of variations of other variables inherently unstable and unpredictable. The set of controllable variables derived through the SVD thus provides a system with greatly reduced dimensionality.

At this point, the *slaving principle* can be used to provide structure in an otherwise chaotic system [Haken 1978]. It states that, although the system as a whole is not entirely controllable, the controllable variables can be used to steer the system's evolution. They provide bounds for the chaotic actions forced by the unstable variables. The unstable variables are considered slaves of the controllable ones. This control system can be used until another critical value is reached, and the dominant mode of operation changes abruptly. It can even be used to force the system past another critical value. Methods for deriving and finding critical values, where the behavior of physical systems changes abruptly, are given in [Jensen 1998]. This is an extension of the basic concepts of robust control, where control strategies are shaped around instabilities and sources of error [Zhou 1996].

A matrix system representation can capture many essential system characteristics. If internal component structure is ignored, transportation models can be used. Material suppliers are sources y and end users are sinks u. Transportation paths and storage depots are represented as limited capacity edges that form a network connecting sources to sinks. This problem can be formulated in terms of graph theory, linear programming, nonlinear differential equations [Haberman 1998, Smulders 1991], or control theory [Zhou 1996].

In terms of graph theory, many methods design systems that maximize flow through a network. In addition to algorithms specifically designed for flow maximization, dynamic programming is a common approach. In the case of stochastic systems, methods generally attempt to optimize the expected flow through the system. These models require knowledge of statistical distributions of the stochastic components, information consistency, and known functions that express supply and demand. These models are too static and deterministic. Pathologies will arise, but the model cannot express how or why.

One way of designing the system would be to try to have the supply match the demand, which could be phrased as a control system:

$$x' = Ax + Bu \qquad y = Cx + Du \quad \text{or} \quad \begin{bmatrix} x' \\ y \end{bmatrix} = \begin{bmatrix} A & B \\ C & D \end{bmatrix} \begin{bmatrix} x \\ u \end{bmatrix} = G \begin{bmatrix} x \\ u \end{bmatrix} \qquad (3)$$

where x is the set of internal state variables, y is the supply, and u is the demand. One then attempts to derive matrices $A, B, C,$ and D to make y follow u. In the linear case, it is possible to solve the equations to optimize a set of known criteria. It is even possible to use stochastic noise variables and define a structured singular value, where the system remains stable and controllable as long as noise remains within limits [Zhou 1996]. Well-defined measures of stability, controllability, observability, and robustness exist in control theory [Zhou 1996].

The matrix formalism is still applicable when the system is nonlinear, even though its application becomes significantly more complex [Brogan 1991]. Note that in analyzing these control systems the singular value decomposition is used to extract the principal components of the system. Singular values (eigenvalues) λ_i express the modes inherent in the system. Sorting the values in order of magnitude allows a threshold T to be set. Singular values larger than the threshold ($\lambda_i > T$) are considered significant and retained. Those smaller than the threshold ($\lambda_i < T$) are not significant and are discarded. This often allows the dimensionality of the problem to be reduced significantly. Details on computing eigenvalues and singular value decompositions can be found in [Press 1992].

[Hagen 1990] expresses dynamic nonlinear systems with multiple operational modalities. These modalities are expressed by system singular values λ_i. Any operation mode is a function of interactions between these modes. The interactions can lead to instability, oscillations, chaotic dynamics, and most other pathologies. Any modality can be approximated by a linearization of the system using a matrix of the λ_i. Different control parameters are relevant for different system modalities. In particular many system parameters become irrelevant, or subservient to another parameter, in specific behavior modes [Hagen 1990]. This can drastically reduce the number of degrees of freedom of a system, as long as underlying dynamics are known.

Although control theory is useful for expressing and discovering many pathologies, it still has significant limitations. Unfortunately in security systems noise inputs are not adequately modeled as stochastic variables. They are at least partially controlled by the plans of an intelligent adversary. The confusion caused by chaotic conditions also leads to difficulties in collecting information and executing plans [Van Creveld 1980]. Internal system variables are subject to inconsistency and corruption. Many significant aspects of the plant are unknown and possibly even unknowable [Van Creveld 1980].

Alternatively, the network can be approached as a nonequilibrium system [Nicolis 1977]. Many biological and chemical systems exist where microscopic flux and chaos is offset by macroscopic order. In this model stable macroscopic regimes emerge and provide a predictable system as long as system variables remain within certain limits. When critical values of system parameters are reached, the internal structure of the system changes radically. In many cases these critical values are due to internal thresholds and effects of positive feedback. This is the basis of many fractal and chaotic interactions seen in nature [Jensen 1998]. Internal thresholds and positive feedback are also present in logistics systems. In the example of medical supplies, when more than a certain percentage of people contract an illness, the illness is more likely to spread. This type of positive feedback relation is hidden from a straightforward control model. Results from nonequilibrium systems are consistent with the pathology taxonomy in [Kott 1999]. Many pathologies are due to incorrect threshold values in a system. These threshold values are critical values where the system modifies its control regime. [Jensen 1998] discusses methods for deriving and verifying critical values where system behavior changes radically.

B. DISCRETE MODELS

[Kauffman 1993] explores the relation between higher order interactions and system adaptation. He finds that in complex systems ordered regimes are frequently separated by chaotic modes that adapt quickly to find new ordered regimes. His work applies differential equations, discrete alphabets, and CA to system analysis. His approach is consistent with the economics study in [Chang 1999], urban planning study in [Portugali 2000], and air operations study in [Brooks 2000a].

These studies all explicitly consider differences in information availability to decision makers in distributed systems. Independent entities interact within a distributed space. It appears that discrete systems and CA are a reasonable approximation of the underlying continuous dynamics [Kauffman 1993]. It is also not necessary for all the underlying dynamics to be understood or modeled [Kauffman 1993, Portugali 2000]. For this reason, it appears that a model of agents in a cellular space is suited for expressing pathologies for systems with unknown underlying dynamics. It is also suited for expressing the interaction between global and local factors.

Some variables may be innately discrete, especially in engineered systems. In other cases, the dynamics may not be sufficiently known (or measurable) for models using differential equations to be practical. It is advisable to model these systems using the CA abstraction [Wolfram 1994, Delorme 1999]. CA's of sufficient size have been shown capable of performing general computation [Delorme 1999]. A CA is a synchronously interacting set of elements (network nodes) defined as a synchronous network of abstract machines [Sarkar 2000]. A CA is defined by

- d, the dimension of the automata
- r, the radius of an element of the automata
- δ, the transition rule of the automata
- s, the set of states of an element of the automata

An element's (node's) behavior is a function of its internal state and those of neighboring nodes as defined by δ. The simplest instance of a CA is uniform, has a dimension of 1, a radius of 1, and a binary set of states. In this simplest case for each individual cell there are a total of 2^3 possible configurations of a node's neighborhood at any time step. Each configuration can be expressed as an integer v:

$$v = \sum_{i=-1}^{1} j_i 2^{i+1} \tag{4}$$

where i is the relative position of the cell in the neighborhood (left = -1, current position = 0, right = 1) and j_i is the binary value of the state of cell i. Each transition rule can therefore be expressed as a single integer r:

$$r = \sum_{v=1}^{8} j_v * 2^v \tag{5}$$

where j_v is the binary state value for the cell at the next time step if the current configuration is v. This is the most widely studied type of CA. It is a very simple many-to-one mapping for each individual cell. The aggregated behaviors can be quite complex [Delorme 1999]. Wolfram's work has found four qualitative equivalence classes for CAs [Wolfram 1994]:

- *Stable* – Evolving into a homogeneous state

- *Repetitive* – Evolving into a set of stable or periodic structures
- *Chaotic* – Evolving into a chaotic pattern
- *Interesting* – Evolving into complex localized structures

These states are useful for modeling complex systems. Under normal operating conditions, stable or repetitive behavior is desirable. When the system has been pushed out of equilibrium, chaotic and interesting interactions are desirable. They enable the system to quickly explore the set of possible adaptations, eventually finding a new configuration adapted to the new environment [Kauffman 1993].

The agents in a cellular space model [Portugali 2000] augments CA by adding agents that are defined as abstract automata. The agents migrate within the cellular space. Their behavior depends on their own state, the state of cells in their neighborhood, and possibly on a small number of global variables. These concepts will be revisited in Chapter 6, which more fully explores the behavior of mobile code systems.

5. CONCLUSION

This chapter has discussed disruptive technologies that are relevant to system security. All four can be used to significantly increase system adaptability:

- Mobile code can reprogram individual platforms autonomously.
- P2P networks provide distributed coordination mechanisms with no centralized control.
- FPGAs are devices that can mimic arbitrary hardware substrates.
- Complex adaptive systems research has created techniques for modeling distributed systems. Their dynamics and possible evolutions can be understood and predicted.

The first two technologies have been identified primarily as security risks. FPGAs have been used to create prototype hardware security solutions. Runtime reconfiguration of FPGAs does present interesting security issues. Complex adaptive systems research provides a set of theoretical tools that have been applied to issues like predicting the spread of e-mail viruses and worms, which we will discuss in Chapter 12.

The rest of this book will look at security issues related to these technologies and, more importantly, possible uses of these tools for creating secure systems.

6. EXERCISES

Exercise 4.1 Map the vulnerabilities given in Chapter 2 Section 1 to each of these disruptive technologies. Explain how these technologies exacerbate or solve security issues related to the vulnerability.

Exercise 4.2 Create an attack graph that describes an exploit that takes advantage of security holes caused by the use of mobile code, P2P networks, and/or FPGAs.

Exercise 4.3 Design an attack that exploits FPGA runtime reconfiguration. Produce a diagram showing how the ideas in [Thompson 1984] could be used to field the exploit.

Exercise 4.4 Design a P2P network that uses code signing and cryptographic primitives to restrict access to programs, nodes, and data.

Exercise 4.5 Contrast the vulnerability to attack associated with using mobile-code with "shrink-wrap" software.

Exercise 4.6 Contrast the vulnerability of P2P networks and centralized systems to Denial of Service (DoS) attacks.

Exercise 4.7 Create a network flow model [Ahuja 1993] of a centralized service and a P2P service using the same physical network. Quantify the vulnerability of each to a Denial of Service attack.

Exercise 4.8 Create psuedocode for a mobile code package that constructs a Distributed Denial of Service (DDoS) attack.

CHAPTER 5

Understanding Networks

Dependability and security are more difficult to guarantee in distributed systems than isolated nodes [Brooks 1998, Jalote 1994, Stallings 1995]. As discussed in Chapter 2, networks like the Internet are subject to disruption through known coordinated attacks including [Molander 1994]:

- Denial of service (DoS) by flooding
- DoS by forging
- Packet sniffing
- Host intrusion
- Attacks on lower level protocols
- Physical attacks
- Distributed Denial of Service (DDoS)

Attacks that circumvent authentication on any node extend the security risks faced by that individual node to the network as a whole. Other attacks, particularly DoS, exploit the distributed structure of networks and present a different risk. The National Information Infrastructure (NII)'s behavior emerges from node interactions, like DDoS attacks where traffic propagation through coupled systems have unforeseen macroscopic effects. These behaviors are difficult to foresee and correct. Similar problems exist in the rest of the critical infrastructure, like the failure of the electric grid in the western United States in the summer of 1996 [CNN 1996].

The ability to tolerate attacks and intrusions is a type of system dependability. Since intelligent opponents can plan attacks, the appropriate fault model is Byzantine faults [Brooks 1998, Lynch 1994]. As detailed in Chapter 2, arbitrary faults can be tolerated by distributed systems if the number of faulty components and system connectivity fulfill known limits. A distributed system fulfilling these criteria is tolerant to attack and will function correctly as long as the known limits are satisfied. Unfortunately, algorithms for identifying which components are faulty require an exponential number of rounds of communications [Barborak 1993]. Another difficulty in building robust network services is the fact that complex systems, like the NII, have a number of failure modes and pathologies.

Progress has been made in modeling macroscopic entities like the NII that are made up of a large number of smaller elements [Portugali 2000, Haken 1978]. The fact that recent studies of Internet traffic detect fractal-like self-similarity in traffic flow across scales [Leland 1994, Grossglauer 1999] supports our supposition that the basic tenets of synergetics [Haken 1978] hold for the NII. The NII is composed of multiple nontrivial components with nonlinear dynamic interactions. Correct system behavior relies on synergetic effects emerging between local and global regimes. NII traffic data at any moment is uncertain and the consequences of corrective actions like routing table modification are equally unknown.

This chapter provides background information on computer networks as currently implemented and understood. There is a strong emphasis on empirical studies of network structure and dynamics. Section 1 provides a brief overview of the Internet Protocol (IP) stack, concentrating on the protocols that are most used and most attacked.

Although most current work concentrates on desktop computers, there is a growing consensus that the desktop market is saturated. On the other hand, the market for embedded computing devices is in its infancy, as is seen in the cell phone boom. Of particular interest are networked embedded systems. Section 2 provides an overview of networks of embedded systems, concentrating on sensor networks and the BACnet (Building Automation and Control networks) standard. In Section 3, we discuss network topologies. The Internet has a different topology from *ad hoc* and cell phone networks. The global structure of the network greatly influences its vulnerability to attack. Finally in Section 4, we discuss the dynamics of network traffic. Empirical analysis has found that network traffic is dominated by statistical distributions with attributes that are difficult for standard statistical techniques to analyze: heavy tails, self-similarity, and infinite variance.

1.   INTERNET PROTOCOL BACKGROUND

Data networks involve machines working together simultaneously at multiple layers. The International Organization for Standardization (ISO) developed the standard Open Systems Interconnect (OSI) reference model consisting of seven layers. The Internet is built using the Internet Protocol (IP) Suite, which only has four layers. These reference layers are sometimes called stacks, since each layer is built on top of services offered by the lower layers. In the Internet world, the term *stack* may also refer to the software implementation of the protocols.

The OSI layers are [Tanenbaum 1996]

- *Physical* – Signaling of bits over a communications channel.
- *Data link* – Put bits into a frame of data that supports error recovery.
- *Network layer* – Route frames of data from source node to destination.
- *Transport layer* – Split session data into packets that can be handled by the network layer, and keep them in order.
- *Session layer* – Maintain a communications session between source and destination.
- *Presentation layer* – Translate data encodings as appropriate.
- *Application layer* – Handle interactions that are specific to a particular program.

The IP layers are [Stevens 1994]:

- *Link layer* – Combining the bottom two layers of the OSI stack.
- *Network layer* – Equivalent to the OSI network layer.
- *Transport layer* – Equivalent to the OSI transport layer.
- *Application layer* – Equivalent to the OSI application layer.

Depending on how you see things, there is either no equivalent to the OSI session and presentation layers in the IP model, or they are folded into the IP application layer.

All IP communications are built around the network layer. The IP network layer receives transport layer data packets and provides a best try attempt to forward these packets to their destination. An IP header (whose format can be found in [Stevens 1994]) is prepended to the transport layer information to create IP datagrams. The IP header always contains the IP address of the source and destination hosts. Datagrams are quickly forwarded through the network to their destination, where the IP header is removed and the transport packet stream handed back to the transport layer.

Link layer IP protocols are mainly techniques for forwarding IP datagrams from one host to the next over a physical channel. IP datagrams are encapsulated in information required by hardware interfaces on both ends of the channel. Under some conditions, the IP datagram may have to be cut into small pieces that are sent individually. The receiving node reconstitutes the datagram. Some other protocols exist for associating IP addresses with hardware addresses in the local network [Stevens 1994].

The Internet suite has two main transport protocols. We will discuss these protocols in more depth, since many of the network vulnerabilities discussed in later chapters are tied to design details of these networks.

The simpler transport protocol is the User Datagram Protocol (UDP). UDP operates packet by packet. Each UDP datagram is treated as an isolated transmission. The data to be transmitted has a UDP packet header prepended to it. The UDP packet is then sent to the destination in one IP datagram. Transmission is done by best effort; it is not reliable. Packets may arrive at the destination in any order, if at all. There are also no flow control mechanisms in place. UDP requests are made. They are forwarded. Congested intermediate nodes may drop UDP packets [Stevens 1994]. If error recovery is needed, it must be coded explicitly in the application layer. This makes the UDP protocol suited to staging DoS attacks, as will be discussed further in Chapter 12. This feature of UDP can also be used to override some aspects of the Transmission Control Protocol (TCP) protocol, which may not suit the requirements of a given application [Wu 2003].

TCP provides a reliable, session oriented, byte stream transmission service to the application layer. As with UDP, data has a header prepended to it and is then inserted into an IP datagram. Unlike UDP, each request is not associated with a single, unique IP datagram. TCP breaks the byte stream sent between the nodes into appropriate sized packet chunks for transport over the network. These packets are reassembled on the destination node and provided to the destination node application layer in the order they were written on the source node [Stevens 1994].

TCP is more complex than UDP, since it guarantees sequential delivery of the byte stream to the destination node. The byte stream is divided into packet-size chunks that are sent separately and recombined into a stream at the destination node. This requires timers to request data transmissions and acknowledgements that confirm successful reception of packets. Packets may arrive out of order and have to be resequenced. Packets may be mistakenly retransmitted, so duplicate packets have to be removed. Checksum values are sent to guard against data corruption [Stevens 1994].

TCP includes flow control. This helps guarantee that the destination always has sufficient buffer space to treat packets as they arrive at the destination. The Nagle algorithm waits for transmitting data until acknowledgements are received. In this way, many small packets can be concatenated into a larger packet and less overhead is incurred. If packets are being dropped, a congestion avoidance algorithm is initiated that reduces the rate packets are sent over the network. Details on how these aspects of TCP work and are implemented can be found in [Stevens 1994,Wu 2003].

To support these complexities, a three-way handshake protocol is used to initialize TCP connections. The source sends a SYN packet to the destination, specifying the port number it intends to use. The destination sends an acknowledgement (ACK) packet. The source then acknowledges receipt of the ACK packet and the connection is established [Stevens 1994]. This information will be important when we discuss DoS countermeasures in Chapter 12.

The IP suite also includes a number of other protocols built on top of these basic services. For example, the Simple Network Management Protocol (SNMP) defines how network managers can collect usage information from devices on the network. The Simple Mail Transfer Protocol (SMTP) controls how e-mail communications take place. We will now discuss how global coordination occurs in the Internet.

The Domain Name System (DNS) is a distributed database used to map hostnames and IP addresses. Applications can request the IP address associated with the hostname or vice-versa. The request is passed through a resolver program located on the host. Each domain maintains a DNS server, which handles requests for the local domain. If a translation is not known, the request moves through the hierarchy to the DNS root servers. Once the IP address of the DNS server for the domain of the address is known, it can be queried directly for the translation. A local cache of translations is kept in order to reduce the number of resolution requests that have to be processed. Chapter 2 discusses vulnerabilities in the current DNS.

One reason why the Internet is robust is its decentralized design. It can be viewed as a conglomeration of Autonomous Systems (ASs). An AS is a subnetwork administered by a single entity. Routing within the AS follows the protocol chosen by the administrator. The Border Gateway Protocol (BGP) controls routing between ASs. An AS can be [Stevens 1994]

- *Stub* – Connected to only one other AS. In which case, BGP does not influence the route taken.

- *Multi-homed* – Connected to more than one other AS, but not carrying traffic when none of its hosts are either source or destination. BGP determines which AS to use for specific outgoing traffic requests.
- *Transit* – Connected to more than one other AS and transferring datagrams between the ASs it is connected to. BGP affects datagrams originating in this AS, as well as transit traffic.

BGP systems exchange information about which ASs they communicate with. This information is updated regularly. The BGP retains a list of the possible paths to destinations. It is possible to prune cycles from the list. Each AS can have its own routing policy. Chapter 2 discusses BGP vulnerabilities.

2. NETWORKS OF EMBEDDED CONTROL SYSTEMS

In spite of the ubiquity of the Internet, networks are evolving towards becoming a fundamentally new type of system. Computing systems up to now have been primarily user-centric. Desktop devices interact directly with a human operator following their instructions. Networks served primarily as communications devices between human users. These communications were often augmented by the existence of databases for transaction processing. Information was retained and processed for later use.

Now, powerful embedded processors are widely available and a pervasive Internet integrates them. This enables creation of the computing environment foreseen in [Weiser 1991]. Computation is becoming a transparent part of daily life, like electricity. The future infrastructure will adapt to current conditions. It must optimize resource utilization while distributing tasks over the network. It will be a large, loosely coupled network with mobile code and data. Data supply and demand will remain stochastic and unpredictable. Applications are in hostile environments with noise-corrupted communication and failure-prone components. Efficient operation cannot rely on static plans.

A. SENSOR NETWORKS

Sensor networks are an example of this new type of system [Brooks 2000, Brooks 2002c, Brooks 2003e, Brooks 2004, Iyengar 2004, Zhu 2004]. They provide distributed systems that interact primarily with their environment. The information extracted is processed and retained in databases as before, but the human is removed from many parts of the processing loop. Devices are designed to act more autonomously than was previously the case. They are also designed to work as a team. Figure 5.1 shows an example sensor network application.

Embedded systems are not new. But sensor networks greatly extend the capabilities of these systems. Up to now, embedded systems were resource-constrained devices providing limited intelligence in a strictly defined workspace. Sensor network research is aiming towards developing self-configuring systems working in either unknown or inherently chaotic environments.

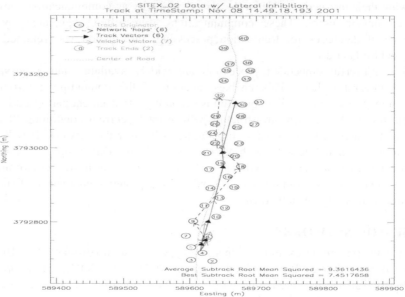

Figure 5.1. Shows an example sensor network implementation. This tracking network was fielded and tested at 29 Palms Marine Base. Distributed tracking results are shown using the lateral inhibition algorithm described in [Brooks 2004].

Sensors require physical interaction with the sensed phenomenon. Proximity to the phenomenon increases accuracy, but may place sensor nodes in danger. Physical interactions are subject to a number of noise factors. The best way to counteract this is by combining multiple measurements [Brooks 1998]. Basic tradeoffs exist between energy and information sharing in cooperative networks of sensors and robots. Radically increased costs result when going from sensing and signal processing to radio communications and mobility [Pottie 1998]. This supports the idea that much processing should be done locally in each sensor node. This requires both *low-level sensing* and *high-level tasking cooperation*. To increase system adaptability, self-configuring networks have been proposed. The network must be able to configure and reconfigure itself to successfully perform surveillance missions in dynamically changing environments. This is especially important for urban and indoor terrains, where obstacles occlude sensor views and cause multi-path fading for radio communications.

Network communications needs to be handled in a new manner. Data is important because of its contents and not because of the machine where it originates. Wireless transmission is expensive, making it attractive to process data close to the source. The problems of multi-path fading, interference, and limited node lifetimes combine to make data paths, even under good conditions, transient and unreliable. The implications this has for network design should not be underestimated.

Similarly, signal-processing technologies need to be aware of transmission delays and the volume of data needed. The resources consumed by an implementation, and the latencies incurred, are an integral part of any sensing solution. In short, all levels of the networking protocols need to be considered as a single gestalt. Beyond this, system design requires new power aware computing hardware and operating systems. Data supply and demand are stochastic and unpredictable. Processing occurs concurrently on multiple processors. Applications are in hostile environments with noise-corrupted communication and failure prone components. Under these conditions, efficient operation cannot rely on static plans. Van Creveld has defined five characteristics hierarchical systems need to adapt to this type of environment [van Creveld 1986, Czerwinski 1998]:

- Decision thresholds fixed far down in the hierarchy.
- Self-contained units exist at a low level.
- Information circulates from the bottom up and the top down.
- Commanders actively seek data to supplement routine reports.
- Informal communications are necessary.

Organizations based on this approach have been successful in market economies, war, and law enforcement [Cebrowski 1998].

The sensor network consists of nodes integrating these abilities. Requests for information form flexible *ad hoc* virtual enterprises of nodes, allowing the network to adapt to and compensate for failures and congestion. Complex adaptive behavior for the whole network emerges from straightforward choices made by individual nodes. Sensor networks are fundamentally different from their predecessors. Some of these differences are a matter of degree:

- Number of nodes required
- Power constraint severity
- Proximity to hostile environment
- Timeliness requirements

In the final analysis, the most important differences are fundamental ones in the way information technology is used. Computer networks are no longer sensitive devices coddled in air-conditioned clean rooms. They are working in hostile conditions. Sensor networks respond to the needs of human users. How they respond, and their internal configurations, are decided independent of human intervention [Brooks 2004, Iyengar 2004, Zhu 2004].

B. BACnet

BACnet is official standard 135 of the American Society for Heating, Refrigeration, and Air-Conditioning Engineers (ASHRAE). American National Standards Institute (ANSI) and ISO have also adopted it. BACnet is an open standard defining the network interfaces for devices used in building automation. It has been a driving factor in the creation of an industry that is starting to deliver on the promise of ubiquitous computing [Weiser 1991].

BACnet provides clear standards for integrating building automation systems into a common network. Of particular interest to ASHRAE is the automation of heating and air conditioning systems. Building owners are also using BACnet as an interface to utility suppliers. Privatization of the energy market has led to a diverse array of electrical power suppliers. Real-time decisions can be made by BACnet systems concerning how much electricity to purchase and from which supplier. Climate control applications also depend on data from building thermostats and air quality control monitors. Monitoring air quality also includes smoke detection, which implies a natural tie-in to fire and security alarms. Security alarms require inputs from a number of possible sensor inputs. Figure 5.2 shows an example display from a building intrusion detection system with multiple sensor inputs. Other BACnet applications include control of lighting systems and elevators.

BACnet provides a common language for interaction among these applications. Twenty-three standard object types have properties that can provide information or accept inputs. Each embedded server contains a set of network-enabled objects that provide services. Communication is possible using any of a number of LAN protocols. BACnet can also interact with the Internet in one of two ways: tunneling messages through an IP connection or using IP directly.

Naturally, connecting embedded systems for building control to the Internet has security implications. A Protection Profile (PP) for BACnet can be found in [Zachary 2001]. Protection Profiles are a key part of the Common Criteria (CC) security standardization effort. The CC evolved from security standardization efforts in Europe, Canada, and the United States, including the U.S. Department of Defense's "Orange Book." In the CC an implementation independent definition of functional and information assurance requirements is defined for a given Target of Evaluation (ToE). The PP is a standardized set of security requirements for a given ToE. Product manufacturers can develop their product to satisfy the PP at a given level and then use an independent testing facility to certify their product's security. The independent testing facility takes the product, subjects it to the threats outlined in the PP, and verifies that the product performs as advertised.

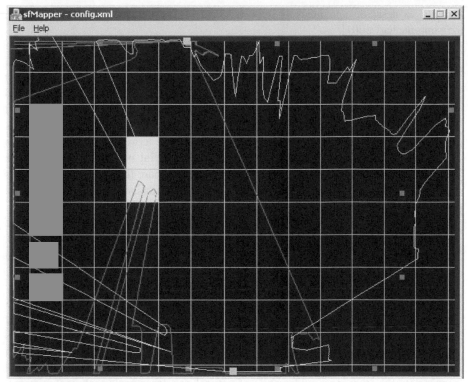

Figure 5.2. Sample display of networked embedded sensors in a smart building. Cameras, motion detectors, pressure sensitive flooring, and ladar sensors can be used to detect and track intruders.

The BACnet PP [Zachary 2001] describes security requirements for building control systems. These include

- Resistance to degradation and denial of service
- Recovery of functionality after an attack
- Robustness to replay attacks
- Maintenance of information integrity
- Reliable system audit of all system activities
- Authentication of users and guarantee of data confidentiality
- Resistance to spoofing

3.   NETWORK TOPOLOGY

An increasing number of networks are being constructed with no central planning or organization. Examples include the Internet, *ad hoc* wireless networks, and peer-to-peer (P2P) implementations like Napster and GNUtella. Most mobile computing implementations fit into this category. Traditional methods of analysis are often inappropriate for these systems since the topology of the system at any point in time is unknown. For these reasons, researchers are turning to statistical or probabilistic models to describe and analyze important classes of networks [Barabási 2002, Krishnamachari 2001].

Random graph theory originated with the seminal works of Erdös and Rényi in the 1950s. Until then, graph theory considered how to analyze either specific graph instances or deterministically defined graph classes. Erdös and Rényi considered graph classes created using a uniform probability for edges existing between any two nodes. Their results were mathematically interesting and found applications in a number of practical domains [Barabási 2002]. In the 1990s, Strogatz and Watts started studying "small world" graphs [Watts 1999]. The term *small world* originates with Milgram's six degrees of separation model of social networks created in the 1960s. Strogatz and Watts' work considers networks where the probability of edges existing between nodes is not uniform. They were specifically interested in clustered graphs, where edges are more likely to exist between nodes with common neighbors. To study this phenomenon, they defined classes of pseudo-random graphs. These graphs combine a deterministic structure and a limited number of random edges. Their results have been used to analyze both social networks and technical infrastructures.

An alternative approach to studying similar systems has been proposed by [Barabási 2002]. His group considered the probability distributions of graph node degree found in graph models of existing systems. This analysis shows that the probability of a node having degree d often follows an inverse power law (i.e., is proportional to $d^{-\gamma}$ where γ is a constant). They explain how this property can emerge from positive feedback in evolving systems. These models appear to be appropriate for studying a wide range of natural and large-scale technical systems. Important results from this model include quantification of the dependability of the Internet [Albert 2000].

Random graph concepts are also widely used in percolation theory [Stauffer 1992]. Percolation theory studies flow through random media. The model of random media is usually built from a regular tessellation of an n-dimensional space. Edges may or may not exist between neighboring vertices of the tessellation with a uniform probability. Applications of percolation theory include oil extraction and analysis of computer virus propagation [Storras 2001], which we will revisit in Chapter 12.

Another random network model, given in [Krishnamachari 2001], is used to study *ad hoc* wireless networks like those used in many mobile networks. A set of nodes is randomly distributed in a two-dimensional region. Each node has a radio with a given range r. A uniform probability exists (in [Krishnamachari 2001] the probability is 1) for edges being formed between nodes as long as they are within range of each other. This network model has obvious practical applications. Many of its properties resemble those of Erdös-Rényi graphs, yet it also has significant clustering like the small world model.

A.   ERDÖS-RÉNYI RANDOM GRAPH

The first model we discuss is the Erdös-Rényi random graph [Bollobás 2001]. It is provided for completeness as it is the most widely studied class, and as a tutorial since it is the simplest class. Erdös-Rényi random graphs are defined by the number of nodes n and a uniform probability p of an edge existing between any two nodes. Let's use E for $|E|$ (i.e., the number of edges in the graph). Since the degree of a node is essentially the result of multiple Bernoulli trials, the degree of an Erdös-Rényi random graph follows a Bernoulli distribution. Therefore as n approaches infinity, the degree distribution follows a Poisson distribution. Figure 5.3 shows different embeddings of an example Erdös-Rényi graph.

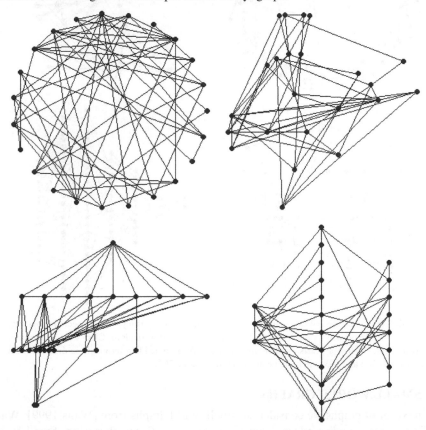

Figure 5.3. Example Erdös-Rényi graph with n equal to 23 nodes and the probability p equal to 0.2.
Clockwise from upper left: nodes in a circle, radial embedding, ranked embedding by geodesic distance from three random nodes, and rooted embedding from a random node.

The expected number of hops between nodes in this graph grows proportionally to the log of the number of nodes [Albert 2001]. Note that Erdös-Rényi graphs do not necessarily form a single connected component. When $E - n/2 \ll -n^{2/3}$ the graph is in a subcritical phase and almost certainly not connected. A phase change occurs in the critical phase where $E = n/2 + O(n^{2/3})$ and in the supercritical phase where $E - n/2 \gg - n^{2/3}$ a single giant component becomes almost certain. When $E = n \log n/2 + O_p(n)$ the graph is fully connected [Jensen 2000]. (Note that the expected number of edges for an Erdös-Rényi graph is $n(n-1) p /2$.)

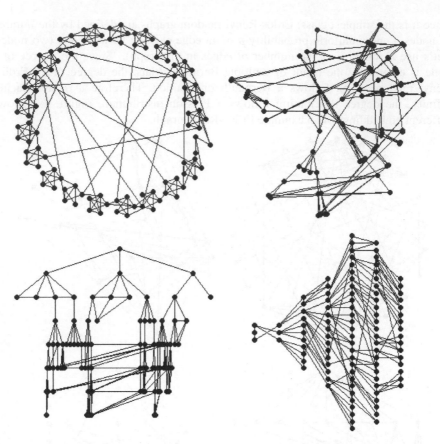

Figure 5.4. Example connected caveman graph with 103 nodes (*n*) starting from connected subgraphs of 5 (*c*) members each. A total of 22 (*e*) edges were rewired at random. Clockwise from upper left to right: "string of pearls," radial embedding, ranked embedding by geodesic distance from nodes 101, 102 and 103, and rooted embedding from node 103.

B. SMALL WORLD GRAPHS

The next set of graphs we consider are small world graphs from [Watts 1999]. Watts studied systems with random connections and significant clustering. Small world graphs have two main characteristics: (*i*) the expected value for the number of hops between any two nodes is small (approaches the expected number of hops for Erdös-Rényi graphs), and (*ii*) a significant amount of clustering among the nodes. The expected number of hops for small world graphs scales similarly to Erdös-Rényi graphs [Watts 1999].

As example small world graphs, consider the *connected caveman model* from [Watts 1999]. To construct these graphs, use the following procedure:

- Construct a set of complete sub-graphs.

- In each sub-graph, one edge is removed and replaced with an edge connecting the sub-graph to the next one; forming a cycle reminiscent of a "string of pearls."
- A fixed number of edges in the system are replaced with random edges.

[Watts 1999] also explores other methods for creating various examples of small world graphs.

This small world model has three parameters: (*i*) *n* the number of nodes in the graph, (*ii*) *c* the number of nodes in each sub-graph, and (*iii*) *e* the number of edges rewired. The node degree distribution in this model is nearly constant with mean value *c* minus one. Variance around the mean is caused by two different sets of Bernoulli trials: (*i*) the probability of an incident edge being rewired to create the "string of pearls" raising (reducing) the node degree by one, and (*ii*) the likelihood of edges attached to the vertex being randomly rewired. Of the three random graph classes, node degree variance in this class is the smallest. Small world graph topologies combine a fixed structure with random effects.

4.   SCALE-FREE GRAPHS

We now consider the scale-free model. It comes from empirical analysis of real-world systems, such as e-mail traffic, the World Wide Web, and disease propagation. Details are in [Albert 2001]. In this model, the node degree distribution varies as an inverse power law (i.e., $P[d] \propto d^\gamma$). These graphs are called scale-free because the power law structure implies that nodes exist with nonzero probability at all possible scales. The expected number of hops for scale-free networks is smaller than the expected number of hops for Erdös-Rényi graphs [Albert 2001]. Scale-free graphs are defined by two parameters: number of nodes *n* and scaling factor γ (see Figure 5.5). Of the random graph classes considered here, node degree variance in this class is the largest.

Many existing systems, like the Internet, are scale-free. Empirical analysis done by different research groups at different times find the Internet's γ parameter value ranging from 2.1 to 2.5 [Albert 2001]. Studies of scale-free networks indicate their structure has unique dependability properties [Albert 2000]. Epidemiological studies show parallels between biological pathogen propagation and computer virus propagation in SF graphs like the Internet [Storras 2001]. We revisit these issues in Chapters 10 and 12.

Figure 5.5 shows how scale-free graphs differ from Erdös-Rényi graphs. The majority of nodes have degree one or two, but there exists a small number of hub nodes with a very large degree. Erdös-Rényi graphs have an almost flat architecture with node degree clustered about the mean. The hub nodes dominate the topology of the scale-free graphs. The ranked embedding illustrates that it is extremely unlikely that a node would be many hops away from a major hub.

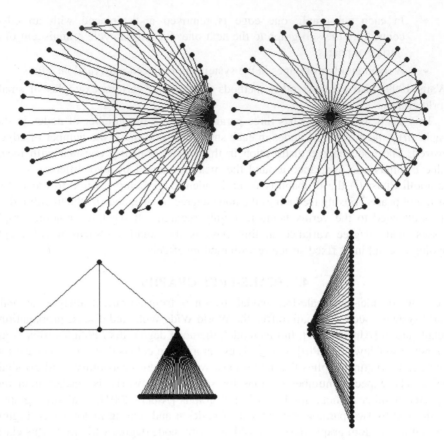

Figure 5.5. Example scale-free graph with $n = 45$ and $\gamma = 3.0$. Clockwise from upper left: nodes in a circle, radial embedding, ranked embedding in order of the geodesic distance from the three largest hubs, and rooted embedding with the root set as the second largest hub.

A. *AD HOC* WIRELESS NETWORKS

Scale-free networks provide a good statistical description of large, evolving, wired networks with no centralized control. Mobile wireless networks are also of importance. *Ad hoc* wireless networks have no fixed infrastructure. Nodes move and communicate with their neighbors. The network topology is purely random in nature, making them suited to analysis as a type of random graph. [Krishnamachari 2001] explains a fixed radius model for random graphs used to analyze phase change problems in *ad hoc* network design.

In [Krishnamachari 2001] the model places nodes at random in a limited two-dimensional region. Two uniform random variables provide the node's x and y coordinates. Two nodes in proximity to each other have a very high probability of being able to communicate. For this reason, they calculate the distance r between all pairs of nodes. If r is less than a given threshold, then an edge exists between the two nodes. Many similarities exist between this graph class and the graphs studied by

Erdös and Rényi, in particular phase transitions for constraint satisfaction problems can be seen. These graphs differ from Erdös-Rényi graphs in that they have significant clustering. Figure 5.6 shows an example range limited random graph.

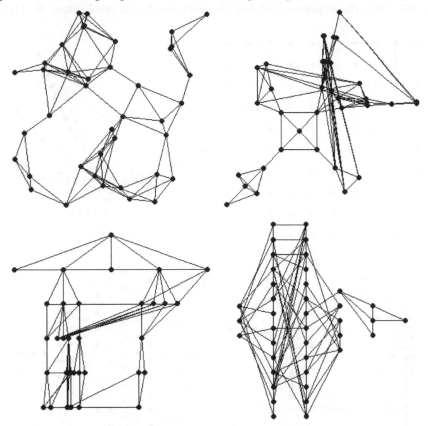

Figure 5.6. Different embeddings of a range limited random graph of 40 nodes positioned at random in a unit square region. The distance threshold was set as 0.25, and within that range edges exist with a probability of 1. Clockwise from upper left: geographic locations, radial embedding, ranked embedding from nodes 38, 39, and 40, and rooted embedding with node 40 as the root.

B. CELL PHONE GRIDS

Percolation theory studies flow through random media. Commonly, the random media is modeled as a regular tessellation of a d-dimensional space where vertices are points connecting edges. It is also possible to consider arbitrary graphs. Two different models exist; site (bond) percolation is where vertices (edges) are either occupied or empty. We discuss only bond percolation; note that it is possible to create dual graphs to convert site (bond) percolation problems to bond (site) problems. These graphs can be considered models of wireless networks with a cellular infrastructure.

This model requires three parameters: x the number of nodes in a row, y the number of nodes in a column, and p the probability of an edge being occupied. Note that n, the total number of nodes, is equal to $x\,y$. Figure 5.7 shows an example graph. We will revisit the importance of these network topologies in Chapters 10, 11, and 12.

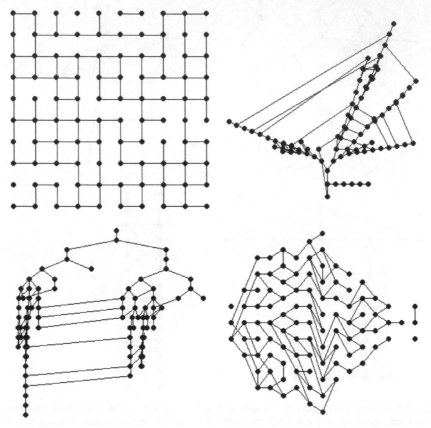

Figure 5.7. Different embeddings of a regular 10 by 10 matrix. Edge probability was set at 0.75. Clockwise from upper left: grid, radial embedding, ranked embedding from nodes 38, 39, and 40, and rooted embedding with node 50 as the root.

5.   TRAFFIC FLOWS

Empirical analysis has shown Internet traffic to be self-similar [Leland 1994] and multifractal in nature [Riedi 1999]. Figures 5.8 and 5.9 illustrate these concepts. Self-similarity describes fractal images that maintain the same structural characteristics over multiple scales [Mandelbrot 1997].

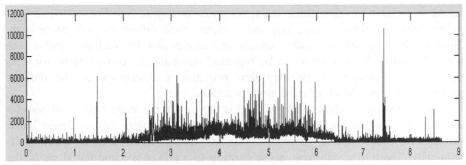

Figure 5.8. Network packet arrival rates. Spikes illustrate the burstiness of the data. Careful examination shows active frequency components at all time scales. The statistical variance of this data is infinite and interactions exist over long time periods.

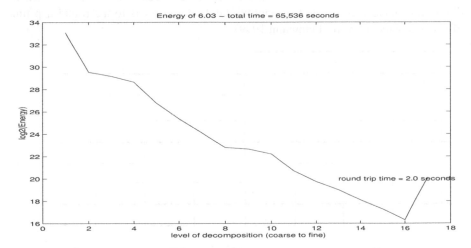

Figure 5.9. Plot of Haar wavelet coefficient magnitudes derived from time series in Figure 5.8 across multiple scales. Where the graph is linear, the process is self-similar across scales. The slope of the line is the fractal dimension of the system. Since the fractal dimension varies across scales (here after decomposition level 16), this process is called multifractal. The change in fractal dimension is tied to the average round trip time of packet in the network [Feldmann 1999].

Many of the concepts we use in this chapter originate with Mandelbrot's study of time series descriptions of markets [Mandelbrot 1997]. Market time series are irregular and bursty. Statistics describing the data vary exponentially s^f as a function of the bin size s used to aggregate the data. The constant exponent f is referred to as the fractal dimension. Figure 5.8 is a plot of the number of packets arriving at a firewall within a given time slice over one day. Note the irregular, bursty nature of the data. Figure 5.9 is a plot of an energy metric of the data in Figure 5.8 over multiple time scales.

The energy metric is computed using the Haar wavelet (see Figure 5.10) decomposition. (Those unfamiliar with wavelets may want to consult a tutorial on the subject, like [Brooks 2001].) The Haar wavelet is used here because it is the simplest wavelet function. Take the time series in Figure 5.8. For each pair j of values, compute their average $a[j]$ and compute their difference $d[j]$. Store both. Note that the original time series consists of j entries and that vectors a and d both have $j/2$ entries. This process can be repeated using the $j/2$ entries of vector a as input. Every iteration of the algorithm provides a description of the data at progressively lower levels of resolution, or scales.

The energy metric shown in Figure 5.9 is the sum of the magnitude of all wavelet components at a given scale. Note how the graph of the metric has an almost linear progression over the first 16 scales. This is what is referred to as traffic self-similarity. The traffic statistics vary according to a power law and the slope of the line is an estimate of the fractal dimension f. Note the change in the slope at scale 16. Systems where the fractal dimension f varies as the scale changes are called multifractal. In the case of network traffic, it has been shown that the fractal dimension changes at a scale that approximately corresponds to the round trip time of packets in the network [Feldmann 1999].

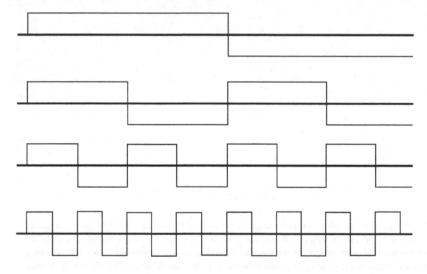

Figure 5.10. The bottom line has 7.5 Haar wavelets. The line above has more than 3 Haar wavelets covering the same region at a lower resolution. The upper two lines continue this progression. Each wavelet is the same function at different scales and translations. A wavelet representation superimposes these individual wavelets multiplied by constant factors.

Time series similar to the one in Figure 5.8 can be produced using random cascades [Feldmann 1998, Mandelbrot 1997]. For example, consider a line with a break somewhere in the middle. Two scaled copies of the line (including break) replace each straight segment in the original line. Orientations for the scaled copies are chosen at random. In the limit, the system produces a jagged multifractal time series. In the case of the Internet where traffic passes through multiple routers, it is not difficult to imagine how the cascade model could mirror reality.

Self-similar time series may be considered the result of a Levy distribution [Mandelbrot 1997, Weisstein 1999]:

$$F[P_N(k)] = F\left[\exp\left(-N|k|^\beta\right)\right] \qquad (6)$$

where F is the Fourier transform of the probability $P_N(k)$ for N-step addition of random variables. When $\beta = 2$, the Levy distribution is Gaussian (normal distribution). Levy distributions often have infinite variance, and may have infinite mean. Many distributions found in Internet traffic have been found to be heavy-tailed and have infinite variance. Because of this, the mathematical tools that worked successfully for telephone networks are incapable of analyzing and predicting traffic flow in the Internet [Willinger 1998]. Our inability to understand and forecast the aggregate behavior of packets in large-scale computer networks has made it difficult to detect network attacks.

Perhaps for these reasons, researchers are finding fractal (or self-similar) models to be more effective to quantify traffic in LAN and WAN packet-switched networks than the traditional models that are predominantly Markovian, cellular automata, or fluid flow-based [Leland 1994, Paxson 1995, Erramilli 1994, Crovella 1997, Lucas 1997, Jerkins 1997]. Self-similarity in these networks is believed to originate from the following sources:

- Packets may enter the network as self-similar processes [Paxson 1995, Crovella 1997, Meier 1991, Willinger 1997, Park 1996].
- The network protocols including the retransmission mechanisms may render traffic to exhibit self-similar dynamics with significant long-range correlations [Peha 1997].
- Traffic passing through a hierarchy of routers work as a random cascade, similar to the model Mandelbrot used to originate the multifractal model to explain economics time series [Feldmann 1998].

The current research on self-similar traffic analysis has largely focused on deriving scaling laws and other multifractal quantifiers under a variety of network topologies and other conditions using a combination of traffic physics models and empirical data [Feldmann 1998, Willinger 1997, Gilbert 1998, Gilbert 1999, Peha 1997, Erramilli 2000]. The current traffic physics models capture the physical sources of self-similarity, LRD, and other characteristics of network traffic.

Figures 5.11 and 5.12 provide evidence supporting the hypothesis that finite dimensional nonlinear stochastic models, similar to those used in analyzing chaotic systems [Bukkapatnam 2000], capture the nuances of traffic data patterns[1]. Our correlation analysis and surrogate data tests show the data contains significant deterministic components. This is evident from the regularities seen in the autocorrelation spectrum (see Figure 5.12a). The autocorrelation spectrum is found

---

[1] These results were obtained in conjunction with Dr. Satish Bukkapatnam.

by cross correlating the time series at different offsets. Frequencies where there is a large autocorrelation value tend to dominate the time series.

The false nearest neighbors test showed that the dynamics may be adequately embedded in a 12–14 dimensional space (Figure 5.12b). This plot is obtained by predicting values in the time series using an average of r other samples from the time series located at offsets of the dominant frequency (found in Figure 5.12a) from the sample. For data that is multi-dimensional, the quality of the prediction should continue to increase until r reaches the dimensionality of the underlying dynamics [Kennel 1992]. Figure 5.12 shows that the error decreases significantly until a dimension of 12–14 is reached. This is consistent with a study performed by Gudonov and Johnson [Gudonov 2001], which found Internet information flow to be a dynamical system with a phase-space of dimension 10–12. Note that these two studies used disjoint datasets taken at different times from different sampling environments.

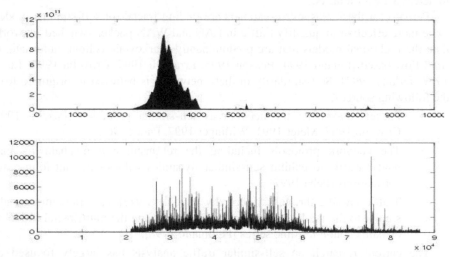

Figure 5.11. Power spectral density (top) and packet arrival time series (bottom). For time series, the x-axis is time in seconds. The y-axis is the number of packets received per second on a node. Data is weekday Internet traffic on a firewall.

The computed fractal dimension values from our datasets are relatively flat and trend near those values. The results also show that the data tend to obey at least two distinct scaling laws one having a dimension in the range of 1.7–3.8, and the other in the range of 5.5–6.2 (Figure 5.13). The consistent increasing trend of fractal dimension values with embedding dimension establishes the presence of significant noise in traffic dynamics.

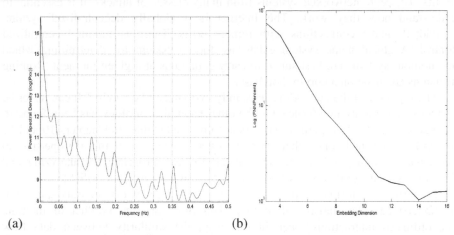

(a)   (b)

Figure 5.12. Representative (a) Autocorrelation plot (b) % false nearest neighbors at various embedding dimensions.

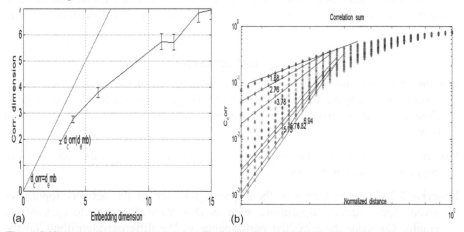

(a)   (b)

Figure 5.13. Representative variations of (a) fractal dimensions with embedding dimensions, and (b) local correlation sums and hence fractal dimension values.

In addition to these models, other approaches exist that model computer network traffic using techniques from statistical physics. The Therminator project at the Naval Postgraduate School modeled network traffic using entropy equations [Donald 2001]. The end result was a display of network state, which skilled users were able to use to verify that the network was performing normally. [Burgess 2000] models networks as thermal reservoirs where fluctuations represent the exchange of information.

6. CONCLUSION

This chapter provides background information on communications networks. It combines some standard material on Internet protocols, with some recent research results. To secure networked systems from many classes of attacks, it is essential to understand how they work. The Internet is a globally decentralized system. Individuals make connections with remote hosts. There is minimal centralized control. A global name system exists, as does a system for determining which autonomous systems are best suited to carry datagrams at a given moment. Routing decisions are made on a hop-by-hop basis.

The topology of the network is constantly evolving and changing. It can never be known with certainty in advance. On the other hand, the topology has been found to have some statistical properties that appear to be predictable. In Chapters 10 and 12 we will provide techniques that attempt to take advantage of these properties. In particular, random graph formalisms appear to be appropriate for analyzing and designing systems of this type where only statistical information is reliable.

Properties of information flows within this evolving network are only starting to be understood. The statistics describing data flows are the product of multiple uncoordinated interactions. Seen in this way, the similarity between data flow statistics and economics data probably should not be surprising. The infinite variance of many of these statistics makes many traditional statistical techniques unusable in this environment. Chapter 12 will discuss network information flow in much more detail.

7.   EXERCISES

Exercise 5.1 Take the list of coordinated attacks given in the introduction to this chapter and compare them to the network properties described in the chapter. Explain how those properties aid in creation of these attacks and hinder detection of attacks.

Exercise 5.2 Which network topologies are suited for the embedded network applications given in Section 2?

Exercise 5.3 Create instances of three graphs for each of the network topologies given. Apply routing algorithms, such as Dijkstra's algorithm, to each of the graphs. Compare the expected performance of the different algorithms on the different topologies.

Exercise 5.4 Repeat Exercise 5.3 but instead of using a fixed graph for the routing, generate a new instance of the graph at every fifth time step. Each new graph instance should have the same statistical properties. How does this affect performance? Suggest routing protocol improvements to deal with uncertainty in the network structure.

Exercise 5.5 Create network simulations (use tools like the Virtual Internet Testbed) for graph structures matching the different topologies listed in Section 3. Create graphs for packet arrival rates for the different topologies. Do this for constant bit rate traffic and traffic generated using a Pareto distribution.

Exercise 5.6 Compute fractal dimension statistics for the data generated in Exercise 5.5.

CHAPTER 6

Understanding Mobile Code [1,2]

This chapter discusses mobile code technologies. Mobile code is a disruptive technology that allows the software configurations on individual nodes to change dynamically. This has frequently been considered a security risk, although there is no reason *a priori* why mobile code packages should be considered less secure than shrink-wrapped software purchased in stores. In fact, viruses have been inadvertently distributed in official releases from some of the largest software corporations. On the other hand, mobile code does allow malicious software to spread more quickly and further than might otherwise be the case.

This chapter discusses mobile code in detail. In chapter 5, we discussed how network behaviors are dominated by multiple interactions in a globally uncoordinated system. In this chapter, we consider how similar effects define the global behavior of mobile code systems. Mobile code paradigms are discussed as are the security issues related to mobile code use. A general model of mobile code is derived. It is used to create simulations that imply different mobile code paradigms may cause different traffic patterns in the network. We finish the chapter by describing the implementation of a mobile code daemon, which supports all of the paradigms discussed. The daemon design integrates standard security tools and authentication.

1. EXISTING PARADIGMS

Table 6.1 shows established mobile code paradigms [Wu 1999, Fuggetta 1998, Milojicic 1999, Tennenhouse 1997]. There has been a clear progression of technology. Initially the client-server approach supported running procedures on a remote node. Remote evaluation augmented this by allowing the remote node to

---

[1] Coauthored with Nathan Orr, Christopher Griffin, and Thomas Keiser.

[2] Portions reprinted, with permission, from:

R. R. Brooks, and N. Orr, "A model for mobile code using interacting automata," *IEEE Transactions on Mobile Computing,* vol. 1, no. 4, pp. 313-326, October–December 2002.

R. R. Brooks, C. Griffin, and A. Payne, "A cellular automata model can quickly approximate UDP and TCP network traffic," *Complexity,* in press.

R. R. Brooks, "Mobile code paradigms and security issues," *IEEE Internet Computing,* vol. 8, no. 3, pp. 54–59, May/June 2004.

T. Keiser, and R. R. Brooks, "Implementation of mobile code daemons for a wired and wireless network of embedded systems," *IEEE Internet Computing,* July 2004.

download code before execution. Code on demand, as implemented in Java, allows local clients to download programs when necessary. Process migration allows processes to be evenly distributed among workstations. Mobile agents permit software to move from node to node, following the agent's internal logic. Active networks allow the network infrastructure to be reprogrammed by packets flowing through the network. Packets of data can be processed while being routed, through execution of encapsulating programs.

Paradigms differ primarily on where code executes and who determines when mobility occurs. Let's consider an example scenario. Given an input data file f on node n_f, a program p on node n_p to be executed, and a user u using node n_u, the paradigms in Table 6.1 would determine the following courses of action [Fuggetta 1996] (this problem is appropriate for neither process migration nor active networks):

- *Client-server* – Data file f is transferred from n_f to n_p. Program p executes on n_p and results are transferred to n_u.
- *Remote evaluation* – Program p is transferred to n_f and executes there. Results are returned to n_u.
- *Code on demand* – Data file f and program p are transferred to n_u and execute there.
- *Mobile agents* – Program p is transferred to n_f and executes there. Program p carries the results to n_u.

Each approach will be efficient at times, depending on network configuration and the size of p and f. The model we propose accepts all of these alternatives. In this model, nodes, files, etc. can be specified at runtime.

Table 6.1. Common Mobile Code Paradigms

Paradigm	Example	Description
Client-server	CORBA	Client invokes code resident on another node.
Remote Evaluation	CORBA factory, SOAP	Client invokes a program on remote node. Remote node downloads code.
Code on Demand	Java, Active X	Client downloads code and executes it locally.
Process Migration	Mosix, Sprite	Operating system transfers processes from one node to another for load balancing.
Mobile Agents	Agent-TCL	Client launches a program that moves from site to site.
Active Networks	Capsules	Packets moving through the network reprogram network infrastructure.

An important distinction exists between *strong* and *weak* code mobility [Fuggetta 1998]. *Strong* mobility allows migration of both code and execution state. Programs can move from node to node while executing. This migration may even be transparent to the program itself (i.e., the program is not aware that it has migrated).

Weak mobility transfers limited initialization data, but no state information, with the code.

The utility of strong migration is debatable since it increases the volume of data transmitted as a process migrates [Zavas 1987]. For load balancing, strong migration is worthwhile only for processes with long lifetimes [Harchol-Balten 1997]. Mobile agents can be implemented using either weak or strong mobility. Differences of opinion exist in the literature as to whether distributed systems that handle migration transparently are [Milojicic 1999] or are not [Fuggetta 1998] mobile code systems. We consider them mobile code systems.

2.   EXISTING IMPLEMENTATIONS

In spite of the differences listed thus far, all mobile code systems have many common aspects. A network aware execution environment must be available. For Java applets, a web browser with a virtual machine downloads and executes the code [Vijaykrishnan 1998]. A network operating system layer coupled with a computational environment provides this service for other implementations [Fuggetta 1998].

Some specific mobile code implementations are difficult to fit into the paradigms in Table 6.1 and warrant further discussion:

- *Postscript* is one of the most successful mobile code applications, but is rarely recognized as mobile code. A postscript file is a program that is uploaded to a printer for execution. It produces graphic images as results.
- *Wave* may be the earliest successful implementation of network aware mobile code. It was implemented in the Ukraine in the early 1970s [Sapaty 1999]. Wave is a programming environment based on graph theory. Network nodes correspond to graph nodes. Network connections correspond to edges. Since distributed computing problems are often phrased in graph theoretical terms [Lynch 1996], it is a very elegant approach.
- *Tube* extends a LISP interpreter to distributed applications [Halls 1997]. As an interpreted system, LISP is capable of meta-programming. Code can be generated and modified on the fly. The distributed interpreter is capable of robust computations and compensating for network errors.
- *Messenger* uses mobile code as the backbone for implementing computer communications protocols [Tschudin 1993]. Protocol Data Units (PDUs) are passed from transmitters to receivers, along with code defining the meaning of the PDUs. This concept is similar to Active Networks [Tennenhouse 1997], but the approach is very different. Instead of concentrating on the mechanics of communication, this approach looks at the semiotics of message passing. Semiotics is the branch of communications that considers the science of sign interpretation.
- *Jini* adds distributed services, especially a name service, to the Java Remote Method Invocation (RMI) module [Sun 1999]. Objects can be invoked on

remote nodes. Jini is intended to extend Java technology to smart spaces, ubiquitous computing, and embedded systems. Some researchers have found difficulties with this approach, since the Java Virtual Machine's 1.5-megabyte memory footprint [MCDowell 1998] is larger than the address space of most widely used embedded processors.

The paradigms discussed have been primarily oriented towards producing prototypes or commercial applications, rather than establishing the consequences of code mobility. In this chapter, we illustrate a model that provides a unified base for the paradigms in Table 6.1.

3.   THEORETICAL MODEL

In the model we present, individual nodes are modeled as abstract machines that are single elements in the global cellular automata (CA). The use of automata in modeling computational devices is well established [Hopcroft 1979]. More recent work creating Discrete Event Dynamic Systems controllers from abstract automata [Phoha 1999] and Petri Nets [Brooks 1999] shows their utility for verifying the stability, controllability, and lack of deadlock in underlying physical systems. We have used this approach to model complex air campaigns [ARL 1999]. It is even more appropriate for mobile code applications.

CA models are powerful tools for studying large, interacting systems. Universal cellular automata can emulate arbitrary Turing machines [Wolfram 1994], guaranteeing that they are capable of executing any computable function. A CA is a synchronously interacting set of abstract machines (network nodes) defined by

- d, the dimension of the automata
- r, the radius of an element of the automata
- δ, the transition rule of the automata
- s, the set of states of an element of the automata

An element's (node's) behavior is a function of its internal state and those of neighboring nodes as defined by δ.

The simplest instance of a CA has a dimension of 1, a radius of 1, a binary set of states, and all elements are uniform. In this simple case, for each cell (automaton) there is a total of 2^3 possible configurations of its neighborhood at any time step. Each configuration can be expressed as an integer v:

$$v = \sum_{i=-1}^{1} j_i 2^{i+1} \tag{7}$$

where i is the relative position of the cell in the neighborhood (left = -1, current position = 0, right = 1) and j_i is the binary value of the state of cell i. Each transition rule can therefore be expressed as a single integer r:

$$r = \sum_{v=1}^{8} j_v 2^v \tag{8}$$

where j_v is the binary state value for the cell at the next time step if the current configuration is v. This is the most widely studied type of CA. It is a very simple many-to-one mapping for each individual cell. The aggregated behaviors can be quite complex [Delorme 1999].

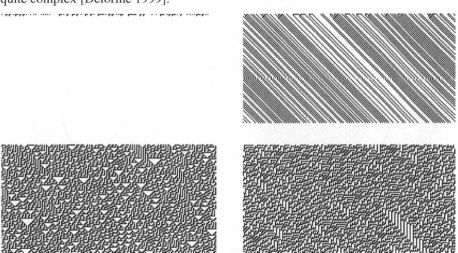

Figure 6.1. Wolfram's four CA complexity classes (clockwise from upper left): stable, periodic, chaotic, and complex. Each pixel on the x-axis is an automaton. The y-axis shows evolution over time.

CAs are especially useful for capturing the complex dynamics caused by interactions among multiple elements, while remaining abstract and tractable. The simple uniform CAs defined by Equations (7) and (8) evolve into one of four complexity classes [Wolfram 1994] (See Figure 6.1):

- *Class 1. Stable* – A permanent fixed state is attained.
- *Class 2. Periodic* – A permanent oscillatory state is attained.
- *Class 3. Chaotic* – A permanent state of chaotic fluctuation is reached.
- *Class 4. Complex* – Complexity evolves for an arbitrarily long time.

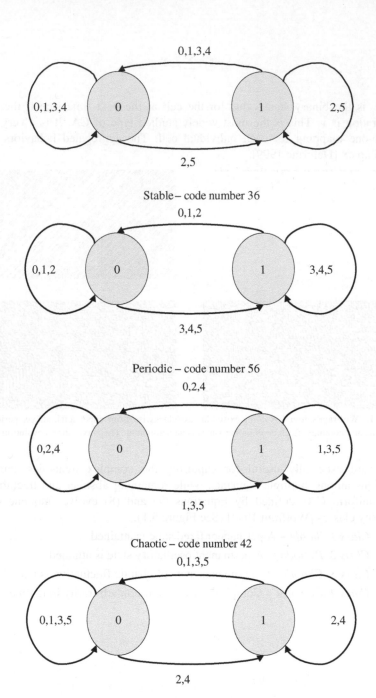

Figure 6.2. Example transition functions for the four complexity classes. ($d = 1, r = 2, s = \{0,1\}$).

Some have theorized that a system's complexity class is related to its ability to adapt to changes. Although stable systems are desirable, a system that is stuck in a stable regime may sometimes be unable to adapt to environmental changes. Chaotic regimes may allow for quick searches of the problem space and allow agile reconfiguration [Kauffman 1993]. Statistical approaches can evaluate CA dynamics [Wolfram 1994]. Particle physics based approaches have also been used to study emergent CA behaviors [Hordijk 1999].

Figure 6.2 graphically illustrates one transition function for each complexity class for one-dimensional CAs where s consists of two states and r is two. For the CA elements in Figure 6.2, the rules are determined by the sum of the states of the elements in the neighborhood. The code value for the numbers is

$$c = \sum_{i=0}^{(2r+1)(k-1)} k^i f[i] \tag{9}$$

They have code values 36 (stable), 56 (periodic), 42 (chaotic), and 20 (complex). Note that trivial transition functions can provide complex interactions and that there is little qualitative difference between the transition functions.

Equations (7) and (8) and the classes in Figure 6.1 all refer to simple one-dimensional automata with binary states and a radius of 1. For the mobile code model, we use nonuniform automata. Each element may have a unique transition function δ. The transition function may even vary over time. Different CAs will have different dimensions. The radius may vary, but remains 1 for the vast majority of cases.

Of primary interest is the design of systems that have globally desirable emergent behaviors, such as intrusion tolerance, based on locally available information. This can be approached in two ways: (*i*) the *forward problem* takes proposed behaviors and determines their global consequences; (*ii*) the *backward* (or inverse) *problem* attempts to derive local behaviors with globally desirable attributes [Gutowitz 1991]. Computer Emergency Response Team (CERT) researchers have identified this as a promising approach to making the Internet more secure from attack [Fisher 1999].

The model we propose is a straightforward tool for evaluating the forward problem. The backward problem is still open. Existing work shows isolated examples of crafting behaviors for global properties [Gutowitz 1991]. Work has been done based on Langton's λ parameter, which measures the fraction of rules producing state 1 in binary automata. Some work indicates that CAs with values of λ near 0.5 tend to have Wolfram class 4 [59]; other studies do not support this conclusion [Gutowitz 1991]. Perhaps the most successful work to date on the backward problem uses learning techniques to find rules with desired properties [Gutowitz 1991]. Genetic algorithms appear to be particularly promising [Hordijk 1999]. A related approach is amorphous computing, where emergent behaviors have been created for practical problems. This approach uses mainly metaphors from biology and physics to create programs that execute in a CA-like environment [Abelson 1999]. We use the model proposed here as a tool for attacking the backward problem to create emergent behaviors that advance network survivability. The work in Chapters 10 and 11 include initial steps in that direction.

The models we use are more complex than the ones expressed by Equations (7) and (8). They build on CA based work for modeling traffic [Nagel 1998] and social [Portugali 2000] systems. This work involves CA environments where entities move from CA element to CA element. These traffic models are referred to as *particle-hopping models*. In [Portugali 2000], a similar concept is referred to as *Free Agents in a Cellular Space* (FACS). We use the FACS nomenclature to avoid confusion with the particle physics concepts in [Hordijk 1999].

The Nagel-Schreckenberg model [Nagel 1998] expresses highway traffic using a one-dimensional CA similar to the one described by Equations (7) and (8). Each element in the CA represents a one-lane highway segment. The segment can be empty (state 0) or contain an automobile (state 1). The radius of the CA depends on the automobile's speed limit. All automobiles move in the same direction through the application of a probabilistic transition rule.

An element's state changes from 1 to 0 when an automobile leaves, and from 0 to 1 at the automobile's new position. If the highway segments (CA elements) in the direction of travel do not contain automobiles (have state 0), the automobile tends to accelerate until it reaches the speed limit. If elements within the radius of the automobile are occupied, the automobile will be forced to slow down. The number of elements the automobile traverses in a single time step defines velocity. This approach qualitatively reproduces important highway traffic attributes, including traffic jam propagation and the formation of "caravans."

Figure 6.3. Output of particle hopping CAs. The *x* dimension is space. Each pixel is a cell. Each row is a time step. Time evolves from top to bottom. White space is empty. Black pixels indicate the presence of a vehicle. The left image is 25% occupied. The right image is 25% occupied. Probability of a vehicle slowing is greater on the right.

Figure 6.3 shows examples from a Nagel-Schreckenberg traffic study. Network traffic can be modeled in a similar manner by allowing each element to represent a computer node in a multihop wireless computer network. Packets move probabilistically from node to node. There is a maximum queue length. The behavior observed in this approach is very similar to Nagel-Schreckenberg results. We integrate these concepts into our approach to model the flow of code, data, and coordination information.

Figure 6.4. The left figure shows an agent traversing the sensor network while approaching the data sink. At the right the agent continues through the CA and a traffic jam has formed above the data sink.

FACS have been used in [Portugali 2000] to study the intermingling of ethnic groups for urban planning. The CA model was expanded to associate agents with CA elements. In the context of urban planning, agents (CA elements) can be city inhabitants of different ethnic groups (neighborhoods in the city). Figure 6.4 shows an example from [Brooks 2002c] where the CA is a sensor network and the agent is a target traversing the network. The central element at the bottom of the image is a data sink. As the target (agent) traverses the sensor field (CA), packets of information are sent in the direction of target travel to cue sensors and propagate track information. Other packets are sent to the data sink to inform users of the target trajectory.

In the context of mobile code, the behavior of the global network cannot be defined purely as an aggregation of individual node behaviors. The behavior of packets traversing the network is also important. In addition to this, mobile code modifies the behavior of its host node. For these reasons, the mobile code model builds on the Nagel-Schreckenberg approach to illustrate network traffic and FACS to illustrate the interaction between mobile code and network hosts.

We call our model Generic Automata with Interacting Agents (GAIA). CA's in the GAIA model are nonuniform. They are defined by the tuple

- d – dimension of the automaton.
- r – radius of the automaton.
- $l[d]$ – vector indicating the number of elements in each dimension.
- Δ – set of transition functions. Each element could have a unique transition function.

- *S[]* – state vector for each automaton.
- *B* – set of behaviors. Behaviors are not tied to specific elements of the CA.

This model is more complex than the CAs discussed earlier but retains the same essential form. The goal is to use this model to study the possibility of network self-organization using mobile code. Study of these CA models should help establish the global emergent behaviors implied by local mobile code activity.

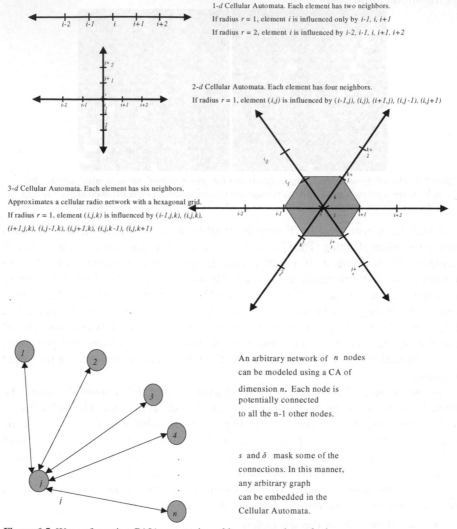

Figure 6.5. Ways of creating GAIAs expressing arbitrary network topologies.

Our approach to mobile code, as shown in Figure 4.1, uses three abstractions: infrastructure, code, and data. There is a fixed infrastructure, which consists of computer hosts and network pipes connecting the hosts. This infrastructure is expressed primarily by the variables *d*, *l[d]*, and *r* in the GAIA tuple. In computer architecture the number of computer connections incident on a node is called the node degree [Hwang 1993], which is expressed by d in our model. The maximum distance between any two nodes is the network diameter [Hwang 1993], which is roughly equivalent to $l[d]$ in the proposed approach. In most models we use r equal to 1, but it could be set to a larger value to model bus architectures. Example network topologies are shown in Figure 6.5. In addition to d, $l[d]$, and r, individual transition functions in Δ are used to complete the description of network topology by either allowing or prohibiting communications between GAIA elements.

In Figure 6.5, the top two diagrams show how elements are connected in one- and two-dimensional GAIA. The middle diagram shows interactions in a regular three-dimensional topology. The three-dimensional topology is appropriate for modeling many communications networks. The bottom diagram shows how to construct a model for an arbitrary network. If there are n nodes in the network, the dimension d can be set to n and all elements of $l[d]$ set to 1. This implies each node is directly connected to every other node. Judicious definition of the elements of Δ prohibits communications between pairs of nodes that are not directly connected. Using this approach, any arbitrary graph structure of n nodes can be embedded in an n-dimensional grid.

Each element of the GAIA has its own instance of the state vector $S[]$. Having the state be a vector is a significant departure from the traditional CA model. In the past, state has always been a single discrete variable. Use of a vector is necessary to concurrently capture multiple aspects of the problem space. For example, behavior of a network will generally depend on the volume of data being handled by the network and the queue length at specific nodes. CA based particle hopping models [Nagel 1998] provide qualitative support for modeling these types of networks. In addition to this, we wish to model the behavior of networks influenced by mobile code.

The presence (or lack) of specific mobile code modules influences the behavior of network nodes as well. Another factor that influences node behavior is whether or not intrusions have been detected. Although it would be possible to use coding schemes to integrate most, if not all, of these factors into a single value, that would serve to complicate rather than simplify the approach.

We force the format of $S[]$ to be uniform for all elements of the GAIA. Constricting the elements of the system to a common state format is standard. The main reason why all elements need a common state definition is to support analysis of the GAIA evolution. For example, visualization of queue length changes across the network, as in Figure 6.3, illustrates network congestion. Visualization of the diffusion of mobile code, or network viruses, across the network helps express the ability of the code to modify network behavior. We also visualize the distribution of entropy [Wolfram 1994] throughout the network. All of these tasks imply the need of a uniform basis for evaluating state for all elements in the GAIA.

The behavior of a specific GAIA element is defined by the interaction among the $S[]$, B, and Δ local to that node. In principle, all elements evaluate their δ concurrently taking as inputs current values of the state vectors and concurrently producing new state vector values for all elements of the GAIA. At each time step, each element of the GAIA evaluates its own transition function δ, which is an element of Δ. Based on the values in the local state vector and the state vectors of all the neighbors, δ determines new values for the local $S[]$. To a large extent, δ is defined by the subset of B present on the local node. Since behaviors are mobile and can move from node to node, δ can vary over time.

$s = \{\text{transition states}\}$
$\delta = \{\text{transition rules}\}$
$s_i^{t+1} = f_i^t(s_{i-1}^t, s_i^t, s_{i+1}^t)$
$f \in \delta$

This model describes a space of interacting automata. In our model, system state and transition rules can also travel from node to node.

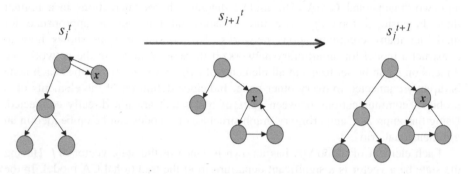

At time t, node j interacts with node $j+1$ providing a new automata for j at time $t+1$

Figure 6.6. CA approach to modeling code migration and virus propagation. Each node's behavior is represented as a finite state machine. At time t, node s_{j+1}^t (middle) transmits the behavior attached at x to node s_j^t (left). Transmission modifies the finite state machine that defines the behavior of s_j by attaching itself at position x on s_j^t. This produces a new finite state machine s_j^{t+1} (right) at time $t+1$. Element behavior includes exchange of code.

Figure 6.6 illustrates the migration of a behavior from node $j+1$ to node j at time step t. In this Figure the local transition function is represented as a finite state machine, which is the parse tree generated from the set of behaviors local to j. At time step t, the behavior attached to the parse tree on node $j+1$ at position x moves to node j. This produces a new parse tree. The migration of this behavior has modified node j's transition function.

Individual elements can also have memory storage beyond a finite number of states and model a Turing or von Neumann machine. Our modifications to the normal CA model reflect the reality of distributed systems for viruses, network intrusions and mobile code applications. Using it, we can model intrusion propagation through a network, and network reconfiguration to battle intrusion. All actions are taken by individual nodes based on $S[]$ and δ, using locally available information.

It is interesting to note the similarities of this model to systems outside computer science. In his dissertation Tschudin discusses parallels among mobile code, computer viruses, biological viruses, and semiotics [Tschudin 1993]. In semiotics there is ambiguity between a sign's meaning and its physical manifestation. Computer code is an excellent example of meaning and essence being intermingled.

Since their inception, computer viruses have been compared to their biological counterparts [Tschudin 1993]. Cells reproduce by having DNA produce RNA, which in turn produces proteins. Many viruses are built from RNA and contain no DNA. Virus RNA is frequently *messenger* RNA that exits from the cell nucleus and creates proteins in the cytoplasm [Fedoroff 1984]. Messenger RNA acts like mobile code modifying the behavior of many parts of the cell. Other genetic artifacts that work in a manner similar to our behavior transmission schema are transposons. They are pieces of DNA that move throughout the genome and modify the genetic code on the cells. Since they do not directly cause the production of protein, they have been called junk DNA. Their ubiquity and importance in DNA modification imply that they may be a basic element of the biological process [Fedoroff 1984]. This hints that mobile code may be an essential element of robust distributed systems.

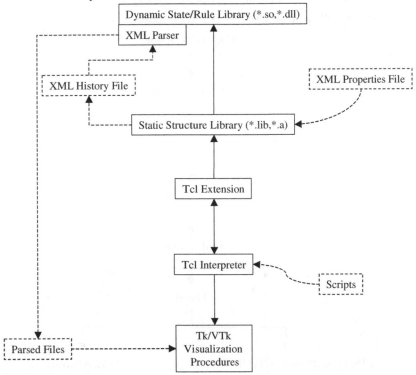

Figure 6.7. CANTOR system architecture. CANTOR was designed to model network traffic in distributed systems, but has evolved to be capable of modeling dynamic discrete event systems using cellular automata.

4. SIMULATOR FOR MODEL

To utilize this model, we have constructed a simulator based on the GAIA model. The simulator consists of a front end that emulates a network with mobile code and a back end that can be used to visualize the evolution of the GAIA. We have named the tool CANTOR (CA ANimaTOR) in honor of the mathematician Cantor's work on self-similar sets. We use this tool to analyze multiple instances of the forward problem [Gutowitz 1991] for designing robust networks safeguarded by mobile code behaviors. CANTOR users can do the following:

- Construct *k*-dimensional cellular grids
- Construct rule based cellular neighborhoods
- Assign evolutionary rules on a cell-by-cell, region by region, or grid basis
- Record evolution of cell states
- Model free agents in the cellular space
- Construct rewritable, swappable, and evolving rules
- Visualize the results in two or three dimensions
- Reprogram the system using a scripting language
- Perform mathematical analysis of cellular grids

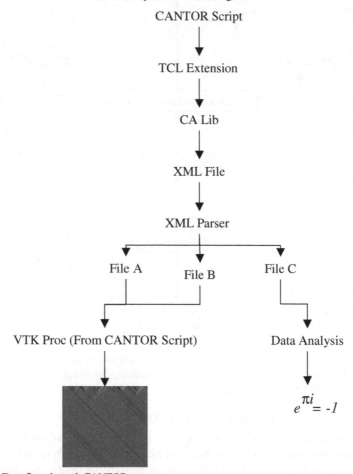

Figure 6.8. Data flow through CANTOR.

The CANTOR design is modular, and portable. Versions exist for Windows NT, Unix, and Linux. The system architecture is shown in Figure 6.7. Figure 6.8 shows data flow in the system. Implementation of CANTOR uses the Tool Command Language (TCL) scripting language and its associated Visualization Toolkit (VTk). The architecture subsystems are:

- *Static Structure Library/Dynamic State/Rule Library:* Models CA internal objects including cells, agents, neighborhood rules, and self-modifying evolution rules. Grid history is contained in XML data files. XML is adaptable. Simulations may require cells with multiple state attributes (i.e., queue length, transmission rate etc.). Visualizations only present one or two attributes simultaneously. XML allows recording of all of the data and selective access using tags. An XML parser is included in the dynamic library, allowing cells to parse their own XML output. Data analysis is also performed by these modules.

- *TCL Extension:* Is a wrapper for the CA library. It allows each function in the CA library to be used as a TCL command.

- *VTk Library:* Is a series of TCL/VTk procedures and scripts designed to graphically display the evolution and interaction of CA/Agents. This library parses XML files output from the CA library and feeds data to a visualization system.

Currently the data analysis routines are only available offline. Plans exist to integrate them into the scripting language. Data analysis tools include entropy analysis and probability and statistical summaries of generations and runs.

5.   MODELS OF PARADIGMS

In this Section we show how the paradigms from Table 6.1 can be phrased as examples of the general mobile code model. The model thus provides a more inclusive paradigm. This approach has many pragmatic aspects. Using abstract automata allows us to quickly construct models of a specific problem for simulation and analysis. The CA shows interactions among distributed components. The CANTOR toolset allows for quick evaluation and comparison of different approaches to a given problem. The tuple elements d, r, and $l[d]$ define network topologies. A network instance that a paradigm will be used in will have a particular topology. The mobile code paradigm itself is described in terms of $S[]$, B, and Δ. We now describe the paradigms listed in Table 6.1.

A.   CLIENT-SERVER

In the client-server paradigm, one computer node has a program that one or more remote computers need to execute. For example, a single database server can service the needs of multiple hosts. A common implementation of client-server is a three-tier approach as outlined in [Stevens 1993]. Figure 6.9 shows the concept. The three layers are clearly shown.

A number of clients (layer 1) send requests to a well-known address (layer 2) that feeds them to a central server (layer 3). The central server is provided with a client-specific address (layer 2) for forwarding results to the client. It would be possible to model this in a number of ways. We provide an example. Since this approach is independent of the network topology, d, r, and $l[d]$ can be arbitrary.

One GAIA element S is specified as the server. We will also specify an element M to act as the second tier of the client-server. We will have M handle both the input to and output from S. M and S may or may not be the same GAIA element. The rest of the elements in the GAIA would be clients (C). We will prohibit the bottom two tiers from being clients.

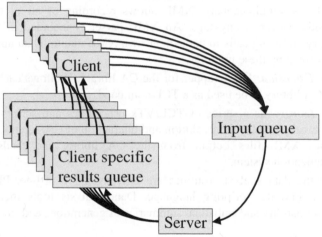

Figure 6.9. A single server services multiple clients. Input requests are received at a central point and queued. Each client has its own output queue.

We define $S[]$ as a vector with the following members:

- *Role* – A nominal variable identifying the GAIA element as M, S, or C.
- *Packet queue length* – The number of packets currently on the node awaiting transmission to a neighboring node. (all elements)
- *Packet list* – The store-and-forward packets are kept in this first in first out (FIFO) temporary data storage. Each packet would be a data structure containing source, destination, and request specific information. (all elements)
- *Outstanding requests* – The number of requests waiting for a response from the server. (all)
- *Serviced requests* – The number of requests that have already been satisfied from the server. (all)
- *Request list* – List of requests that have yet to be services (second tier and server).

- *Internal state* – Each node needs a set of states (e.g., waiting for request, processing request, etc.) for interaction with its transition function δ. (all nodes).

State elements that are not relevant for a given GAIA type are set to a known default value.

Three different transition functions exist in this model:

- *Client* – Starts in an idle state. When a request is made, it triggers a request behavior that propagates through the network and transitions to a waiting for response state. While in that state, it can make further requests. Each time a request is made the number of outstanding requests is augmented. When a response to a request is received, the number of outstanding requests is decremented and the number of serviced requests incremented. If the number of outstanding requests reaches zero, the client returns to an idle state.

- *Middle tier* – Starts in an idle state. As requests are received, the original request behavior terminates and a new request behavior started that serves to signal the server. It maintains outstanding and serviced request counters, like the client does. It moves to a waiting for response state when a service request is received. When a service results behavior is received it moves to a responding to server state. In this state, it terminates the results behavior and starts a new one. In addition to this, the outstanding requests queue is maintained.

- *Server* – Starts in an idle state. It receives requests from the middle tier and terminates the request behavior. When results are available, a response behavior is initiated. While there are requests to be serviced, the server remains in an active state. The server maintains counters and lists in the same manner as the second tier.

In these definitions, we have specified neither how clients formulate requests nor how the server formulates responses.

Most of these transition functions are essentially FIFO queues. They could be implemented either as a finite state machine, as shown in Figure 6.10, or as a stack machine as shown in Figure 6.11. For the finite state machine, queue length relates directly to the state of the automaton. The maximum queue length is exceeded when a request is received and the machine is in state n. For the stack machine, queue length corresponds to stack depth. The stack machine abstraction does not provide any advantages over finite state machines for expressing limited queue lengths.

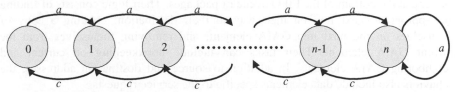

Figure 6.10. A finite state machine for a queue capable of storing n elements.

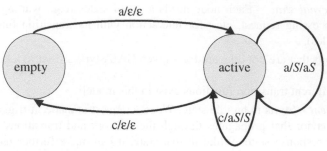

Figure 6.11. A stack machine for a queue.

To construct a simulation that analyzes client-server performance versus other designs, it would be possible for (*i*) clients to produce requests with either uniform or Poisson probability distributions and (*ii*) the server to reply to requests in a FIFO manner following an exponential probability distribution.

Another issue that has not been dealt with is packet transmission over the network. There are two ways of modeling this. It could be either expressed in the transition function or as mobile behaviors. It is worth noting that it is trivial to insert elements into the GAIA, which are not directly involved in the client-server mechanism and only relay packets between neighboring elements.

To express packet transmission in the transition function, each element is made responsible for exchanging packets with its neighbors. Packets have source and destination addresses. Per default, packets originate at their source and travel to their destination following a simple greedy heuristic. They move from their local position to the next node, which has not reached its maximum queue length, along the shortest path to the destination. At each time step, the packet at the bottom of the FIFO packet queue is potentially transferred to its neighbor. Transfer of packets follows the general form of the Nagel-Schreckenberg particle-hopping model described in Section 3. This simple behavior is present in every node and can be expressed as a finite state machine (Figure 6.10) or stack machine (Figure 6.11). By performing a cross product operation between this finite state machine and the transition functions described above, the two functionalities can be merged in a straightforward manner.

If more complex routing behavior is desired for packets, they could also be expressed as behaviors. In this client-server model, we have defined behaviors for request and results propagation. These behaviors originate at the sending GAIA element. They execute once on each element they visit. The execution occurs when they are at the bottom of the FIFO queue of packages. Their logic consists of finding the appropriate next hop on their way to their destination; creating a copy of themselves on the next hop GAIA element; and removing themselves from the current GAIA element. Their tasks can include bookkeeping on current and neighboring GAIA elements. In addition to source and destination addresses, the behaviors also include data elements specific to the service requests.

B. REMOTE EVALUATION

Remote evaluation is similar to client-server, except that the remote node may have to download code before execution. A common implementation of this is the use of remote procedure calls (RPCs) on UNIX systems. Remote evaluation is similar to the client-server approach given above, except for three things: (*i*) no second tier is used, (*ii*) the system is not limited to a single server, and (*iii*) the program executed is not generally resident on the server beforehand. The model given here builds upon the client-server model.

The packet transfer model can be taken from Section 5.A with no modification. The client model requires little modification. The difference is that there is more than one server. Clients can make calls to any available server.

Similarly, servers work as in Section 5.A with a minor modification. The modification is that if the behavior requested is not present it must be downloaded from another node. The request for code could be handled using a client-server approach. For the sake of simplicity, we do not designate a single server; we treat all nodes as peers. In which case if a client node *a* requests execution of a program *p* on server node *b*, server node *b* may have to play the role of a client when requesting delivery of *p* from another node *c*. Upon completion of execution *b* returns results to *a*.

In the simplest model for remote evaluation, all elements of the GAIA play the role of client or server as needed. The state vector *S[]* is given by

- *Packet queue length* – As with client-server.
- *Packet list* – As with client-server.
- *Client outstanding requests* – The number of requests waiting for a response from a server.
- *Client serviced requests* – The number of requests that have already been satisfied from a server.
- *Server outstanding requests* – The number of requests waiting to be serviced by this node.
- *Server serviced requests* – The number of requests that have already been serviced by this node.
- *Request list* – List of requests that have yet to be serviced by this node.
- *Internal state* – Each node needs a set of states (e.g., waiting for request, processing request, etc.) for interaction with its transition function δ.

This state structure reflects the fact that each node is both client and server.

In this approach there is only one transition function. Each node starts in an idle state. When necessary it performs client processing as described in Section 5.A. No middle tier exists; so middle tier processing is not included. If the node receives a request, it performs the server processing as in Section 5.A. If the code requested is not present, it performs client processing to retrieve the code before servicing the request. To allow concurrent client and server processing, a cross product is formed of the client and server finite state automata in Section 5.A.

Simulation of this approach is straightforward by implementing the GAIA. GAIA elements are chosen at random to play the role of client or server. Specific network configurations can be implemented as needed. Deterministic schemes can then be used to test specific load models. Remote evaluation was an evolutionary extension to client-server in that the code evaluated no longer had to be present on the server beforehand.

C. CODE ON DEMAND

A common implementation of code on demand is a web browser. It is a simplification of remote evaluation. The server and client nodes are identical. A single user node can request code and data from any machine on the network. In some ways, it is the inverse of the client-server model.

Code on demand can be phrased in GAIA by modifying remote evaluation. Each node potentially contains a web browser. It can request code or data from other nodes on the network. The nodes respond by transmitting the information to the requesting node.

States and transition functions are the same as for remote evaluation. The differences are

- Code always executes on the node that originates the request.
- Since results are computed at the node requesting the data, results do not have to be transmitted after computation has completed.

Every node can potentially place a request. The number of nodes that can provide code and/or data to satisfy the request can be limited. For example, in [Brooks 2000] the code repository is a single node.

D. PROCESS MIGRATION

Sections 5.A through 5.C describe widely used mobile code paradigms, which incrementally increase user independence from physical location. In contrast to this, process migration has been implemented and used primarily by research laboratories [Milojicic 1999]. It differs greatly from the methods in Sections 5.A through 5.C. Among other things, it uses strong mobility to transfer program state along with code and data.

Processes move from node to node in an attempt to find an equitable distribution of resources. Process migration is in many ways a precursor of the mobile agent paradigm, which will be described in Section 5.E.

Since processes are not tied to their host nodes, we model them as instances of behaviors. Process behaviors are mobile. They include (*i*) the program being executed, (*ii*) its state information, and (*iii*) associated data files. A process looks at the load on the local computer node (element) and all nodes (elements) in the immediate neighborhood. If the current load exceeds a threshold value and there exists a neighboring node with a lighter load, it moves to the neighbor with the lightest load. Processes may be large; transporting a process from one node to another may require multiple time steps.

Each node has a state vector *S[]* with the following members:

- *Outgoing packet list* – If a process is large, it must be cut into multiple packets for transmission from a node to its neighbor. Multiple processes may have to migrate simultaneously. All packets awaiting transmission are stored on a common FIFO queue.
- *Outgoing packet queue length* – Number of packets currently on the queue.
- *Incoming packet list* – This list temporarily stores packets that make up a process until it is entirely transferred.
- *Incoming packet queue length* – Number of packets currently on the list.
- *Maximum load* – An integer signifying the resources available at this node for use by processes.
- *Current load* – Resources currently consumed by processes on the node.
- *Process list* – A list of behaviors currently active on the node.

E. MOBILE AGENTS

We define mobile agents as processes capable of moving from node to node following their own internal control logic. As such, mobile agents are an extension of the model proposed for load balancing. The difference is that their control logic is not limited to moving to neighboring nodes in response to load increases. In principle, this model could encapsulate arbitrary control logic.

The mobile agent approach has the constraint that data sources are generally not mobile. When agents move they transport only the data, which is part of their internal state. They are often proposed as models where they harvest data from large distributed data resources. An example study of when this approach is efficient is given in [Qi 2001].

The state vector $S[]$ is the same for mobile agents as for process migration, except that the load variables are removed. The transition functions for nodes (elements) are identical to the process migration transition functions.

F. ACTIVE NETWORKS

In some ways, active networks can be considered as a way of merging the functionality of process migration and mobile agents. It could also be considered as a radically new approach. The DARPA active networks research initiative contained a number of related programs [Tennenhouse 1997].

One active network approach is to encapsulate all the data in a packet containing the programs that modify the data. In this way, data can be modified while being routed through the network. This approach is a modification of the process migration approach with two differences:

- The processes are small.
- Migration is not done for load balancing. It follows its own logic.

Another active network approach is to use packets to reprogram the infrastructure. Packet routing methods are dynamically modified when packets alter the infrastructure while traversing the network. This is radically different from the other approaches we have considered.

The packets are behaviors that move from node (GAIA element) to node (GAIA element). Packet source is defined as the node where the packet originates. For the sake of argument, we will consider that each packet has a destination that is known *a priori*. In practice some packets, for example network management packets, may move through the network with no fixed destination.

In this approach, the next hop for each packet is determined by the node where the packet is currently located. The logic used by a node to determine the next hop can, however, be modified by the packets currently on the node. For example, the choice of packet for transmission could be changed from following a FIFO logic to a priority queue.

The state vector would be the same as mobile agents. The transition function for the node (GAIA element) determines which neighbor receives the packet. No single transition function exists. In fact, it must be possible for packets to modify the transition function dynamically.

Packet behaviors are basically compilers, which parse the local nodes behavior and generate a modified behavior. If node behaviors are limited to the set of regular languages, then packets could be defined as Mealy machines. Mealy machines are regular languages that map one regular language to another [Hopcroft 1979]. Nodes defined as stack machines or Turing machines will require more sophisticated techniques for parsing and generating node behaviors.

It is advisable to keep behaviors in all these models as simple as possible. We have not set arbitrary limits on behaviors in an attempt to have this approach mirror reality.

6. SIMULATION STUDIES OF MODELS

Here we will now illustrate differences between the mobile code approaches and the traffic patterns that they produce. Results in this Section are all from CANTOR simulations using a very simple network topology. The topology is a straight line with each processor (except those on the edges) having two neighbors it can communicate with. In Section 8, we will compare the fidelity of CANTOR simulations to simulation results from a standard simulation tool.

For all images showing the evolution of CA models, we will use the same axes. Each pixel along the x-axis is a client. Each pixel represents the state of a single processor. No messages go beyond the boundaries since messages are exchanged only between nodes active in the simulation. Nodes are numbered left to right from 0 to n. Messages for lower (higher) numbered nodes go left (right). The y-axis shows how the system evolves over time. Each line of the image shows the state of the entire network at a given time step. Time step zero is the top line of the image. Network evolution proceeds from top to bottom. Except where indicated differently, the parameters for simulations are

- Mean time between requests, 75 generations.
- Mean processing time, 1 generation.
- Maximum queue length, 14.
- Retransmits enabled.

- Probability of transmission failure, 0.05.
- No packet dropping.
- 300 generations.
- One-dimensional network of 200 nodes.

A. CLIENT-SERVER

Figure 6.12a shows the graphical results of a CANTOR client-server network simulation with a long mean time between requests by clients following a Poisson distribution and low mean time to process the requests following an exponential distribution at the server. The very light gray background color indicates an empty network queue. Darker grays indicate an occupied network queue. Lighter shades of gray show a longer queue. The line down the middle of the image indicates the location of the server node. Note the transient congestion forming in the network. This is an example of data bursts forming spontaneously in the system.

Figure 6.12b shows a network where the mean time between requests is much less (25 generations) and the mean time required to process requests is longer (3 generations). The results are consistent with what one would expect from a queuing theory analysis: significant congestion forms around the server.

Often entropy [Weisstein 1998] is used to analyze cellular automata and identify disordered regions. We find that entropy charts of networks help identify bifurcations of network behavior. If x_i^t is the queue length of cell i at generation t, then the maximum likelihood estimator for the probability of a cell having queue length q at generation t is

$$p_q^t = \frac{1}{N} \sum_{i=1}^{N} \chi(x_i^t) \qquad (9)$$

where

$$\chi(x_i^t) = \begin{cases} 1 & x_i^t = q \\ 0 & \text{else} \end{cases} \qquad (10)$$

and N is the number of cells in the model. The entropy for generation t can be computed as

$$H(t) = - \sum_{0 \le q \le q_{max}} p_q^t \log(p_q^t) \qquad (11)$$

Figure 6.13 shows entropy for several client-server examples.

In the legend of Figure 6.13, P indicates the Poisson mean time between transmissions, and E indicates the mean time to service a request by the server. In this example, we observe three qualitatively different regimes:

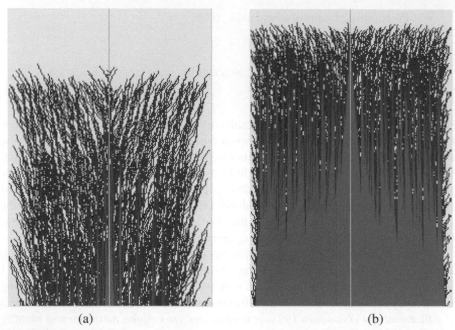

(a)   (b)

Figure 6.12. (a) Low arrival rate, high processing speed. (b) Higher arrival rate, lower processing speed.

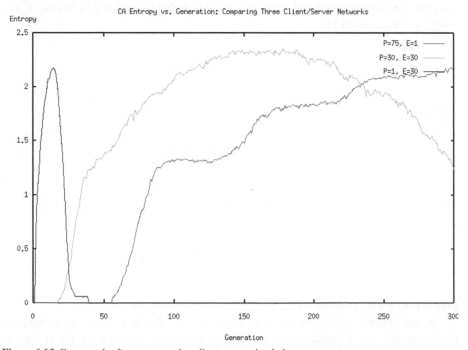

Figure 6.13. Entropy plot for representative client-server simulations.

- When the server is slow, a long queue forms quickly around the server and congestion from this queue saturates the network (Figure 6.12b), as shown by the line that peaks on the far left in the entropy plot (Figure 6.13).

- When the server is fast and jobs are generated quickly, the congestion that occurs is caused by network traffic and is distributed throughout the system (Figure 6.12a), as shown by the line that peaks in the middle of the entropy plot.

- When the server is fast and jobs are generated slowly, there is little congestion. Queue formation is transient, as shown by the line where entropy continues to increase in the entropy plot.

Similar effects are observed in other mobile code paradigms, which are discussed in the following Sections. For all cases if jobs are generated more quickly than the server can process them, the final state will be a deadlocked system with full queues.

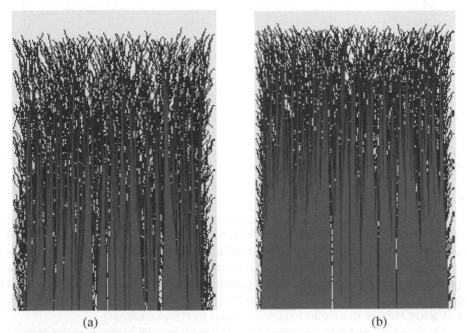

(a)   (b)

Figure 6.14. (a) Remote evaluation without significant congestion. (b) Remote evaluation with significant congestion.

B. REMOTE EVALUATION

Figure 6.14 shows results from simulations of the remote evaluation paradigm. Figure 6.14a has the mean time between requests set to 30 generations. In Figure 6.14b, the mean time between requests is 15 generations, and mean processing time is 3 generations. The entropy plots for remote evaluation shown in Figure 6.15 are very similar to the client-server entropy plots. Remote evaluation is very similar to client-server. The difference is that there is not a central server and processing is spread throughout the network. Instead of having a central bottleneck, a number of smaller bottlenecks occur.

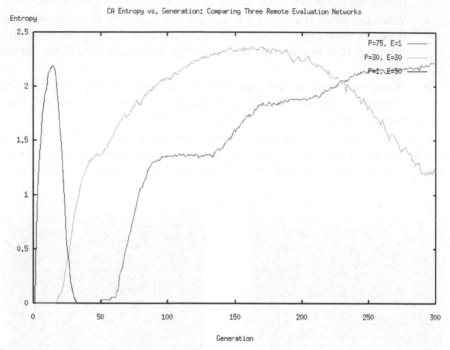

Figure 6.15. Entropy plot for remote evaluation.

C. CODE ON DEMAND

Code on demand extended remote evaluation by allowing arbitrary nodes on the network to request and execute code. The GAIA models for code on demand show a marked difference in qualitative behavior with the client-server model.

Figure 6.16a shows results from a code on demand network with a high Poisson mean time to generate requests. Mean processing time is not applicable to code on demand, since results remain on the local host. Figure 6.16b shows the same network with a low Poisson mean time to generate requests (16 generations).

Figure's 6.17 and 6.18 compare the three paradigms. Differences in the entropy plots of the three scenarios are evident. As the figure indicates, the disorder produced in the code on demand network seems to be greater than that of the other two networks. In both client-server and remote evaluation, computation requests are serviced remotely. The server has a queue that is serviced following an exponential distribution. In the code on demand model, requests are serviced by sending the program instantaneously. The delay introduced by the wait at the remote node appears to reduce disorder in the network. For code on demand, the behavior of the global system is dependent only on the network traffic. Processing is done locally and the time required to process requests is of no consequence to the behavior of the network as a whole.

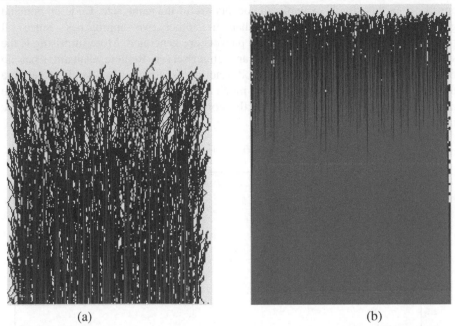

(a)   (b)

Figure 6.16. (a) Code on demand with minimal congestion. (b) Code on demand with significant congestion.

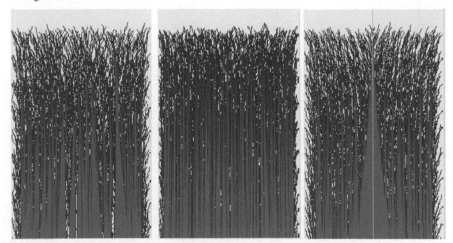

Figure 6.17. From left to right: Remote evaluation, code on demand, client-server with moderate congestion.

Disorder is a function of queue length variance in the system. In practice, queue lengths are uniform under two conditions: (*i*) if the system is underutilized queue lengths are uniformly low, (*ii*) if the system is overloaded queue lengths are uniformly high as the system becomes congested. This implies that high entropy is indicative of an active system with transient congestion and no major bottlenecks. Using this argument, Figure 6.18 implies that code on demand is a more efficient approach. In this simple example all packets are of the same size. Code on demand generates significantly less traffic than the other two approaches. Since all processing is done locally, no response packets are generated. More surprising is the similarity between remote evaluation and client-server. Remote evaluation has no central server bottleneck. It has 200 nodes acting as servers. One would expect the throughput of remote evaluation to be much higher. This does not appear to be the case. Evidently in this configuration, the congestion bottleneck is network traffic rather than server throughput.

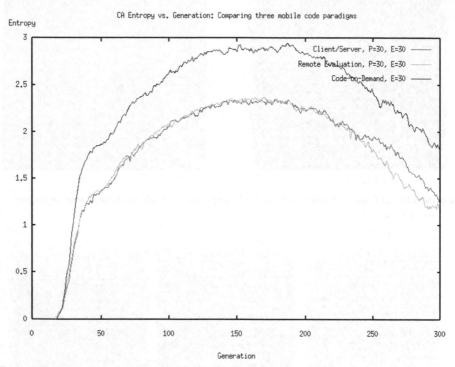

Figure 6.18. Entropy for remote evaluation, client-server, and code on demand.

D. PROCESS MIGRATION

For process migration, each node has the same transition function, which resembles the Nagel-Schreckenberg particle-hopping model. Each process is chopped into a sequence of packets and put on a queue. Packets on the outgoing queue are transferred to the neighboring node chosen by the process. Once all packets associated with a process have been completely transferred to the neighboring node, the migrated process is put on the process list. One packet per time step can be transferred. There is a small probability that a packet will need to be retransmitted.

Process behaviors follow a simple logic. When they start on a node they add their load to the current load. When they leave a node, they remove their load from the current load. They migrate to the neighbor with the smallest load. Figure 6.19 illustrates scenarios with high and low process arrival rates. Note that instead of showing packet queue length, Figure 6.19 shows the number of processes active on each node. The network disorder caused by process migration differs from the other networks we have modeled as well. The system shown in Figure 6.19a has a mean process load of 1 using an exponential distribution. The maximum load supported by a node is 5, and the mean process duration is 10 generations following an exponential distribution. The mean time between process initiations is 80 (Poisson distribution). In Figure 6.19b the system is the same as in Figure 6.19a, except the time between process initiation is 10 (Poisson). These show scenarios with high and low process arrival rates. Retransmission was not included in the process migration and mobile agent scenarios.

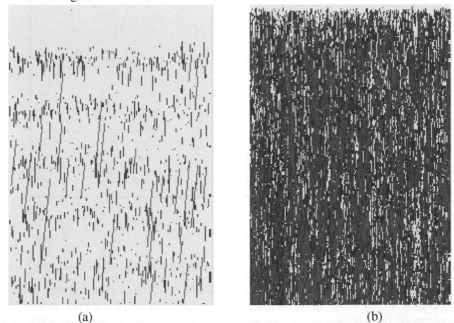

(a)   (b)

Figure 6.19. Process migration. (a) Low process creation rate. (b) Process migration, high process creation rate.

The network disorder caused by process migration differs from the other networks we have modeled. Figure 6.20 shows entropy plots for three process migration networks. The top line shows the entropy when the mean time between process arrivals following a Poisson distribution is 5 time steps. The system reaches a high state of disorder and remains at a constant high entropy. The line in the middle shows a mean time parameter of 20 time steps. The entropy is lower, and it varies significantly over time. The bottom line shows a system with a mean process arrival time of 50. The entropy is lower and shows a significant, regular oscillation.

We have analyzed the cause of this oscillation and determined that the period of oscillation is a function of the mean time between process generation, while the amplitude is a function of the ratio of mean process lifetime to mean time between process creation. Figure 6.21 shows a set of entropy curves in which the mean time between generations is fixed at 50 generations and the mean process lifetime is varied from 5 generations to 100 generations.

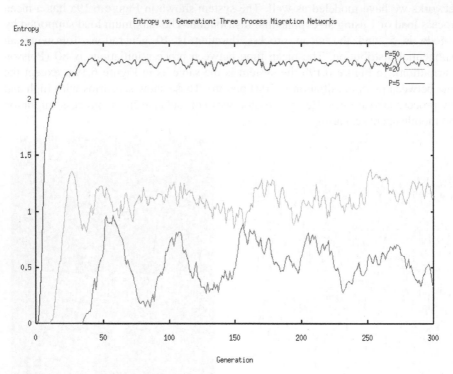

Figure 6.20. Entropy for process migration.

As the figure shows, the period of oscillation is related to the mean time to generation of 50 generations. We see that peaks seem to be forming around the generations of multiples of 50. The amplitude of oscillation decreases as a function of the ration of mean lifetime to mean time to generation of new processes. As the network becomes cluttered the peaks become less obvious.

E. MOBILE AGENTS

Agent behaviors potentially follow arbitrary logic. In our model, few restrictions exist on the internal structure of the behaviors implementing the mobile agents. In this analysis, an agent is given an arbitrary itinerary. The itinerary consists of a list of nodes to be visited and processing to be done. The processing times vary according to a uniform distribution. Figure 6.22 shows results from a simulated network of mobile agents. These diagrams show process queue length.

Figure 6.22a has mean process load 1 (exponential distribution), mean process duration on each node 8 generations (exponential distribution), and mean time between process initiation 50 (Poisson). Figure 6.22b has mean process load 1 (exponential distribution), mean process duration on each node 8 generations (exponential distribution), and mean time between process initiation 10 (Poisson). Note that the generality of the mobile agent concept means that other types of mobile agents are possible.

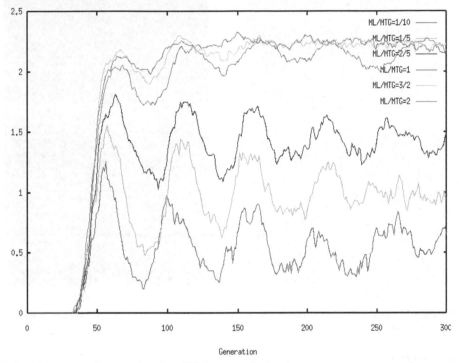

Generation

Figure 6.21. Entropy shape as a function of lifetime to production time.

Figure 6.23 shows the entropy plots for representative mobile agent networks. The entropy plot resembles the entropy of process migration systems in many respects. For a large number of agents, this similarity is reasonable. For medium and small numbers of agents, the entropy is higher for the agent system than for process migration. This is reasonable since the system is not attempting load balancing. We can see a similar oscillation in the mobile agents. We believe that this oscillation is caused for the same reasons that it is in the process migration model, and that it is a simulation artifact with no inherent meaning.

7. MODELS OF NETWORKING PATHOLOGIES

In addition to the mobile code paradigms, a number of network pathogens and pathologies rely on code mobility. We feel they need to be described as well to provide an adequate picture of mobile code. Because they are generally handled in a separate body of literature, we are placing them in a separate Section. Worms and viruses are clearly applications of mobile code. Although Denial of Service (DoS) attacks do not use mobile code per se, they are distributed systems that resemble the client-server family of paradigms enough to deserve consideration here. The models presented in this section are specialized instances of the paradigm models given in Section 5.

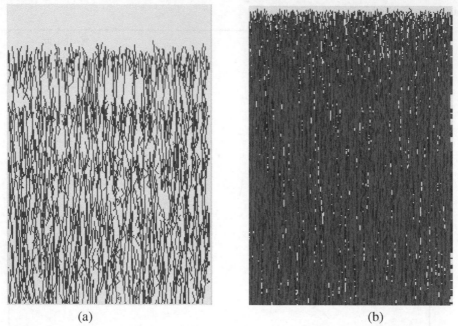

(a) (b)

Figure 6.22. (a) Mobile agent network with low congestion. (b) Mobile agent network with high congestion.

A. WORM

A worm is a network program that creates new copies of itself on a computer system. Worms most frequently attempt to create multiple copies of themselves on multiple computers [Stallings 1995]. We consider worms as mobile agents. These agents not only move from node to node, but they also create new instances of themselves.

B. VIRUS

A virus is a program that lives within another program. When the host program runs, the virus logic is activated first. The virus logic searches for another program to infect, and copies itself into that program [Stallings 1995]. This can best be modeled as an instance of an active network. The logic carried in a packet modifies the host node by inserting into the host node logic that infects packets as they pass through the host node.

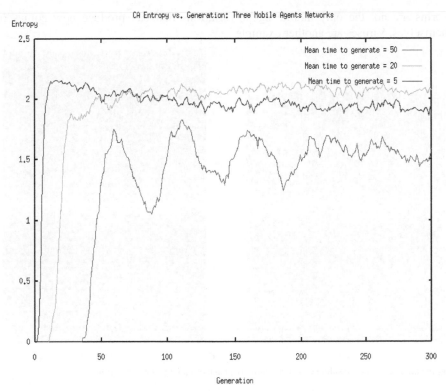

Figure 6.23. Entropy plots for mobile agent networks.

C. DISTRIBUTED DENIAL OF SERVICE

A DoS attack is an instance of the client-server paradigm. A client floods a server with requests until the server can longer function. Distributed Denial of Service (DDoS) attacks are examples of the remote evaluation paradigm. A single client tasks multiple nodes on the network to flood a given victim node with requests until the victim can no longer function.

8. SIMULATION STUDIES OF PATHOLOGIES

In this section we present representative simulation results for the worm and DDoS pathologies. No virus simulations are given since they closely resemble the worm results.

A. WORM

Figure 6.24 shows sample runs of networks with worm infections. Figure 6.24a has the same parameter settings as Figure 6.22a. Figure 6.24b has the mean time to process initiation set to 15 generations. Figure 6.25 shows the entropies of other representative networks that have been infected with worms. The reader will note the increased traffic that results from a worm versus a regular mobile agent. Note that worms are not the only mobile agent variations that can produce new copies of themselves. Viruses are another example.

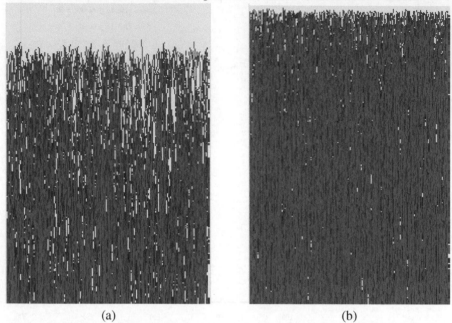

(a)   (b)

Figure 6.24. (a) Slow spreading worm infection. (b) Fast spreading worm infection.

B.   DISTRIBUTED DENIAL OF SERVICE

Figure 6.26 shows example DDoS attacks. The node in the center is the server in these images. The light colored nodes represent zombie processes that attempt to cause congestion around the server. In Figure 6.26a 10% of the nodes are zombies. For nonzombie nodes, the mean time between request initiation is 40 (Poisson), andmean time to service request is 3 (exponential). For Figure 6.25b 25% of the nodes are zombies. For nonzombie nodes the mean time between request initiation is 40 (Poisson), and mean time to service request is 3 (exponential). Each zombie generates a request for service from the server at each time step. In both images, congestion forms quickly around the server. Congestion can be seen moving quickly towards the server. This attack exploits the congestion weakness of the client-server paradigm.

The entropy plot shown in Figure 6.27 shows that the entropy profile of a DDoS attack is qualitatively similar to a client-server entropy plot. The difference is that the DDoS system becomes disordered more quickly and that entropy dies off more quickly as congestion isolates the server from its clients.

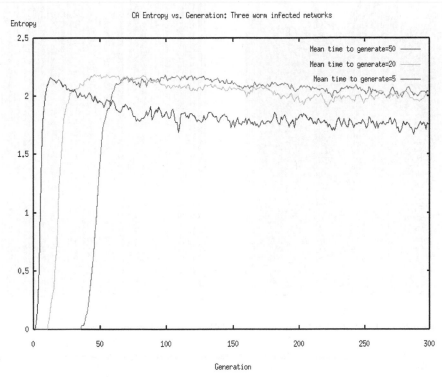

Figure 6.25. Entropy plots for worm infected networks.

9.   COMPARISON OF NETWORK SIMULATIONS

The mobile code model in Sections 3 through 8 best expresses large and decentralized mobile code systems with no centralized control. It combines simple packet traffic models with abstract automata representations of programs. This simple abstraction permits analysis of interactions between network communications and local software modification.

The simulation results in Sections 6 and 8 have many interesting implications. The simulations indicate that different mobile code approaches will tend to generate different traffic patterns. The simulations also show the importance of transient congestion formation in the network. These short-lived traffic jams are underestimated by more traditional queuing theory approaches. They provide cumulative probabilities for queues on individual nodes having a given length, but underestimate the existence of short-lived disturbances.

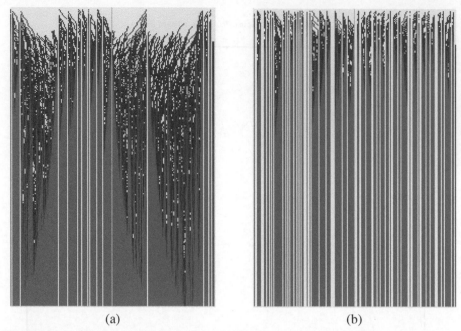

Figure 6.26. (a) DDoS attack with few zombies. (b) DDoS attack with many zombies.

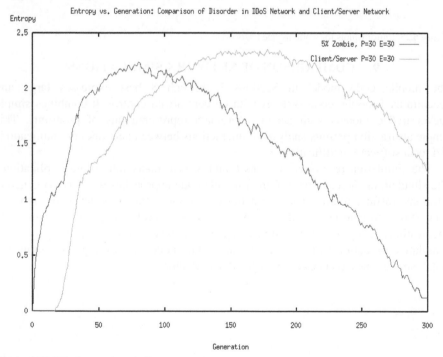

Figure 6.27. DDoS entropy analysis.

Finally, the mobile code simulations provide an intuitive understanding of the use of entropy as a measure of network health. Entropy is a measure of disorder. It is at a minimum when all entries have the same value. It is at a maximum when each entry is unique. We use entropy as a metric for network disorder computed using the queue lengths of the nodes. Nodes will have a uniform queue length in two cases: (*i*) a uniform low queue length indicates that the network is underutilized and (*ii*) a uniform high queue length indicates that congestion is disrupting the network. Entropy is high when transient queues are forming and dispersing spontaneously. This is when the network is working and traffic throughput is high, but there are no serious bottlenecks that cause major disruptions. High entropy values indicate a healthy network.

What is missing from Sections 3 through 8 is empirical evidence that these results correspond to the behavior of network implementations. In this section, we construct CANTOR models of the Transmission Control Protocol (TCP) and User Datagram Protocol (UDP) protocols and compare the results of CANTOR simulations using these models with a high fidelity network simulation tool ns-2 [VINT 2002].

The ns-2 simulator is part of the Virtual InterNetwork Testbed (VINT), which is a high fidelity network simulation package. It is an open source system containing full software implementations of the IP protocol stacks. Graph structures of networks can be constructed. Traffic sources and sinks defined for the network. IP protocols modified. Simulations run. Traffic recorded and analyzed. A network animation tool, nam, is also provided for displaying the network traffic.

A. CANTOR UDP MODEL

Our UDP network model is a lattice with each node receiving and transmitting UDP packets. The state of a network node at position x is given by the tuple

$$\left\langle q_i^x : q_i \in \mathbb{N} \right\rangle_{|x-i| \geq r}$$

where r is the radius of the cellular automata. Each q_i^x is the length of the queue containing packets for the neighbor at position i in the lattice. Hence, the cumulative queue length for any given cell is the sum of the elements in the tuple. The bandwidth of the connection from node x to node i is given by β_i^x, which is expressed in packets per CA time step.

Each q_i^x is updated independently at each time step using the formula

$$\varphi\left(q_i^x\right) = \min\left\{ q_{i,\max}^x, q_i^x + \sum_{|x-j| \leq r} \chi_i\left(q_x^j\right)\beta_x^j - \lambda\left(q_x^i\right)\psi\left(q_i^x\right)\beta_i^x + \gamma_i \beta_i^x \right\} \tag{12}$$

where

- $q_{i,\max}^x$ is the maximum queue length for communications from node x to node at i.
- χ_i is 1 (0) when q_x^i is nonempty and has packets for x to put in queue q_i^x (otherwise).
- ψ is 1 (0) when q_i^x is nonempty and has packets for node i (otherwise).
- λ is 1 (0) when q_i is already at its maximum.
- γ_i is a random variable modeling packet generation.

When an indicator function is 1 and an entire packet cannot be transferred in one generation, then it remains 1 until the whole packet is transferred to its destination. There is a difference between hop destination and final destination. If a packet arrives at its final destination, then it is not part of the packet queue. Packets making hops en route to their final destination are counted in the packet queue. The function χ_i indicates the existence of packets that hop to a neighbor and then continue, while ψ indicates the existence of any packets that can leave the queue.

The random variable γ_i is the most complicated part of the model. It should model network background traffic in a true network and tuned to match the network being modeled. [Willinger 1998] suggests that for Internet traffic, packet bursts are generated according to a Poisson distribution and burst duration has an exponential distribution. In our simulations, we applied this insight.

The update rule for UDP is

Input: Cell State STATE, Neighbors NEIGHBORS;
Output: None;
1. {Check neighbors for new packets}
2. **for all** NEIGHBOR $\in$ NEIGBORS **do**
3.   QUEUE $\leftarrow$ NEIGHBOR. L_m;
4.   **for all** PACKET $\in$ QUEUE **do**
5.   {drop tail system}
6.   **if** PACKET.p_d = STATE. λ **or** PACKET.p_n = STATE. λ **then**
7.   **if** STATE.$q = q_{\max}$ **then**
8.   POP STATE.L_m;
9.   **if** PACKET.$p_d \neq$ STATE. λ **then**
10.   PACKET.$p_n \leftarrow$ (NEIGHBOR $\in$ NEIGBORS closest to PACKET.p_d)
11.   PUSH PACKET ON STATE.L_m;
12.   **break**; {If packet final destination, stop.}
13.   {Generate packets if needed}
14.   GeneratePacket(STATE,NEIGHBORS);

The packet generation algorithm is

Input: Cell State STATE, Neighbors NEIGHBORS;
Output: None;
1. **if** STATE. γ **then**
2.   {drop tail system}

3. **if** STATE.$q = q_{max}$ **then**
4.   POP STATE.L_m;
5.   PACKET $\leftarrow$;{Create new packet}
6.   PACKET.$p_i = \lambda$;
7.   PACKET.$p_s = \lambda_s$;
8.   HOP_DEST $\leftarrow$ (NEIGHBOR $\in$ NEIGBORS closest to server)
9.   PACKET.p_n = HOP_DEST;
10. PACKET.p_t = DATA
11. PUSH PACKET ON STATE.L_m;

B. CANTOR TCP MODEL

The TCP traffic model is more complicated because we have to consider full duplex traffic and the sliding window algorithm [Stevens 1994]. We combined the update rules for the acknowledgements and data packets. The length of the queue waiting acknowledgements from node i is α_i^x and the set of queues is

$$\left\langle \alpha_{|x-i|<r}^x \right\rangle$$

The update rule for TCP/IP networks is a set of two equations:

$$\varphi(q_i^x) = \min\left\{ q_{i,\max}^x, q_i^x + \sum_{|x-j|\leq r} \chi_i\left(q_i^j\right)\beta_x^j - \lambda\left(q_x^i\right)\psi\left(q_i^x\right)\beta_i^x + \gamma_i\alpha\left(\alpha_i^x\right)\beta_i^x \right\} \quad (13)$$

$$\eta(\alpha_i^x) = \alpha_i^x + \gamma_i\alpha\left(\alpha_i^x\right)\beta_i^x - \kappa\left(q_x^i\right)\beta_x^i \quad (14)$$

where

- $\alpha = \max\{0, \alpha_{\max} - \alpha_i^x\}$ indicates that enough acknowledgements have been received for new packets to be sent.
- κ is 1 (0) if node i has (does not have) any packets for node x.
- $\alpha_{\max}$ allows different window sizes for different connections.

The sliding window algorithm is encoded into the extra terms appended to the random variable β_i^x. The control term α_i^x allows us to vary the packet generation rate to match network speed. Full duplex packet acknowledgement is encoded in the coupling of equations (13) and (14). Packet dropping issues are integrated into both the UDP and TCP models by using the *max* function. Decoupling the acknowledgement and the data queues lets us model the network more accurately, as it associates different queues to each element of the duplex link. It would be desirable to evaluate this model against an actual network to compare both its quality and the quality of the ns-2 simulator.

The update rule for TCP is

Input: Cell State STATE, Neighbors NEIGHBORS;
Output: None;
1. {Check neighbors for new packets}
2. **for all** NEIGHBOR ∈ NEIGBORS **do**
3.   QUEUE ← NEIGHBOR. L_m;
4.   ACK_QUEUE ← NEIGHBOR. L_n^{ACK} ;
5.   **for all** PACKET ∈ QUEUE **do**
6.   {drop tail system}
7.   **if** PACKET.p_d = STATE. λ **or** PACKET.p_n = STATE. λ **then**
8.   **if** STATE.q = q_{max} **then**
9.   POP STATE.L_m;
10.   **if** PACKET.p_d ≠ STATE. λ **then**
11.   PACKET.p_n ← (NEIGHBOR ∈ NEIGBORS closest to PACKET.p_d)
12.   PUSH PACKET ON STATE.L_m;
13.   **break**;
14.   **for all** PACKET ∈ ACK_QUEUE **do**
15.   {drop tail system}
16.   **if** PACKET.p_d = STATE. λ **or** PACKET.p_n = STATE. λ **then**
17.   **if** STATE.q = q_{max} **then**
18.   POP STATE. L_n^{ACK} ;
19.   **if** PACKET.p_d ≠ STATE. λ **then**
20.   PACKET.p_n ← (NEIGHBOR ∈ NEIGBORS closest to PACKET.p_d)
21.   PUSH PACKET ON STATE. L_n^{ACK} ;
22.   **else**
23.   STATE.W_{ACK} ← STATE.W_{ACK} – 1;
24.   GeneratePacket(STATE,NEIGHBORS);
25.   STATE.W_{ACK} ← STATE.W_{ACK} + 1;
26.   **if** STATE.W_{ACK} < 2 **then**
27.   GeneratePacket(STATE,NEIGHBORS);
28.   STATE.W_{ACK} ← STATE.W_{ACK} + 1;
29. {Generate packets if needed}
30. **if** STATE.W_{ACK} = 0 **then**
31.   GeneratePacket(STATE,NEIGHBORS);
32.   STATE.W_{ACK} ← STATE.W_{ACK} + 1;

C. SIMULATION COMPARISONS

The packet is the basic block of transmission in our model. A packet is a four-tuple consisting of

- Packet source
- Packet destination
- Next hop
- Packet type (data or acknowledgement)

Packets are generated by each cell according to a Poisson distribution, whose mean can be set. Packets are generated for a random amount of time following an exponential distribution. This is identical to packet generation using an exponential traffic source in ns-2 [VINT 2002].

Bandwidth issues are not directly considered in the model used here; each generation of the cellular automata corresponds to the time it takes a cell to transmit one packet to its neighbor using a fixed bandwidth channel. Under our current model all nodes transmit data at the same rate.

We present quantitative and qualitative results, and use two methods for comparing our model against ns-2. The first compares the average queue length of the network nodes at a given time step. This is the finest level of comparison possible. It is senseless to compare individual queue lengths since the two models make pseudo-random choices when generating packets. Our second measurement compares the network entropy over time of the two models. As noted previously, a network that is neither under-used, nor flooded will exhibit high entropy, as node queue length changes quickly in response to data transmissions. We are not the first to suggest that entropy can be used as a measurement for the health of a network. This observation was also made in [Burgess 2000].

The first comparison uses a simple UDP packet sink network. Nodes were connected in a line, with addresses starting at 0 and increasing to node n-1. The sink is in node 25 and all other nodes generate packets. Each node generates bursts of packets; each burst had duration an exponential random variable with mean 0.5 seconds. Bursts occurred with according to a Poisson pseudo-random variable with mean 1 second. To simplify the cellular automaton model, we assumed a bandwidth restriction of 1 packet per second (i.e., 1 packet per generation could be transferred from each cell); in the ns-2 simulation each packet was 100 bytes in size. This allowed us to ensure that the cellular automaton and ns-2 models were using similar parameters. Each model was run 50 times and the results for average queue length and entropy at each generation were computed.

Figure 6.28 compares average queue lengths for CANTOR and ns-2 simulations. Each simulation ran for 30 seconds (600 time steps) and data was taken at each time step. For the graphs in this Section, the abscissa measures time in 1/20 of a second, or 1 cellular automaton time step. We computed the mean queue length for the nodes at each time step and averaged these values over 50 runs to obtain the value shown.

Figure 6.29 shows the difference between the mean queue lengths shown in Figure 6.28. The difference between average queue lengths between CANTOR and ns-2 remains approximately 1 packet per generation.

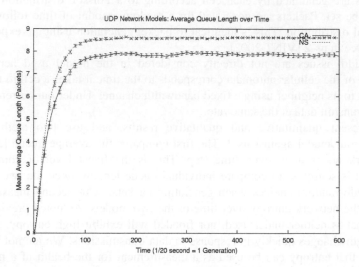

Figure 6.28. Average mean queue lengths for CANTOR and ns-2 simulations. The mean queue length of the network nodes was computed at each time step. Means were averaged over the 50 runs.

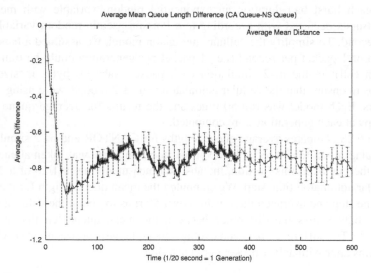

Figure 6.29. The difference in the averaged mean queue length for ns-2 and CANTOR UDP simulations over time.

Figure 6.30 shows the entropy measure for the two UDP simulations. The entropy lines are similar, showing that overall the behavior being modeled by the two networks is similar, i.e., the cellular automaton model expresses behaviors like the ns-2 implementation.

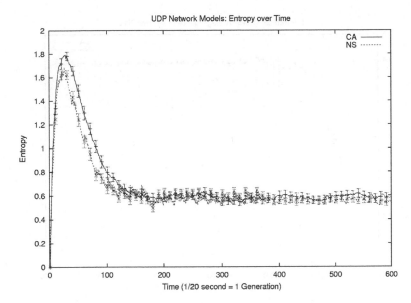

Figure 6.30. Network entropy over time for the two UDP network simulations.

We now consider a simple TCP packet sink network. Again, nodes are connected in a line with addresses progressing from 0 to n-1. The central node 25 housed the sink. All other nodes generate packets. Each node generates bursts of packets; burst duration follows an exponential distribution with mean 0.5 seconds. Bursts occur according to a Poisson distribution with 3 second mean. All connections had a bandwidth restriction of 1 packet per 1/20 second (1 packet per time step). Each packet was 100 bytes in size. Again, the CANTOR and ns-2 simulations use close to identical parameters. Each simulation was run 50 times and the average queue length and entropy computed at each time step. Figure 6.31 compares the average queue lengths of the two TCP network simulations. Each simulation was run for 30 seconds (or 600 time steps) and data was taken at each time step.

Figure 6.32 shows the entropy of the TCP simulations. The entropy measure trends similarly for both simulations, showing that the behavior of the two networks is similar. Both tools capture the same network behaviors. Note that the CANTOR TCP model is less true to the higher fidelity ns-2 implementation than the CANTOR UDP model.

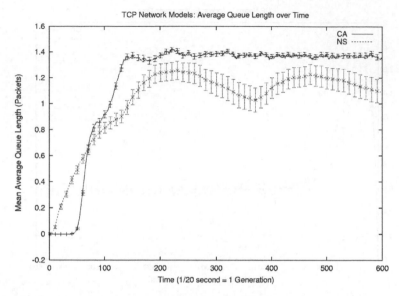

Figure 6.31. Average mean queue length of the TCP network simulations over time.

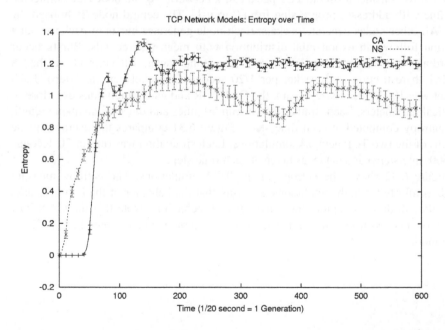

Figure 6.32. Entropy of the TCP simulations over time.

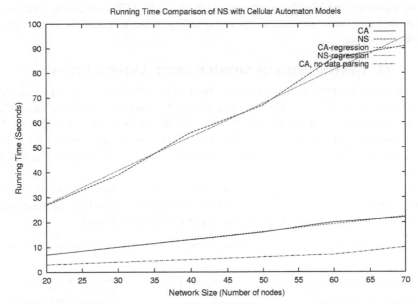

Figure 6.33. Time required to run a network simulation using our TCP/IP CA model and ns-2, as a function of network size. The lines with higher slope are for ns-2. The lower slope lines are for the CA.

The CANTOR UDP model is significantly more faithful to the higher fidelity ns-2 simulation than the CANTOR TCP model. This is not surprising, since the TCP guarantee for end-to-end packet delivery is not explicitly contained in our CA model. The actual TCP implementation is much more sophisticated than the simple sliding window algorithm and acknowledgement system we model. It is likely that the oscillations associated with the ns-2 simulations in Figures 6.31 and 6.32 result from ns-2's higher fidelity implementation of the TCP/IP protocol. On the other hand, the traffic patterns produced by the two simulations is closer than one would expect given the simplicity of the CA update rules.

Figure 6.33 compares the execution time of ns-2 and CANTOR simulations as a function of network size. It indicates that the CA model scales better with network size. (The lines with higher slope are running times for ns-2 and the corresponding regression.) The computed regression had slope 0.31 for the CA and 1.3 for ns-2. The CA simulation is roughly four times faster than ns-2 yet provides a relatively accurate picture of network congestion.

The observed speedup is not surprising given the simplicity of the CA models. What is surprising is the CAs ability to predict traffic congestion on the same order of magnitude as ns-2, which is a full implementation of TCP. The CA model simulates large-scale networks quickly to obtain an impression of how protocols interact with network dynamics. CAs can be used to quickly compare multiple alternative protocols. Higher fidelity protocols can then be used to refine and tune the most promising alternatives. The CA approach is also useful for determining which factors dominate network performance. This study indicates that the sliding window algorithm may be the most important factor in TCP congestion formation. We also find that these simulations show the utility of the CA models for analyzing distributed systems.

10. TAXONOMIES OF MOBILE CODE AND SECURITY

In this Section, we present the taxonomy from [Orr 2002] and use it to illustrate mobile code security issues. The taxonomy was developed to find commonalities between mobile code paradigms (see Section 1). We based it intentionally on the security incident taxonomy from [Howard 1998] given in Figure 2.1. The correspondence of mobile code implementations to security issues can be naturally discussed in this manner.

As shown in Figure 6.34, in the mobile code taxonomy a transmission is a set of messages sent between two entities. An entity may be either a host thread bound to a specific machine or a user thread that may migrate from node to node.

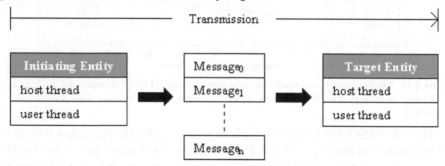

Figure 6.34. A transmission is a message exchange between two entities.

A message (see Figure 6.35) is the basic unit of communication. It contains an instruction and a payload. Many instructions request some type of service from the target. These messages typically contain an empty payload. In most cases, the target responds with a new message containing the appropriate instruction and payload. Payloads may contain a concatenation of many payload types. For example a thread migrate request for a mobile agent with strong mobility would typically contain a payload containing code, data resources, and execution state.

An itinerary (see Figure 6.36) is a set of related transmissions, and a system's behavior (see Figure 6.37) is defined as a set of related itineraries. Figure 6.37 thus presents the entire taxonomy showing the relationship between its parts.

The paradigms and mobile code implementations in Sections 1 and 2 are all limited instances of this taxonomy. For example, code on demand is limited to code requests moving from the initiating host to the target, followed by a code migrate message in return. Another example is mobile agents, which are a series of code (and state) migration requests where the agent determines the itinerary.

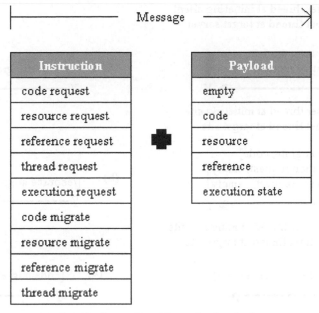

Figure 6.35. A message consists of an instruction with associated payload.

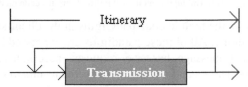

Figure 6.36. An itinerary is a set of transmissions.

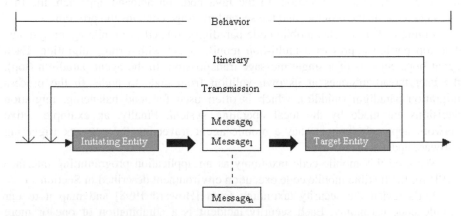

Figure 6.37. A behavior is defined by a set of related itineraries defining a complex network activity.

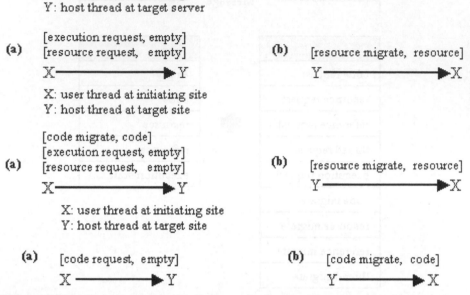

Figure 6.38. The three paradigms in the client-server family of mobile code expressed using the taxonomy: (top) client-server, (middle) remote evaluation, (bottom) code on demand.

Figure 6.38 shows the mobile code paradigms in the client-server family, which we discussed in Section 5. All of these paradigms are expressed by two messages. In client-server, the first message has two requests: access to node services, and execution of services. The second message returns the results of execution. In remote evaluation, the first message contains the program to be executed and the second message the results of execution. In the Java code on demand approach, the first message requests the program and the second message contains the program.

Figure 6.39 illustrates mobile code paradigms related to mobile agent systems. The top portion expresses a multi-hop mobile agent with strong migration. Each agent hops consists of a single message transmission. In the agent paradigm (top), the user thread migrates at its own volition from node to node. In the process migration paradigm (middle), which is often used for load balancing, migration decisions are made by the local operating system. Finally, an example active network approach (bottom) has a mobile agent traversing the network triggering software updates in its wake.

We used this mobile code taxonomy as an application programming interface (API) for the flexible mobile code execution environment described in Section 11.

Let's revisit the security taxonomy from [Howard 1998] and map it to our mobile code taxonomy. Each security incident is a combination of one or more attacks perpetrated by a group to fulfill its objectives. Attacks use tools to exploit system vulnerabilities and create an unauthorized result. Each unauthorized result is produced by an event. Events are the actions an attacker takes to exploit the vulnerabilities of specific targets. Figure 6.40, adapted from [Howard 1998], enumerates the most common possibilities for every element of the taxonomy.

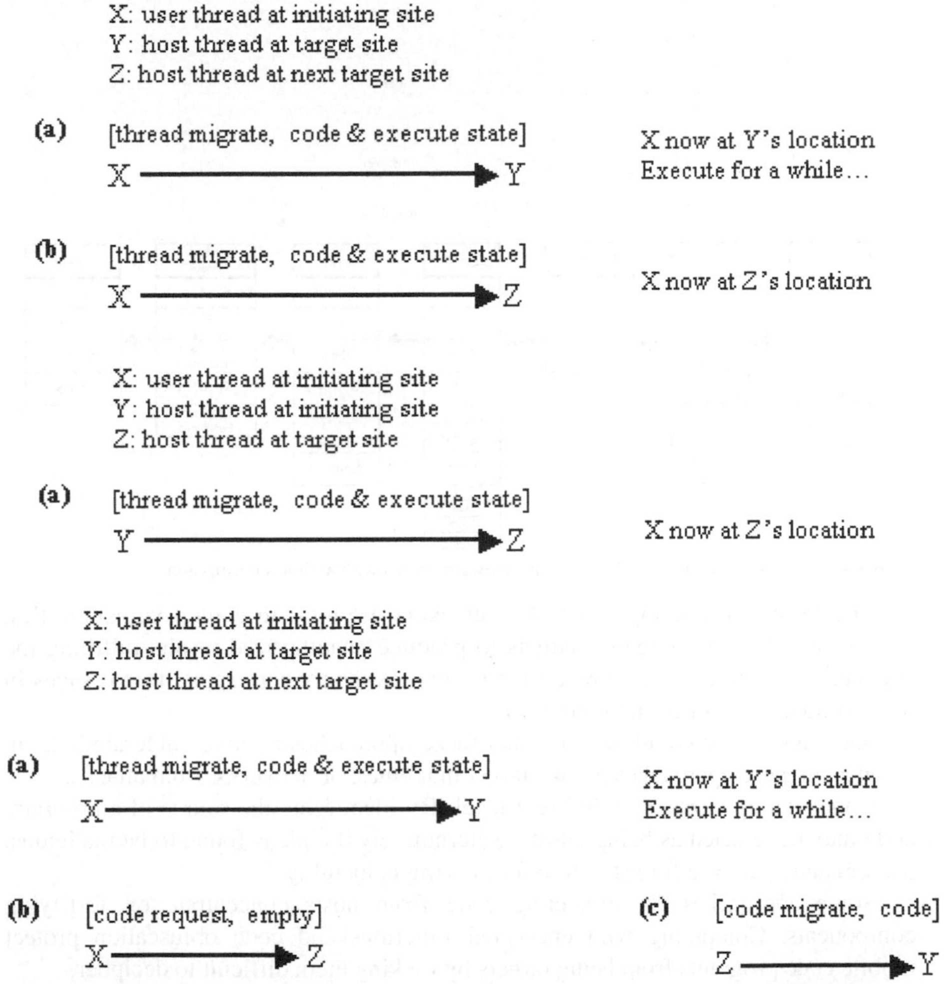

> X: user thread at initiating site
> Y: host thread at target site
> Z: host thread at next target site

(a) [thread migrate, code & execute state]

X ———————————————► Y

X now at Y's location
Execute for a while…

(b) [thread migrate, code & execute state]

X ———————————————► Z

X now at Z's location

> X: user thread at initiating site
> Y: host thread at initiating site
> Z: host thread at target site

(a) [thread migrate, code & execute state]

Y ———————————————► Z

X now at Z's location

> X: user thread at initiating site
> Y: host thread at target site
> Z: host thread at next target site

(a) [thread migrate, code & execute state]

X ———————————————► Y

X now at Y's location
Execute for a while…

(b) [code request, empty]   **(c)** [code migrate, code]

X ————► Z   Z ————► Y

Figure 6.39. Three paradigms in the mobile agent family of mobile code expressed using the taxonomy: (top) multi-hop mobile agent, (middle) process migration, (bottom) a type of active network.

The behavior of a malicious mobile code package results in a single security incident. The itinerary of the package behavior is a set of transmissions. Each transmission used by the malicious code is an attack, and every message is a security event. Each instruction is an action applied to a payload, which is a potential target. Unauthorized mobile code executions produce unauthorized results.

Where do mobile code security measures fit in? A sandbox contains code execution. It protects a target machine from unauthorized access. A firewall's goal is to protect a target subnetwork from unauthorized access. Proof carrying code's goal is to allow target machines to reject offensive code before executing the code.

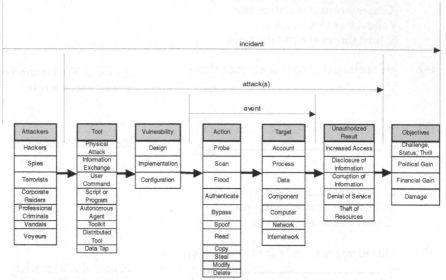

Figure 6.40. Security taxonomy adapted from [Howard 1998] with author's permission.

The security taxonomy shows that attackers use tools to exploit vulnerabilities. Actions are then taken against targets to produce unauthorized results fulfilling the attacker's objectives. Note how events in this taxonomy correspond to messages in the taxonomy illustrated in Figure 6.37.

Although a case could be made that these approaches remove vulnerabilities, in essence all these approaches protect target machines, or networks, from attacks.

Code signing works at a different level. By identifying the source of a program, code may be rejected as being unsafe. Alternatively if code is found to be malicious, the signature can be a forensics tool for proving culpability.

Some approaches for protecting code from hosts concentrate on fortifying components. Computing with encrypted functions and code obfuscation protect mobile code programs from being targets by making them difficult to decipher.

Tamperproof hardware makes system corruption impossible, removing an entire class of vulnerabilities. This allows both host and code to trust the tamperproof component. In the ideal case, this protects both from being targets of attack.

The use of itineraries, redundancy, and audit trails work at an entirely different level. Although each single event in a mobile code intrusion is of relatively minor importance, the consequences of the aggregate behavior can easily become catastrophic. These approaches look at aggregates of messages, and thus work closer to the incident or behavior levels of the taxonomies.

Most security measures fortify potential targets of attacks. While this is important and necessary, consider the larger picture. Many e-mail viruses do not perform actions that are forbidden by a sandbox. Worms primarily exploit software implementation errors. It is unlikely that software design will advance in the near future, if ever, to the point where we automatically foresee the abuses of software features or consistently produce bug-free systems.

Our network infrastructure enables distributed attacks. Increasingly fortifying individual machines on the network does not fortify the network. A metaphor can be made between worms/viruses and *blitzkrieg*. The advent of *blitzkrieg* made fortification of individual positions insufficient. In much the same way, fortifying individual processors is no longer sufficient. Distributed attacks have become widespread. Distributed countermeasures are needed to defend against them. Concentrating on fortifying individual processors is like building a stronger Maginot Line after World War II.

11. MOBILE CODE DAEMON IMPLEMENTATION

This Section presents lightweight mobile code daemons that were originally implemented to support wireless sensor networks. Current implementations work on both wired and wireless networks. The daemons run on multiple operating systems and architectures, implementing a common execution environment as discussed in Section 2. A peer-to-peer indexing scheme is introduced here. It is used to find mobile code packages as needed. Daemon API calls are automatically dereferenced to find the proper package for the node OS and hardware.

The mobile code daemon is built on the Remote Execution and Action Protocol (REAP), which defines message passing between nodes. On top of this packet protocol we developed a framework for object serialization (preparation for transmission), transmission, and restoration. A higher layer of abstraction is provided by a messaging API derived from the taxonomy in Section 10.

The API handles remote process creation and monitoring, file operations, and index operations. These daemons act as middleware for robust distributed infrastructures needed by applications like those described in Section 2. For example, a battery-powered wireless sensor network was fielded where nodes had a minimal software suite that was extended as required using mobile code. Since nodes in the same region have a similar environment, programs usually travel a small number of hops during a download. The daemon allows nodes to easily reconfigure their software configuration dynamically.

Another application is a dynamic battle management scenario. A distributed process, such as target allocation, consists of multiple tasks that may be performed at different locations. The enemy attempts to disrupt the target allocation process using DoS attacks. The system uses the mobile code daemon for introspection and reallocates tasks to new nodes as required. Once again, the mobile code daemon provides the infrastructure needed for adapting to a chaotic environment. In this case, the daemon allows the network to reconfigure its global topology dynamically.

The mobile code daemon framework is built on the mobile code taxonomy. In the taxonomy, a transmission is a set of messages sent between threads on hosts. A system's behavior is defined as the itineraries followed by its transmissions. The daemon thus supports all paradigms simultaneously.

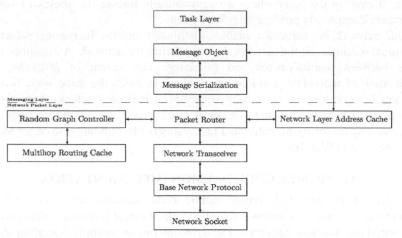

Figure 6.41. REAP daemon architecture.

The daemon structure has several core modules: foundation classes, the networking core, the random graph module, the messaging core, the packet router, the index server, the transaction manager, the resource manager, and the process manager. We discuss each in turn.

Before discussing the daemon in detail let's consider its underlying framework, which abstracts many systems programming abstractions out of the core system into a set of libraries. We have our own threading and locking classes that access the threads library of the underlying operating system. We rely on a set of templated, multithreaded linked list, hash, and heap objects throughout the code. In addition, classes exist for singleton objects, the union-find problem, and object serialization. Lastly, a polymorphic socket library allows different networking architectures to emulate stream sockets, regardless of the underlying network protocol or topology. These socket libraries are explained with the the networking core.

The daemon can use several networking protocols, including: TCP/IP, diffusion routing [Intanagonwiwat 2000], and UNIX sockets. The socket framework eases insertion of new protocols. An abstract base class socket includes the familiar network I/O calls. Nodes are assigned protocol-independent unique addresses. Opening a new socket involves looking up the network-layer address of a node in local cache and opening the lower-level socket. When a cache miss occurs, a higher-level protocol finds the network-layer address. The appropriate socket object is allocated based upon the network-layer address of the destination.

Diffusion routing was challenging because it is not a stream-oriented unicast protocol. It has a publish-subscribe interface and is essentially a multicast datagram protocol. Thus, we had the choice of rewriting the REAP socket protocol as a datagram protocol or building a reliable stream protocol on top of diffusion. We found it simpler to write a reliable stream protocol on top of diffusion. In essence, it was a simplified userspace TCP stack. The userspace stack employs the standard three-way handshake protocols for socket open and close. It also employs a simple delayed-ACK algorithm. This system is implemented as an abstract child of the socket base class. Our diffusion driver provides a userspace TCP implementation. The diffusion driver performs a role equivalent to the IP layer. It receives datagrams from the diffusion daemon through callback functions, parses the headers to make sure the datagram has reached the correct destination, and either discards the contents, or passes it to the TCP layer. These steps were necessary since we could not otherwise prohibit diffusion datagrams from reaching socket objects they were not destined for.

Early on in the project, it became clear that persistent connections between nodes were needed. The transfer of a shared object could require thousands of packets, and session setup time was too long when using TCP and diffusion. To counteract this we kept sockets open when possible. The first implementation opened directly to a destination and did not support multi-hop routing. Socket timeout counters were used to close underutilized sockets. This method has inherent scalability problems, and a better solution was needed.

The better solution is a multi-hop packet routing network built on a random graph of sensor nodes. Adding new edges to the graph, a random number is generated to decide whether or not to add a clique edge. Then a random node from the node cache is chosen based on two filter criteria: the chosen node must have a minimum path length of two to this node, and its minimum path length must be less than or equal to the clique radius for a clique edge or greater than the clique radius for a nonclique edge.

Table 6.2. REAP Packet Format

Offset	Word Contents		
0	Protocol	Version	Command Code
4	Source Node ID		
8	Source Process ID		
12	Source Task ID		
16	Source Ticket ID		
20	Destination Node ID		
24	Destination Process ID		
28	Sequence Number	Max Sequence	
32	Packet Size	Options	TTL
	Extended Header (0–60 bytes)		
	Data (0–65495 bytes)		
	CRC Checksum		

The messaging system implements the core REAP protocol. At its lowest levels, this consists of a packet protocol used to transmit serialized objects. The packet class is essentially a variable-sized opaque data carrier that sends itself from node to node and performs data and header checksumming. The layout of a REAP packet is shown in Table 6.2. The header contains enough information to route packets, specify the upper-level protocol, and handle multi-packet transmissions where the number of packets is known *a priori*. The options field consists of a 4-bit options vector and a 4-bit header extension size parameter. The time to live (TTL) field is used in the new multi-hop protocol to eventually destroy packet routing loops that might form.

Higher level messaging functionality is handled by a set of classes that do object serialization and by a base message class. The serialization class in REAP provides a fast method of changing common data types into network byte-ordered, opaque data. The key advantage to this serialization system is that it handles only common data types, and thus has much lower overhead than technologies such as XDR and ASN.1.

The base messaging class provides a simple interface to control destination address, source transaction information, possible system state dependencies for message delivery, and message transmission. In addition, it defines abstract serialization and reordering functions that are implemented by all message types.

The serialization class sits beneath the base message class and does the physical work of serializing data, packetizing the serialized buffer, and injecting packets into the router.

On the receiving end, packets are received by an object serialization class and inserted at the proper offset in the receive buffer. A union-find structure keeps track of packet sequence numbers, and once all packets have been received, the message is delivered to a message queue in the destination task structure.

The function run takes a task structure as an argument and is generally intended to perform some action on the destination of the message. An example of this is discussed with the index server.

The daemon packet router performs many tasks. The primary one is to use its internal routing tables to move packets from source to destination. The other primary function of the router is to coordinate the dissemination of multi-hop routing data. The current method of determining multi-hop paths is through broadcast query messages. We gradually increase the broadcast TTL until a route is found, or a TTL upper limit is reached, at which point the node is assumed down. This methodology helps reduce flooding, while making optimal paths likely. A simple optimization allows a node to answer a multi-hop query if it has an answer in its routing table. Although this system is essentially a heuristic, it tends to work well because failed intermediate nodes are easily bypassed when their neighbors find that they cannot reach the next hop. Of course, this can lead to much longer paths through the graph, but support is integrated to warn of intermediate node failures, and multi-hop cache expire times help to reduce this problem by forcing refreshes occasionally. The multi-hop refreshes are carried out in unicast fashion, and a broadcast refresh is only used if a significant hop count increase is detected.

Packet routing uses the two destination fields in the packet header. First, a check determines if the destination node address is the current node or one of several addresses defined for special purposes, such as broadcast to clique members. The next check determines whether the destination process identifier is the current process. If not, then the packet is forwarded across a UNIX domain socket. If both of these tests are true, the packet is delivered to the appropriate task. Because packets do not contain sufficient routing data for delivery to a specific task, we recreate the high-level message object in the router to determine the message's final destination.

Every REAP task registers itself with the router during initialization. Once registered, the task can receive messages bound for any active ticket. Several special tickets are defined for handling task status messages and task-wide requests. Other tickets are ephemeral and allocated as needed.

The index system implements a distributed database of resources available on the network. Each database record describes an object of one of these types: index server, file, executable, library, pipe, memory map, host, or task. Every record has an associated canonical name and resource locator. Both are stored as strings. Besides this, metadata allowing for both data and metadata replication are present. The goal is to have a distributed cluster of index servers that transparently replicate each other's index records and have a resource control system that transparently replicates the actual data as well. More information about index design is given in Chapters 9 and 10.

The index system has the following: client, server, database, and messaging protocol. The client builds query messages, sends messages, and either waits for a response or returns a response handle to the client for asynchronous calls. The server is a pool of threads that poll for incoming messages. When a thread receives a message, it runs the query embedded in the message on the local database, and sends the results back to the client. The query system is based upon a fairly extensible parse tree. The query language permits complex Boolean filtering on most any variable defined in an index record. The index server is essentially a lightweight SQL server tailored to resource location.

Once the query message reaches the server, it is received by a server thread, and the run function is called. This function performs a query against the index database object and sends back a result message to the source node. Once these actions are complete, the run function returns, and the index server deallocates the query object. The index server itself is nothing more than a pool of threads that accept a certain type of message and then allow the messages to perform their actions. In this sense, the REAP messaging system is an instance of the mobile agent paradigm.

Another feature of the index system is a system to select code based on destination system architecture and operating system. System architecture and operating system are polymorphic class hierarchies. Every index record contains an enumeration defining its membership in each hierarchy. When a system requests object code or binary data, we ensure that it is compatible with the destination system. Every index query can filter on architecture. When a query indicates that architecture and/or operating system are a concern, then C++ dynamic_cast calls are made to ensure compatibility. Because we are using the C++ dynamic casting technology, supported architectures and operating systems are determined at compile time. It would not be difficult to use strings and runtime-defined polymorphic hierarchies.

All REAP operations use their transaction address, which is the 4-tuple (node, process, task, ticket). These globally unique addresses permit flexible packet routing. A major goal of REAP is to permit network-wide interprocess communication through a simple high-level interface, without introducing high overhead.

All threads and major tasks have their own task structure, which is registered with the packet router. The task structure primarily handles message I/O and allocates tickets. Every active ticket has an incoming message queue, making it possible to receive messages for specific tickets. Message type filtering is supported at the task level. Messages that do not satisfy the filter are not delivered to the task and are deallocated.

The transaction management system also uses a publish-subscribe model for this task monitoring. Tasks may request status information from another task by subscribing to its status information service. Status messages published by tasks are sent to the subscribed task. An interesting application of this technology could include monitoring the progress and system load on a cluster of nodes and scheduling jobs to distribute the load to meet predefined criteria.

The resource management framework is tightly coupled with the index. When a client program needs a resource, a query is sent to the index. Query results can be passed to the resource manager, which attempts to open one of the resources listed in the result set. If possible, one resource from each canonical name in the result set will be opened. Thus, the resource manager can overcome node failures by looking for other copies of the same resource. The current implementation attempts to open one instance of every canonical name in parallel and continues this process as timeouts occur. Eventually, an instance of every canonical name will be opened, or the resource manager will run out of instances of a resource in the index result set.

The resource control system is a client-server framework. It consists of two REAP message types: a resource operation message and a resource response message. There are two types of resource objects: a client object and a server object. For any given resource, there will exist exactly one server object, and one client object per task with an open handle to the resource. When a given client wants to perform an operation on the resource, it sends a resource operation message to the server object's transaction address. The server calls the run method of the message, and through a set of polymorphic calls, it performs I/O operations on the server object. Finally, a response message will then be sent to the originating node.

The client and server resource objects are based upon an abstract interface that defines several common methods that can be used on UNIX file descriptors. The major base operations are open, close, read lock, write lock, unlock, read, write, and stat. In all cases, blocking and nonblocking versions are provided, and blocking functions are simply built on top of the nonblocking code.

As a simple performance improvement, client and server caching objects perform both data and metadata caching. Since our distributed resource interface is essentially the virtual filesystem interface that UNIX-like kernels give to applications, standard locking semantics apply. Thus, our caching module simply looks at open file descriptors to determine the caching strategy. For the multiple readers and single writer, we allow client-side caching. For all other cases we disable client-side caching. Thus, our caching semantics are identical to the Sprite Network Filesystem [Nelson 1988]. The REAP framework makes our implementation very simple because our mobile-agent based messages can easily turn on and off client caches with minimal overhead. We have built client and server objects to support a distributed shared memory architecture. They employ the abstract client-server caching model to increase performance.

The final major component of the REAP framework is process creation and management, which consist almost entirely of message types. The primary message type is a process creation message, containing an index record pointing to the binary to execute. It also contains argument and environment vectors to include as well. A second message is the associated response message that contains the transaction address of the newly created process. Finally, task-monitoring messages monitor the progress of a task using the publish-subscribe model discussed.

We provide two simple pseudocode examples to illustrate how the mobile code daemon middleware is used in practice. The examples represent the two major families of mobile code paradigms (client-server and mobile agent).

Remote evaluation is a member of the client-server mobile code family. It is used by CORBA factories and SOAP. Local thread (X) transmits three concatenated messages to remote thread (Y). A message containing the executable code is concatenated to a client-server style transmission. After execution, Y sends possibly NULL execution results to X. This is accomplished using the following pseudocode:

```
//Locate appropriate host
   Host = IndexQuery(Service_name);
//Construct appropriate data inputs if needed
   Payload=ConstructPaylodMessage();
//Transfer code and data to remote host
//   and wait for response
   Response=RunCommandWait(Host,Code,Payload);
```

The mobile agent paradigm uses two threads for each hop. Thread X executes locally and composes a thread migrate message containing agent code and state. This message is transmitted to thread Y on the remote host, where execution continues. A set of n hops requires n transmissions between up to $n+1$ threads. The agent decides when and where to migrate. This is accomplished using the following pseudocode:

```
//Do local processing and collect data
   Payload = LocalCommands();
//Locate appropriate host for next hop
   Host = IndexQuery(ServiceName);
//Move agent (named code) to next hop and execute.
   RunCommand(Host,Code,Payload);
```

The REAP mobile code daemon permits us to experiment with many different mobile code paradigms over a fault-tolerant multi-platform framework. Because it provides a simple cross-platform, distributed interprocess communication framework, it is very useful for developing collaborative distributed processes. This approach can mimic all the major mobile code paradigms. Furthermore, its polymorphic code selection system permits us to use the optimal algorithm on a given system without significant user interaction. Finally, the distributed resource management system allows us to reduce bandwidth and permit concurrent use of resources without breaking normal concurrency rules.

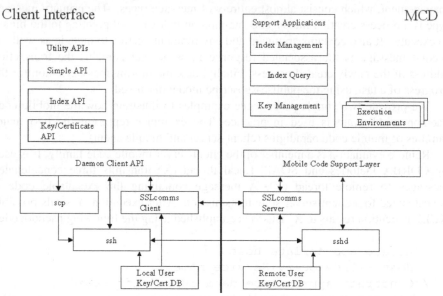

Figure 6.42. Architecture of version 2.0 of the daemon, which was designed to leverage SSL and SSH encryption infrastructure.

An updated version of the daemon (v. 2.0) was written to leverage the security infrastructure provided by secure sockets layer (SSL) and secure shell (ssh) implementations. This version was designed to work on wired IP networks, since the TCP substrate used by SSL and ssh is not appropriate for the wireless networks we use. The indexing, API, and messaging framework used in the original daemon were maintained. Serialization and many other parts of the original daemon were not longer, needed since ssh tools (notably scp) can be leveraged to perform these tasks. A new aspect of the system is integration of key management into the index structure. This version of the daemon includes many of the security tools described in Chapters 7, 8, and 9. Design and implementation of the distributed index system is handled in detail in Chapter 10.

12. CONCLUSION

The Internet is a large system of loosely coupled components. The robustness of this approach is probably a major reason for the success of the IP protocol suite. It has now evolved into a large system of loosely coupled software distribution and consumption nodes. Writing software to physical media and shipping the media causes unnecessary delays and cost. These delays are especially intolerable for distributing software upgrades and patches. This is the essential difference between mobile code and shrink-wrapped software.

In this chapter we have presented existing mobile code paradigms and implementations. We then presented a model that allows us to compare mobile code approaches. The model is based on modeling interactions between abstract automata. Simulations based on the model can be used to show how the different approaches will scale. They also show that transient queue formation is an important issue for these large systems and an issue that is largely ignored by current analytical approaches. By comparing models of TCP and UDP produced using our approach with a higher fidelity model, we have shown that our approach provides important performance information and scales better. The model applies both to commercial and malicious software designs.

Based on the model we presented a mobile code taxonomy, which is based on a taxonomy of security incidents. Comparing the two taxonomies illustrates that current network security research is dangerously myopic, concentrating primarily on securing individual machines.

Finally, we presented the design and implementation details of a mobile code daemon that supports all existing mobile code paradigms. The indexing system used by the daemon can be constructed using a peer-to-peer infrastructure. In later chapters, we show how the combination of mobile code and peer-to-peer technologies makes a more robust infrastructure.

13. EXERCISES

Exercise 6.1 Take the mobile code paradigms and map them onto the security taxonomy from [Howard 1998]. Identify potential points of attack and security vulnerabilities.

Exercise 6.2 Use the taxonomy to describe mobile code approaches that do not fit within established paradigms.

Exercise 6.3 Sketch a possible network attack using mobile code that would be immune to current mobile code security approaches. Explain why it is immune.

Exercise 6.4 Develop a queuing theory model for the client-server system. Use the parameters given for our client-server simulation to calculate expected queue length. Compare to the simulation results permitted. Explain the differences.

Exercise 6.5 Contrast the positive and negative aspects of the CA based simulation tool and detailed network simulation tools.

Exercise 6.6 Implement a simple daemon that accepts and executes programs transmitted from a remote source.

Exercise 6.7 Implement a simple daemon that transmits executable files on request.

Exercise 6.8 Design an interface between the programs implemented in Exercises 6.6 and 6.7.

CHAPTER 7

Protecting Mobile Code[1, 2]

Most security research has concentrated on protecting hosts from malicious code. Little has been done to protect code from malicious hosts [Sander 1998, Jansen 1999, Hohl 1997]. Methods recorded in the literature include

- *Computing with encrypted functions* – It has been shown that it is possible in some cases to execute encrypted functions on encrypted data [Sander 1998]. The host performing the computation has no way of interpreting data inputs, outputs, or program structure, securing the program from both malicious corruption and reverse engineering. The drawback is that it is neither certain that this approach could work for arbitrary functions, nor known how to execute encrypted functions except for a few classes of functions.

- *Code obfuscation* – With obfuscation, the object code is deliberately scrambled in a way that keeps it functional but hard to reverse engineer [Hohl 1997]. In addition to this, code (data) is modified to remain valid only for a short period of time. In theory, the time needed for reverse engineering will be longer than the period of time the code (data) is valid. This approach retains the advantages of code encryption [Sander 1998] and can be applied to arbitrary functions. Unfortunately, it is difficult to quantify the time needed to reverse engineer the obfuscated code and robustly establish the code validity time periods.

- *Itineraries* – Itineraries can be kept of the nodes visited by a mobile code package. If a code package starts behaving incorrectly, it may be possible to infer the platform that corrupted it. Other packages that the platform has handled would then become suspect [Jansen 1999].

- *Redundancy* – Multiple code packages can work in parallel on multiple hosts and compare their results. The aggregate system can thus detect tampering that causes isolated anomalies [Jansen 1999].

---

[1] Coauthored with Dr. Vijaykrishnan Narayanan, Dr. Mahmut Kendemir, Dr. John Zachary, and Hendra Saputra.

[2] Portions reprinted, with permission, from:
H. Saputra, R. R. Brooks, N. Vijaykrishnan, M. Kandemir, and M. J. Irwin, "Code protection for resource-constrained embedded devices," *LCTES '04 Conference on Languages, Compilers, and Tools for Embedded Systems*, June 2004. Accepted for publication, March 2004.

- *Audit trail* – Partial results can be logged throughout a distributed computation. This forms an audit trail, which can help determine which hosts are malicious [Jansen 1999].
- *Tamperproof hardware* – Viruses or other methods cannot corrupt hosts that are tamperproof. In many cases, this means that mobile code packages can execute on these nodes without fear of tampering or corruption [Loureiro 2000].

This chapter discusses multiple techniques for protecting mobile code from either malicious hosts or compromise during transmission over the network. The first five sections discuss methods related to program obfuscation and computing with encrypted functions, which are designed to hinder reverse engineering of mobile code packages. Section 6 discusses hardware support mechanisms for protecting programs from malicious hosts. A small trusted computing base is used to verify the trustworthiness of the entire host. While the methods discussed can be usefully applied to counteracting specific threat models, the problem of securing software packages moving through a hostile environment is difficult. Research in this area is in its infancy and major advances are to be expected.

1. CONTROL FLOW MODIFICATION

The Java programming language architecture uses a virtual machine (VM) as an interpreter to execute program class files. Program instructions in the class file are written in an architecture neutral, standardized, intermediate bytecode format. This approach is intended to increase the interoperability of compiled files and make the language hardware independent. The drawback of this approach is that it is relatively easy to use decompilers to recover a good approximation of the original program source code.

There are many reasons why software developers may want to hinder decompilation and reverse engineering of their programs. Reverse engineering provides competitors access to the intellectual property encoded in the program, such as subject area expertise and programming techniques. Malicious programmers may even use this knowledge to tamper with the original program. The resulting program may allow eavesdropping on financial transactions or insert a logic bomb into a benign program.

This section discusses techniques for modifying the control flow of programs stored in class files in order to hinder reverse engineering of programs. Reverse engineering requires physical possession of the class file. Due to the intentionally mobile design of the Java infrastructure, class files and applets are often relatively easy to obtain.

A number of commercial and freeware Java decompilation tools are readily available [Nolan 1998]. Although software license agreements often forbid reverse engineering of the software, there is no effective enforcement mechanism for this prohibition.

It is possible to use standard encryption techniques to protect programs, with the producer encrypting the file and the end user decrypting the program using standard public or private key algorithms [Menezes 1997]. This solution introduces a number of logistical issues, such as key management. It also leaves the decrypted code vulnerable to inspection by the end user.

On the other hand, code obfuscation, while not having the hard computational security guarantees of encryption, allows end users to execute code that is not easily reverse engineered. In Table 3.1 we present the obfuscation taxonomy proposed in [Collberg 1997]. Different metrics for comparing obfuscation technologies are presented in [Collberg 1998]:

- *Potency* – Compares the relative complexity of the obfuscated and original programs. Complexity may be measured by the number of instructions, the maximum nesting level for loops and decisions, data structure complexity, number of dependencies between blocks, structure of the inheritance tree, etc. This metric can be measured objectively, but may not always be useful. For example, an obfuscator could add 1000 nested for loops enclosing a null statement to a program. This would increase the complexity, but not make the program more difficult to reverse engineer.

- *Resilience* – Compares the difficulty of automatically counteracting an obfuscation approach. This is measured by combining the amount of time it takes to program an automatic de-obfuscator and the runtime needed by the de-obfuscator to reduce the potency of the obfuscation technique. This metric is clearly related to the quality of the obfuscation approach, but would be hard to measure objectively.

- *Stealth* – Compares the ability to recognize the presence of obfuscation constructs between approaches. The more difficult the obfuscations are to detect, the more difficult they are to remove. This metric is again related to the quality of the obfuscation technique, but appears to be rather subjective in practice.

- *Cost* – Compares the runtime requirements of the obfuscated and original programs. These requirements can be in the form of execution time, or storage space.

As presented in Table 3.1, the primary types of program obfuscation are

- *Layout obfuscation* – Removes or changes information that is not needed for class file execution. This information includes comments, formatting information, and identifier names.

- *Data transformation* – Change the data structures used by the program. This includes using odd data encodings, storing data in counterintuitive ways, and performing random reorderings of data structures.

- *Control transformation* – Modify the program control flow. This includes aggregating instructions in a nonstandard way, randomizing the order computations are performed, and changing the algorithms directly.

Many classes of control transformations are presented in [Collberg 1997]. The obfuscator can insert dead or irrelevant code into programs. It can add instructions supported by the object code but not the higher-level language. It is also possible to insert redundant termination clauses into loops.

We now discuss advanced control-flow obfuscation methods from [Chinoda 2000], which is effective against the current generation of decompilers. This approach does not modify the existing control flow of the program. They are enclosed in a complex graph of irrelevant control mechanisms. Many easily detectable and trivial obfuscation constructs are intentionally included in the complex graph. They are removed by the decompiler, which assumes that they are irrelevant.

There are three trivial transformations in [Chinoda 2000]:

- Predicates that are always true
- Predicates that are always false
- Conditional predicates where both paths taken are identical

Using these trivial transformations a number of irrelevant control statements are inserted into the program with associated dead code and bogus branches. Care is taken that the actual control flow is not compromised. In addition, goto bytecode statements are inserted into the class file. Since goto Java bytecode instructions have no equivalent Java source instruction, their presence makes decompilation difficult.

Tests have shown that many decompilers detect the trivial constructs and remove them from the program. The assumption is that they are a poorly implemented attempt at obfuscation. By encasing actual changes in the control flow in predicates of the first and third types, the decompiler is tricked into removing relevant control flow constructs.

This approach has been implemented and compared with a commercial obfuscator. Comparisons were made using the two objective metrics from [Collberg 1998]. For the cost metric, this approach required more storage than the commercial product. Its effect on execution time was less. Its resilience metric was found to be superior to the commercial product. Details on the comparison test can be found in [Chinoda 2000].

2. BYTECODE MODIFICATION

We now consider issues securing of mobile code packages against reverse engineering and execution by unauthorized users. In particular, let's consider program execution on resource constrained embedded devices [Wolf 2001]. Embedded applications need to consider stringent memory size and energy resource limitations. This section introduces a resource-conscious solution for secure programming of remote devices.

Some embedded devices need to be reprogrammed frequently to support software upgrades or to adapt to changing operational needs. [Moore 2003] presents an example sensor network application, where the functionality of sensor nodes needs to change based on newly sensed events. The constraints imposed by limited memory necessitate reprogramming the device as opposed to storing all envisioned codes locally. However, the flexibility of field upgrades also makes the code vulnerable to eavesdropping and execution in an unauthorized device. Tampering with code traversing the network is also possible. In sensor networks for military applications or natural disaster management, code protection is essential. Two aspects of security need to be addressed: authentication and privacy. Authentication is the verification of the source of information (in our context both programs and data). Privacy is restricting access to information to authorized entities.

Cryptography is the accepted tool for achieving these goals [Schneier 1996]. A cryptosystem has a plaintext space, a ciphertext space, and a key space. Functions map data between the plain and ciphertext spaces using the key. If both mappings use the same key, the process is symmetric cryptography. If the keys differ, the process is public key cryptography [Rothe 2002]. Cryptosystems use mapping functions, whose solution without the key is of provably high computational complexity. Unfortunately, for many constrained embedded systems, cryptography is expensive in terms of time, power, and computational resources [Perrig 2001].

To overcome the resource needs of cryptosystems, a multitiered approach is sometimes used. Computationally expensive public key methods are used to exchange a symmetric key at infrequent intervals. The less expensive symmetric key cryptography is used to frequently exchange symmetric hash functions. Data is exchanged after one execution of the hash function. On reception, the hashed data is sent through the hash function again, restoring the data to its original state [Toxen 2003]. In this case, hashing is a form of obfuscation. Obfuscation serves a role similar to cryptography, but is less computationally intensive and has no computational complexity guarantees.

In this section, we discuss an obfuscation-based approach for securely programming remote embedded Java devices. Java is discussed because (*i*) in the embedded domain, a variety of system and operating configurations are prevalent, making the use of architecturally neutral Java bytecodes attractive; (*ii*) Java is supported in embedded devices ranging from smart cards to cell phones. Our goal is to permit mobile devices to be reprogrammed by transmitting the bytecodes associated with the new functionality while preventing unauthorized mobile devices from correctly executing these bytecodes.

In this approach, the programming system and the authorized embedded node exchange a Java bytecode substitution table using standard encryption techniques. Two protocols are given in Section 3 for bytecode table exchange: one uses symmetric and the other public keys. The substitution table is used to encode the bytecodes to be transmitted and to interpret the received bytecodes on the authorized embedded system. Unauthorized bytecode installations will cause an error during the verification process since lack of substitutions almost certainly lead to stack overflows/underflows. However, similar to all substitution ciphers, our scheme is vulnerable to frequency attacks by an eavesdropper. Hence, we design our substitution table such that the frequency information is minimized.

We validated our approach using a set of Java applications and show that the proposed technique is a performance effective solution as compared to the Advanced Encryption Standard (AES) based on Rijndael's algorithm [Daemen 2000]. Our experiments show the robustness of the substitution-based approach to frequency attacks using an entropy metric [Fletchner 1984].

This complements prior art for protecting mobile code. Approaches used for providing security for Java bytecodes include proof carrying code [Necula 1998], modified class names [Chander 2001, Shin 1998], the use of encryption [Algesheimer 2001], and filters [Balfanz 1997]. In [Chander 2001] and [Shin 1998] bytecodes are changed to make some classes and methods more restrictive. For instance, to prevent a window consuming attack, they modify the frame class to safe$frame class that controls every window generation. Proof-carrying code [Necula 1998] transmits a proof of safety with the application code. A drawback to this approach is the size of the proofs, which may increase exponentially with program size.

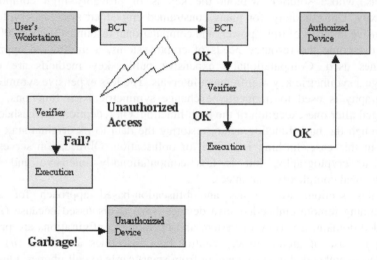

Figure 7.1. Interaction between user and mobile device.

The suggested approach is competitive with other methods for protecting Java class files from reverse engineering using decompilation [Nolan 1998]. One method is to encrypt and decrypt the code at the server and client end, respectively, to limit access to authorized devices. However, encryption/decryption is expensive, especially in resource-constrained environments. Another approach requires end-users requesting code to send information describing the execution platform to the server distributing the code. The server would compile the code and send native code to the client instead of a class file containing bytecodes. This may complicate the decompilation process, but decompilers also exist for native code [Nolan 1998]. This approach is unattractive when a large variety of platforms need to be supported, due to the increased load on the server. Code obfuscation is an attractive alternative to make reverse engineering using decompilation difficult. In this technique, the class files are transformed to an obfuscated class file that produces the same output, but there is more to decompile. In contrast to data-flow or control-flow obfuscations [Low 1998] that confuse decompilers, our approach to obfuscation changes the opcode assignments associated with the bytecodes.

We use a bytecode conversion table (BCT) instead of encrypting the class file. The BCT is a list of bytecode pairs <Op1, Op2>, where Op1 is the original bytecode and Op2 is the corresponding substitution. This conversion table is used by the sender to transform the original code into an encrypted code that is sent to the mobile devices.

Figure 7.1 illustrates interactions between the user device (e.g., Workstation) that distributes the code and authorized and unauthorized mobile devices. The authorized mobile device can retrieve the original code from the substituted code using the same BCT. After the mobile device restores the incoming class file, it verifies the restored-class file using the bytecode verifier in the Java virtual machine (JVM) and successfully executes the code. On the other hand, an unauthorized device exposes the incoming code directly to the verifier, which can lead to two possible scenarios. The lack of substitution leads with a very high probability to stack overflows/underflows detected by the verifier preventing the code from being executed. In fact, in our experiments, the substituted classes always failed the verification phase. Even codes that pass the verifier will not execute correctly. In addition to protecting the unauthorized use of the code, this scheme also protects unauthorized malicious code from being installed in the device in cases that the verifier detects problems. This approach protects embedded devices from unauthorized access. It also protects code from reverse engineering and execution on unauthorized machines.

While using substitution to obfuscate information may seem an easy solution, the main challenge is in thwarting attacks based on frequency analysis. Frequency attacks are common to all substitution ciphers. By counting the frequency of symbols in the ciphertext and exploiting homeomorphisms in the plaintext, substitution ciphers can be broken. Symbol frequency and homeomorphisms describe structure in the plaintext domain that substitution ciphers carry over into the ciphertext domain. In our case, it is possible for an eavesdropper to utilize the frequency of bytecode usage in applications as a means to deciphering the substitution text. For example, the usage of stack manipulating bytecodes tends to exhibit a higher frequency across different applications [Radhakrishnan 1999]. In Section 4, we show how to use the metric of entropy in evaluating the resilience of the chosen substitution to frequency attacks and investigate different alternatives for substitution using this metric.

3.   PROTOCOL FOR EXCHANGING BYTECODE TABLES

The confidentiality of a class file is achieved by using the BCT, assuming that the attacker does not have access to the BCT. This table acts as an encryption algorithm. Thus, a critical aspect of our system is to securely transmit this table between the programming system and the authorized device. In order to do that, we use a cryptography algorithm. Although cryptography itself is a costly process, we only need it when we change the contents of the BCT. This is less computationally intensive as compared to using encryption for the entire application code. Here we show two different approaches for securely transmitting the BCT.

A simple public key protocol for bytecode table exchanges is given in Figure 7.2. In the protocol description, we use the following variables:

WR – Workstation private key

WU – Workstation public key

IR – Internet device private key

IU – Internet device public key

The new bytecode table is established on workstation W. To put the table into use W sends to Internet device I a packet containing the data structure:

1. Encrypted with IU{
   1. New byte table
   2. Time stamp
   3. Sequence #
   4. Encrypted with WR{ Hash of 1.1-1.3}
}

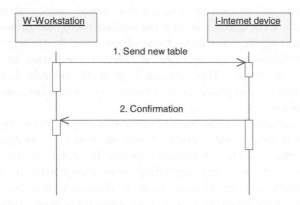

Figure 7.2. Example public key protocol for replacing bytecode table on an Internet device. The workstation sends the encrypted table, and the Internet device sends a response.

I receives the packet and decrypts the contents using private key IR. A hash value of the decrypted contents is computed. This value is compared with the value in 1.4 decrypted using the workstation public key WU. If they are equal, this verifies that the message originated from W and has not been tampered with. In response, I sends to the following message to W:

Encrypted with WU{
1. Sequence # +1
2. Encrypted with IR {Hash of message 1}
}

W uses this message to verify that I received the message in an unaltered form and installed the bytecode table.

The symmetric key variant of the protocol is shown in Figure 7.3. This protocol uses the variable:

SK – Shared symmetric Key known only by W and I

As before the bytecode table is constructed on W. To install the bytecode table, W sends this message to I:

Encrypted with *SK*{

1. Time stamp

2. Sequence #

3. New bytecode table

}

I decrypts the message and installs it. To verify receipt, *I* sends the following data structure to *W*:

Encrypted with *SK*{

1. Sequence # + 1

2. Hash of message 1

}

W uses this data structure to verify correct receipt and installation of the bytecode table on *I*.

Both protocols presented have the bytecode table update process initiated by the workstation. If it should be desirable for the Internet device to formulate the bytecode tables, the roles of the two entities could be reversed. The sequence number could also be replaced with a random nonce. That would not significantly affect the protocol's security.

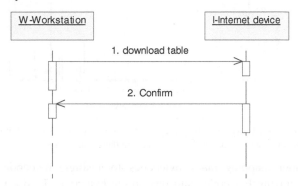

Figure 7.3. Example symmetric key protocol for replacing bytecode table on an Internet device. The workstation sends the encrypted table, and the Internet device sends a response.

4.   ENTROPY MAXIMIZATION OF BYTECODE MAPPINGS

We will now consider options for defining BCT substitutions to reduce the information available for frequency attacks.

The one-to-one bytecode mapping substitutes one bytecode with another, an example, one-to-one mapping maps 0x4b (astore_0) to 0x2a (aload_0). This neither changes the class file size nor hides the instruction frequency in the program. However, these substitutions cause verification problems. For example, mapping bytecodes that load operands onto the stack to unused bytecodes in the virtual machine causes code reaching an unauthorized mobile device to have a stack underflow during verification when instructions that consume stack data are encountered.

Figure 7.4 contrasts the original frequency profile (top) of a representative Java class file (scanner) with the frequency profile (bottom) after the (1-1) mapping is applied. The new frequency profile is a simple permutation of the original one. This provides some protection if bytecodes of similar frequencies are interchanged. However, it is vulnerable to frequency-based attacks.

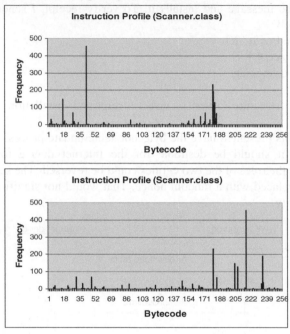

Figure 7.4. (Top) Original bytecode frequency profile for scanner class. (Bottom) Bytecode frequency profile after a (1-1) mapping is performed on the scanner class.

Now, consider mapping many bytecodes to a single bytecode. We combine infrequently occurring bytecodes into one single bytecode. To do this, we need to use extended bytecodes. An extended bytecode uses two bytes to represent an opcode. The first byte is the opcode of the extended instruction, and the following byte identifies the original bytecode. This mapping combines many rarely occurring bytecodes into a single bytecode that occurs more frequently. Although this transformation modifies the frequency profile as seen in Figure 7.5 (top), it does not obscure the rates that frequently occurring bytecodes are used. However, as will be shown later, this technique is useful when combined with other approaches. The size of the resulting substituted class file is slightly larger due to the additional byte in each extended bytecode. Consequently, the field associated with the code size in the Java class file is also modified when this mapping is used.

We next consider one-to-many (1-M) mappings, which considers bytecodes that occur most frequently. This property can be exploited by frequency-based attacks. To make these attacks difficult, different occurrences of a frequently used bytecode are assigned to different unused bytecodes. For instance, the frequently occurring aload_0 bytecode can have three different opcodes associated with it. Our ability to reduce the frequency of these bytecodes is limited by the availability of unused bytecodes in the JVM. Note that the (M-1) mapping increases the number of unused bytecodes, which can make the (1-M) mapping more effective. Figure 7.5 (bottom) shows the frequency profile of the (1-M) mapping on the same class used in Figure 7.4. The frequency profile is flatter and contains less information for attackers to use.

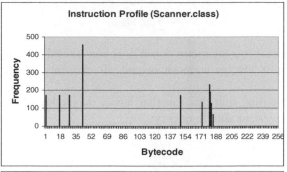

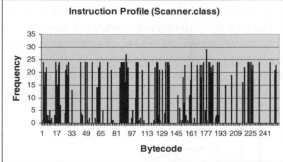

Figure 7.5. (Top) Bytecode frequency profile for the scanner class after applying the (M-1) mapping. (Bottom) Bytecode frequency profile for the scanner class after applying the (1-M) mapping.

The resilience of the system to frequency-based attacks is increased by combining these individual mappings. We will consider these combinations:

- One-to-many, many-to-one, and one-to-one combination - OM: A (1-M) mapping is followed by a (M-1) mapping and a (1-1) mapping. This encoding is done in a single pass on transmitted class files. (1-M) and (M-1) mappings flatten the instruction profile. The (1-1) mapping shuffles the profile.

- Many-to-one, one-to-many, and one-to-one combination – MO: A (M-1) mapping is followed by a (1-M) mapping and a (1-1) mapping.

Note that the OM and MO combinations apply the same mappings in a different order.

To compare the quality of the obfuscation provided by these mappings, we borrow concepts from information theory. To measure the quality of data coding, Shannon employed the concept of entropy to measure the presence of structure in data streams [Fletchner 1984]. Structure in data streams implies predictability. Predictable events provide less information than unexpected events. This logic supports using the frequency of symbols in a text as a measure of their information content. For example, a symbol (in our case bytecode) that occurs 50% of the time provides less information than one occurring 10% of the time. Using p_a to represent the frequency of symbol a (where a $\in \Sigma$, and Σ is the alphabet used) as a fraction of the data stream, the entropy of the data stream is defined as

$$-\sum_a p_a \log p_a \tag{15}$$

where log is the base two logarithm. Since p_a is constrained to values between 0 and 1, the logarithm is always nonpositive and all elements of the summation are nonnegative.

It is easily verified that this function has a maximum when all symbols are equally likely, i.e., occur with frequency:

$$\frac{1}{|\Sigma|} \tag{16}$$

This occurs when a histogram of the occurrences of symbols in a representative set of strings is flat. The entropy (information content) is maximized at that point and the amount of structure is minimized. These insights are well established and the basis of data compression techniques. In this work, we use entropy as a measure of resilience to frequency-based attacks. Lack of structure in the data streams makes it more difficult to decipher the information content of the data streams.

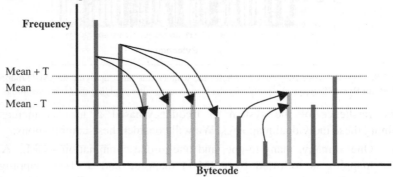

Figure 7.5. Flattening the profile.

To evaluate the effectiveness of our mapping schemes, we used 52 classes from the following Java application benchmarks:
- SPEC JVM98 http://www.specbench.org/osg/jvm98/
- Volano mark http://www.specbench.org/osg/jvm98/
- UCSD http://www-cse.ucsd.edu/users/wgg/JavaProf/Javaprof.html
- DigSim http://www.cs.berkely.edu/~jfoster/cs252-project/benchmarks.html

We flattened the bytecode usage frequency histogram using two parameters:
- The mean frequency of all bytecodes, easily computed as 1 over the total number of bytecodes

- A threshold T indicating the tolerance to variations in the flattened profile from the mean

All bytecodes with frequencies in the range Mean-T to Mean+T are considered balanced (see Figure 7.5). Bytecodes with frequency greater than Mean+T are used in (1-M) transformations and assigned to M other bytecodes. M is the frequency of that bytecode divided by the mean. This is done for all bytecodes with frequencies greater than Mean+T as long as there are unused bytecodes available. Bytecodes used with frequency less than Mean-T are merged using the (M-1) mapping. For (1-1) mappings, bytecodes are chosen with minimal difference in their frequencies. The results from these steps are used to create the BCT.

Table 7.1. Entropy Values Resulting from Different Mapping Schemes

Class file	Entropy				
	Original	1-M,1-1	OM	M-1,1-1	MO
ParameterFrame	4.17	6.08	6.02	4.14	6.55
Parser	4.49	6.41	6.22	4.35	6.76
Plasma	4.75	6.37	6.16	4.65	6.86
Probe	4.62	6.37	6.32	4.62	6.99
QubbleSort	3.86	4.79	4.73	3.79	5.21
RuntimeConstants	3.01	5.5	5.5	3.01	5.95
Scanner	4.29	6.22	5.96	4.16	6.63
SchematicPanel	3.71	6.11	6.03	3.67	6.71
SelectionSort	4.18	4.72	4.63	4.05	5
ShakerSort	3.97	4.64	4.54	3.88	5.17
ShellSort	4.36	4.9	4.74	4.24	5.29
P	3.42	6.41	6.4	3.42	6.92
Q	4.65	6.37	6.28	4.63	6.75
Vmark2_1_2_0	4.95	6.49	6.27	4.82	6.84
Averages	4.12	5.64	5.55	4.06	6.07

The BCT can be derived using either the profile of an individual Java class or the profile of a set of Java classes. While the use of a custom BCT for a single class creates a flatter profile, it is more practical to create the BCT for a large set of applications. The latter approach allows the BCT setup cost to be amortized across several class file transmissions. In our experiments, we use the profile obtained across all class files in the benchmark sets given to create the BCT.

To test the resilience of the mapping schemes to frequency attacks, we computed the entropy values of the substituted Java class files. This was done for 52 different class files, but we only show results from representative class files in the benchmark suites in Table 7.1. The last row in Table 7.1 is the averaged results from all 52 class files tested. We do not include a column for the (1-1) mapping. It has by definition the same entropy as the original file. A higher entropy value indicates that the file contains less information for use in frequency attacks. All combinations except (M-

1, 1-1) increase the entropy, and thereby hinder frequency-based attempts to crack the obfuscations. Using (M-1) before applying the (1-M) transformation results in the highest entropy values and produces the most robust mapping. This is because the (M-1) mapping frees additional slots of bytecodes that are subsequently used in the (1-M) mapping.

In addition to preventing frequency attacks, the substituted class files failed the verification process in all 52 classes tested using all the mapping schemes. The verification failed for a variety of reasons such as illegal target of jump or branch, illegal location variable number, illegal instruction found at offset, and inability to pop operand off an empty stack location.

Table 7.2. Entropies of Different Mapping Schemes Measured by Tracking All the Class Files

Entropy of 1-M, M-1, and 1-1				Entropy of M-1, 1-M, and 1-1			
Original	1-1	1-M,1-1	OM	Original	1-1	M-1, 1-1	MO
5.19	5.19	7.38	7.17	5.19	5.19	5.08	7.95

Attackers could also cumulate frequency information across multiple transmissions. Table 7.2 shows entropy values cumulating the frequency profiles across all applications. Since the mappings are based on the global mean across all profiles, these entropy values are expected to be higher than those of individual applications. Individual class files may have behave differently than the global trend. Histograms of the OM and MO profiles are shown in Figure 7.6 and Figure 7.7. It is evident from these figures that the higher entropy metric of 7.95 for MO translates to a flatter histogram than the 7.17 entropy value for OM.

Let's consider the impact of these mappings on performance. Specifically, we measure the time required for performing the substitutions at the sender and reversing substitutions at the receiver and contrast it with a commonly used AES algorithm, Rijndael [Daemen 2000]. With the encryption algorithm, encryption is performed at the sender and decryption at the receiver. Table 7.3 compares results obtained using the MO mapping that provided the best entropy value with results from using AES. AES is considered an efficient encryption technique. MO averages about five times faster than the encryption approach when executed on the same SPARC workstation. Note that there are corresponding energy savings due to the reduction in computation. These savings are important in resource-constrained environments. We do not include the time for BCT setup, as it is negligible when amortized over sending multiple programs.

Results from analyzing the impact of the MO mapping on the size of the substituted class files are in Table 7.4. The average size increase is less than 1.7%.

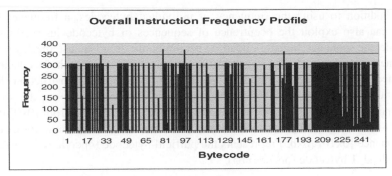

Figure 7.6. Overall bytecode frequency profile using O-M

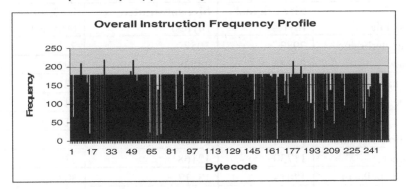

Figure 7.7. Overall bytecode frequency profile using M-O.

Table 7.3. Performance Comparison between the MO Mapping and Rijndael

Class File	T_sub (uSecond)	T_desub (uSecond)	T_encr (uSecond)	T_decr (uSecond)
Parameter Frame	306	264	1079	1060
Parser	2309	1946	6425	6348
Plasma	417	324	1267	1284
Probe	262	219	973	986
Qsort	157	133	494	509
Runtime Constants	1026	874	4704	4645
Scanner	1620	1361	3302	3232
Schematic Panel	1250	1053	3547	3513
SelectionSort	124	108	436	426
ShakerSort	155	130	482	475
ShellSort	140	119	466	459
P	7146	5185	6449	6644
Q	2626	1925	3096	3071

In addition to using the frequency of individual bytecodes, a frequency-based attack can also exploit the occurrence of sequences of bytecode instructions. For example, the sequence (iload_0, iload_1) is commonly used because the Java virtual machine is stack-based. To illustrate the utility of this approach in considering sequences of instructions, we find the frequency of two sequence instructions before and after applying the MO mapping strategy. Figure 7.8 shows the original frequency profile and the x-axis represents the sequences starting from [0x0] [0x0 – 0xFF] followed by [0x1][0x0 – 0xFF] until [0xFF] [0x0 – 0xFF]. Here, for example, the sequence [0x1b] [0xb5] represents the putfield bytecode (opcode = 1b) followed by the iload_1 bytecode (opcode=b5).

Table 7.4. Size Comparisons between Original Class Files and Substituted Class Files

Class File	Size original (bytes)	Size substituted (bytes)	Differences (+bytes)
ParameterFrame	2983	3057	74
Parser	24146	24938	792
Plasma	3737	3868	131
Probe	2605	2649	44
QSort	724	755	31
RuntimeConstants	17852	17858	6
Scanner	11730	12168	438
SchematicPanel	12814	13117	303
SelectionSort	547	567	20
ShakerSort	684	723	39
ShellSort	583	613	30
P	24689	24931	242
Q	11397	12691	1294

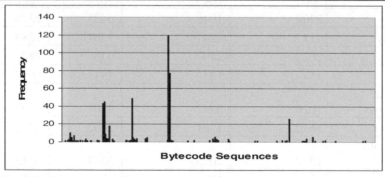

Figure 7.8. Original frequency profile of bytecode sequences for Scanner.class.

Figure 7.9 shows how the frequency profile changes from Figure 7.8 when we apply the MO mapping. The profile is obfuscated by the mapping. For example, the highest frequency in the new profile is obtained for the bytecode sequence (putfield, iload_1) as opposed to (aload_0, aload_1) sequence in the original profile. However, since the profile still reveals frequency variations, we also consider an approach using instruction folding.

Instruction folding is a method used by bytecode processors to combine commonly occurring sequences into one single operation [McGhan 1998]. Sequence mapping takes advantage of this approach in conjunction with other techniques discussed earlier to reduce the frequency information of bytecode sequences. Figure 7.10 shows the influence of applying sequence mapping for the pair (putfield, iload_1) on the profile given in Figure 7.9. Sequence mapping also helps reduce the size of the class file and affects the frequency profile of individual bytecodes. In general, sequence mapping is an effective mechanism to hide the frequency information associated with larger sequences of instructions.

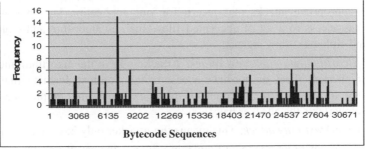

Figure 7.9. Frequency profile of bytecode sequences for Scanner.class using M-O.

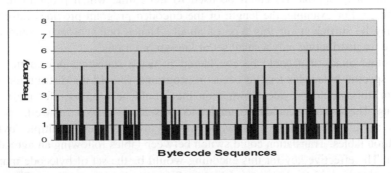

Figure 7.10. Impact of sequence mapping on profile shown in Figure 7.9.

Cryptanalysis is used to determine the security of encryption techniques. Attacks are divided into classes based on the types of information available to the attacker [Schneider 2004]:

- *Chosen plaintext attack*: The attacker knows some set of plaintext – ciphertext pairs for plaintexts of the attacker's choice. An example of a chosen plaintext based attack is differential cryptanalysis [Biham 1991]. Our approach can be vulnerable to this attack where an opponent can choose a set of plaintexts and receives the associated encoding. Inferring the mapping in this case would be trivial. However, to obtain the associated encoding, the attacker needs either access to the translation table or to know the plaintext being transmitted. Due to the use of standard encryption for transmitting the translation table, access to the translation table is restricted. The second vulnerability is mainly an issue only when the codes being transmitted are limited to a known few codes.

- *Known plaintext attack*: The attacker knows some plaintext-ciphertext pairs. The difference between known plaintext and chosen plaintext based attacks is the set of the plaintext-ciphertext pairs that the former has, and is out of the attacker's control. On the other hand, in the chosen plaintext based attack, the pairs are based on the plaintext that the attacker chooses. One example of known plaintext based attack is linear cryptanalysis [Matsui 1994]. The vulnerabilities to this attack are similar to those discussed for the chosen plaintext approach in the worst case.

More appropriate attacks of concern for our application are ones where the attacker has access to a set of encrypted files, such as algorithm-and-cipher based attacks and ciphertext-only attacks:

- *Algorithm-and-ciphertext attack*: Attackers have the algorithm and a set of ciphertext. They do not have access to the plaintext. In this situation, they try to use a large amount of plaintext until the output matches the ciphertexts the attacker has.

- *Ciphertext-only attack*: This means the attacker only has a set of ciphertext.

In the case where an opponent knows in advance the set of programs that could be used, many approaches could be used to determine which program has been transmitted. For example, the length of the encoded program provides information that may be sufficient for this type of attack. Hence our approach would not be suitable for distributing only a small set of known programs.

Another attack that could be considered is using statistical information about where specific bytecodes tend to occur in programs. Should the distribution not be uniform, this would provide information that could be used to infer parts of the mapping. The approach could be extended to consider these issues as well.

A useful extension of this work would involve using multiple bytecode translation tables. Translation could switch between tables following an agreed upon pattern. The effective key for this encoding would be the set of bytecode mappings and the pattern used to choose the table in effect at any given moment. This would effectively transform the approach into a type of block cipher. This should be feasible when enough storage is available and use approximately the same amount of resources as the approach described here.

Note that this approach is presented as a form of data obfuscation. This is an appropriate label since it provides some protection against the information being accessed by unauthorized parties, but is less secure than standard encryption techniques. It is appropriate for use in resource-constrained environments, where encryption would be impractical. When the information is valuable enough and resources are available, encryption methods such as RSA or AES would be a more appropriate choice.

On the other hand this approach is probably more secure than techniques in widespread use, like the use of hash functions proposed in [Toxen 2003]. The approach proposed is more secure than many obfuscation approaches because it is not sufficient to know the algorithm being used. The unauthorized user must still find a way of determining the bytecode mapping. In this way, the bytecode mapping itself could be considered a cryptographic key. The approach proposed can also easily be integrated with other Java obfuscation techniques, such as control flow obfuscation [Low 1998].

The simplest substitution method is called mono-alphabetic substitution cipher [Schneider 2004]. This method substitutes a letter into a fix symbol or letter. This kind of method is vulnerable to every cryptanalysis attack described in the last section. To reduce this vulnerability, one could use more than one permutation table and create a poly-alphabetic substitution cipher [Schneider 2004, DoA 1990]. The permutation table that is used to map a letter depends on the position of that letter. This helps to balance the frequencies of alphabets and makes frequency attacks more difficult than using just mono-alphabetic substitution ciphers. However, when using poly-alphabetic substitution ciphers, an attacker with the knowledge of the number of permutation tables and the usage order of these tables will be able to break these codes. In these cases, frequencies of pairs or triplets of alphabets are used to determine the number of permutation tables and usage order.

Our approach to bytecode substitutions is based on applying the ideas of alphabetic substitution for secure code and transmission. In our bytecode substitution approach, multiple substitutions are applied one after another in order to make frequency attacks difficult. Further, the use of instruction folding helps in balancing the frequency of sequences of bytecodes (note that frequency attacks on sequences are a major concern in the case of poly-alphabetic substitution).

5. BYTECODE STEGANOGRAPHY

Let's now consider another application of the approaches given thus far. Control flow obfuscation requires inserting dead code into programs. In Sections 3 through 4, we have considered the possibility of using nonstandard bytecode tables to transmit Java class files in order to hide their content and protect them from unauthorized access. What if we used programs written using different BCTs as dead code during control flow obfuscation?

This approach would allow us to hide a sensitive program (hidden code) within an ordinary program (basic code). Inspection of any class file intercepted during transmission over the network would reveal a normal program that has been obfuscated. If done correctly, the basic code should still execute normally. This approach is a form of steganography for mobile code.

An approach to inserting hidden code into basic code must

- Not modify the basic code's ability to execute
- Be resilient to decompilation [Collberg 1998]
- Be able to execute the hidden code, with the proper additional information. The additional information is a BCT and start address

Two types of insertion are possible. First, code could be inserted as dead code during control flow obfuscation. This is straightforward.

Second, portions of the hidden code could be mapped so that they match portions of the basic code. To do this, it is necessary to create a mapping table that contains a new BCT for the hidden code so that the new bytecode values match a nontrivial portion of the basic code. Portions of the code that are identical by coincidence can be mapped onto each other. Control flow instructions return instructions, and variable length instructions can be mapped onto each other, and can invoke getfield, getstatic and putfield instructions. The mapping table (see Figure 7.13) also needs to contain some offset values and definitions of a few special commands.

For the mapping to be accepted by the verification pass of the Java virtual machine, substitutions must only exchange bytecodes within certain equivalence classes. Care must be taken to avoid the following errors:

- Stack verification
- Register conflict name
- Uninitialized register
- Constant pool
- Field name verification
- Exception table index

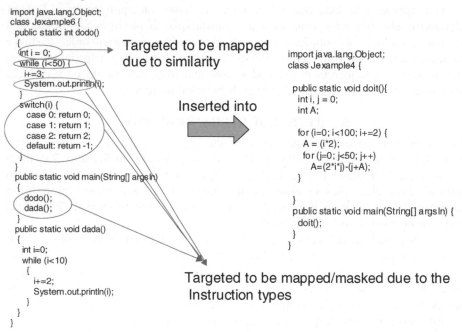

Figure 7.11. Example of insertion of hidden code into basic code.

Figure 7.11 and Figure 7.12 illustrate a simple example of this approach. The hidden code is on the left and the basic code on the right in Figure 7.11. In this example only one instruction is mapped from the hidden code into the basic code. Several other instructions are mapped into portions of the obfuscated basic code that would not execute. Figure 7.12 shows the output when the merged program files are sent through a decompiler. The bottom part of Figure 7.12 contains instructions that were not included in the normal decompiler output.

```
Warning #2002: Environment variable CLASSPATH not set.
//
// SourceAgain (TM) v1.10 (Core Java 1.2 Trial)
// (C) 1998 Ahpah Software Inc
// Please visit our website at http://www.ahpah.com for purchasing information.
//

import java.io.PrintStream;

class Jexample4 {

    // Please visit http://www.sourceagain.com for product information.

    public static void doit()
    {
        int int2 = 0;
        int int1;

        for( int1 = 0; int1 < 100; int1 += 2 )
        {
            int int3 = int1 * 2;

            for( int2 = 0; int2 < 50; ++int2 )
            {
                int3 = 2 * int1 * int2 - (int2 + int3);
                If( 0 == 1 )
                    int1 += 3;
            }
        }
    }

        // Please visit http://www.sourceagain.com for product
    information.

        public static void main(String[] String_1darray1)
        {
            doit();
        }

        // Please visit http://www.sourceagain.com for product
    information.

        public static void Jexample4_dada()
        {
            int int1 = 0;

            while( int1 < 10 )
            {
                int1 += 2;
                System.out.println( int1 );
            }
        }
}
```

The portion of the hidden code that will not be touched by the control flow

Leftover from the hidden class file's methods. In the current approach, we change the original method name for the leftovers, with no changes in the instruction levels

Figure 7.12. Decompiler output when given the merged programs from Figure 7.11.

Figure 7.13 shows the mapping table structure used in this approach.

Of particular interest is the fact that this process need not be limited to inserting a single hidden program into the basic code. The merged code can now become the basic code for a second round of the approach. The same code segment can in theory be part of multiple programs and have very different interpretations when each hidden program uses a different BCT. To insert multiple programs, it is often necessary to modify the mapping tables from earlier rounds.

Computation of a mapping table that creates nontrivial overlaps between two arbitrary programs is computationally challenging. Changing any given bytecode value mapping can radically change the size of the amount of overlap possible between the hidden and basic code. This problem is a combinatorial optimization problem that can be mapped directly to the knapsack problem. The knapsack problem is NP-complete, so to be certain that the optimal mapping is found would require an exhaustive search of the problem space. In this case, the problem space is the number of potential bytecode values squared (assuming that instruction folding is not considered). In practice, good approximations could be found using any of the meta-heuristics presented in [Brooks 1998]. In particular, genetic algorithms (GAs) present an attractive approach to finding good mapping tables for finding mappings that enable large overlaps between the hidden and basic code. This is an interesting twist on the concept of genetic programming [Jacob 2001].

```
u2 this_class
u2 super_class
END_OF_CLASS_INFO
        u2 access flags
        u2 name_index
        u2 descriptor_index
        u2 starting_point   → indicate the first instruction/location for extracting the hidden code
        CODE               → fix-length inst opcode, [byte1...byte4];
                             var-length inst opcode [size] [.....]
                             SPECIAL_GOTO, byte1, byte2 (change to a new offset)
                             OBFUSCATED_CODE, byte1 (for obfuscated code, #of nodes)
        EXCEPTION_TABLE
END_OF_METHOD
        .

        .
        CODE
        .


END_OF_METHOD
END_OF_FILE
```

Figure 7.13. Mapping table data structure for the code steganography approach.

Let's now consider cryptanalysis attacks on this approach, assuming that a mapping table enabling a nontrivial overlap has been found. For chosen plaintext and known plaintext attacks, the attacker is faced with the same NP-complete problem that we had to approximate to find the mapping table. Except that we can stop when a sufficiently good approximate answer is found. The attacker has to find the exact approximation that we chose to use. Meta-heuristic approaches will be of no use in solving this problem. The attacker is reduced to performing a brute force search of all potential mapping tables. Note that this is exactly the type of computational hardness guarantees found in cryptography.

The ciphertext based attacks are even more intractable. The attacker needs to verify all possible programs that can be extracted using all possible mapping tables on the merged file. Since the known plaintext attacks are NP-complete, it is easy to see that these attacks belong to an even more challenging complexity class.

There are many possible applications of this concept. It extends the previous concepts for securely reprogramming remote devices. It is even more difficult to reverse engineer software when its presence is unlikely to be detected. Another application is for distributing software packages where the pricing policy allows for more than one level of functionality. A single package could be distributed, but the advanced features could only be accessed to users that receive the information needed to access them. In fact, the same compiled code could be executed with differing results based on the mapping table in use. When large overlaps among programs are found, significant compression is also to be expected.

6.   USE OF SECURE COPROCESSORS

Thus far we have concentrated on protecting mobile code by making it difficult to reverse engineer and execute. An alternative way to protect mobile code is to allow it to execute only on trustworthy hosts.

An essential concept in computer and network security is the trusted computing base (TCB). The attack in [Thompson 1984], where he inserted a Trojan horse into a compiler that inserted similar Trojan horses into all programs it compiled, illustrates that for any nontrivial operation there is some set of hardware and software that needs to be trusted. In chapter 9, we present detailed information on one approach to maintaining trust in the network. This includes methods for verifying that hosts have not been corrupted.

To adequately verify that the host is trustworthy, the computation should be performed on a TCB. For the verification to have any practical advantage the TCB needs to be significantly smaller and hopefully less expensive than the host it verifies. To remain trusted, the TCB requires some form of physical protection.

Tamper-resistant hardware is a pragmatic solution to this type of security problems. It makes public key cryptography more secure by shielding the private key from inspection. There is a cost associated with outfitting hosts with tamper-resistant hardware, but it continues to fall.

Tamper-resistant hardware may contain a CPU, bootstrap ROM, secure nonvolatile memory, and special-purpose circuitry (e.g., encryption and decryption routines) in a tamper-resistant epoxy and wire mesh package. This packaging can withstand many physical attacks, including penetration, chemical decomposition, temperature manipulation, and laser-based manipulation [Yee 1994]. With devices of this level of complexity, the problem of assuring trustworthiness throughout the bootstrap process is nontrivial. Alternatively, a field programmable gate array

(FPGA) can be tamperproofed; providing what is essentially a hardwired secure subsystem. The security of these devices is sufficient to guard against most forms of intrusion.

Let's apply these ideas to maintaining host integrity and authenticating users. The system must (*i*) ensure the host operating system boots properly and is not altered, (*ii*) ensure RAM is protected against unauthorized access, and (*iii*) perform crypto-paging of data to disk storage. These tasks can be done using tamper-resistant hardware.

This is possible using a computer card – smartcard tamper-resistant hardware configuration. The computer card is securely installed in the remote host. It can perform host integrity checks. It has the storage and CPU bandwidth necessary to encode and decode information from the remote repository. The smartcard authenticates users of the remote host, including their security level or domain.

Secure remote execution of mobile code depends on having a trusted hardware base where secure computation can occur. Tamper-resistant hardware to provide a minimal trusted base. Small, protected tamperproof components can "bootstrap" trust in the rest of the remote system. Cryptographic alternatives may be possible and warrant further research. These concepts are explored more fully in Chapters 8 and 9.

7. CONCLUSION

This chapter explored approaches to protecting mobile code packages that are executed remotely. A number of technological solutions were proposed for different threat models.

To protect code that is to be executed without authentication from reverse engineering, obfuscation techniques were given. We discussed control flow obfuscation techniques in detail.

To reprogram embedded devices securely there are a few alternatives. The use of cryptographic techniques is to be encouraged for those applications where the hardware can support the computational load and guaranteeing security of the systems is worth the expense. We presented an alternative approach that changes the meaning of bytecode values, providing a new form of obfuscation. The security of the approach was discussed in detail.

We then expanded this approach to present a technique that combines program obfuscation and steganography. When using an obfuscation program, another program can be used as the dead code that is inserted into the original program. Using the bytecode mapping approach discussed in Sections 2 through 4, it is possible for the programs to share code.

The final approach we discuss uses tamperproof hardware as a TCB. This TCB can be leveraged to monitor another larger system that it is attached to.

These concepts are discussed further in Chapters 8 and 9.

8. EXERCISES

Exercise 7.1 Take four sample programs and construct their control flow diagrams. Construct a larger, more complicated control flow web. Embed the original programs in the larger control flow web. Ensure that the original programs still execute properly in the obfuscated form.

Exercise 7.2 Exchange results from Exercise 7.1 among students. Attempt to extract the original programs from the obfuscated program.

Exercise 7.3 Write a program to create histograms of letter and punctuation (including white space) usage from text files. Use the program to create histograms from large text files all written in the same language. Compare the histograms.

Exercise 7.4 Write a program to create histograms involving the usage frequency of sequences of letters and punctuation marks. The program should accept as input the sequence length. Use the program to create histograms from the same text files as Exercise 7.3. Compare the histograms.

Exercise 7.5 Create simple ciphers by substituting letters in large text files. Use the histograms to help decrypt the ciphertext.

Exercise 7.6 Use the histograms from Exercise 7.3 to create a mapping where all letters occur with the same frequency. Write a program that uses this mapping to encode and decode text. Verify that the program works. Compare the size of the plaintext and ciphertext.

Exercise 7.7 Repeat Exercise 7.6 but use histograms of letter sequences from Exercise 7.4.

Exercise 7.8 Repeat Exercises 7.3 through 7.7, but use program source code as input. Again, restrict yourself to the same programming language.

Exercise 7.9 Construct a program that finds potential character mappings for one large text file onto another. What is the largest sequence of characters that map successfully from one program to the other that you can find?

Exercise 7.10 Repeat Exercise 7.9 but allow one of the text files to be cut into pieces.

Exercise 7.11 Create a table of costs, benefits, and the appropriate threat models for all of the security approaches discussed in this chapter.

CHAPTER 8

Protecting Mobile Code Platforms[1, 2]

Individual nodes are subject to a number of known security risks. Computer security systems identify entities (users or software agents) that access the system, determine the tasks each entity should be able to perform, and enforce policies restricting entities to performing only approved tasks [Tanenbaum 1997]. Designing systems that incorporate these concepts is challenging. Moreover, even a correct design will almost certainly have implementation flaws that introduce security risks into the system [Knight 1998]. These problems exist with all computer systems and are not unique to systems using mobile code; but, by allowing easier dissemination of software, mobile code heightens the risks.

Authentication is performed when a user initiates a computing session. In most existing systems, a user is identified in one of three ways: by knowledge (ex. password), by possession (e.g., smart card), or by biometrics (e.g., fingerprint) [Zimmerli 1984]. Each method has drawbacks. Combinations of methods have been attempted with moderate success. Authentication over networks is problematic. Some systems send passwords in clear text through the network. Most secure systems rely on cryptography to secure a token or digital signature identifying the user [Stallings 1995]. Determining the data and programs a user should access is normally done on a case-by-case basis. The most common enforcement mechanism is defining access rights for individual files. Mechanisms exist for restricting access by classes of users or on an individual basis by using Access Control Lists (ACLs) [Tanenbaum 1997]. Methods of enforcing access vary. Multics enforced access

---

[1]Coauthored with Hendra Saputra, Eric Swankoski, Dr. Vijaykrishnan Narayanan, Dr. Mahmut Kandemir, and Dr. John Zachary.

[2] Portions of this chapter are reprinted, with permission, from:
H. Saputra, N. Vijaykrishnan, M. Kandemir, M. J. Irwin, R. R. Brooks, S. Kim, and W. Zhang, "Masking the energy behavior of DES encryption," *Proceedings of IEE*, Accepted for publication.
E. Swankoski, R. R. Brooks, N. Vijaykrishnan, M. Kandemir, and M. J. Irwin, "A parallel architecture for secure FPGA symmetric encryption," *RAW 2004*.
J. Zachary, R. R. Brooks, and D. Thompson, *Secure Integration of Building Networks into the Global Internet*, NIST GCR 02-837, National Institute of Standards and Technology, U.S. Dept. of Commerce, Gaithersburg, MD, Oct. 2002.

control through hardware. All enforcement mechanisms, even Multics', are subject to errors due to implementation mistakes [Tanenbaum 1997, Knight 1998].

A number of generic security attacks have been identified that take advantage of these vulnerabilities. These attacks are [Stallings 1995, Tanenbaum 1997]

- *Scavenging* – Is possible when systems do not correctly erase information from memory or disk as resources are returned to the system. Programs scan newly allocated buffers to recover information.

- *Worms* – Occur when a program executes multiple copies of itself. The Internet Worm [Stallings 1995] used mobile code to spread through the Internet.

- *Trapdoors* – Are ways of accessing a system that bypass normal security checks.

- *Viruses* – Are portions of programs that insert themselves into other programs. The Melissa virus [Computer 2000] is an example. Viruses generally have three sections: (*i*) a reproductive part that finds new host programs into which they attach themselves, (*ii*) an identification section that marks the host as infected to stop reinfection, and (*iii*) a function that performs some hidden task that is usually malicious [Ludwig 1991].

- *Trojan horses* – Perform actions other than those expected by the user. These actions are most often malicious.

Many attacks are combinations of these generic attack methods or exploitations of specific implementation errors [Knight 1998]. Worms and viruses are usually attached to some type of Trojan horse. This circumvents user authentication by having a correctly authorized user execute the program. It is difficult for a computer system to know *a priori* that the actions taken by a program are not those desired. Most methods for stopping Trojan horses are untenable since they hinder many activities that are required for normal use of a system. The use of mobile code has exacerbated these attacks, making it possible for attacks like the Love Bug virus to seriously compromise numerous corporate computer networks within a single day [Computer 2000].

When code executes, it runs on a single host. Research on mobile code security has concentrated on protecting isolated hosts from the consequences of executing malicious mobile code [Sander 1998]. Code moving from node to node adds a global dimension to system intrusions and node failures.

The four main current approaches to protecting remote hosts from malicious mobile code are [Rubin 1998]

- *Sandbox* – Limits the instructions available for use. Java uses this method. Its virtual machine restricts an applet's ability to read and write on the local disk, as well as communicate with other nodes. In spite of this, malicious applets can circumvent restrictions [Rubin 1998]. This has been primarily possible due to implementation and design errors on specific virtual machines [Knight 1998].

- *Code signing* – Ensures that code is from a trusted source. Microsoft's ActiveX uses this approach [Rubin 1998]. This assumes that when the source of software is a reputable supplier, it is relatively risk-free to use the software. The code is as secure as "shrink-wrap" software. Code is given either unrestricted access to the machine or no access at all.

- *Firewall* – Limits the machines that can access the Internet. It forces nodes to go through gateways that scan and filter mobile code before the code enters a secure zone. The halting problem provides a hard limit to the ability of a system to scan and determine the safety of a given mobile code module [Rubin 1998]. Alternatively, a subset of machines can be allowed to run mobile code, with the knowledge that they will eventually be compromised.

- *Proof carrying code* (PCC) – Carries an explicit proof of its safety. The producer of the code is obliged to construct an explicit proof that the code is safe. The proof is put into a signature that is transmitted along with the code. Upon receipt, the host verifies the proof before executing the code. This system has been tested with typed assembly language [Crary 1999]. Problems exist since many information flow characteristics can never be proven [Rubin 1998].

The first three approaches are in widespread use. Netscape and Sun browsers use a hybrid approach that combines use of a sandbox and code signing [Rubin 1998]. Firewalls are in widespread use, but have serious limitations on their ability to detect malicious code. Current literature indicates that PCC is, for the moment, only possible for small programs [Tenenhouse 1997] and used only by its creators [Rubin 1998]. It is not clear that generic implementations of PCC will ever be possible.

In the mobile code approach we discuss, each participating node has an active daemon. Figure 8.1 shows the class structure of version 1 of the daemon. It has three main threads: (*i*) a network listener that accepts packets, (*ii*) a network transmitter that receives packets, and (*iii*) a master thread. The master thread reassembles messages from packets and spawn worker threads to perform the tasks defined by the messages when the messages are complete.

The master thread and its worker threads are sub-classes of a vthread class. The vthread class catches all exceptions and serves to isolate the daemon from any programming errors that occur within the worker threads. One of the most common uses of worker threads is to execute arbitrary mobile code packages. The mobile code packages can be packaged as dynamic link libraries, shared objects, or executables. The vthread is a simple wrapper that works as a sandbox to limit what a mobile code package can do. In this chapter we discuss novel methods for protecting hosts running mobile code daemons from a number of attack vectors.

The discussion in this chapter interacts with the trust establishment techniques described in Chapter 9. Trust establishment uses encryption to guard access to programs and data. Part of the adaptation approaches considered in this book looks at the ability of hardware to adapt to software and vice-versa. Some fault isolation and call masking responsibility may be implemented in hardware. Multics has shown the utility of implementing security via hardware interfaces [Tanenbaum 1997].

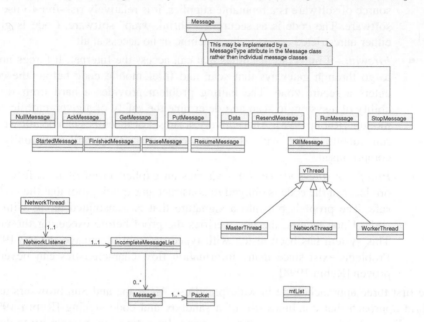

Figure 8.1. UML structure of version 1 of the mobile code daemon.

The rest of this chapter is structured as follows. In Sections 1 and 2, we discuss applications of networked resource limited processors. Section 3 discusses custom cryptography circuits implemented on FPGAs. Inserting dedicated cryptography components into secure distributed systems is an attractive method for adding security without affecting system performance. We finish this chapter by discussing creating secure processor instruction sets to foil resource-monitoring attacks. The concept of integrating security into the processor instruction set is an important advance in the security art.

1. SMART CARD APPLICATIONS

The term *smart card* is used for a number of computing devices containing a small CPU with a form factor similar to the ubiquitous credit card. The CPU generally has a small amount of Read Only Memory (ROM) associated with it. These devices are relatively inexpensive. Their resemblance to credit cards has led to their quick acceptance by consumers. The presence of a CPU in the device allows them to be potentially more secure than standard credit cards, whose magnetic stripe can be easily copied. It is possible for the CPU in the smart card to use a secured communications protocol to authenticate the other end of the communication, before sharing information.

Smart cards are currently being used for many applications:

- As a more secure form of credit card

- For long distance telephone calls
- As identity cards
- As tokens for user authentication on computer systems
- As tickets for mass transit

Envisaged future applications for smart cards include their use to help guarantee the security of medical records.

Unfortunately, smart cards are vulnerable to both invasive and noninvasive attacks. Specifically, noninvasive attacks using power and timing measurements to extract the cryptographic key has drawn a lot of negative publicity for smart card usage. The power measurement techniques rely on the data-dependent energy behavior of the underlying system. Further, power analysis can be used to identify the specific portions of the program being executed to induce timing glitches that may in turn help to bypass key checking. Thus, it is important to mask the energy consumption when executing the encryption algorithms.

With increased usage of smart cards, the financial incentive for security attacks becomes attractive. For example, the smart card usage in North America surged by 37% in 2000, particularly in the financial segment where security is a prime issue. There are various classes of security attacks that can be broadly classified as: microprobing, software attacks, eavesdropping, and fault generation. Microprobing is an invasive technique that involves physical manipulation of the smart card circuit after opening the package. Software attacks focus on protocol or algorithm weaknesses, while eavesdropping techniques hack the secret keys and information by monitoring the power consumption, electromagnetic radiation and execution time. The fault generation techniques induce an intentional malfunction of the circuit by using techniques such as varying the supply voltage, inducing clock glitches, and exposing the circuit to ionizing radiation.

Since smart cards are small, portable devices these vulnerabilities could counteract the possible security benefits provided by smart cards. In Sections 4 through 6 of this chapter we will discuss methods for preventing information leakage through noninvasive attacks.

2.   BUILDING CONTROL SYSTEMS

As mentioned in Chapter 5, the Building Automation Control Network (BACnet) is an international industry standard for networking devices responsible for monitoring and controlling intelligent buildings. In many buildings BACnet systems are used to control

- Heating ventilation and air conditioning
- Fire detection and alarm
- Lighting
- Security monitoring and alarm systems
- Smart elevators
- Interfaces to utility companies, including purchasing decisions

Unauthorized modification of these systems could have potentially serious consequences. There are also obvious financial incentives for compromising these systems.

A security analysis of the BACnet standards was performed and documented in [Zachary 2002]. The analysis produced an analysis of BACnet's security features and a Protection Profile (PP) [CC 1999] listing the security needs of BACnet Broadcast Management Devices (BBMDs). We will summarize these results in this section.

BBMD's control message broadcast among BACnet devices connected to different Internet Protocol (IP) subnets. BACnet/IP devices can be connected directly to IP networks. Other BACnet devices need to either pass through a BACnet/IP router device to access the IP network, or use a packet assembler / disassembler (PAD) to create a virtual BACnet network as an overlay network on top of IP. BACnet networks and virtual networks do not need a BBMD if all communications are either point-to-point to nodes in tables statically maintained on each BACnet node or confined to local IP subnets. This approach has obvious scalability problems. Introducing a new BACnet node to the network may require manual reconfiguration of every other node on the network. By supporting broadcast operations between IP subnets, the BBMD supports information and node discovery on a distributed BACnet network.

Each BBMD listens for broadcast messages on its network and forwards them to peer BBMD devices located on other IP subnets. Each BBMD maintains a broadcast distribution table (BDT) that is a list of its peer BBMD devices located on other subnets. A protocol exists for maintaining the tables. When a broadcast is received by the BBMD, it can either forward the message directly to the nodes on the remote subnet or to the BBMD on the remote subnet, which then performs a local broadcast.

The PP defines security levels for BBMD devices, but ignores how security is enforced. This is done to support market competition among device providers, who can provide devices to independent laboratories for evaluation against the PP criteria. We now summarize the security characteristics listed in the BBMD PP [Zachary 2002]. To be secure a BACnet BBMD should be able to

- Detect and resist attacks leading to degradation or denial of service
- Recover from attacks
- Resist replay attacks
- Maintain information confidentiality and integrity
- Maintain an audit trail
- Authenticate peer nodes and foreign devices when they are introduced to the network

A number of secure usage assumptions are made, such as that the system is implemented and used in good faith. Issues involving insider threats are typically ignored in evaluating system security compliance.

The list of threats considered in the PP is listed in detail. The attack models considered include

- BACnet administrators making errors
- Message traffic flow characteristics and message contents being analyzed by the attacker
- Individual nodes being compromised, failing, or functioning incorrectly
- Attackers tampering with packets in the network, masquerading as nodes, or creating a map of the network
- Attackers staging a DoS attack

Each organization is assumed to have consistent security policies that support the goals of the system. The policy defines the roles, accountability, and authentication of all parties related to the BACnet system. Policies also describe how data and node integrity is to be established and maintained.

These policies should enable the system to maintain its security goals, which are also outlined in detail. Access controls for the system are to be defined. Significant failures of components need to be detected and alarms raised when events, like violations of access controls, compromise security. Of particular interest is maintaining the confidentiality and integrity of node configuration information. It should be possible to verify the security of nodes and restore them to a trusted state, should a compromise occur. It is assumed that the nodes are in a physically secure environment and that malicious personnel do not have access to the nodes.

To enforce the security policies, the system must have some minimal functionality. Audits need to be available to store and retrieve security related events. Access rights need to be enforced, and this requires a system for user authentication. Many security functions need to be mandatory; forcing limits to be set on the ability to manipulate security rules. Methods need to be in place to ensure data integrity and avoid the danger of replay attacks. Plans for guarding against performance degradation and assuring system security are mandatory. They need to be provided with the device.

The original BACnet standard suggested using Data Encryption Standard (DES) encryption with 56 bit keys to secure communications among BACnet devices. The analysis in [Zachary 2002] suggested modifying the standard to require using Advanced Encryption Standard (AES) encryption with 128 bit keys. This is due to the sensitive nature of some BACnet applications and the vulnerability of DES to brute force attacks, like the one outlined in [EFF 1998]. Public key cryptography may have some usefulness for BACnet devices, but have more onerous computational requirements. There would also be the implicit need of a public key infrastructure that would have to be maintained. If public key cryptography were to be used, its best application would be to establish session keys for later communications.

3.   FPGA CRYPTOGRAPHY ENGINE

We have discussed two important applications that use inexpensive, resource constrained devices on computer networks. In many cases remote reprogramming of these devices would be attractive. Securing these devices is a nontrivial task. As we discussed in Chapter 3, encryption is the tool of choice for ensuring the security attributes of confidentiality, authentication, access control, and nonrepudiation [Stallings 1995]. We now discuss techniques for implementing cryptography algorithms for use in resource-constrained devices. Of particular interest is the use of field programmable gate arrays (FPGAs) to take advantage of the latent parallelism of these algorithms. We will present an interesting parallel implementation of symmetric key encryption on FPGA hardware.

The recent availability of powerful FPGA hardware makes them suitable for use as cryptography engines, partly because many cryptographic algorithms were designed to be easily implemented in hardware. Research indicates that software-based encryption is inefficient when compared to hardware implementation; a Pentium 4 implementation of modern encryption is not only more than ten times slower than a hardware solution but also consumes considerably more energy [Rivest 1992] .

A desirable cryptographic system has three attributes:

- It must be secure. It must only be decipherable by those with specific knowledge, in this case, the cryptographic key. Adversaries should not be able to intercept and understand the transmission.
- It must be efficient. In a resource-constrained environment, such as a mobile device, it must operate on limited battery power while still maintaining adequate performance.
- It must be flexible. It should respond to and adapt to changes in its environment. Ideally, energy consumption should be scalable, and the device should be reprogrammable to maintain security. Also, it may need to communicate with separate entities requiring separate keys.

Static RAM-based FPGAs have all these attributes.

Secure transactions require strong algorithms, like AES (the Rijndael algorithm) or the cipher block chained Triple Data Encryption Standard (3DES), to protect the transmission. Older, simpler, and less secure algorithms, such as the original DES may still be acceptable for applications like securing personal electronic mail. Important messages and transmissions can be authenticated using secure hash algorithms. Hashing algorithms are one-way functions, which produce a digital signature of a given length, based on an input of nearly any size. Since they are many-to-one functions, they cannot be decoded in the sense that the input can be recovered; however, they can verify that a particular message was not tampered with en route. For our purpose, we evaluate the secure hash algorithm (SHA-1) and MD5.

FPGAs are relatively cheap and easy to program. They have a low cost-performance ratio. Static RAM-based FPGAs, known for their programmability and low cost, are suited to hardware-based encryption. Reprogrammability allows the FPGA to be modified with new keys or new algorithms. FPGAs are not without security vulnerabilities, such as differential power analysis or internal adversaries. We discuss differential power analysis in more detail later in this chapter.

A.   EXISTING IMPLEMENTATIONS

Most recent implementations of encryption algorithms have focused on the current standard, which is AES-128. AES-128 encrypts 128 bits of data using a 128-bit key; encryption takes 11 cycles to complete. Pipelined approaches achieve an effective throughput of 128 bits per cycle since at any given time, 11 encryptions are active at various stages. However, pipelined approaches have disadvantages. They are not flexible. They use a constant amount of power while encrypting and cannot be scaled down in resource-constrained environments. Encrypting with a separate key requires an additional pipelined encryptor or a reconfiguration of the key, which negatively affects power consumption and performance. We propose a parallel architecture to remedy these shortfalls and perform a case study of our own pipelined and parallel designs. We detail the results of this comparison with respect to consumed area, power consumption, throughput, and effective system security.

Many high-performance FPGA block ciphers have been implemented. Most work has been done on DES and AES. AES work is more prominent since adoption of the Rijndael algorithm as the standard. Work on pipelined DES has faded since its security became weaker with the advent of greater computing power. Triple DES is inherently sequential, and a logical extension of DES. Much of the work related to DES applies directly to Triple DES.

Advances in computing power and FPGA architecture have been reflected in recent encryption engine designs. Many implementations achieve throughput of more than 10 Gbps. The Xilinx implementation of DES using JBits achieves significant throughput advances by removing the key schedule and mode select hardware from the datapath [Patterson 2000]. Thus, any desired key change or mode switch requires a reconfiguration of the chip. Though not a pure reconfigurable DES core, this compromise allows its throughput to exceed the previous record-holding Sandia National Laboratories DES application specific integrated circuit (ASIC) chip [Jarvinen 2003].

Most AES designs are conventional pipelines similar to pipelined DES. Throughput is dependent on the target device, as a pipelined Virtex-E device achieves a throughput of 4.12 Gbps [Enriquez 2003] whereas a pipelined Virtex device can achieve a throughput of 12.2 Gbps [Chodowiec 2001]. The most recent high-performance AES implementation uses a Virtex-II device and achieves a throughput of 17.8 Gbps [Jarvinen 2003]. Other factors affect performance as well, such as design entry method (Verilog or VHDL), design optimizations, and implementation optimizations. A multithreaded approach proposed by Alam and Badawy uses multiple pipelined units to achieve a throughput of 7.68 Gbps on a Virtex-II device; this approach is inefficient because it requires a very large device to achieve maximum performance [Alam 2002]. This underutilizes I/O resources and fragments the FPGA's logic cells. Table 7.1 summarizes existing symmetric key implementations. It includes industry cores from Helion Technology as industry benchmarks.

As hashing algorithms are generally part of a larger scheme, such as IPSec, implementation of hardware-specific solutions is not as common as symmetric key algorithms. We consider implementations of the standard SHA-1 and MD5 algorithms against leading industry intellectual property producers: CAST, Inc., and Helion Technology [Alam 2002, Oldfield 1995]. We are able to provide accurate comparisons, as both companies implement algorithms on the same Xilinx FPGAs we will use: the Spartan-3 and the Virtex-II Pro. Table 8.2 summarizes secure hashing implementations.

Table 8.1. Summary of FPGA Symmetric Key Encryption Implementations

Design Origin	Implementation	Architecture	Throughput
Belfast, DSiP Labs	Pipelined DES	Virtex	3.87 Gbps
Xilinx	Pipelined DES	Virtex	10.7 Gbps
Sandia National Labs	Pipelined DES	ASIC	9.28 Gbps
Tampere University, DCS Lab	Pipelined 3DES	Virtex	364 Mbps
Rodriguez, Saqib, Diaz	Pipelined AES	Virtex-E	4.12 Gbps
GMU	Pipelined AES	Virtex	12.2 Gbps
Helsinki UT	Pipelined AES	Virtex-II	17.8 Gbps
University of Calgary	Multithreaded AES	Virtex-II	7.60 Gbps
Helion Technology	Pipelined AES	Spartan-3	10.0 Gbps
Helion Technology	Pipelined AES	Virtex-II Pro	16.0 Gbps
Helion Technology	Pipelined AES	ASIC	25.0 Gbps
Helion Technology	Single Iterative AES	Virtex-II Pro	1.700 Gbps
Helion Technology	Single Iterative AES	Spartan-3	1.000 Gbps

Table 8.2. Summary of Related FPGA Secure Hashing Algorithm Implementations

Design Origin	Implementation	Architecture	Throughput
CAST	SHA-1	Virtex-II Pro	632.5 Mbps
CAST	SHA-1	Spartan-3	313.1 Mbps
CAST	MD5	Virtex-II Pro	631.5 Mbps
CAST	MD5	Spartan-3	312.0 Mbps
Helion Technology	SHA-1	Virtex-II Pro	874.0 Mbps
Helion Technology	SHA-1	Spartan-3	543.0 Mbps
Helion Technology	MD5	Virtex-II Pro	744.0 Mbps
Helion Technology	MD5	Spartan-3	488.0 Mbps

Since it is the current standard, we focus on the Rijndael algorithm for software performance comparisons. As a general rule, software encryption has much lower performance than hardware encryption. We present results from a single algorithm and assume that the performance trend holds for other algorithms. AES performance on comparisons can be found at [Lipmaa 2004, Schulman 2003]. The fastest implementation known is an assembly language approach compiled for the IA-32 architecture; on a Pentium 4 running at 3.2 GHz encryption speeds can reach a throughput of about 1.6 Gbps. While gigabit throughput looks reasonable on the surface, research from Agere Labs notes that the IA-32 architecture consumes more than 100 times more silicon area than a comparable hardware approach as well as consuming more than 100 times more power [Alam 2002]. Note that in the past, performance of the DES and 3DES algorithms has followed a similar pattern of trailing hardware solutions by an order of magnitude. Hashing algorithms, such as SHA-1 and MD5, perform relatively better in software than their symmetric key counterparts; however, software performance still lags behind hardware solutions. Table 8.3 summarizes AES software implementations.

Table 8.3. Summary of Related Software AES Implementations

Design Origin	Entry Method	Architecture	Instruction Count	Throughput
Helger Lipmaa	Assembly	IA-32 (P4, 3.2 GHz)	254	1.538 Gbps
Helger Lipmaa	C (gcc 3.0.2)	IA-32 (P3 1.3 GHz)	348	466.5 Mbps
Helger Lipmaa	C (gcc 3.0.2)	AMD Athlon (2.25 GHz)	319	861.0 Mbps
Brian Gladman	Assembly	IA-32 (P3 1.3 GHz)	280	579.8 Mbps
Denis Ahrens	C (gcc 3.3 –O2)	PowerPC 7400, 500 MHz	401	159.0 Mbps
Denis Ahrens	C (gcc 3.3 –O2)	Power PC 7457, 1.25 GHz	385	415.0 Mbps
Mckinley	Assembly	IA-64 Itanium, 800 MHz	124	825.8 Mbps
Mckinley	Assembly	IA-64 Itanium 2, 1.5 GHz	124	1.548 Gbps

Consider the key scheduling methods used in symmetric key algorithms. The structure of AES has 10 rounds; DES and Triple DES have 17 rounds. Each round has an associated key. Initially, DES and Triple DES use a key derived from the original plaintext key via an algorithmically specified permutation. Similarly, AES uses the plaintext key for the first round. Both algorithms use modified keys in each successive round.

The pipelined architectures duplicate the internal functions of the block ciphers. This effectively prevents temporal isolation of the key, as each round has a constant key output. Essentially, in the structure of a pipelined AES implementation, the key is always present in the chip in its pure form, making it vulnerable to attack and interception through differential power analysis. The same holds for DES and Triple DES. It has been shown that pipelined symmetric encryption methods are inherently insecure, as they are vulnerable to differential power analysis attacks [Schneier 1996]. Figure 8.2 indicates security vulnerabilities in pipelined encryption devices; important data is present in lines that remain constant with the life of each encryption key. Parallel devices do not share this vulnerability as we show later. Note that the lines marked with an "X" are static. This makes them more vulnerable to differential power analysis. Block 1 receives the plaintext key; a compromise of this line results in a compromise of the entire system.

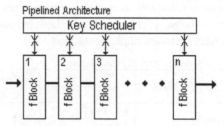

Figure 8.2. Pipelined security vulnerabilities.

A controlled physical random function could allow each chip to individually generate a device-specific signature. These algorithms are based primarily on delay analysis of self-oscillating loops to generate distinct hardware signatures that are deterministic within the context of a single device. Research has been done in the implementation of controlled physical random functions in FPGAs, and results indicate the signatures can be reliably used to distinguish between separate devices [Gassend 2002, Gassend 2003]. However, these circuits have not yet been perfected. We can use principles of these physical random functions to create an obfuscated key; however, it is unlikely that physically obfuscated keys are ideal for use in high-speed encryption applications.

B. PARALLEL ENCRYPTION ENGINE FOR DES

Let's consider a parallel architecture as a method of achieving maximum utilization of the FPGA's logic cells and I/O resources. Symmetric key block ciphers consume a very large amount of silicon area with respect to their I/O usage; for example, a memoryless 128-bit AES encryptor [Menezes 1997] uses roughly 12 times the silicon area as an arbitrary 64-bit multiplier despite having the same amount of I/O usage. Typically, large FPGAs are required for these block ciphers and have by definition a higher numbers of I/O pins.

Pipelined architectures require considerably more area than a single parallel encryption block; however, fully parallel encryption architectures require more area than a pipelined architecture. Parallel blocks allow flexibility when designing an encryption system and have security advantages. If two pipelined architectures cannot fit within a given device, an arbitrary amount of FPGA resources, both logic and I/O, will remain unused as the pipelined block cannot be split. However, individual parallel blocks are considerably smaller and can be used to reduce fragmentation and increase utilization of the FPGA's logic and I/O resources.

Parallel architectures have performance and utilization advantages in area-constrained devices. If the available area is an integer multiple of the area required for a pipelined architecture, pipelined systems have a performance advantage. However, for spaces larger or smaller than this, pipelined systems are inefficient. Note we make the assumption that additional I/O resources are always available. In a black-and-white area comparison, pipelined architectures are smaller than fully parallel architectures, because the key hardware must be duplicated for each block. In the case of AES, the key-scheduling module is large. This represents a direct tradeoff between area and security of the system.

It is important for system security and functionality that keys are separated. This requires each parallel block to have its own key hardware, to spatially isolate keys. This allows multiple independent encryptions to process simultaneously. As a consequence, parallel encryption suffers an area penalty.

Figure 8.3 shows differences between parallel and conventional pipelined architectures. Each block in the parallel architecture is a self-contained encryption unit. The dotted lines indicate the smallest possible unit that can encrypt a block of data. A fully parallel encryption architecture utilizes n blocks, where n is the number of rounds of the specified block cipher. Note that a pipelined implementation requires all n functional blocks whereas a parallel block requires only one. Thus we define a parallel encryption block as a single round function block and a key control module. Furthermore, we define a pipelined encryption as having one key control module and n round function blocks. In the parallel case, more than n blocks requires an additional I/O allocation. The parallel encryption blocks each have their own independent key hardware. This illustrates the property of n independent encryption sessions utilizing n independent keys. Also, it follows logically that only one independent encryption block must be present for encryption to proceed. We can see then that the use of n independent keys requires a minimum of n parallel blocks.

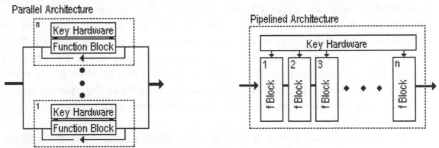

Figure 8.3. Overview of parallel and pipelined architectures.

DES uses a 56-bit key and operates on 64-bit blocks of data. Encryption and decryption are symmetric. They use the same functions with a reversed key schedule. Basic DES operations include permutations, compressions, expansions, and shifts using 32-bit operands. The data blocks in DES are split in half. DES has 16 rounds. A round consists of three 32-bit XOR operations, three 32-bit permutations, and eight 4-bit substitutions. Following an initial permutation, 15 identical rounds are performed; the last round is slightly different. An ending permutation finishes the computation [Patterson 2000, Henriquez 2003, Chodowiec 2001]. This allows for easy pipelining, as identical hardware can be duplicated 15 times in succession. The design may not pipelined for several reasons, the most notable being the ease of expansion to Triple DES.

Though the initial and final permutations are not essential for the security of DES, they are implemented. The round function is implemented once and once only. The same hardware is used 16 times per encryption or decryption operation. This reduces area by approximately a factor of 16 as opposed to a larger, pipelined version, and it has the added effect of greatly reducing the size and complexity of the key management control logic. The round function itself is self-contained. It is designed to ease the use of lookup tables, which optimizes both speed and area.

We utilize our proposed parallel architecture to build, at a small penalty to area, a high-throughput, high security cryptoprocessing environment. A parallel architecture provides a high level of controllability, as each data block in the encryption queue can theoretically select its key or keyset. This architecture includes 17 separate parallel DES blocks. Based on available space, more or less than 17 blocks can be implemented; 17 represents a zero-latency design. Additional I/O resources would allow other configurations, such as 34, 51, and so on; only designs with multiples of 17 have zero latency. It is feasible to use an encrypted header to indicate the desired key; also, in the case of DES, this header can select between encryption and decryption. An initial key setup period is required; this time period ranges from a minimum of 1 cycle to a maximum of n cycles, where n is the number of parallel blocks implemented. The security of the header need not be equivalent to that of the data itself; invalid or tampered headers would not compromise the data.

The single DES encryption block was synthesized on three separate FPGA architectures, and as expected the Virtex-II Pro device provided the best performance. It also had the lowest area of the three devices, which is notable despite the slight differences in the Virtex and Spartan logic cell design. Table 8.4 summarizes synthesis and translation for both an iterative single DES block and a parallel DES architecture consisting of 17 single DES blocks. We include results for the Virtex-E device, a device that is larger and cheaper than the Spartan series. This comparison is important, as cost is an issue for many end markets; however, we study only performance.

The Spartan-3 and Virtex-II Pro devices allow near-gigabit throughput. The Virtex-E's performance leaves something to be desired, but in low-cost applications it becomes more attractive. The relatively small size of the DES implementation provides interesting possibilities on all three architectures. A single DES cryptoprocessor synthesized on a Virtex-II Pro FPGA has an extremely high throughput at 11.754 Gbps. The option to use either DES or Triple DES allows a tradeoff between area and security with little effect on overall throughput. The scaleable throughput T_s can be quantified by letting N equal the number of parallel blocks implemented and F_{sys} equal the system clock frequency. We have

$$T_s = ((64) * F_{sys}) * (N/17) \tag{17}$$

Table 8.4. Performance Comparison of DES on Virtex-II Pro and Spartan-3 FPGAs

Algorithm	Target Device	System Frequency	Area (Slices)	Throughput
DES (Single)	Virtex-II Pro 50	221.831 MHz	366	835.13 Mbps
DES (Single)	Virtex-E 1000	118.864 MHz	365	447.488 Mbps
DES (Single)	Spartan-3 5000	168.805 MHz	337	635.50 Mbps
DES (Processor)	Virtex-II Pro 50	183.664 MHz	5559	11.754 Gbps
DES (Processor)	Virtex-E 2000	80.959 MHz	5707	5.181 Gbps
DES (Processor)	Spartan-3 5000	136.108 MHz	5571	8.711 Gbps

The number of available I/O pins limits the effective throughput, as each multiple of 17 requires an additional 128 pins. Assuming a fixed number of pins for control and system operation and an 8-bit data header, each block of data requires 144 bits for input and output. This allows up to 17 blocks of throughput at no penalty; implementing more than 17 blocks with 144 I/O pins has no gain. Required I/O can be quantified by letting P_S equal the number of system pins required for proper operation, giving

$$P_{IO} = (144) * \lceil (N/17) \rceil + P_S \tag{18}$$

Maximum throughput is attained when the number of parallel blocks implemented is an integer multiple of 17.

C. PARALLEL ENCRYPTION ENGINE FOR TRIPLE DES

Triple DES increases the security of DES greatly by expanding the key length from 56 to either 112 bits (2 key Triple DES) or 168 bits (3 key Triple DES). The Triple DES algorithm consists of three single DES operations in sequence: encryption with key 1, decryption with key 2, and encryption with key 3 to produce the ciphertext. A pipelined-block design is used for Triple DES; the single DES hardware is duplicated three times in succession. Minimal control logic is needed. The output of the first encryption block triggers the operation of the second decryption block, and the output of the second decryption block triggers the operation of the final encryption block. Also the output of the first block indicates it can accept a new block of data to encrypt. This allows for throughput levels identical to single DES provided keys do not change. Figure 8.4 shows the expansion of single DES into Triple DES; note that it is a combination of feedback and nonfeedback modes applied to single DES blocks.

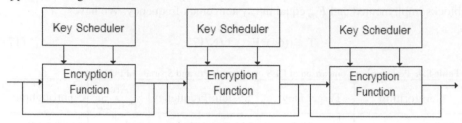

Figure 8.4. Expansion of DES to 3DES.

A single Triple DES block can be replicated and scaled to create a controllable high-throughput parallel cryptoprocessor. Conventional pipelined architectures replicate the internal round structure; typical DES pipelines include hardware for 16 rounds. The downside of this approach is the complexity of key hardware, as more hardware is required to store and select individual round keys. Additionally, sequential encryptions are required to use the same key. In a multi-user environment, this may not be desirable. A higher security approach would allow each sequential encryption the option of using any one of the keys (or keysets, in the case of Triple DES). Table 8.5 summarizes the synthesis and translation for both an iterative single 3DES block and a parallel 3DES architecture consisting of 17 Triple DES blocks. Again, the Virtex-E may be attractive to applications where performance is not the key issue.

Table 8.5. Performance Comparison of 3DES on Virtex and Spartan FPGAs

Algorithm	Target Device	System Frequency	Area (Slices)	Throughput
3DES (Single)	Virtex-II Pro 50	234.852 MHz	926	884.15 Mbps
3DES (Single)	Virtex-E 1000	111.433 MHz	905	419.512 Mbps
3DES (Single)	Spartan-3 1000	168.805 MHz	923	635.50 Mbps
3DES (Processor)	Virtex-II Pro 50	141.044 MHz	15859	9.026 Gbps
3DES (Processor)	Virtex-E 2000	85.222 MHz	15519	5.454 Gbps
3DES (Processor)	Spartan-3 2000	100.440 MHz	15394	6.428 Gbps

The Spartan-3 and Virtex-II Pro devices allow near-gigabit throughput. Performance similarity is due to the straightforward expansion of DES into 3DES. The small size of the Triple DES implementation provides interesting possibilities. Given that Triple DES takes up about 3.5% of the Virtex-II device and each single DES encryption or decryption operation has a latency of 17 cycles, each Triple DES block could be duplicated 17 times to create a high-throughput zero latency cryptoprocessor. This would allow 51 separate keys to be used at the added expense of key setup time. A high-level design incurs some hardware overhead, including the data input and output multiplexers and tri-state buffers. The synthesized clock frequency is decreased to 141.044 MHz, resulting in a throughput of 9.026 Gbps. After an initial key setup period (where separate keys are loaded if required), there is a constant zero-latency effect on the cryptoprocessor. As a single-chip cryptoprocessor this approach would be an excellent high-performance option. Importantly, we see now that the option to use either DES or Triple DES allows a tradeoff between area and security with little effect on overall throughput. It should be noted that the equations used for single DES hold for Triple DES as well; the only difference is the approximate size increase of three.

D. PARALLEL ENCRYPTION ENGINE FOR AES

AES became the new encryption standard in May 2002. It operates on all combinations of data input and keys with lengths of 128, 192, and 256 bits. This design uses a data input length of 128 bits with a key length of 128 bits. A block of data is placed into a 16-byte array and proceeds through 10 rounds of encryption. Basic operations include byte substitutions, independent row byte shifts, column Galois field multiplications, and key additions. Row shifting and column multiplication use 32-bit operands (one 4-byte row or one 4-byte column) [Alam 2002, Oldfield 1995]. Similar to DES, this design is not pipelined. Space limitations make pipelining prohibitive on a mid-size FPGA. AES is not symmetric for encryption and decryption. The mathematical operations are different and require different hardware [Alam 2002].

The AES design uses reusable function hardware, with minimal unnecessary hardware duplication. As with DES, AES lends itself to reusable function blocks. The four row shifting operations are separate modules, since each operation is a separate shift. All row shifting is done through routing channels; no logic resources are used. They are similar to DES permutations, though entire bytes are shifted rather than individual bits. The column multiplication operations use four separate modules, allowing each column multiplication to proceed in parallel. The byte substitution is a 256x8 ROM lookup, and it is duplicated 16 times to also allow maximum parallelism. Also, we can use Virtex Block RAMs to implement the byte substitution tables. This saves a considerable amount of space, since a fully combinatorial implementation of a single encryption block requires 1280 Virtex-II SLICEs for substitution tables alone. A dual-ported Block RAM is used to implement two substitution boxes. This requires 8 Block RAMs per block; a fully parallel block would use 80 Block RAMs. The substitution boxes associated with the key scheduler are implemented combinatorially for performance reasons. All other internal functions are combinatorial. This allows for a parallel architecture, which to some degree sacrifices hardware efficiency for throughput.

The security of AES has been well researched and is widely considered to be more secure than Triple DES. Its longer key length adds to its security capabilities; additionally, key lengths of up to 256 bits allow an even higher level of security. In this design, the 10-round structure and 128-bit block size allow the AES algorithm to encrypt data much faster than a similar Triple DES implementation. Also, AES provides more efficient use of hardware; its performance and security capabilities far offset its somewhat larger area.

The AES implementation duplicates some hardware to achieve higher performance. The byte substitution ROM is implemented 16 times; these modules are reused each round during encryption and decryption. An extremely area-constrained design could theoretically use only one byte substitution ROM with a huge penalty to throughput. Also, the column multiplication function is repeated four times. This is not as much of an issue since a single multiplication operation requires roughly half the area of a single byte substitution ROM. The largest component is the key scheduler, which is not duplicated. The bulk of the key scheduler is comprised of four byte substitution ROMs and four 32-bit XORs.

The encryption module is able to attain gigabit throughput, but as a comprehensive module the system must operate at or around the decryption frequency (depending on synthesis results). The overall throughput is reasonable at about 2.0 Gbps. Note that the decryption operation initially incurs a 10-cycle key setup penalty once per key lifetime. The keys are generated sequentially but must be used in reverse order. It should also be noted that encryption and decryption could occur in parallel with a comprehensive module provided the inputs arrive on subsequent cycles. Also, it is assumed that decryption key setup occurs prior to the bulk of the encryption or decryption operations. For this paper, we consider only encryption performance.

Since the design does not waste hardware, we can also construct a dedicated high-throughput AES encryption processor based on duplicated single AES encryption modules. Unconventional approaches have been proposed before, including multithreaded and pipelined approaches. This architecture is similar to a multithreaded approach in that synchronization between "threads" need only occur to prevent data collision at the output. Assuming all modules are identical, collisions are impossible, as a collision would require data arriving simultaneously to two separate units. This is prevented because the input bus is shared.

For a fully parallel encryption architecture, we do not include any decryption modules. Additionally, the inclusion of decryption would reduce the maximum hardware utilization to 50%. At best, it would interleave encryption and decryption operations, likely increasing the overall latency for both operations.

Tables 8.6 and 8.7 summarize the synthesis and translation on the Spartan-3 and Virtex-II Pro platforms. The primary issues for the Virtex-E and Spartan-3 devices involve cost and performance tradeoffs. These issues are the same as for DES and 3DES.

We can quantify the throughput of the AES encryption processor by letting N equal the number of parallel blocks implemented and F_{sys} equal the system clock frequency:

$$T_{AES} = ((128)*F_{sys})*(N/10) \tag{19}$$

We quantify the throughput of nonparallel AES decryption over time as follows:

$$T_{DEC} = ((128)*F_{sys})/(10+(10/O_D)) \quad\quad\quad (20)$$

where O_D indicates the number of decryption operations performed with the same key. Throughput of the decryption operation approaches that of the encryption operation provided the key does not change; the initial 10-cycle latency becomes less significant over time.

Table 8.6. Performance of AES Encryption and Decryption on Virtex-II Pro FPGAs

Algorithm	Target Device	System Frequency	Area (Slices)	Throughput
Iterative Encryption	Virtex-II Pro 50	199.960 MHz	1736	2.327 Gbps
Parallel Processor	Virtex-II Pro 50	179.533 MHz	21997	22.98 Gbps
Pipelined Processor	Virtex-II Pro 50	221.141 MHz	12728	28.31 Gbps
Iterative Decryption	Virtex-II Pro 50	199.960 MHz	2795	2.327 Gbps

Table 8.7. Performance of AES Encryption and Decryption on Spartan-3 FPGAs

Architecture	Target Device	System Frequency	Area (Slices)	Throughput
Iterative Encryption	Spartan-3 5000	157.873 MHz	1826	1.837 Gbps
Parallel Processor	Spartan-3 5000	130.647 MHz	22670	16.722 Gbps
Pipelined Processor	Spartan-3 5000	164.739 MHz	12729	21.087 Gbps
Iterative Decryption	Spartan-3 5000	127.858 MHz	2796	1.487 Gbps

Table 8.3 summarized current AES implementations. The pipelined memoryless AES implementation proposed in [Jarvinin 2003] is the fastest published implementation of the AES-128 algorithm with a reported throughput of 17.8 Gbps. Our memoryless parallel encryptor achieves a throughput of 18.8 Gbps and the Block RAM parallel encryptor achieves a throughput of 17.8 Gbps. Our parallel architectures are larger; however, they are able to utilize 10 different keys. Also, individual parallel blocks can be placed as area permits where a pipelined architecture cannot fit.

Place and route results indicate a memoryless parallel AES encryption processor with all its control logic can fit in a Virtex-II Pro 50 (XC2VP50). It is large, occupying nearly all of the available slices, but is able to achieve extremely high throughput. The implementation that uses Block RAM resources to implement substitution boxes uses roughly half of the device's logic resources and roughly one third of the device's Block RAM resources.

E. SECURE HASH FUNCTION ENGINE

Secure hash algorithms are used for code or data verification. The receiver of encrypted data can verify that the transmission was not tampered with en route by computing a hash of the data and comparing it with a hash value included by the transmitter.

The MD5 algorithm is suitable for application in hardware and on 32-bit processors. It takes any message less than 2^{64} bits in length and produces a 128-bit digital signature of that message. It is computationally infeasible to find two messages that produce the same signature. The operations in MD5 consist of four separate nonlinear functions as well as some 32-bit additions, left circular rotations, and XOR operations. There are 4 rounds, each consisting of 16 operations. The latency of a single MD5 block is then 64 cycles. The design is reasonably compact, and the only real memory requirement is storage for 64 independent 32-bit additive constants.

SHA-1, though similar to MD5, expands the security by adding an additional 16 operations (1 additional round) and produces a 160-bit digital signature. The basic operations of SHA-1 also consist of four nonlinear functions, additions, XOR operations, and circular rotations. Computation proceeds in 5 rounds, consisting of 16 operations each. The latency of a single SHA-1 block is 80 cycles. Much like MD5, it is computationally infeasible to find two messages that produce the same digital signature. Also, tampering with a message en route will almost certainly produce a different signature. The storage requirements of SHA-1 are variable and can be increased for an increase in throughput. Each 512-bit message block is used to generate 80 32-bit additive constants, which are generated and used sequentially. The message itself comprises the first 16 values; each value after that utilizes 4 of the previous 16 values. These are stored in registers to allow SHA-1 to proceed with less computational delay.

MD5 throughput is less than SHA-1, the more secure algorithm. It may seem that there is no reason to consider MD5, but AES operates on 128-bit blocks so that an MD5 hash could be encrypted in a single AES encryption. The 160-bit SHA-1 hash would require two AES encryptions.

The SHA-1 throughput is higher mainly due to its more streamlined and elegant design. The 80 round constants, generated from the message itself, are created and stored immediately on algorithm initiation. There is no delay in generating these constants each round, but only in selecting the appropriate value. Additionally, the functions used to update the hash do not vary with each round, but only every 20 rounds. This is in sharp contrast to MD5, where each round is related only to 4 others in its group. That is, the first operation is related to the 4th, 8th, and 12th, but no others. Also, shift operations in SHA-1 are fixed and require no control logic or selection multiplexing. This results in a speed improvement, as many actions can be done in parallel. The addition operations performed each round are identical, and register updates are done in parallel.

MD5's structure does not lend itself well to a streamlined architecture. The 64 round constants in MD5 occupy less physical hardware than their SHA-1 counterparts but require physical storage. (SHA-1 round constants can be calculated on the fly, resulting in performance degradation.) The four separate sub-functions of MD5 vary function to function by shift amounts, message sub-block ordering, round constants, and nonlinear functions. The general structure of the sub-functions is similar, but the operations involved are distinctly different. Since each round updates a separate register and proceeds differently depending on its operands, multiple selection multiplexers must be used at some point to ensure correctness. Maximum parallelism can be achieved by performing additions prior to or concurrently with selections, as things like the round constant and message sub-block are known prior to the current round. Minimizing sequential additions results in a clock frequency gain of approximately 20%.

Neither SHA-1 nor MD5 is pipelined or parallel because the algorithms process sequential 512-bit blocks of the same message; results of the first 512-bit block are required to correctly continue. Separate messages could be hashed in parallel, requiring additional hardware with essentially no throughput gain. The problem stems from the fact that messages are rarely identical sizes, and collisions at the output queue would be inevitable.

Table 8.8. Performance Comparison of SHA-1 and MD5 on Virtex-II Pro and Spartan-3 FPGAs

Algorithm	Target Device	System Frequency	Area (Slices)	Throughput
SHA-1	Virtex-II Pro 50	97.914 MHz	1722	626.650 Mbps
MD5	Virtex-II Pro 50	71.134 MHz	1249	569.072 Mbps
SHA-1	Spartan-3 5000	86.797 MHz	1404	555.50 Mbps
MD5	Spartan-3 5000	60.498 MHz	1505	483.98 Mbps

The throughput of MD5 is always less than SHA-1 and the security of MD5 is less than SHA-1 as well. MD5 has an area advantage over SHA-1, but only in extremely constrained environments. The main advantage of MD5 is its convenient output hash size of 128 bits, requiring only one AES or two DES encryptions. When used for code signing with these block ciphers, the throughput of the system would increase overall with MD5. However, when used for code signing exclusively there would be no need to implement any parallel symmetric encryption blocks. The slow speed and sequential nature of MD5 would be a severe bottleneck. However, if code signing were indicated piecewise – such as in the network header – then the benefits of parallel encryption could be realized, as code-signed data could be inserted in the output queue.

F. ASIC IMPLEMENTATIONS

For further comparison, we synthesize three variations of AES in 130-nm cell-based ASICs. Generally, cell-based approaches provide significant performance gains over FPGAs without the longer and more expensive design cycle of full-custom ASICs. We implemented a single AES encryption block, a pipelined AES approach, and a parallel AES approach. Given that the three main reasons for implementing a parallel approach are key flexibility, space flexibility, and security, implementing a parallel device in a cell-based ASIC is illogical. This is supported by our results. Table 8.9 gives the performance of cell-based ASIC synthesis.

ASIC performance is, as expected, better than other approaches. However, ASIC cost is prohibitive. In a large-scale deployment where performance is a prime concern, ASICs would be optimal solution. Additionally, if the keys are stored in on-chip registers, reconfiguration could be done dynamically. Note that this is not optimal from a security perspective.

Table 8.9. ASIC Performance of AES-128 Implementations

Implementation	Cells	Total Area	System Frequency	Throughput
AES (Single)	1550	46877.558	353.35 MHz	4.111 Gbps
AES (Parallel)	5232	522881.250	303.03 MHz	38.78 Gbps
AES (Pipelined)	3923	304442.406	370.37 MHz	47.407 Gbps

A pipelined ASIC approach handling upwards of 47 gigabits per second would require multiple system inputs to achieve optimal performance. Considering that modern processor clock frequencies are more than eight times the synthesis speed of these ASIC approaches, it would seem on the surface that ASIC approaches cannot keep up with processor speeds. However, the I/O bandwidth of modern processors is not enough to overwhelm the ASIC encryption processors. Though bandwidth varies throughout the system, general limitations (such as limited width I/O ports) ensure that a single processor will not experience bottlenecks as a result of the cryptographic processor.

G. COMPARISON OF PARALLEL AND PIPELINED AES

Pipelined encryption architectures are the fastest solution. However, when the primary design goal is not performance, parallel implementations provide a flexible and dynamically reconfigurable encryption environment that protects sensitive data. Pipelined approaches do not adequately protect the cryptographic keys. Also, pipelined approaches are limited in their scaling of energy consumption and area usage. The parallel architecture provides solutions to these challenges.

Recall the general architecture of AES encryption and decryption. Operations include byte substitution, Galois field multiplication, row shifting, and bitwise XOR. An individual encryption round involves 20 byte substitution operations and 4 each of the other operations. An area-constrained approach would implement one of each and drastically limit throughput. Additionally, the sequential nature of each round prohibits explicit parallelism. Noting that 16 byte substitutions are done for the encryption and 4 are done for each of the key operations, it would be logical to implement 2. Row shifting, Galois field multiplication (the MixColumns operation), and bitwise XOR operations do not occupy considerable area; duplicating these functions does not come with a large penalty. To increase performance while still minimizing area, we implement 20 byte substitution modules and 4 each of the remaining modules. This allows each individual round of encryption to execute in a single cycle. It should be noted that pipelined architectures also employ this methodology to implement the encryption round function.

Utilizing a feedback mode, we can effectively perform a single encryption in 11 cycles by implementing a single round of the key scheduling function as well as a single round of the encryption function. This provides an excellent tradeoff between performance and area. The key scheduler provides a different key value each cycle; this is important to protect sensitive data like cryptographic keys. Additionally, the key is not stored in its plaintext form; we instead perform the XOR on logically equivalent partial values.

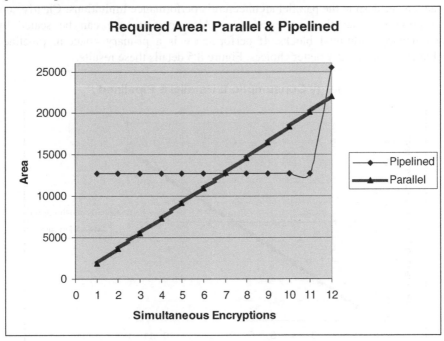

Figure 8.5. Required area: parallel and pipelined.

To provide a high-performance as well as high-security alternative, we can duplicate this self-contained encryption block an arbitrary number of times. Twelve blocks is sufficient to provide a zero-latency approach; an additional cycle is added to allow for distribution of inputs to multiple encryption blocks. This approach allows us to use 12 separate keys (or 17, in the case of DES or 3DES). Thus, we can have multiple users, a single user using different keys, and so on. If particular users are inactive at any time, their encryption mechanism(s) can be sent into sleep mode to save power. Sleep mode is accomplished by gating the clock. In this manner, the parallel architecture achieves flexibility in terms of multiple keys as well as energy consumption. If n blocks are utilizing the same key at any one time, the energy consumption can be scaled by shutting down up to $n-1$ encryption blocks.

Having outlined the basic architectural differences between the two, we consider the performance of the two approaches. We consider area, energy consumption, throughput, and security. Clearly, previous results indicate that parallel architectures provide flexibility in all these areas. Pipelined architectures have a distinct advantage in terms of throughput, area and energy consumption. However, the scalability of the approaches must be considered. Consider Figures 8.5, 8.6, and 8.7.

The flexibility of the parallel architecture is apparent, as are its performance disadvantages. As expected, the pipelined architecture outperforms the parallel architecture in terms of energy consumption, area, and throughput. However, its specifications are rigid. In an area-constrained environment, some level of parallel architecture could be implemented where pipelined architectures cannot fit. This is an advantage despite the parallel architecture's performance limitations. Clearly, any encryption is better than no encryption. Also, performance can be scaled by implementing additional blocks. If performance is a primary concern, pipelined architectures are clearly better choices. Figure 8.5 details these results.

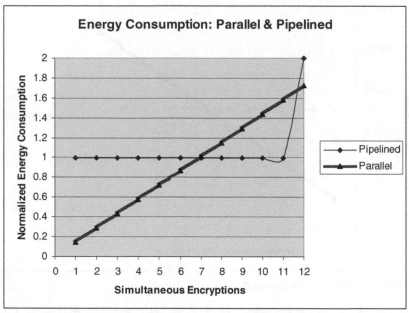

Figure 8.6. Energy consumption: parallel and pipelined.

In an energy-constrained environment, pipelined encryption may not be able to function at all as the entire device is needed to operate. However, parallel architectures can operate in reduced modes, saving energy. By definition, operating in a reduced mode requires the area to implement the inactive blocks. As is shown in Figure 8.6, parallel architectures have the capability to operate at far less power than pipelined; however, to match the throughput, parallel architectures must consume almost twice the power of pipelined architectures. This property may be desirable in a changing environment; for example, a solar-powered system might be able to operate at full power during the day but only has limited power during the night. We can visualize a scenario where the number of active encryption blocks dynamically changes to meet power consumption requirements.

The most drastic difference between the two architectures is in throughput as shown by Figure 8.7. Parallel architectures only maintain a throughput advantage in very area-constrained environments; this follows from Figure 8.5 as well as our original hypothesis. The feedback mode utilized by the parallel architecture requires a lower clock frequency. Pipelined architectures have single-use input and output ports and do not require feedback.

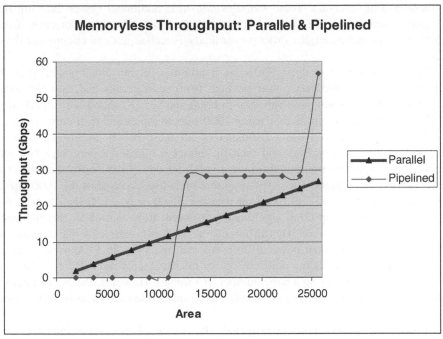

Figure 8.7. Memoryless throughput: parallel and pipelined.

4.   DIFFERENTIAL POWER ANALYSIS

Power analysis attacks use the variations in power consumption of different operations. The power consumption of an operation depends on the inputs (for cryptography: plaintext and secret key). Different operand values cause different switching activities in the memory, buses, datapath units (adders, multipliers, logical units) and pipeline registers of processors (smart cards, BACnet devices, etc.). Among these components, the processor datapath and buses exhibit more data-dependent energy variation than memory components [Ye 2000].

Power analysis attacks have varying degrees of sophistication. Simple Power Analysis (SPA) [Kocher 19987] uses only a single power consumption trace for an operation. From this power trace, an attacker can identify the operations performed (e.g., whether or not a branch at point p is taken or if an exponentiation operation is performed). Combining power consumption information with knowledge of the underlying algorithm can be used to reveal the secret key. For example, if a branch is taken when a particular bit of a secret key is zero, the attacker can identify this bit by monitoring the power consumption difference between a taken and not taken branch. Protecting against this type of simple attack can be achieved fairly easily by restructuring the code. For example, a restructured algorithm in [Coron 1999] eliminates branch conditions that can reveal secret key information. Also, techniques that randomly introduce noise into power measurement can mislead simple power analysis. For example, dummy modules can be inserted in the system and activated at random time intervals. These modules consume additional power skewing the original power profile. However, such techniques only provide protection from simplistic approaches. Higher-order power analysis techniques can circumvent these mechanisms.

Differential power analysis (DPA) is a common higher-order power analysis approach. This scheme uses power profiles from several runs and uses the data-dependent power consumption variation to break the key [Kocher 1998]. In [Goubin 1995], the secret key is guessed by using 1000 sample inputs and their corresponding 1000 power consumption traces. A mean of all these power consumption traces represented as M is obtained, and then the attacker guesses a particular key and based on the input determines a theoretical value for one of the intermediate bits (b) generated by the program. The outcome of this bit is used to separate the 1000 inputs into two groups ($G1$ and $G2$) based on whether $b = 0$ or $b = 1$. If the mean of the power profiles in Group $G1$ is significantly different from that of M, this indicates that the guess was correct. This difference is a manifestation of the consequent downstream computational power differences that used the bit b. As evident from the above discussion, random noises in power measurements can be filtered through the averaging process using a large number of samples. However, the use of random noises can increase the number of samples to an infeasible number to be of practical concern.

Many researchers have investigated the potential for both invasive and noninvasive attacks against smart cards. An overview of these techniques is presented in [Dhem 2001, Komerling 1999]. In particular, the retrieval of secret information from a smart card through its leakage called side-channel analysis is an important class of attack. Analyzing the power profile of an encryption process is a popular side-channel attack. [Kocher 1998] provides a detailed description of the SPA and DPA techniques. The difference between these two attacks is that DPA is more sophisticated and involves statistical analysis using a larger sample set.

There have been prior attempts to address the SPA and DPA attacks [Biham 1999, Coron 1999, Goubin 1999, Kocher 1996, Kocher 1998, Moore 2002]. These counter measures can be classified into three types as in [Goubin 1999]. First, random timing shifts and noise can be added so that computed means for power consumption do not correspond to the same instruction. However, the difficulty in this process is to ensure that the random technique is not vulnerable to statistical treatment using large samples. While complete protection is difficult to achieve in this way, it may become infeasible for an attacker to break the key. The second countermeasure technique is to modify the underlying software implementation or algorithm [Coron 1999, Dhem 2001, Goubin 1999]. For instance, the use of nonlinear transformations of S-box operations is proposed in [Goubin 1999] to avoid some DPA attacks. However, it is observed in [Dhem 2001] that software countermeasures are difficult to design.

The third form of countermeasure involves replacing some of the critical instructions such that their energy consumption behavior does not leak any information. Our approach is in this category. Dual-rail logic has been identified as one of the most promising ways to provide protection to SPA and DPA [Dhem 2001]. The use of dual-rail encoding and self-timed circuits is also proposed in [Moore 2002]. The use of self-timed circuits can alleviate problems arising from clock glitches induced in synchronous circuits while the dual-rail logic masks the power consumption differences due to bit variations. Our contribution is the actual modification of an embedded processor to implement this technique and the addition of secure instructions to its instruction set. However, the use of dual-rail logic can increase overall power consumption by almost two times as observed in our experiments. In fact, power is an important constraint for smart card markets such as the GSM industry and specific constraints on maximum power are imposed by the GSM specification for different supply voltages [Dhem 2001].

A. SECURE INSTRUCTION SET

Our energy masking approach is to eliminate operation input dependencies. We focus on four operations that are critical in DES encryption: assignment, bit-by-bit addition modulo two (XOR), shift, and indexing. We do not mask all the operations, but only the operations that use the secret key and operations that use data generated from prior secure operations. The compiler analyzes the code and identifies how variables are used. Then, for operators that use secure variables, the compiler employs secure versions of the corresponding instructions. It should be emphasized that it is not sufficient to protect only the variables annotated as sensitive by the programmer. Variables whose values are based on the values of the protected variables also leak information. Consequently, they also need to be protected. We do this using a technique called forward slicing [Horwitz 1990]. In forward slicing, given a set of variables and/or instructions (called *seeds*), the compiler determines all the variables/instructions whose values depend on the seeds. The complexity of this process is bounded by the number of edges of the control flow graph of the code being analyzed. After the variables whose values are affected by the seeds are determined, the compiler uses secure instructions to protect them.

DES is a widely used symmetric cryptography algorithm. DES [DES 1993] uses 64 binary bits for the key, of which 56 bits are used in the algorithm while the other 8 bits are used for error detection. Similar to other cryptography algorithms, the security of the data depends on the security provided by the key used to encrypt or decrypt the data. Although the DES algorithm is public, one will not be able to decrypt the cipher unless they know the secret key used to encrypt that cipher.

The plaintext is permuted before it goes to the encryption process. The core of the DES encryption process consists of 16 identical rounds, each of which has its own sub-secret key, called K_n ($n = 1,2,..16$). Each K_n is 48 bits produced from the original secret key using key-permutation and shift operations. Each round consists of 8 S-box operations, which use the 48-bit input derived from the permutated input and sub secret key K_n (Figure 8.8). Each S-box operation takes 6 bits from the 48-bit input that is divided into 8 blocks. These 6-bits are used to index a table. This table lookup operation consequently generates 4 bits (for each S-box). These 32 output bits (4 x 8 S-boxes) are then used as an input combination for the next round.

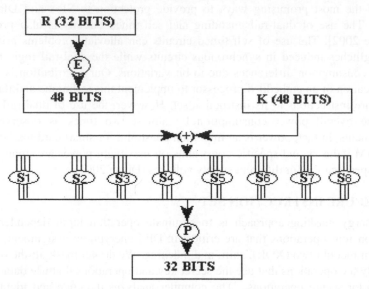

Figure 8.8. S-box operations (f(R, K)) .

The complete encryption process of DES is in Figure 8.9 (left). Here, (+) denotes bit-by-bit addition modulo 2. From this algorithm, we can identify the operations that can reveal the secret key. These operations are key permutation, left-side and right-side assignment operations, and key generation. Next, we identify the instructions used to implement operations and consider their secure versions.

Data Initial Permutation (L0,R0) = Permute IP(Data) Key Permutation (C0,D0) = Permute K1(Key) = denotes insecure assignment	Data Initial Permutation (L0,R0) = Permute IP(Data) Key Permutation (C0,D0) ← Permute K1(Key) ← denotes secure assignment
M⁻¹ Rounds **Left Side Operation** Lm = Rm-1 M⁻¹ **Key Generation** Cm = Rotate(Cm-1,n) Dm = Rotate(Dm-1,n) Km = Permute K2(Cm,Dm) **Right Side Operation** E[R]= Permute E(Rm-1) f(Rm-1,K) = S(E(R)(+) Km) Rm = Lm-1 /+\ f(Rm -1 K)	M⁻¹ Rounds **Left Side Operation** Lm ← Rm-1 M⁻¹ **Key Generation** Cm ← Rotate(Cm-1,n) Dm ← Rotate(Dm-1,n) Km ← Permute K2(Cm,Dm) **Right Side Operation** E(R)← Permute E(Rm-1) f(Rm-1,K) ← S(E(R) <+> Km) Rm ← Lm-1 <+> f(Rm -1 K)
Output Inverse Permutation Output=Permute IP (R16,L16)	**Output Inverse Permutation** Output=Permute IP (R16,L16)

Figure 8.9. Modified DES algorithm

Figure 8.9 shows how we modified DES operations. Figure 8.9 (left) shows the original DES operations. The first step is permutation of the plaintext. This operation does not use the secret key and thus does not have to be secure.

The next operation is key permutation. It obviously needs to be secure. Figure 8.9 (right) shows how we modify this operation. The symbol "=" corresponds to the original assignment (i.e., insecure assignment) operation, and the symbol "$\leftarrow$" indicates that the assignment operation is secure.

The next step contains the operations within each round. Since some of these operations require the secret key, and the operations are repeated in every round using the data generated from the previous round, we need to secure all operations inside this block. Note that the modified left side operation uses a secure assignment operation, although it does not operate on the secret key directly. This is because it uses the data generated from the previous round (for $\geq 2^{nd}$ round) that uses the secret key. In the right side operation, all the instructions need to be secure. Each round uses four types of secure operations: secure assignment, secure shift, secure bit-by-bit addition modulo two and secure indexing. Note that the S symbol in the Figure represents the S-box operation.

The last operation is the output inverse permutation. This operation does not need any secure instruction although it uses data generated from secure instructions as it reveals only the information already available from the output cipher. The following section explains how our secure instructions are implemented.

B. SECURE INSTRUCTION IMPLEMENTATION

Our target 32-bit embedded processor has five pipeline stages (fetch, decode, execute, memory access and write back) and implements the integer instructions from the Simplescalar instruction set architecture [Ye 2000]. Its ISA is representative of current embedded 32-bit RISC cores used in smart cards such as the ARM7-TDMI RISC core. We augment our target instruction set architecture with secure versions of select instructions. To support these secure operations, the hardware should be modified.

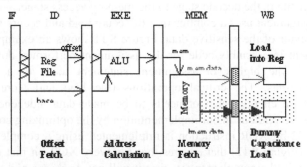

Figure 8.10. Secure load architecture (dotted portion is augmented).

An assignment operation typically involves loading a variable and storing it into another variable. We will consider the parts of the load operation that are of interest.

Energy consumption at all stages of the pipeline (Figure 8.10) is independent of the loaded data until the memory access stage (revealing the data address is not considered as a problem). The memory access itself is not sensitive to the data being read. However, the output data bus switching depends on the data being transmitted. Consider different scenarios for the 1st bit (d0) of the 32-bit data read from the cache. If the values of d0 in two successive cycles are 0 and 1, it consumes more power than the case when the values are 0 and 0 in these two cycles. Specifically, for an internal wire of 1 pF and a supply voltage of 2.5 V, the first case consumes 6.25pJ more energy than the second case. The output from the memory access stage is fed to the pipeline register before being forwarded for storing the data in the register file. Thus, based on whether a bit value of 1 or 0 is stored in the pipeline register bits, a different amount of energy is consumed. Finally, the energy consumed in writing to a register is independent of the data as the register file can be considered as another memory array.

The secure version of the load operation masks these energy differences due to bit dependences through the following modifications to the architecture. The buses carrying the data from a secure load are provided in both their normal and complementary forms. Thus, instead of a 32-bit bus, we use a 64-bit bus. The number of 1's and 0's transmitted in the bus will always both be 32. However, this is not sufficient for masking energy differences that depend on the number of transitions across the bus. But this modification along with a precharged bus can mask this difference. All 64-bus lines are pre-charged to a value of 1 in the first phase of the clock. In the next evaluating phase, the bus settles to its actual value. Exactly, 32 of the bus lines will discharge to a value of zero. In subsequent cycles, energy is consumed only in precharging 32 lines independent of the input activity. The next modification involves propagating the normal and complementary values until the write back stage. The complementary values are terminated using a dummy capacitive load. The required enhancements to the underlying processor architecture are illustrated in Figure 8.10. Similarly, a secure version of the store operation involves passing along both the normal and complementary forms of the data read from the register file in the decode stage to the memory access stage.

A secure assignment uses a combination of secure load and secure store to mask the energy behavior of the sensitive data. Figure 8.11 shows an example use of the secure assignment in assembly code for the assignment performed during the "left side operation." The high-level assignment statement leads to a sequence of assembly instructions. The critical operations (the load and store instructions highlighted) whose energy behavior needs to be made data independent are then converted to secure versions in our implementation by the optimizing compiler.

The secure 32-bit XOR instruction is implemented using a complementary pre-charged circuit (Figure 8.12) that ensures that for every XOR bit that discharges in the required circuit, the complementary circuit will not discharge and vice-versa. In the first clock phase (when $v = 0$), all (64 = 32 original + 32 complementary) the output nodes of the XOR circuit are pre-charged to one. In the next phase (when $v = 1$), half discharge and the other half remain one. In subsequent cycles using the XOR, energy is consumed for charging 32 output nodes regardless of the data.

During the S-box operation, a 6-bit value is used to index a table. This operation is performed by a load operation with the 6-bit value serving as the offset in our underlying architecture. Note that our current secure load operation does not mask the energy difference due to differences in the offset. As these 6 bits are derived from the key, it is also important to hide the value of this offset. When the 6-bit value is added as an offset to the base address of the table, the addition operation will consume an energy based on the 6-bit value. To avoid this, we align the base address of the table so that the 6-bit value serves as the least significant bits of the lookup and the most significant bits are determined at compile time. Further, the inverted value of this 6-bit index is propagated to mask the energy consumption. Thus, the load operations used for indexing are replaced by the secure indexing that generates the memory address using our secure version.

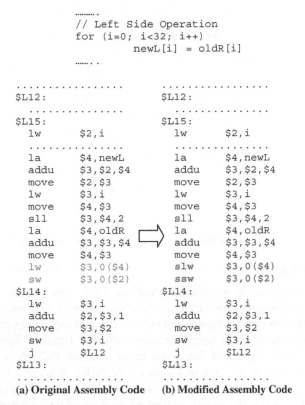

```
............
// Left Side Operation
for (i=0; i<32; i++)
        newL[i] = oldR[i]
........
```

```
...............                     ................
$L12:                               $L12:
...............                     ................
$L15:                               $L15:
    lw      $2,i                        lw      $2,i
...............                     ................
    la      $4,newL                     la      $4,newL
    addu    $3,$2,$4                    addu    $3,$2,$4
    move    $2,$3                       move    $2,$3
    lw      $3,i                        lw      $3,i
    move    $4,$3                       move    $4,$3
    sll     $3,$4,2                     sll     $3,$4,2
    la      $4,oldR                     la      $4,oldR
    addu    $3,$3,$4                    addu    $3,$3,$4
    move    $4,$3                       move    $4,$3
    lw      $3,0($4)                    slw     $3,0($4)
    sw      $3,0($2)                    ssw     $3,0($2)
$L14:                               $L14:
    lw      $3,i                        lw      $3,i
    addu    $2,$3,1                     addu    $2,$3,1
    move    $3,$2                       move    $3,$2
    sw      $3,i                        sw      $3,i
    j       $L12                        j       $L12
$L13:                               $L13:
...............                     ................
(a) Original Assembly Code    (b) Modified Assembly Code
```

Figure 8.11. Code level representation of the left side operation.

To use the augmented architecture, the compiler tags selected operations as secure. Secure instructions can be implemented using either the unassigned opcodes (bits in the instruction identifying the operation) in the processor architecture or by augmenting the original opcodes with an additional secure bit per operand. In our implementation, we use the second option to minimize the impact on the decoding logic. Whenever a secure version of the instruction is identified both the normal and complementary versions of the appropriate segments of the processor become active. For example, for the secure XOR operations, the data values (both source data and result data) are present in normal and complementary forms in the internal data buses. Further, the required and complementary versions of the circuit operate together. Since the additional parts consume extra power, the clock to the complementary versions is gated to reduce energy consumption. The details of the gating (note that the complementary version of the circuit is provided with a clock v gated with secure signal – secure v - for the evaluation phase) for the XOR unit implementation are shown in Figure 8.12. Thus, as opposed to energy consumption of 0.06pJ in the secure mode, the XOR unit consumes only 0.03 pJ in the normal mode. Additional savings in energy also accrue during the execution of normal versions due to gating of the additional buses and the pipeline registers.

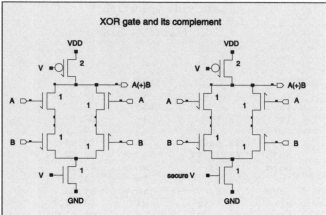

Figure 8.12. XOR circuit and its complement. v is the clock. A and B are inputs to the XOR function.

C. DES RESULTS

To evaluate this approach, we implemented the DES algorithm in software and captured the energy consumption in each cycle using a cycle-accurate energy simulator. We discuss only processor and buses since memory power consumption is largely data-independent. The simulator uses validated transition-sensitive energy models for both the buses and functional units obtained through detailed circuit simulation and is within 9% of actual values [Ye 2000]. It accurately captures the differences in energy consumption due to data transitions. Working with the simulator lets us monitor the energy consumed in every cycle (along with details of actual instructions executed) and helps quickly identify the benefits of modifying the underlying processor architecture. Current measurement based approaches would be limited by the sampling speed of the measuring devices and it would be more difficult to correlate the operations and sources of energy consumption. The processor modeled for our simulation results is based on 0.25-micron technology using 2.5 V supply voltage.

First, we show the energy behavior of the original DES algorithm to demonstrate the type of information it leaks. Figure 8.13 shows the energy profile of the original encryption process revealing clearly the 16 rounds of operation. This result reiterates that the energy profile can show what operations are being performed. Next, we present a (differential) energy consumption trace for two different secret keys to demonstrate that the energy consumption profiles can reveal more specific information.

Figure 8.14 shows the difference in energy consumption profiles generated for two different secret keys using the same plaintext. This illustrates that it is possible to identify differences in even a single bit of the secret key. Similar observations on energy differences can also be made using differences in one of the internally generated key-related variables.

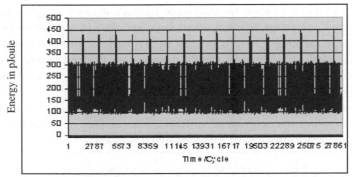

Figure 8.13. Energy consumption trace of encryption (every 10 cycles).

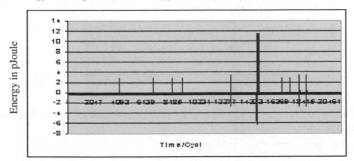

Figure 8.14. Difference between energy consumption profiles generated using two different secret keys (vary in bit 10), 1st round.

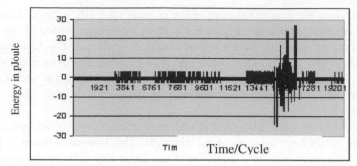

Figure 8.15. Difference between energy consumption profiles generated using two different keys before masking process.

Figures 8.15 and 8.16 show the difference between the two energy consumption traces generated using two different secret keys and the same plaintext before and after the energy masking. These traces are shown only for the first round of DES algorithm for clarity. The graphs clearly demonstrate that the secure instructions mask the energy behavior of the key related operations. While the effectiveness of the algorithm is shown using differences between profiles generated from two different keys, the results hold for other key choices. Specifically, the mean of the energy consumption traces generate different internal (key related) bits will not exhibit any differences that can be exploited by DPA attacks.

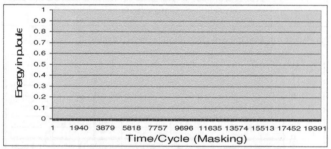

Figure 8.16. Difference between energy consumption profiles generated using two different keys after masking process.

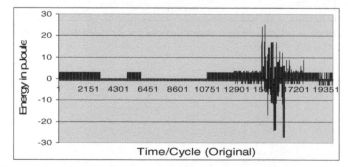

Figure 8.17. Difference between energy consumption profiles generated using two different plaintexts before masking process.

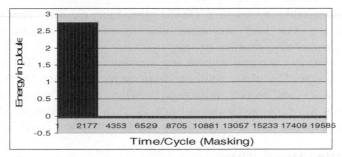

Figure 8.18. Difference between energy consumption generated using two different plaintexts after masking process.

Figures 8.17 and 8.18 show the difference between the energy consumption traces generated using two different plaintexts but the same secret keys.

The first operation in the DES is plaintext permutation. Since this process is not operated in a secure mode, the differences in the input values result in the difference in both the energy masked and original versions. The other operations in the first round are secure; as a result, there are energy consumption power differences.

However, the proposed solution is not without drawbacks. The energy masking requires that the same amount of energy be consumed independent of the data. Thus, additional energy is consumed in the circuits added for the complementary portion of the circuit as shown in Figure 8.19. However, this additional energy is 45 pJ per cycle (as compared to an average energy consumption of 165 pJ per cycle in the original application). Note that we add excessive energy even in places where the differential profile in Figure 8.15 shows no difference. This is because the same secure instruction is used for parts of the input that are the same for both the runs. Of course, in portions where the data was identical we have nothing to mask but we need to be conservative to account for all possible inputs in a statistical test using large samples.

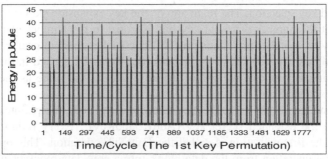

Figure 8.19. Additional energy consumed due to the energy masking operation during the 1st key permutation.

It must also be observed that our approach of using selective secure instructions helps to reduce the energy cost as compared to a naïve implementation that balances energy consumption of all operations. For example, looking at the code segment shown earlier in Figure 8.11, we increase the energy cost of only one of the four load operations executed in the segment. On the other hand, the naïve approach would convert all the four load operations into secure loads thereby consuming significantly more energy than our strategy.

The total energy consumed without any masking operation is 46.4 μJoule. Our algorithm consumes 52.6 μJoule while the naïve approach consumes 63.6 μJoule (all loads and stores are secure instructions). When all instructions are secure instructions, it will consume almost as twice as much as the original, 83.5 μJoule. This scheme is the one used in current dual-rail solutions [Dhem 2001].

D. AES IMPLEMENTATION

Due to DES weaknesses, such as short key length, a new encryption standard called AES has been introduced. The AES Rijndael algorithm is symmetric cryptography that has independent block length and key length. Both are of length multiple of 32 bits with the minimum of 128 bits and maximum of 256 bits. Similar to DES, Rijndael runs in several rounds. The number of rounds (Nr) depends on the length of the key (K) and the data block (D) as shown in Table 8.10.

All operations in Rijndael use a data block and key block that are represented as an array of bytes. The representation of data block is a two dimensional array, in which there are 4 rows and the number of columns is the length of data block divided by 32 (called N_b). The key block is also represented similar to the data block (the number of row is 4 and the number of column is key length/32, called N_k).

Table 8.10. Number of Rounds

Nr	D = 128	D = 192	D = 256
K = 128	10	12	14
K = 192	12	12	14
K = 256	14	14	14

The basic operation of Rijndael encryption consists of three steps. The first step is an initial round key addition. This step contains two substeps: the key expansion and the round key selection. The main aim of the key expansion step is to expand the key such that the number of round key bits is equal to the number of block length multiplied by the number of rounds plus 1. The subkey used in each round will be the sub set of this expanded key, for instance the first subkey used in the first round will be the first key block (the size of the key block is the same as the data block size) of the expanded key.

The second step is Nr-1 rounds. Yet before these rounds, the plaintext should be XORed with the extended secret key (AddRoundKey). Every round has similar operations. The first operation is called the ByteSub operation. This operation is a transformation operation from the data block into a new data block using an S-box. The substitution table (S-box) is invertible and composed of two transformations: the multiplicative inverse in GF (s8) and an affine transformation over GF (2). The second operation is the ShiftRow transformation that shifts cyclically every row of the output of the ByteSub operation based on a particular offset. The third operation is the MixColumn operation. The MixColumn operation then will XOR every column of the output from ShiftRow with a fixed polynomial c (x). The final operation for each round is the round key addition (AddRoundKey). This round key addition takes the output from MixColumn and then XORs them with the round key generated from the initial round key addition.

The last step of Rijndael encryption is similar to the operations that happen in each round (1st round through Nr-1th round) except it does not contain the MixColumn operation. Figure 8.20 shows all the operations in Rijndael encryption (left side) as well as the secure versions (right side).

From Figure 8.20 we see that all operations use the secret key or data that have been modified by the secret key. So to mask the energy consumption behavior, we need to mask all of those operations. The operations Rijndael has are similar to ones DES has, such as XOR, table lookup, and shift.

Initial Round Key Addition KeyExpansion(KeyxKey)	Initial Round Key Addition sKeyExpansion(KeyxKey)
AddRoundKey(Data,xKey) **MthRounds(Mac Nr-1)** ByteSub(Data) ShiftRow(Data) MixColumn(Data) AddRoundKey(Data,K)	sAddRoundKey(Data,xKey) **MthRounds(Mac Nr-1)** sByteSub(Data) sShiftRow(Data) sMixColumn(Data) sAddRoundKey(Data,K)
Final Rounds ByteSub(Data) ShiftRow(Data) AddRoundKey(Data,K)	**Final Rounds** sByteSub(Data) sShiftRow(Data) AddRoundKey(Data,K)

Figure 8.20. Modified Rijndael algorithm.

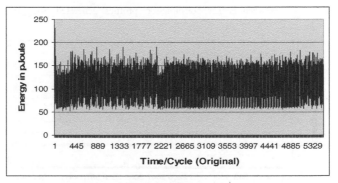

Figure 8.21. Energy consumption trace of AES encryption

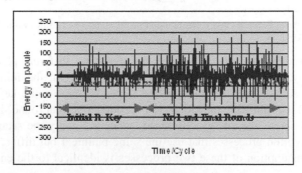

Figure 8.22. Difference between energy consumption profiles generated using two different secret keys.

E. AES EVALUATION

Lets use the same procedure to evaluate AES as we did for DES. Figure 8.21 shows the original energy consumption of Rijndael encryption with key length 256 and data block length 128.

Figure 8.22 shows the differences in energy consumption between two different keys with the same plaintext (the length of the plaintext is only one data block). We can see the energy difference in the initial round key addition. This occurs since that operation uses the secret key. For the remaining operations (Nr rounds) we also see differences in energy consumption since these rounds use the extended secret key generated by the initial round key addition.

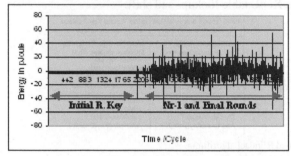

Figure 8.23. Difference between energy consumption profiles generated using two different plaintexts.

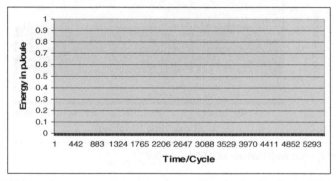

Figure 8.24. Difference between energy consumption profiles generated using two different secret keys after masking.

Figure 8.23 shows the energy differences if we use different plaintext but the same secret key. In this scenario, the energy consumed in the initial round key addition is the same, since the initial round depends only on the key. The energy consumed in all the following operations (Nr-1 round and final round) is different.

Figure 8.24 shows the energy differences when we apply the secure instruction set to two encryption processes that use the same plaintext but different secret key. The energy consumption of these two processes is identical to the energy masking operations.

While using our secure operations on the same plaintext consume the same amount of energy, this is not true if we apply it to the same secret key, see Figure 8.25. This phenomenon is similar to the one that we have explained in the DES section. The difference comes from loading the same plaintext.

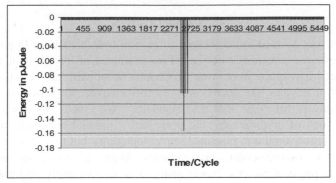

Figure 8.25. Difference between energy consumption profiles generated using two different plaintexts after masking.

F. PARALLEL CRYPTOGRAPHY ENGINE POWER ANALYSIS

It should be noted that the Rijndael algorithm was chosen as the AES partly because of its inherent resistance to differential power analysis. Our parallel architecture provides specific advantages over pipelined architectures with respect to these attacks. The presence of static key lines in the pipelined encryption datapath, which include the plaintext key as well as each of the round keys, expedites the job of power profiling by providing an easy medium for data-dependent collection. The presence of static lines themselves does not present a security vulnerability. However, in each cycle, variable input data (the data to be encrypted) is paired with a static key for computation. This is precisely what differential power analysis requires. We have shown in Sections 4.D and 4.E that a selective dual-rail solution can be applied to pipelined AES encryption architectures without a substantial area or energy consumption penalty.

Parallel architectures provide an alternative to dual-rail logic by making key values fully transient. In each cycle, variable input data is paired with variable key data. Note that the primary difference is that the key values in parallel architectures are fully dynamic. Thus, differential power analysis, while not fully prevented, is greatly complicated. Though it is very difficult to quantify, it is suspected that the difficulty of conducting differential power analysis attacks on such parallel architectures is greatly increased. Also, the dynamic nature of the data makes invasive probing extremely difficult if not impossible. As an added precaution, parallel architectures can also utilize selective dual-rail logic to mask the power consumption of sensitive operations. This effectively makes the differential power analysis resistance of parallel and pipelined architectures identical; however, the area and key flexibility of parallel architectures still provide an attractive alternative. Also, in a multi-user environment, energy conservation techniques have the added effect of randomizing the power profile. Such irregular operation modes, coupled with the added flexibility of encryption-by-encryption key flexibility, can make parallel architectures resistant to power analysis without requiring energy-intensive dual-rail logic.

5. CONCLUSION

This chapter was devoted to the security of mobile code platforms. In particular, we discussed resource-constrained devices. Two examples of this class of device with important security aspects were given. In Chapter 9, we will further explore security applications of devices like smart cards. In this chapter, we provided an in-depth security analysis of the BACnet standard. We then discussed hardware implementations of cryptography and presented a parallel approach that provides throughput at rates similar to pipelined implementations, but provides flexibility that is needed for resource-constrained systems. Many of these systems will be vulnerable to physical attacks. Power analysis is an extremely important class of attack. We showed that the implementation of a secure instruction set can be an effective countermeasure to these attacks.

FPGAs are attractive platforms for both cryptography engines and systems with custom instruction sets. The secure instruction set concept is an attractive idea for computer security. By integrating security into the software, compilers, and underlying hardware implementations it is possible to remove entire classes of vulnerabilities.

6. EXERCISES

Exercise 8.1 List network security issues and vulnerabilities for both smart cards and BACnet.

Exercise 8.2 Discuss the use of Protection Profiles in the design of secure devices.

Exercise 8.3 Compare pipelined, parallel, and ASIC AES implementations. Under which circumstances would each be preferable? Include discussions of Figures 8.5 and 8.6. Provide quantitative support.

Exercise 8.4 Outline a secure instruction set solution to a vulnerability other than power analysis.

Exercise 8.5 Outline a secure instruction set solution that uses parallel encryption circuits.

CHAPTER 9

Maintaining Trust on the Network[1, 2]

Vertrauen ist gut. Kontrolle ist besser.
(Trust is good. Control is better)
– German proverb

The Internet allows global exchange of information and software among computer nodes and users. This has greatly increased productivity and communications in networked enterprises. One negative aspect of this global interchange of information is the ease of undesirable disclosure and dissemination of confidential information. Another drawback is the vulnerability of systems to manipulation by viruses and hostile programs [Ludwig 1991, Knight 1998, Garber 2000]. Methods are needed to protect network nodes from hostile programs, and data (programs) from malicious software [Stallings 1995, Rubin 1998, Sander 1998].

This chapter discusses technology for negotiating trust in open systems. We define trust as a guarantee that the network node will not improperly manipulate data objects and that the data objects will not maliciously manipulate the host. To establish trust we start with a few basic assumptions:

- A network node in its initial configuration, known by a central authority, is trustworthy.

- A data object in its initial configuration, known by a central authority, is trustworthy.

- A user should be able to access only those portions of the data object, which the central authority agrees to divulge.

- The central authority is assumed to be trustworthy.

- Public key encryption is reliable, and each entity has a private key initially known only to itself [Schneier 1996, Stallings 1995].

We make no assumptions about communications confidentiality. A few other assumptions may be necessary, such as some well-defined portions of the system being implemented in read-only memory (ROM) and cannot be modified. When assumptions are made they are stated explicitly.

---

[1] Coauthored with Dr. John Zachary

[2] Portions of this chapter are reprinted, with permission, from:
J. M. Zachary and R. R. Brooks, "Bidirectional mobile code trust management using tamper resistant hardware," *Mobile Networks and Applications*, vol. 8, pp. 137-143, 2003.

Interfaces and wrappers resemble cell walls providing internal system structure and filtering information between components. The walls need to protect hosts from code and vice-versa. To do this, we integrate code signing and sandboxing [Rubin 1998] into formal security proofs. Wrappers and interfaces impose local constraints on resources and interactions with global consequences.

In addition to a wrapper protecting the host from malicious code, technologies are needed for protecting mobile code from being compromised by hosts. In this chapter, we discuss an approach for ensuring mutual protection. This approach considers four entities: users, daemons, code (and data), and a code repository. Figure 9.1 shows the entities and their interactions. Our approach is built on four atomic actions: secret transmission, source verification, inspection, and introspection. Protocols use combinations of these actions to guarantee the trustworthiness of other components.

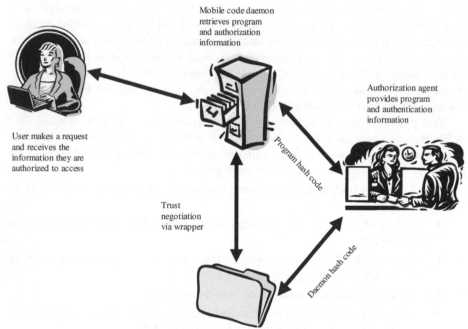

Figure 9.1. Interactions among entities.

The security of systems using mobile code is a critical issue for the National Information Infrastructure (NII). Systems including software mobility are an integral part of the modern network infrastructure. We are interested in code mobility, where data, programs, and state all are mobile. Our security mechanisms are applicable to both specialized mobile computing frameworks and legacy systems. Two main issues exist: securing mobile code from hosts and securing hosts from mobile code. While the latter component dominates research literature and the popular press, both components are essential to mobile computing security. A general model of mobile code security is given in Figure 9.2. Mobile code security is a *security pipeline* with one stage feeding into the next.

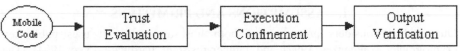

Figure 9.2. Mobile security pipeline.

Our approach uses the three security modes shown in Figure 9.2. Authentication and deciding whether or not to accept and execute mobile code is part of trust evaluation. Code signing and digital signatures (e.g., Microsoft's Authenticode system for ActiveX) are examples of trust evaluation. Execution confinement prevents mobile code from improperly accessing or modifying the execution environment. This includes restricting access to the local file system and network connections. The Java "sandbox" is an example. Output verification checks program results to ensure that answers are within given bounds. An example of verification for distributed systems can be found in [Brooks 1998].

This chapter describes in detail the "trust evaluation" security mode from Figure 9.2 in the context of mobile code security. While most research on mobile code security focuses on protection remote hosts from malicious or faulty mobile code, our method also considers the protection of mobile code from malicious remote hosts.

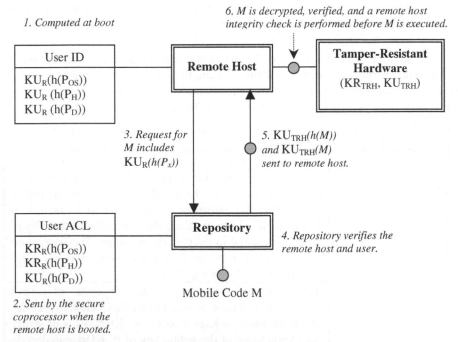

Figure 9.3. Mobile code and remote host trust management process.

1. ASSUMPTIONS AND PRIMITIVES

Our method considers protection of both host and code. It uses public-key cryptography [Menenzes 1997] and tamper-resistant hardware [Yee 1994]. The following assumptions are made:

1. Trust negotiation is identity-based, i.e., all entities are familiar with one another. Unknown entities are actively excluded from the system.

2. Security is based on a secure Public Key Infrastructure (PKI) technology. Each entity E has a public key (KU_E) and a private key (KR_E).

3. A secure one-way hash function (h()) maps an input file to a fixed width output string.

4. The repository is trustworthy. We assume controls and security mechanisms are in place assuring that the repository cannot be compromised.

5. Mobile code and the remote host state are trustworthy in an original "pristine" state. The registration of mobile code and remote hosts with the centralized repository includes extracting signatures for each mobile code program and class of remote host. This set of signatures represents entity states that have not been compromised.

6. The network infrastructure is untrustworthy. Network channels are noisy and insecure. Hostile agents can monitor transmissions between the repository and remote hosts.

Assumptions 2 and 3 are defined by the atomic operations used. Assumptions 1, 5, and 6 define the scope of the problem. Assumptions 1 and 5 combine to provide a pragmatic definition of trust. It avoids undecidable problems, such as whether or not a program contains viruses or undesirable side effects.

Table 9.1. Atomic Operations Used for Secure Transmission over Insecure Networks and Verification of Information against Tampering

Secret transmission	To secretly transmit a message P from sender σ to receiver ρ, σ uses the public key of ρ to encrypt P, expressed as $G = KU\rho$ (P). While $U\rho$ is public knowledge, the information contained in G is hidden from outside observers since the key privately held by ρ, $KR\rho$, is required to decrypt the message. The decryption occurs when ρ receives G and is expressed as $P = KR\rho$ (G) (i.e., $P = KR\rho$ ($KU\rho$ (P))).
Source verification	This process is the functional opposite of secret transmission. σ uses its own private key, $KR\sigma$, to encode[1] an information package P as $G = KR\sigma$ (P). Any entity with knowledge of the public key of σ, $KU\sigma$, can decode G. This guarantees that G originated from σ.
Inspection	A one-way hash function, such as MD5 or SHA-1

---

[1] We use the term *encode* rather than e*ncrypt* to stress that the information can be obtained by any entity with knowledge of the public key of the sender.

	[Menezes 1997], is used to generate a code or data signature. This is denoted as h().
Introspection	An entity hashes itself.

Four atomic security operations are used. They use PKI and one-way hashing functions [Schneier 1996] to ensure data and code authenticity. These atomic operations are discussed in Table 9.1. We assume they are secure and reliable.

An example of mobile code trust evaluation is shown in Figure 9.3. We consider trust management and evaluation to be integrity checking as an adjunct to authentication. In Figure 9.3, the tamper-resistant hardware (TRH) is present in the remote host prior to any requests for mobile code. The TRH contains a public and private key, KU_{TRH} and KR_{TRH}, for encryption and decryption. When the remote host is booted, the TRH performs an integrity check of the remote host software, hardware, and mobile code daemon.

Encrypted verification results are transmitted to the repository. When the remote host requests a mobile code package, the user ID[1], if applicable, is securely transmitted to the repository (R) along with the encrypted remote host signatures sent at boot time in order to perform user and remote host verification and security level determination. The mobile code is then encrypted and sent to the remote host along with a hashed value of the mobile code. The TRH performs a check of the mobile code to ensure that the mobile code was not tampered with during transmission.

2.   MOBILE CODE VERIFICATION

Malicious mobile code is a major security concern due to the unpredictable effects of viruses and Trojan horses, and their ability to propagate. In this chapter, we assume the repository of mobile code is highly secure and centralized. The mobile code programs stored in the repository are uncorrupted "shrink-wrap" software. The mobile code can be modified and replaced with mobile code containing malicious routines during transmission. The method we propose assures the remote host that mobile code was not modified during transmission. Our single-hop assumption can be extended to multi-hop instances in which mobile code goes from remote host to remote host. The current discussion is concerned with the single-hop situation. We assume identity based trust management. An initialization step registers mobile code with a code repository. Remote hosts are registered with the repository as well. Further work may relax this assumption to allow requests for mobile code from unknown remote hosts. In the current context this assumption provides an intuitive definition of trust. Two trusted entities can interact and be certain they are protected from other unknown entities. Protection from insider attacks and assurance of software correctness are important orthogonal issues.

Let H be a remote host running a mobile code daemon. TRH, see Chapter 7, is attached to H to provide a minimal trusted computing base. The TRH is a proxy for the user, the software consumer. R is a repository to which remote hosts issue

---

[1] The user ID could be captured via a smart card connected to the TRH.

requests for mobile code. R is the software provider. P is a mobile code package requested by H from R. Only R and TRH are assumed to have public and private keys. The trust negotiation procedure is split between the repository and the remote host. At the repository, the mobile code is encoded using the private key of the repository. This encoding guarantees that the mobile code package P came from the repository and not from another source. A one-way hash algorithm is run on the encrypted version of P. Both the encoding and the hash value are encrypted with the public key of the remote host and transmitted. The remote host uses its private key to decrypt the encoding and the hash value. The encoding is then hashed on the remote host and compared to the hash value received from the repository. By checking the two hash values, the remote host can determine if the mobile code encoding was altered during transmission. If satisfied, the remote host then uses the public key of the repository to reverse the encoding of the program for execution. The security of this procedure is formally proven in Table 9.2.

Table 9.2 A Frmal Proof of the Security of our Method for Checking the Origination and Integrity of a Mobile Code Program Given our Assumptions

At the repository

Action	Description	Justification
$T_1 = KR_R(P)$	R uses its private key KR_R to encode P.	Any entity with knowledge of the public key of R can decode T_1 to recover P. This guarantees that R sent P.
$T_2 = h(T_1)$	Compute a hash value of T_1.	This step provides a fixed-length signature of the encoded program P.
$T_3 = KR_R(T_2)$	R uses its private key KR_R to encode the hash signature T_2.	This step guarantees that the hash signature was generated by R.
$T_4 = KU_{TRH}(T_1)$	R encrypts T_1 using the public key of the tamper-resistant hardware (TRH).	Only TRH has the corresponding private key, which is needed to decrypt T_4.
$T_5 = KU_{TRH}(T_3)$	R encrypts T_3 using the public key of the tamper-resistant hardware (TRH).	Ibid.

(Transmit T_4 and T_5 from R to H over an insecure network.)

At the remote host

Action	Description	Justification
$T_1 = KR_{TRH}(T_4)$	The TRH decrypts T_1 using its private key.	Ibid.
$T_3 = KR_{TRH}(T_5)$	The TRH decrypts T_3 using its private key.	Ibid.
$\tau_2 = h(T_1)$	Compute a hash value of T_1.	Compute a fixed length

		signature of the encoding of P.
$T_2 = KU_R(T_3)$	The TRH decodes T_2 using the public key of R.	This step provides a guarantee to the TRH that T_2 was sent by R.
$Compare(T_2, \tau_2)$	Compare the hashed encoding of P created on R with the hashed encoding of P created on H.	This verifies to TRH that T_1 was not modified during transmission from R to H.
$P = KU_R(T_1)$	The TRH decodes P using the public key of R.	This step provides a guarantee to the TRH that P was sent by R.

Through this process, the remote host is certain that the mobile code was sent by the repository and was not tampered with during transmission. The mobile code that was sent by the repository is bit-wise identical to the mobile code that the remote host received. Assuming that the mobile code is trustworthy in its initial state and the repository is secure, the remote host can trust that the mobile code was not intercepted and altered to provide malicious intent by a third-party agent during transmission. Encryption with public key of the TRH safeguards the code from reverse engineering by a third party.

3.   HOST VERIFICATION

Let's use the same definitions and assumptions as in the previous section. We define H as the aggregation of three components, P_{MCD}, P_{OS}, and P_H. P_{MCD} is the mobile code daemon running on the remote host. P_{OS} is an image or signature of the operating environment on the remote host (discussed later in the document). P_H is a set of hardware signatures such as the ID of the microprocessor, the size of RAM, and/or the IP address of the network card. Additionally, smartcards used with the TRH allow us to identify users by P_{User}.

When the remote host starts, the TRH calculates hash value encodings of P_{MCD}, P_{OS}, and P_H. These values, $KR_{TRH}(h(P_M))$, $KR_{TRH}(h(P_{OS}))$, and $KR_{TRH}(h(P_H))$, are securely transmitted to the repository (using the public key of the repository). This information allows the remote host to request mobile code from the repository.

R contains a user access control list (ACL) mapping P_{User} and mobile code packages to security levels or domains. Each user should possess a smartcard that that the TRH can use to authorize access to mobile code packages with appropriate security levels.

Table 9.3. A Formal Procedure for Verifying a Remote Host and its Integrity to a Mobile Code Program.

Remote Host (Remote Host Authentication)

Action	Description	Justification
$S_1 = h(P_{MCD})$	Compute a hash value of S_1.	This step provides a fixed-length signature of the encoded mobile code daemon.

$S_2 = h(P_{OS})$	Compute a hash value of S_2.	This step provides a fixed-length signature of the encoded operating system.
$S_3 = h(P_H)$	Compute a hash value of S_3.	This step provides a fixed-length signature of the encoded hardware IDs.
$S_4 = KR_{TRH}(S_1)$	TRH uses its private key to encode the mobile code daemon running on H.	Any entity with knowledge of the public key of TRH can decode S_4. This guarantees that TRH sent $h(P_{MCD})$.
$S_5 = KR_{TRH}(S_2)$	TRH uses its private key to encode the operating system of H.	Same as S_4. This guarantees that TRH sent $h(P_{OS})$.
$S_6 = KR_{TRH}(S_3)$	TRH uses its private key to encode the hardware IDs of H.	Same as S_4. This guarantees that TRH sent $h(P_H)$.
$S_7 = h(P_{User})$	Hash the signature of the user's property.	This step provides a fixed-length signature of the user's credentials.
$S_8 = KR_{TRH}(S_7)$	TRH uses its private key to encode the hashed value of the user's identification and security level.	Same as S_4. This guarantees that TRH sent the hashed user credentials.
$S_9 = KU_R(S_4)$	TRH encrypts S_4 using the public key of R.	Only R has the private key, which is needed to decrypt S_4.
$S_{10} = KU_R(S_5)$	TRH encrypts S_5 using the public key of R.	Ibid.
$S_{11} = KU_R(S_6)$	TRH encrypts S_6 using the public key of R.	Ibid.
$S_{12} = KU_R(S_8)$	TRH encrypts S_7 using the public key of R.	Ibid.

(Transmit S_9, S_{10}, S_{11}, and S_{12} to R over an insecure network.)

Code Repository (Remote Host Authentication

Action	Description	Justification
$S_4 = KR_R(S_9)$	R decrypts S_4 using its private key.	The repository R decrypts the remote host signatures from H using its own private key.
$S_5 = KR_R(S_{10})$	R decrypts S_5 using its private key.	Ibid.
$S_6 = KR_R(S_{11})$	R decrypts S_6 using its private key.	Ibid.

$S_8 = KR_R(S_{12})$	R decrypts S_7 using its private key.	Ibid.
Compare(S_4, h($KR_{TRH}(P_{MCD})$))	Compare the hashed encoding of the mobile code daemon created by the TRH to the hashed encoding of the mobile code daemon stored on R.	
Compare(S_5, h($KR_{TRH}(P_{OS})$))	Compare the hashed encoding of the operating system created by the TRH to the hashed encoding of the operating system stored on R.	This verifies to R that the request for a mobile code package came from the remote host H with TRH.
Compare(S_6, h($KR_{TRH}(P_H)$))	Compare the hashed encoding of the hardware ids created by the TRH to the hashed encoding of the hardware ids stored on R.	
UserLevel = Lookup(S_8)	Lookup the user credentials in the user access control list.	Perform user authentication. Map the user's security level to mobile code's ACL to find the appropriate version of the mobile code package to send.
Generate T_4 and T_5 from Section 2 on the repository to construct an encrypted version of the mobile code/data package for verification on the remote host.		
$S_{13} = KU_{TRH}(S_4)$	R encrypts S_4 using the public key of TRH.	Only the TRH has the private key that can decrypt S_4.
$S_{14} = KU_{TRH}(S_5)$	R encrypts S_5 using the public key of TRH.	Ibid.
$S_{15} = KU_{TRH}(S_6)$	R encrypts S_6 using the public key of TRH.	Ibid.

(Transmit S_{13}, S_{14}, S_{15}, T_4, and T_5 to H)

Remote Host (Integrity Check)

Action	Description	Justification
$S_{16} = KR_T(S_{13})$	TRH decrypts S_{13} using its private key.	Ibid.
$S_{17} = KR_T(S_{14})$	TRH decrypts S_{14} using its private key.	Ibid.
$S_{18} = KR_T(S_{15})$	TRH decrypts S_{15} using its private key.	Ibid.

Compare(S_{16}, S_4)	Compare the encoding of the hashed value of the mobile code daemon received from the repository that that computed previously by the TRH.	
Compare(S_{17},S_5)	Compare the encoding of the hashed value of the operating system received from the repository that that computed previously by the TRH.	Ensure that the requesting remote host is identical to the receiving remote host. If so, the TRH passes control of M to H.
Compare(S_{18}, S_6)	Compare the encoding of the hashed value of the hardware IDs received from the repository that that computed previously by the TRH.	
The TRH performs the second stage of the procedure given in Section 2 to validate the mobile code package has not been tampered with.		

Encryption and decryption on the remote host is performed by the tamper-resistant hardware using the public and private keys of the tamper-resistant hardware. The remote host does possess neither a public nor a private key. This adds security. The tamper-resistant hardware can not be modified physically without erasing its keys.

Our framework uses signatures of the remote host state to authenticate the remote host to the repository. Authentication is provided by the host components P_H, P_M, and P_{OS}.

This is predicated on the intractability of the problem of finding two distinct files with the same cryptographic hash value. That is, given a program P and a one-way hash function h(P), it is computationally hard to discover P' such that:

$$P \neq P' \text{ and } h(P) = h(P') \tag{21}$$

Given this fact, we can store a secure database of parameters and their associated hash values. We focus on ensuring remote host system integrity by capturing state information of the mobile code daemon running on the host in P_M as well as operating environment state information in P_{OS}.

A simple scheme for generating P_{OS} for the Windows NT operating system is based on a signature generated from the set of key Windows system files. Table 9.4

lists the set of key Windows system files and their associated CRC-32[1] hash values. Run-time memory scans similar to virus scanning are included as a component of the signature.

A signature for each of these files is generated executing a one-way hash function implemented in the tamper-resistant hardware. The hashed value captures the operating system version and any service packs that may have affected the given file. The set of signatures is then concatenated into a single *meta-signature* (e.g., 4feb14df3899d4e9 ba610d37...4b485c2c), encrypted, and sent to the mobile code repository for comparison to a stored value of the same meta-signature. We are currently analyzing Windows NT™ and Linux in the context of security scenarios to determine the system files and other file system attributes that should be included in the host integrity check. The Linux process file system, /proc, provides useful information about the kernel and current processes currently running on a host.

Table 9.4 Windows NT System Files and CRC-32 Hash Values in Hexadecimal

SYSTEM FILE	CRC-32 VALUE
Services.exe	4feb14df
Winlogon.exe	3899d4e9
Smss.exe	ba610d37
Psxss.exe	e3fa3ea2
Os2ss.exe	a9b4cc9a
Csrss.exe	ac59e7c4
Ntdll.dll	aa1a74f8
Kernel32.dll	126cca3a
User32.dll	34839f81
Gdi32.dll	df50b638
Psxdll.dll	2a30804d
Ntoskrnl.exe	51e53f1e
Hal.dll	dcdcbf7b
Win32k.sys	4b485c2c

4.   MULTI-LEVEL SECURITY

Actual users on remote hosts need to be authenticated as valid system users with known security levels or domains. The security levels of a user and the remote host may determine whether and which version of a mobile code package is executed. The repository must rely on the user identity and remote host signatures P_M, P_{OS}, and/or P_H to ultimately decide on requests for mobile code.

As an example, users may be granted one of four security levels: normal, classified, secret, and top secret. A user is issued a tamperproof smart card with their identity and security level encrypted with KU_R, the public key of the code repository.

---

[1]CRC-32 is not an appropriate hash function in the context of a secure environment. The MD5 and SHA-1 algorithms discussed in Chapter 8 are appropriate. We use CRC-32 as an example only.

Additionally, a remote host may have a given security level that determines the decision and version of a mobile code program appropriate for that host. This information is transmitted to the repository along with host properties as part of the request for a mobile code package. Using this information, the code repository decides which version of a mobile code package to send to the remote host. For each mobile code package, there is a corresponding access control structure that correlates user security level and remote host security level with a mobile code package version. Table 9.5 gives an example.

In this example, version four is the most restricted mobile code package as it grants access privileges only to users with *Top Secret* clearance on *Classified* hosts. On the other hand, version one grants access to any user on an unclassified public access machine. Uses with an *Unclassified* security level are not permitted to run this mobile code program on a *Classified* machines. Our approach to controlling access is based on ACLs associated with each package with more than one level of security control.

The different package versions are separated since it is likely that they will not be stored on the same storage subsystem. In the case of Top Secret security access, it is likely that requests will necessarily go through additional levels of authorization, but this scenario is outside the scope of this paper. Additionally, logging capabilities can be added to this method to track mobile code package requests and usage on a per-user and per-security level basis. Anomalies in request and usage patterns may indicate malicious intent in the mobile network.

Table 9.5. Example of an Access Control Structure for a Mobile Code Program.

SECURITY LEVEL OF USER	SECURITY LEVEL OF REMOTE HOST		
	Unclassified (Public Access)	Unclassified (Restricted Access)	Classified
Unclassified	V_1	V_1	N/A
Secret	V_1	V_2	V_3
Top Secret	V_1	V_2	V_4

5. CONCLUSIONS

We developed a bidirectional trust negotiation method for a mobile computing environment. Our method is bidirectional in the sense that both the mobile code and remote host can be relatively assured of the trustworthiness of the other computational entity. Our method relies on a tamper-resistant hardware mechanism connected to the remote host to perform secure computations. We also rely on the security of public-key encryption and one-way hash functions..

Further research needs to be done in two areas. First, it would be useful to eliminate reliance on tamper-resistant hardware. Mobile cryptography methods may be possible substitutes for a trusted computing base on the remote host. This would likely not affect the use of smart cards for user authentication; the greatest effect would be on platforms such as servers and embedded systems.

It would be useful to improve the granularity of the user authentication process. Currently, we assume a user's security level corresponds to an appropriate version of a mobile code package. However, this can be extended in several different directions. The first direction is to define the security level of a mobile code package based on the remote host and the user in combination. Alternatively, a mobile code package may be decomposed into different sections. For example, a given mobile code program may use different versions of an algorithm for given security context (e.g., classified, secret, top secret).

6.   EXERCISES

Exercise 9.1 Make a diagram expressing the protocols given in this chapter. Analyze the protocols for replay and man-in-the-middle attacks. Suggest improvements to remove any vulnerability that is found.

Exercise 9.2 Consider vulnerabilities to the host verification process. Specifically, consider corruption that does not affect the files on disk. What problems exist for detecting corruption in memory? Are there any current programming features that would have to be disabled?

Exercise 9.3 Discuss the reliance of this approach on tamper-resistant hardware. Consider the attacks from Chapter 8 and discuss vulnerabilities that may exist.

Exercise 9.4 Translate the protocol descriptions in this chapter to the formalisms given in the Chapter 3 discussion of cryptography.

Exercise 9.5 Draft a security architecture combining the approaches in this chapter with the technologies in Chapters 7 and 8.

CHAPTER 10
Designing Peer-to-Peer Systems[1, 2]

Peer-to-peer (P2P) networks are networks where all participants function simultaneously as both client and server. This has led to the term *servents* being used to describe nodes in P2P systems. The two most widely known P2P implementations are Napster and GNUtella. Both were designed to support distributed file sharing. Napster has a single index. In 2001 on connecting to Napster, each user workstation would upload a list of filenames, usually multi-megabyte MP3 music files, it could share. To retrieve a file the user queried Napster's index and received a list of potential offerors. File exchanges occurred between individual nodes distributed at random across the Internet. This is very efficient, but has a single point of failure. A court order stopped the central index and the entire system.

A GNUtella network of n nodes has n indexes. Each node keeps track of the files stored locally. The network has no single point of failure. To stop the GNUtella service, it would be necessary to stop every node running GNUtella on the Internet. This is a desirable survivability property. A global search of the GNUtella network involves flooding the network with search packets. This is an inefficient approach and scales poorly.

We consider Napster and GNUtella extremes of a range of possible P2P designs. GNUtella illustrates the desirability of this approach for implementing a survivable infrastructure. The decentralized nature of the network provides an excellent framework for adaptation to disruptions, like those caused by a packet flooding Distributed Denial of Service (DDoS) attack. Especially if the system can use mobile code to dynamically change the roles of individual nodes at runtime.

Each node in a P2P system has a large degree of autonomy. Nodes join and leave the infrastructure of their own volition. There is little, if any, centralized control. The exact topology of the system can never be known with certainty. This makes analysis of these networks challenging. And the lack of convincing analysis makes the rational design of P2P networks difficult.

We will use random graph formalisms to analyze P2P systems. This approach can also be used for others whose exact structure is never known. This is true for

[1] Coauthored with Amit Kapur, Dr. N. Gautam, and Dr. S. Rai.
[2] Portions of this chapter are reprinted, with permission, from:
A. Kapur, N. Gautam, R. R. Brooks, and S. Rai, "Design, performance and dependability of a peer-to-peer network supporting QoS for mobile code applications," *Proceedings of the 10th International Conference on Telecommunications Systems*, pp. 395-419, Sept. 2002.

large-scale networks, like the Internet. It is also true for other classes of systems, like mobile *ad hoc* networks, whose structure is undefined by definition. All that is needed is a reasonably good statistical definition of the system structure. Given the ability to predict network behavior based on the statistical properties of individual nodes, it becomes possible to derive the statistics needed for the nodes to produce globally desirable behaviors. It is our hypothesis, which we have yet to prove, that this type of flexible structure can be designed to have very desirable survivability characteristics.

This chapter presents design principles for peer-to-peer networks. First we present background on graph theory and random graphs. The random graph discussion includes the presentation of stochastic connectivity matrices for predicting the behavior of systems designed using random graphs. We then discuss how to estimate the expected number of hops between nodes in the network. This information is used to derive

- The dependability of P2P networks
- The Quality of Service of P2P networks
- The number of indexes needed to attain the optimal Quality of Service by the P2P system

1. GRAPH THEORY BACKGROUND

A graph is traditionally defined as the tuple [V, E]. V is a set of vertices, and E is a set of edges. Each edge e is defined as (i, j) where i and j designate the two vertices connected by e. In this paper, we consider only undirected graphs where $(i, j) = (j, i)$. (Many systems are modeled using directed graphs (di-graphs) where $(i, j) \neq (j, i)$.) An edge (i, j) is incident on the vertices i and j. We do not consider multi-graphs where multiple edges can connect the same end-points. We use the terms *vertex* and *node* interchangeably. *Edge* and *link* are also used synonymously.

Many data structures have been used as practical representations of graphs. Common representations and their uses can be found in [Aho 1974]. For example, a graph where each node has at least one incident edge can be fully represented by the list of edges. Another common representation of a graph, which we explore in more depth, is the connectivity matrix. The connectivity matrix M is a square matrix where each element $m(i, j)$ is 1 (0) if there is (not) an edge connecting vertices i and j. For undirected graphs this matrix is symmetric. Figure 10.1 shows a simple graph and its connectivity matrix.

A *walk* of length z is a set of edges, which can be expressed as an ordered list of z edges $((i_0, j_0), (i_1, j_1), \ldots, (i_z j_z))$, where each vertex j_a is the same as vertex i_{a+1}. A *path* of length z is a walk where all i_a are unique. If j_z is the same as i_0, the path forms a *cycle*. As a matter of convention, the diagonal of the matrix can consist of either zeros or ones. Ones are frequently used based on the simple assertion that each vertex is connected to itself. We use a convention where the diagonal is filled with zeros, since the diagonal indicates a cycle in the graph. Cycles are not relevant to most of the characteristics we consider.

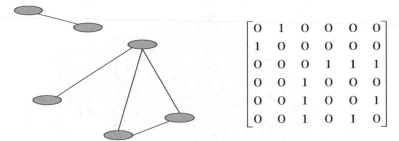

$$\begin{bmatrix} 0 & 1 & 0 & 0 & 0 & 0 \\ 1 & 0 & 0 & 0 & 0 & 0 \\ 0 & 0 & 0 & 1 & 1 & 1 \\ 0 & 0 & 1 & 0 & 0 & 0 \\ 0 & 0 & 1 & 0 & 0 & 1 \\ 0 & 0 & 1 & 0 & 1 & 0 \end{bmatrix}$$

Figure 10.1. On the left is a graph of six nodes. On the right is its associated connectivity matrix. Row j of the matrix corresponds to the jth node from the top.

A connected component is a set of vertices such that from any vertex in the component there is a path to all other vertices in the component. (In the case of digraphs, this would be a fully connected component.) A complete graph has an edge directly connecting any two vertices in the graph. A complete subgraph is a subset of vertices in the graph with edges directly connecting any two members of the set.

An interesting property of connectivity matrices we use is the fact that element $m^z(i,j)$ of the power z of graph G's connectivity matrix M (i.e., M^z) is the number of walks of length z from vertex i to vertex j that exist on G [Cvetovic 1979]. This can be verified using the definition of matrix multiplication and the definition of the connectivity matrix. Iterative computation of M^z until $M^z = M^{z-1}$ can be used to find the connected components in a graph.

2.   RANDOM GRAPH BACKGROUND

We are interested in P2P networks primarily because of what they lack: central control and single points of failure. Since nodes join and leave the network with no central organization, random network models are appropriate for studying the topology of P2P systems. In fact since the Internet itself grows with minimal centralized coordination, random graph formalisms also model many aspects of the Internet. We consider four random graph models, some of which are due to advances in statistical physics [Albert 2001] and sociology [Watts 1999].

A.   ERDÖS-RÉNYI

The first model is the traditional Erdös-Rényi random graph [Bollobás 2001]. As we described in Chapter 5, these graphs are defined by the number of nodes n and a uniform probability p of an edge existing between any two nodes. To construct a probabilistic connectivity matrix for this graph, create an n-by-n matrix with all elements on the diagonal set to 0 and all the other elements set to p. If n is 3 and p is 0.25, we get

$$\begin{bmatrix} 0 & 0.25 & 0.25 \\ 0.25 & 0 & 0.25 \\ 0.25 & 0.25 & 0 \end{bmatrix} \tag{22}$$

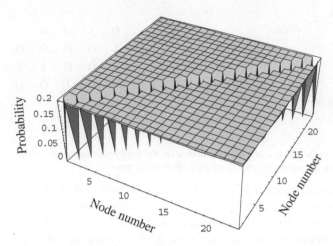

Figure 10.2. A three-dimensional plot of the probabilistic connectivity matrix for Erdös-Rényi graphs with n=23 and p=0.2. The diagonal values are zero. All other edges have the same probability.

B. SMALL WORLD

Next we consider small world graphs from [Watts 1999]. As we noted in Chapter 5, small world graphs have two main characteristics: (*i*) the expected value for the number of hops between any two nodes is small (approaches the expected number of hops for Erdös-Rényi graphs), and (*ii*) a significant amount of clustering among the nodes. As example small world graphs, we use the *connected caveman model* from [Watts 1999]. [Watts 1999] also explores other methods for creating examples of small world graphs. Our approach would also be applicable to those cases.

A connectivity matrix for a small world graph is constructed by following essentially the same algorithm used to create a graph instance. For the connected caveman model that we use as an example small world graph (defined by n the number of nodes, c size of the fully connected components, and e number of rewired edges)

- Create an n-by-n matrix
- To reflect the fully connected components of size c, populate the diagonal of the matrix with c-by-c blocks of value one. If n is not a multiple of c, the last block will not be c by c. It will be n mod c by n mod c. This gives us a block diagonal matrix.
- Set diagonal values to zero.
- Connect the fully connected components. Do the following for all blocks: Block starting address is j and last address $k = j + c$. Set elements (k-1, k) and (k, k-1) to zero. Set elements (k+1,k) and (k, k+1) to zero. Set element (n-1, n) and (n, n-1) to zero, and (1,n) and (n, 1) to one.
- Count all the zeroes and ones in the matrix excluding the diagonal. The probability of gaining a connection by the rewiring step becomes

$2e/$(number of zeroes). The probability of losing a connection by the rewiring step becomes $2e/$(number of ones).

- For all elements of the matrix except diagonals (which remains zero), if the element is one (zero) subtract (add) the probability of losing (gaining) a connection.

The resulting matrix expresses the probabilities of edges existing in the connected caveman model. For other examples, similar algorithms can easily be constructed. For our example, the matrix for ($n=6$, $c=3$, $e=1$) is

$$
\begin{bmatrix}
0 & 5/6 & 5/6 & 1/9 & 1/9 & 5/6 \\
5/6 & 0 & 1/9 & 1/9 & 1/9 & 1/9 \\
5/6 & 1/9 & 0 & 5/6 & 1/9 & 1/9 \\
1/9 & 1/9 & 5/6 & 0 & 5/6 & 5/6 \\
1/9 & 1/9 & 1/9 & 5/6 & 0 & 1/9 \\
5/6 & 1/9 & 1/9 & 5/6 & 1/9 & 0
\end{bmatrix}
\tag{23}
$$

It is possible to change step 4 of the small world probabilistic connectivity matrix generation procedure to choose block elements at random. It is worthwhile describing how this is done. Among other things, all nodes in the matrix created in this manner have probabilities that are permutations of each other. Perform the procedure above except step 4. At the end of the procedure, modify the matrix as follows

- All edges connecting components in the cluster have the same probability of being chosen $1/[c\,(c-1)]$.
- This value is subtracted from all nondiagonal elements in the block representing the cluster on the diagonal.
- Each node in the current cluster has the same probability of being selected $(1/c)$ for connection to the next cluster. Each node in the next cluster also is equally likely $(1/c)$ to receive an edge.
- To represent this, each element potentially connecting the two clusters has a probability of $1/c2$ added to it.

Note that when n is not zero modulo c, the block size of the final subgraph is not c but rather n modulo c. The values given above then become $1/[c'\,(c'-1)]$ and $1/(c'\,c)$, where $c' = n$ modulo c. Notice that since each row is a permutation of the same probabilities, both this graph description and the Erdös-Rényi graph description are regular. The regular matrix description for ($n=6$, $c=3$, $e=1$) is

$$
\begin{bmatrix}
0 & \frac{2}{3} & \frac{2}{3} & \frac{2}{9} & \frac{2}{9} & \frac{2}{9} \\
\frac{2}{3} & 0 & \frac{2}{3} & \frac{2}{9} & \frac{2}{9} & \frac{2}{9} \\
\frac{2}{3} & \frac{2}{3} & 0 & \frac{2}{9} & \frac{2}{9} & \frac{2}{9} \\
\frac{2}{9} & \frac{2}{9} & \frac{2}{9} & 0 & \frac{2}{3} & \frac{2}{3} \\
\frac{2}{9} & \frac{2}{9} & \frac{2}{9} & \frac{2}{3} & 0 & \frac{2}{3} \\
\frac{2}{9} & \frac{2}{9} & \frac{2}{9} & \frac{2}{3} & \frac{2}{3} & 0
\end{bmatrix}
\tag{24}
$$

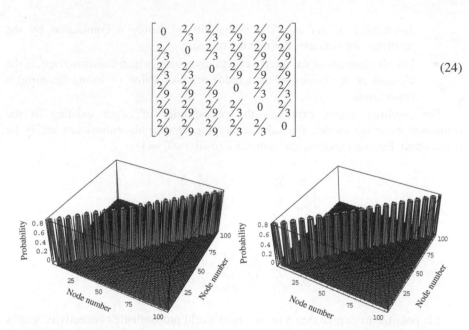

Figure 10.3. Three-dimensional plot of matrices for connected caveman model with $n=103$, $c=5$, and $e=22$. Left: first method given. Right: regular matrix. Note how clear the clustering is and how low the probability of other connections is.

C. CELL PHONE GRIDS

As discussed in Chapter 5, percolation theory studies flow through random media. We use percolation theory concepts to study the coordination of peer-to-peer systems in networks with a very regular infrastructure. This model requires three parameters: x the number of nodes in a row, y the number of nodes in a column, and p the probability of an edge being occupied. Note that n, the total number of nodes, is equal to $x\,y$. The matrix construction method is only valid for finite problems. Once the matrix has been constructed, however, scaling analysis can be performed to consider infinite ranges. Figure 5.7 shows an example graph.

Excluding edge effects in this tessellation, each node (i, j) has four immediate neighbors: $(i+1, j)$, $(i, j+1)$, $(i-1, j)$, and $(i, j-1)$. Each vertex is assigned the unique row position $(i + (j-1)\,y)$ in the connectivity matrix. (This assumes that i (j) ranges from 0 to x (y) and makes the matrix row major. Readers that are dogmatic about C or FORTRAN can change these conventions at will [Press 1992].) Vertices outside the range ($[1..x, 1..y]$) are ignored, since they are out of bounds. In the connectivity matrix all positions are set to 0, except that for each node (i, j) the positions in its row $(i + (j-1)\,y)$ that correspond to its neighbors:

$$
i\text{-}1 + (j\text{-}1)\,y \qquad i\text{+}1 + (j\text{-}1)\,y \qquad i + (j\text{-}2)\,y \qquad i\text{-}1 + (j)\,y \tag{25}
$$

are set to p. The matrix corresponding to a 3-by-3 grid with probability of 0.75 is

$$\begin{bmatrix} 0 & 0.75 & 0 & 0.75 & 0 & 0 & 0 & 0 & 0 \\ 0.75 & 0 & 0.75 & 0 & 0.75 & 0 & 0 & 0 & 0 \\ 0 & 0.75 & 0 & 0 & 0 & 0.75 & 0 & 0 & 0 \\ 0.75 & 0 & 0 & 0 & 0.75 & 0 & 0.75 & 0 & 0 \\ 0 & 0.75 & 0 & 0.75 & 0 & 0.75 & 0 & 0.75 & 0 \\ 0 & 0 & 0.75 & 0 & 0.75 & 0 & 0 & 0 & 0.75 \\ 0 & 0 & 0 & 0.75 & 0 & 0 & 0 & 0.75 & 0 \\ 0 & 0 & 0 & 0 & 0.75 & 0 & 0.75 & 0 & 0.75 \\ 0 & 0 & 0 & 0 & 0 & 0.75 & 0 & 0.75 & 0 \end{bmatrix} \quad (26)$$

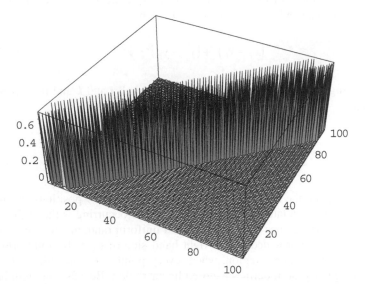

Figure 10.4. Three-dimensional plot of the connectivity matrix for a 10-by-10 grid with n=0.75. It is a band-diagonal matrix.

D. *AD HOC*

Ad hoc wireless networks, which have no fixed infrastructure, are suited to analysis as a type of random graph. In [Krishnamachari 2001] the model used places nodes at random in a limited two-dimensional region. Two uniform random variables provide a node's x and y coordinates. Two nodes in proximity to each other have a very high probability of being able to communicate. We use the model from [Krishnamachari 2001], except that they create an edge with probability one when the distance between two nodes is less than the threshold value. We will allow the probability to be set to any value in the range [0..1].

We construct range limited graphs from the following parameters:

- n – The number of nodes
- *max_x (max_y)* – The size of the region in the x (y) direction

- r – The maximum distance between nodes where connections are possible
- p – Probability that an edge exists connecting two nodes within the range

Construction of range limited random graphs proceeds in two steps: (*i*) sort the nodes by either their x (or possibly y) coordinate and use order statistics to find the expected values of that coordinate, and (*ii*) determine probabilities for edges existing between nodes based on these expected values.

To construct the connectivity matrix for range limited graphs, we consider the position of each node as a point defined by two random variables: the x and y location. Without loss of generality, we use normalized values for the x, y, and r variables limiting their range to [0..1]. To calculate probabilities, we sort each point by its x variable. For the n nodes, rank statistics provide expected value $j/(n+1)$ for the node in position j in the sorted list. Using Euclidean distance, an edge exists between two nodes j and k with probability p when

$$\left(x_j - x_k\right)^2 + \left(y_j - y_k\right)^2 \le r^2 \tag{27}$$

By entering the expected values for nodes of rank j and k and reordering terms, this becomes

$$\left(y_j - y_k\right)^2 \le r^2 - \left(\frac{j}{n+1} - \frac{k}{n+1}\right)^2 \tag{28}$$

We assume that the random variables giving the x and y positions are uniformly distributed and uncorrelated. The probability of this occurring is the probability that the square of the difference of two normalized uniform random variables is less than the constant value c provided by the right hand side of (28). Two uniform random variables describe a square region, where every point is equally likely. Expression (28) is an inequality, so it defines a closed linear region. Because the right hand side is squared, two symmetric regions are excluded from the probability. The limiting points are when y_j or y_k are equal to the constant on the left hand side of (28). Algebraic manipulation provides the equation $2c-c^2$ for the probability of (28) occurring. An example matrix for six nodes in a unit square with $r=0.3$ and $p=1.0$ is:

$$\begin{bmatrix} 0 & 0.134 & 0.0167 & 0 & 0 & 0 \\ 0.134 & 0 & 0.134 & 0.0167 & 0 & 0 \\ 0.0167 & 0.134 & 0 & 0.134 & 0.0167 & 0 \\ 0 & 0.0167 & 0.134 & 0 & 0.134 & 0.0167 \\ 0 & 0 & 0.0167 & 0.134 & 0 & 0.134 \\ 0 & 0 & 0 & 0.0167 & 0.134 & 0 \end{bmatrix} \tag{29}$$

Figure 10.5 shows a three-dimensional plot of an example matrix. The approximation is achieved by this approach is good, but far from perfect.

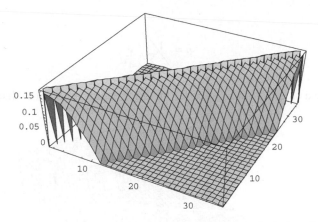

Figure 10.5. Three-dimensional plot of the connectivity matrix for a range limited graph of 35 nodes with range of 0.3.

E. SCALE-FREE

The final model we consider is the scale-free model. As described in Chapter 5, the node degree distribution varies as an inverse power law (i.e., $P[d] \propto d^{\gamma}$). These graphs are called scale-free because the power law structure implies that nodes exist with nonzero probability at all possible scales. Scale-free graphs are defined by two parameters: number of nodes n and scaling factor γ.

An algorithm for constructing these graphs based on positive feedback that produces graphs with $\gamma \approx 3$ can be found in [Barabási 1999]. Barabási's use of positive feedback plausibly explains how SF systems emerge and why they are widespread. Another algorithm for producing scale-free graphs with arbitrary scaling factors is in [Volchenkov 2002]. This later algorithm does not explicitly contain positive feedback. We present a method for constructing scale-free networks that uses positive feedback to produce graphs with arbitrary scaling factors. Utilizing the mechanism believed responsible for creating scale-free networks has two advantages: (*i*) it may produce graphs closer to those found in reality, and (*ii*) it helps explain how scale-free systems work.

Creating a probabilistic connectivity matrix for scale-free graphs is more challenging. Remember that scale-free graphs are characterized by n the number of nodes and γ the scaling factor. The first step is to compute a probability distribution for node degree d. Remember $P[d] \propto d^{-\gamma}$. We compute the probability distribution, by finding a constant factor so that all probabilities sum to 1. Set

$$P[d] = bd^{-\gamma} \tag{30}$$

Since node degree ranges from 1 to n-1

$$1 = \sum_{d=1}^{n-1} bd^{-\gamma} \tag{31}$$

thus

$$b = 1 \Big/ \sum_{d=1}^{n-1} d^{-\gamma} \qquad (32)$$

We now have a closed form solution for the node degree probability distribution.

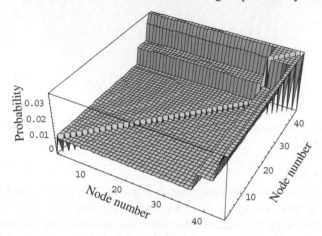

Figure 10.6. Three-dimensional plot of the connectivity matrix for a scale-free graph with $n=45$ and $\gamma=3.0$. Note the zero diagonal and the high probability of connections to the hub nodes. Connections between hub nodes are virtually assured. Connections between nonhub nodes are very improbable.

The next step is determining how many edges are incident on each node. First construct a vector v of n-1 elements, whose values range from 0 to 1. Each element k of the vector contains the value

$$v[k] = \sum_{d=1}^{k-1} b d^{-\gamma} \qquad (33)$$

Vector element $v[0]$ has the value zero and element $v[n-1]$ has the value one. Each element represents the probability of a node of degree less than or equal to k existing.

Each row of the probabilistic connectivity matrix represents the expected behavior of $1/n^{th}$ of the nodes of the class under consideration. We now construct a vector v' of n elements, the value of $v'[k]$ states how many edges are incident on node k. Set $v'[k]$ to the index of the largest element of v whose value is less than or equal to k/n. [1]

---

[1] It is possible to use the mean, or a weighted average of the index values that point to elements in the range $(k-1)/n$ to k/n. Since equation 8 can give values greater than one, constraining matrix element values to the range $[0..1]$ flattens the degree distribution. Using the maximum index value counteracts this tendency.

The elements of the connectivity matrix are probabilities of connections between individual nodes. These values are computed using the insight from [Barabási 1999] that scale-free networks result from positive feedback. Nodes are more likely to connect to other nodes with many connections. The value of each matrix element (k, i) is therefore

$$P[k,i] = \frac{v'[i]v'[k]}{\sum\limits_{m \neq k} v'[m]}$$ (34)

The likelihood of choosing another node i to receive a given edge from the current node k is the degree of i divided by the sum of the degrees of all nodes except k. Summing these factors would give a total probability of one for the row. Since k has degree $v'[k]$ these probabilities are multiplied by $v'[k]$, so that the total of the probabilities for the row is k. This finishes the derivation of Equation (34).

To construct the matrix, we modify the values given by Equation (34) in two ways. Since the node degrees have an exponential distribution, the values of the bottom rows are often much larger than the other degrees. The result of (34) for values of k and l close to n can be greater than one. To avoid having elements of the matrix with values greater than one (i.e., probability greater than one), we compute the matrix elements in a double loop starting with k (outer loop) and i (inner loop) set to n-1. The values of k and i are decremented from n-1 to zero. If the value of equation (34) is greater than one then the corresponding element is set to one and the value copied from $v'[k]$ for computing row k is decremented by one. This keeps all matrix elements in the range zero to one, so that they represent probabilities.

The other modification of element values that deviates from (34) forces the matrix to be symmetric. When computing a row k and $k < n$-1, all elements for $i > k$ are set to be the same as the values computed for element (i, k). If the value of element (i, k) is one, the value copied from $v'[k]$ is again decremented. In some cases this may force the sum of row k to deviate from $v'[k]$. If the deviation is significant enough, the resulting connectivity matrix may only have a degree distribution that approximates the scaling factor γ. An example connectivity matrix for n=10 and γ=2.0 is

$$
\begin{bmatrix}
0 & \frac{1}{22} & \frac{1}{22} & \frac{1}{22} & \frac{1}{22} & \frac{1}{22} & \frac{1}{10} & \frac{1}{10} & \frac{2}{9} & \frac{9}{10} \\
\frac{1}{22} & 0 & \frac{1}{22} & \frac{1}{22} & \frac{1}{22} & \frac{1}{22} & \frac{1}{10} & \frac{1}{10} & \frac{2}{9} & \frac{9}{10} \\
\frac{1}{22} & \frac{1}{22} & 0 & \frac{1}{22} & \frac{1}{22} & \frac{1}{22} & \frac{1}{10} & \frac{1}{10} & \frac{2}{9} & \frac{9}{10} \\
\frac{1}{22} & \frac{1}{22} & \frac{1}{22} & 0 & \frac{1}{22} & \frac{1}{22} & \frac{1}{10} & \frac{1}{10} & \frac{2}{9} & \frac{9}{10} \\
\frac{1}{22} & \frac{1}{22} & \frac{1}{22} & \frac{1}{22} & 0 & \frac{1}{22} & \frac{1}{10} & \frac{1}{10} & \frac{2}{9} & \frac{9}{10} \\
\frac{1}{22} & \frac{1}{22} & \frac{1}{22} & \frac{1}{22} & \frac{1}{22} & 0 & \frac{1}{10} & \frac{1}{10} & \frac{2}{9} & \frac{9}{10} \\
\frac{1}{10} & \frac{1}{10} & \frac{1}{10} & \frac{1}{10} & \frac{1}{10} & \frac{1}{10} & 0 & \frac{1}{5} & \frac{4}{9} & 1 \\
\frac{1}{10} & \frac{1}{10} & \frac{1}{10} & \frac{1}{10} & \frac{1}{10} & \frac{1}{10} & \frac{1}{5} & 0 & \frac{4}{9} & 1 \\
\frac{2}{9} & \frac{2}{9} & \frac{2}{9} & \frac{2}{9} & \frac{2}{9} & \frac{2}{9} & \frac{4}{9} & \frac{4}{9} & 0 & 1 \\
\frac{9}{10} & \frac{9}{10} & \frac{9}{10} & \frac{9}{10} & \frac{9}{10} & \frac{9}{10} & 1 & 1 & 1 & 0
\end{bmatrix}
\tag{35}
$$

3. NUMBER OF HOPS BETWEEN NODES

An important issue in all the network attributes we consider is the expected number (and variance) of hops between nodes in the network. First we provide background on approximations for estimating the average number of hops and their variance. This includes defining important variables. We then describe two methods for estimating the expected number of hops in random graphs. An experimental approach is given first, followed by an approach based on graph theory and linear algebra.

The variable q_h represents the expected number of nodes that can be reached in h hops from a node, and z_h represents the expected number of nodes *first* reachable with exactly h hops from any node. The symmetry of Erdös-Rényi graphs forces the expected value of q_h (z_h) to be the same for every node in the graph. For scale-free and small world graphs, we consider average values. A derivation using generating functions in [Newmann 2001] indicates that q_h can be approximated using the average number of nodes one hop (q_1) and two hops (q_2) away. The estimate from [Newmann 2001] using our notation is

$$
q_h = \left(\frac{q2}{q1} \right)^{h-1} * q_1
\tag{36}
$$

Further analysis uses the *clustering coefficient* C to express the cliquishness of the network ($C = 1$ for a complete graph, $C = 0$ for a tree). C can be visualized as the probability of a node being part of a triangle in an Erdös-Rényi graph. In [Watts 1999], clustering coefficient is defined as the average of the number of edges between nodes in the subgraph of nodes immediately adjacent to a given node divided by the total number of edges possible given the degrees of the nodes. This definition has been deprecated [Watts 2001] in favor of these new definitions from [Newmann 2001a]:

C = 3 * (Number of triangles in network) / (Number of connected triples of vertices)

$$(37)$$

C = 6 * (Number of triangles in network) / (Number of paths of length two)   (38)

The deprecated and new definitions are equivalent, except the new definition computes the ratio over the entire graph instead of at each node. This provides a more stable result.

To estimate q_2, [Newmann 2001a] introduces a mutuality factor M. It is the mean number of paths of length two leading to nodes first reached in two hops. Mutuality M provides the density of "squares" as opposed to the clustering coefficient C referring to the "fraction of transitive triples" (triangles) in the network. M accounts for the overcount of nodes two hops away relying solely on C. Mathematically,

$$M = \frac{\text{mean number of vertices two steps away}}{\text{mean paths of length two to those vertices}} \quad (39)$$

An analytical estimator for M in terms of C making independence assumptions is:

$$M = \frac{average\left[\dfrac{k}{1+C^2(k\text{-}1)}\right]}{k_{ave}} \quad (40)$$

[Newman 2001a] derives the following best estimator of q_2, where the summation is over all degree values and p_k is the probability of a node having that degree:

$$q_2 = M(1-C)\sum_k (k^2-k)p_k \quad (41)$$

A. EMPIRICAL ESTIMATE

We developed a new algorithm for computing C. Here we define A as the connectivity matrix of a network where each element a_{ij} of A is 1 if an arc exists between i and j, and 0 otherwise. The algorithm is based on the fact that each element a_{ij} of a graph's connectivity matrix raised to the power k contains the number of walks of length k from i to j. The connectivity matrix A is squared giving matrix A^2. We compute two sums: all nondiagonal elements of A^2 and nondiagonal elements of A^2 where the corresponding element of A is nonzero. The second sum is the numerator and the first sum is the denominator of the cluster coefficient C. The results are identical to the approaches in [Newmann 2001a, Albert 2001]. We find this approach easier to understand and implement.

We extend the concept of Newman's mutuality factor M beyond two hops, making it a vector $M[h]$ where h is the number of hops. In this new notation, the original factor M becomes $M[2]$. To illustrate the influence of this parameter, Figure

10.7 shows representative values of $M[h]$ for the random graph classes. Note that overcounts are important for values of h greater than 2. Also, note the tight error bars. Variance increases significantly after the peak, since the number of nodes first reachable with this number of hops drops off steeply making the sample size smaller.

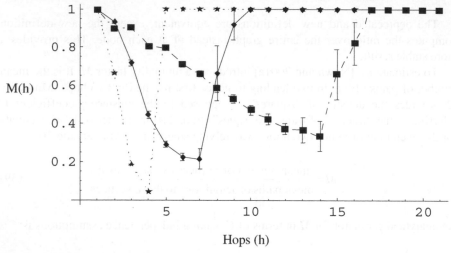

Figure 10.7. $M[h]$ for random graph classes. All statistics are from graphs of 100 nodes and average node degree of 4. Sample size was 35. In order of peaks from left to right, we have scale-free, Erdös-Rényi, and small world graphs.

We extend these results in the literature to derive an estimate of the number of nodes reachable after exactly h hops. The average number of nodes reachable after one hop is by definition k_{ave}. For the second hop, every node reached by one hop has $(k_{ave} - 1)$ degrees free. [Newmann 2001a] improves this estimate by summing over all values of k weighted by their probability. On the average, C of the nodes attached to the $k_{ave}*(k_{ave} - 1)$ degrees were already reached by one hop. This follows from the definition of C. This leaves $(1-C)$ percent available for connecting to new nodes. Using this logic we get the following recursion equations:

$$q_h = (k_{ave}-1)\, q_{h-1}\, (1-C) * M[h] \tag{42}$$

$$\text{stopping criteria, } q_1 = k_{ave} \tag{43}$$

Giving for $h > 1$,

$$q_h = (1-C)^{h-1} (k_{ave}-1)^{h-1} k_{ave} \prod_{i=2}^{h} M[i] \tag{44}$$

A more accurate estimate takes into account the greater likelihood of connecting to a node with a higher degree [Newmann 2001a] ($h > 1$, for $h = 1$ it is unchanged, $p(i)$ is the probability of a node with degree i):

$$q_h = (1-C)^{h-1} \left(\prod_{i=2}^{h} M[i] \right) \sum_{i=1}^{n-1} i(i-1)^{h-1} \, p_i \tag{45}$$

Figure 10.8 shows how well this estimate works compared to actual results and the generating function estimate. For Erdös-Rényi and scale-free graphs this estimator is closer to the actual than the generating function approach. The nonrandom portion of small world graphs is problematic. The middle line is the set of actual values, with error bars. The top line is the generating function estimate. The bottom line is the estimator derived here. The estimators used the fact that $n = 100$.

The expected number of hops between any two nodes chosen at random can now be estimated as:

$$\mu_{hops} = \left(\frac{q_1 + 2(q_2-q_1) + 3(q_3-q_2) + \dots}{n} \right) \tag{46}$$

$$\mu_{hops} = \frac{1}{n} \left[k_{ave} + 2 \left((1-C)M[2] \left(\sum_{i=2}^{n-1} p_i i(i-1) \right) - k_{ave} \right) + \right.$$

$$\sum_{h=3}^{Maxhops} h \left(\left((1-C)^{h-1} \left(\prod_{i=2}^{h} M[i] \right) \sum_{i=2}^{n-1} p_i i(i-1) \right)^{h-1} \right.$$

$$\left. \left. - \left((1-C)^{h-2} \left(\prod_{i=2}^{h-1} M[i] \right) \sum_{i=2}^{n-1} p_i i(i-1) \right)^{h-2} \right) \right]$$

Given the mean (μ_{hops}) and the distribution of the hop count, the standard deviation can be computed using the following formula:

$$\sigma_{hops} = \sqrt{ \frac{\sum_{i=1}^{n} \sum_{j=1}^{n} \left(h_{ij} - \mu_{hops} \right)^2}{n^2 - 1} } \tag{47}$$

where, h_{ij} is the number of hops from node i to node j and n is the number of nodes in the network.

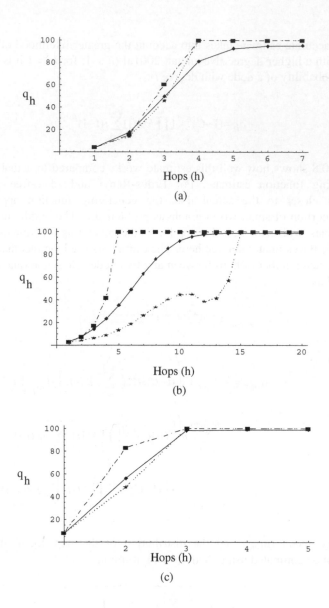

Figure 10.8. Estimates for the 3 networks. (a) Estimate for Erdös-Rényi. (b) Estimate for small world. (c) Estimate for scale-free. Same parameters as for Figure 10.7.

Table 10.1 compares analytical and Matlab simulation results for the mean and standard deviation of number of hops for 3 networks: Erdös-Rényi graph, small world, and scale-free. The number of nodes and average arc degree for the 3 networks were: Erdös-Rényi graph, 25 nodes and 3 average arc degree; small world, 25 nodes and 4.4 average arc degree; and scale-free, 25 nodes and 5.28 average arc degree. Ten different networks were created for each of the 3 types with the same above-mentioned topology. In Matlab the hop distribution was computed using

Dijkstra's shortest path algorithm. It shows that the analytical and simulation results for mean and standard deviation of hops are quite close, hence validating our analytical model.

Table 10.1. Comparison of *Mean* and *Standard Deviation* for Three Networks

	Simulation		Analytical	
	Mean	*Std. Dev.*	*Mean*	*Std. Dev.*
Erdös-Rényi graph	2.7307	1.2985	2.7478	1.3409
Small world	2.5543	1.2044	2.58	1.296
Scale-free	1.9091	0.7518	1.904	0.747

B. ANALYTICAL ESTIMATE

Recall that each element (j,k) of the random connectivity matrix is a probability and constrained to values between zero and one. It represents the likelihood of an edge existing between nodes j and k. The product of two probabilities values gives the likelihood of their two associated events occurring together when independence is assumed. So the likelihood of edges existing simultaneously from node j to node k and node k to node l, is (j,k) (k,l). This assumes that the events are independent. Throughout this paper we make this explicit assumption with no loss of generality. As we have shown in constructing the matrices for scale-free and small world graphs, we can construct probability matrices where the values of the probabilities explicitly state the influence of statistical dependencies.

Now consider the likelihood of a path of length two existing between nodes j and l. This can be calculated by summing the values of (j,k) (k,l) for all possible intermediate nodes:

$$\sum_{k=1}^{n}(j,k)(k,l) \tag{48}$$

Note that this is the equation used in matrix multiplication to calculate element (j,l) of M_1M_2 by multiplying row j of M_1 by column l of M_2. At this point, it is important to consider computation of this value. Remember that values used are probabilities (with an assumption of independence and the results need to be probabilities as well. Numerically the probability of either of two independent events j and k occurring is $P_j + P_k - P_jP_k$. The probability of three events j, k, and l occurring can be computed recursively as $P_l + (P_j + P_k - P_jP_k) - P_l(P_j + P_k - P_jP_k)$. As the number of events increases the number of factors involved increases, making this computation awkward for large matrices. An equivalent computation to (48) is

$$1 - \prod_{k=1}^{n}\left(1 - P_{jk}P_{kl}\right) \tag{49}$$

Equation (16) is easier to compute and suggested for use in all matrix multiplications discussed in the application sections.

As a matter of convention, the diagonal values (P_{jj}) of connectivity matrices can be set either to one or zero. Frequently they are set to one, signaling implicitly that each graph vertex is connected with itself. This is often reasonable. For our applications, we generally have found the diagonal value of zero more appropriate. The applications we will discuss concern the likelihood of paths existing between nodes. The value P_{jj} expresses the probability of a path connecting node j with itself. The existence of a loop within the graph should not increase the probability that two nodes in the graph are connected. Constraining the diagonal values to the value zero discounts the influence of loops in our calculations. For some random graph classes, like scale-free graphs, it is advisable to add a post-processing step to multiplication where each element (j,k) is set to the maximum of (j,k) and (k,j) to guarantee that the matrix remains symmetric.

Theorem. Element (j,k) of M^z is the probability of a walk of length z existing between nodes j and k.

Proof. The proof is by induction. By definition, each element (j,k) is the probability of an edge existing between nodes j and k. M^2 is the result of multiplying matrix M with itself. Equation (49) is used to calculate each element (j,k) since all values are probabilities. This calculates the probability of a path of length two existing between nodes j and k by exhaustively enumerating the likelihood of the path passing through each intermediate node in the graph. Using the same logic, M^z can be calculated from M^{z-1} using matrix multiplication to consider all possible intermediate nodes between nodes j and l. Where M^{z-1} has the probabilities of a walk of length $z-1$ between j and k, and M has the values defined previously.

Example 1. Probabilities of walks of length three in an Erdös-Rényi graph of four nodes for $p=0.6$ and 0.65:

$$M = \begin{bmatrix} 0 & 0.65 & 0.65 & 0.65 \\ 0.65 & 0 & 0.65 & 0.65 \\ 0.65 & 0.65 & 0 & 0.65 \\ 0.65 & 0.65 & 0.65 & 0 \end{bmatrix} \quad M^2 = \begin{bmatrix} 0 & 0.666 & 0.666 & 0.666 \\ 0.666 & 0 & 0.666 & 0.666 \\ 0.666 & 0.666 & 0 & 0.666 \\ 0.666 & 0.666 & 0.666 & 0 \end{bmatrix}$$

$$M^3 = \begin{bmatrix} 0 & 0.679 & 0.679 & 0.679 \\ 0.679 & 0 & 0.679 & 0.679 \\ 0.679 & 0.679 & 0 & 0.679 \\ 0.679 & 0.679 & 0.679 & 0 \end{bmatrix}$$

$$M = \begin{bmatrix} 0 & 0.6 & 0.6 & 0.6 \\ 0.6 & 0 & 0.6 & 0.6 \\ 0.6 & 0.6 & 0 & 0.6 \\ 0.6 & 0.6 & 0.6 & 0 \end{bmatrix} \quad M^2 = \begin{bmatrix} 0 & 0.59 & 0.59 & 0.59 \\ 0.59 & 0 & 0.59 & 0.59 \\ 0.59 & 0.59 & 0 & 0.59 \\ 0.59 & 0.59 & 0.59 & 0 \end{bmatrix}$$

$$M^3 = \begin{bmatrix} 0 & 0.583 & 0.583 & 0.583 \\ 0.583 & 0 & 0.583 & 0.583 \\ 0.583 & 0.583 & 0 & 0.583 \\ 0.583 & 0.583 & 0.583 & 0 \end{bmatrix} \tag{50}$$

4. DEPENDABILITY OF PEER-TO-PEER SYSTEMS

Given the expected number of hops in terms of the number of nodes and degree distribution, consider approximating dependability for paths of h hops for random graphs with arbitrary degree distributions using the same statistics. Assume each link has the same probability of failure f. Note that, ignoring node failures, the dependability a of a serial path through the graph can be calculated using the fact that it can only work if all components work. This is given by the equation (a_h is the dependability of an h hop serial system):

$$a_h = (1-f)^h \tag{51}$$

This can be compared to the dependability of a parallel system of h components. In which case, the system fails only if all h components fail concurrently. Using the same variables a and f as previously, this gives

$$a_h = 1 - f^h \tag{52}$$

For serial systems as the number of components increase, system dependability decreases rapidly and asymptotically approaches zero. The redundancy in parallel systems causes dependability to increase quickly and asymptotically approach one, as the number of components increases. Obviously, degradations in component dependability adversely affect both approaches.

All classes of random graph structures can have nonnegligible amounts of redundancy. We now analyze how this redundancy affects communications between nodes in the P2P graph structures. The statistics we have discussed should enable us to predict path dependability in these systems.

We have established ways of dividing random and pseudo-random graphs into partitions for indexing, authentication, etc. When this is done, we have parameters that describe the graph. Given these parameters, we can calculate statistics that describe clustering and mutuality in the graph.

To determine system dependability as a function of the number of P2P indexes (partitions), we need only calculate communications dependability as a function of the number of hops. We modify a to determine a new factor $\hat{a}$ that takes into account the network redundancy. Network redundancy provides multiple possible paths between two neighboring nodes. The single hop dependability adjusted to consider alternate paths of exactly r hops is $\hat{a}_r$, giving the following formula:

$$\hat{a} = 1 - \prod_{r=1}^{n-(h+1)} (1 - \hat{a}_r) \tag{53}$$

so that a better estimate of the dependability of an h hop path would be given by $\hat{a}^h$. We modify Equation (53) by considering redundant paths. In graph classes multiple paths of varying lengths between two nodes frequently exist, and they can be used as alternatives to the shortest path of length h connecting the nodes. We attempt to quantify this effect by computing the expected amount of redundancy for individual edges (1 hop paths) in the graph. Methods for computing the likelihood of redundant paths of varying lengths are described. These probabilities are then used to calculate a more realistic availability estimate for the h hop path using the modified per hop availability.

The variable $\hat{a}$ is used for the per hop availability of an edge, taking into account redundancy in the random graph. From equation (51) a^r is the dependability of a path of r hops with no redundancy. Let's consider two adjacent nodes i and j. Equation (52) defines $\hat{a}_r$ as the dependability of a path of r hops connecting nodes i and j parallel to the edge (path of length 1) connecting the nodes. Equation (54) takes into account the probability that this path exists:

$$\hat{a}_r = a^r P[q_r \mid q_1] \tag{54}$$

$P[q_r \mid q_1]$ is the probability that a path of r hops exists between two nodes given that a path of 1 hop (an edge) exists connecting the nodes. We now have paths of differing lengths connecting two nodes in parallel. Remembering that h is the expected number of hops between two nodes in the network, our estimate of the dependability of the file transfer path becomes $\hat{a}^h$. This estimate has two weak points: (*i*) it is pessimistic in that it only considers redundancy for a single hop, and (*ii*) it is optimistic in that it makes a tacit assumption that the paths of differing lengths share no edges.

For the sake of brevity, we introduce notation $P_{x...y}$ for $P[\{q_x \wedge ... \wedge q_y\}]$. For example $P[\{q_3 \wedge q_2 \wedge q_1\}]$ (the probability a node belongs to the set of nodes where paths of lengths 3, 2 and 1 connect it to another node) can be expressed as $P_{3,2,1}$ and $P_{2,-1}$ means $P[\{q_2 \wedge \neg q_1\}]$ (the probability that a node belongs to the set of nodes with a path of length 2 and none of length 1 connecting it to another node).

Consider the effect of two hop paths:

$$\hat{a}_2 = a^2 P[q_2 \mid q_1] \tag{55}$$

$P[q_2 \mid q_1]$ is the probability that a path of two hops exists between two nodes given that an edge connects the nodes. This differs subtly from the cluster coefficient. C is the percentage of two hop paths already reached in one hop. $P[q_2|q_1]$ is the percentage of one hop paths that also yield two hop paths. It can be computed by modifying the procedure for computing the cluster coefficient in Section 3.A. It suffices to swap the roles of M^2 and M.

The variable $\hat{a}_3$ depends on $P[q_3|q_1]$, which we decompose into distinct cases depending on the existence (or absence) of paths of length 2:

$$\hat{a}_3 = a^3 P[q_3 \mid q_1] = a^3 \frac{P_{3,1}}{P[q_1]}$$

$$= \frac{(1-f)^3}{P[q_1]} \left(P_{3,2,1} P[q_2] + P_{3,-2,1} P[\neg q_2] \right)$$

(56)

$P[q_2]$ is q_2/n. $P[q_1]$ is q_1/n. The top right hand object in Figure 10.9 is two contiguous triangles, and occurs with probability $P[q_2|q_1]^2$.

The probability of a rectangle occurring can be calculated by the following procedure:

- First calculate M^2.
- Elements of M^2 that are greater than one, with corresponding element of M equal to zero, are rectangle vertices.
- $P_{3,-2,1}$ is the number of columns of M^2 with elements that meet this criterion divided by n.

This procedure provides the final information needed to compute $\hat{a}_3$. Equation (56) can be completed giving

$$\hat{a}_3 = \frac{(1-f)^3}{q_1} \left(P_{3,2,1} q_2 + P_{3,-2,1} (n - q_2) \right)$$

(57)

All $P_{i,-(i-1),\dots,-2,1}$ where the number of hops i is odd describe the probability of the node being a vertex of a polygon with an even number of sides $2(i-1)$. All sides are edges of the graph.

Estimation of $P_{i,-(i-1),\dots,-2,1}$:

- Initialize L' to the connectivity matrix L.
- Perform the following for $i-1$ iterations:
- Initialize L'' to equal L'
- Set diagonal elements of L' to zero
- Set all nonzero elements of L' to one
- Set all elements $l_{i,j}$ of L' to $l_{i,j} * l_{j,i}$
- Multiply L' by L giving L'
- Count the columns of L' with elements greater than one and the corresponding elements of L^{i-1} to L equal to zero.

- Divide this sum by n giving $P_{i,-(i-1),...,-2,1}$.

These values can be computed using an instance of the random graph class. As with $M[h]$, a more reliable value is found by computing the mean over several instances of the graph classes. If the number of hops is even, this procedure will not work. In which case, estimate $P_{i,-(i-1),...,-2,1}$ by averaging $P_{i+1,-i,...,-2,1}$ and $P_{i-1,-(i-2),...,-2,1}$.

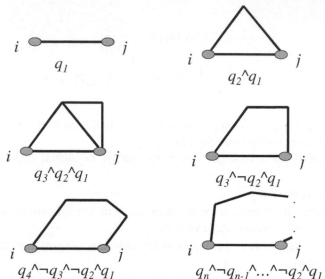

Figure 10.9. Geometric figures implied by the existence of paths of different lengths. If paths of length q_n and q_{n+1} exist, a triangle is implied. Paths of length q_i and q_j with $i > j$ and no paths of length k $i > k > j$. Implies a polygon with $(i-j)+2$ sides.

To compute $\hat{a}_n$ we follow a similar approach to computing $\hat{a}_3$. The value of $\hat{a}_n$ is $(1-f)^n P[q_n|q_1]$, and

$$P[q_n \mid q_1] = \frac{P_{n,n-1,1}P[q_{n-1}] + P_{n,-n-1,1}P[\neg q_{n-1}]}{P[q_1]}$$

$$P_{n,n-1,1} = P_{n,n-1,n-2,1}P[q_{n-2}] + P_{n,n-1,-n-2,1}P[\neg q_{n-2}] \qquad (58)$$

$$P_{n,-n-1,1} = P_{n,-n-1,n-2,1}P[q_{n-2}] + P_{n,-n-1,-n-2,1}P[\neg q_{n-2}]$$

Equation (58) is recursive and continues until each element is a sequence exhaustively enumerating the existence or nonexistence of all paths of length 1 to r. The probability of each atomic element is the product of the probabilities of the polygons whose union defines the object. For example, $P_{4,-3,2,1}$ describes the union of a triangle and a rectangle. It is equal to $P[q_2|q_1]$ times $P_{3,2,1}$.

When the recursion of Equation (58) terminates, each factor contains a variable of the form $P_{j,...,1}$, where j and 1 delimit a list of path lengths, some of which are negated. The limits of the list $(j,1)$ are never negated. This term needs to be translated into a probability.

Calculation of $P_{j,\dots,1}$:

- Initialize probability $P_{j},\dots,1$ to 1.
- Start with 1 and count the number of negated paths until the next nonnegated one. Call this number k.
- If k is 0, the polygon described is a triangle. $P_{j},\dots,1$ becomes $P_{j},\dots,1$ * $P[q2|q1]$.
- If k > 0, the polygon described has 3+k sides. The probability of it being a part of the figure described by $P_{j},\dots,1$ is described by $P_{k/2},^-(k/2-1),\dots,^-2,1$. We have already described how to estimate this value for even and odd k. $P_{j},\dots,1$ becomes $P_{j},\dots,1$ * $P_{k/2},^-(k/2-1),\dots,^-2,1$.
- Replace one with the next nonnegated path length. If that path length is less than j, start again at step two. Else, terminate the calculation.

We now compute an estimate for $\hat{a}$ the expected value of the dependability of an edge in a random graph. Considering the system as a set of parallel paths of differing lengths gives:

$$\hat{a} = 1 - \prod_{j=1}^{diameter} \left(1 - \hat{a}_j\right) \tag{59}$$

The path dependability for the *h* hop path becomes $\hat{a}^h$.

This method has several shortcomings:

- It implicitly assumes independence for paths through the graph.
- Computation of Equation (34) has a combinatorial explosion. For paths of length j, 2^j factors need to be considered.
- Tables of $P_{i,\dots,1}$ statistics are not readily available. The estimates we describe are computable, but computation requires many matrix multiplications. Stable statistics require computation using several graph instances. For large graphs, the amount of computation required is nonnegligible.
- It ignores the existence of multiple redundant paths of the same length increasing per hop dependability. This factor is important.

Most of these can be overcome by realizing that the additional dependability afforded by a path drops off exponentially with the number of hops. It should be possible to stop the computation when a^r becomes negligible. Another factor to consider is that the diameter of the graph scales at worst logarithmically for these graph classes. The algorithm scales as the exponential of a logarithm making it linear. This approach reveals the redundancy inherent in these systems and how it can be effectively exploited.

Alternatively, $P[q_r]$ can be taken directly from the probabilistic connectivity matrices. For the Erdös-Rényi graph all nondiagonal elements have the same value, which is $P[q_h]$. For small world and scale-free graphs, the average of all elements in M^h is a reasonable estimate of q_h. We suggest, however, using the minimum nondiagonal element value in the matrix. The average will be skewed by large values for connections in the clusters for small world graphs and large values for hub nodes in scale-free graphs. The minimum value is the most common in both graph classes and provides a more typical estimate of the probability of connection between two nodes chosen at random.

5. VULNERABILITY TO ATTACK

Empirical evidence that the Internet is a scale-free network with a scaling factor close to 2.5 is discussed in [Albert 2001]. [Albert 2000] analyzes the resiliency of the Internet to random failures and intentional attacks using a scale-free model. Simulations show that the Internet would remain connected even if over 90% of the nodes fail at random, but that the network would no longer be connected if only 15% of the best-connected hub nodes should fail. In this section, we show how this problem can be approached analytically. The techniques given here allow an analytical approach to the same problem:

- Construct a matrix that describes the network under consideration.
- The effect of losing a given percentage of hub nodes can be estimated by setting all elements in the bottom j rows and left j columns to zero, where j/n approximates the desired percentage.
- Compute C^2 and see whether the probabilities increase or decrease. If they decrease, the network will partition.
- Find the percentage where the network partitions.

Theorem. The critical point for scale-free network connectivity arises when the number of hub nodes failing is sufficient for every element of the square of the connectivity matrix to be less than or equal to the corresponding element in the connectivity matrix.

Proof. Using the algorithm given here, hub nodes correspond to the last rows and columns in the probabilistic connectivity matrix. When a hub node fails, all of its associated edges are removed from the graph. This is modeled by setting all values in the node's corresponding row and column to zero. Matrix multiplication is monotone decreasing. If all elements of matrix K are less than all elements in matrix K', then, for any matrix J, $JK < JK'$. When all two hop connections are less likely than one hop connections, then three hop connections are less likely than two hop connections, etc. Using the same logic as with Erdös-Rényi graphs, this will cause the network to tend to be disconnected. Therefore when enough hub nodes fail so that all elements of M^2 are less than the corresponding elements in M the corresponding networks will be more likely to be disconnected. Q.E.D.

This approach can also be applied to finding the number of nodes or edges that need to be disabled in order to fracture other network classes.

6.   QUALITY OF SERVICE OF PEER-TO-PEER SYSTEMS

As described in [Oram 2001], many technologies can be classified as P2P. The two most widely known implementations are Napster and GNUtella. We describe existing P2P implementations in Chapter 5.

We are interested in P2P networks primarily because of what they lack: central control and single points of failure. Since nodes join and leave the network with no central organization, random network models are appropriate for studying the topology of P2P systems.

On the same lines as Napster and GNUtella, we consider a P2P network where the nodes represent computers, workstations, or servers storing mobile code (analogous to audio files in Napster) and the arcs represent physical or logical connectivity between two nodes. However, one of the main differences is that we use a protocol with a "time-out" parameter for abandoning a search. Let's study the question: what is an appropriate number of indexes for a P2P network? We analyze this problem in terms of performance, scalability, and survivability. Recall that Napster has one index that stores the locations of all its files. It is efficient, but has a single point of failure. GNUtella provides n indexes for n nodes. It lacks single points of failure, but does not scale well. We consider Napster and GNUtella as the extreme cases of a continuum. The number of indexes varies in the range of 1 to n. Another question studied in this chapter is what is the appropriate time-out value to use?

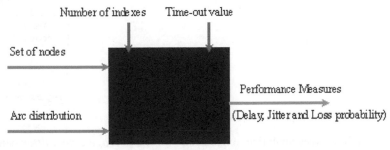

Figure 10.10. Given the number of nodes and arcs in a network, we show how to compute performance measures. This gives us an objective value to optimize the number of indexes and time-out values for use in the network.

Before designing and implementing a network, it is necessary to thoroughly analyze its performance and dependability. These two issues are critical in P2P networks because of their complex topologies and the chaotic environments they operate in. In P2P networks, it is of interest to know how long it will take to retrieve a file (in our case mobile code) and what percentages of the requests are lost. These issues become more critical with each additional hop a request needs to travel, since nodes may become unavailable due to random failures or attacks.

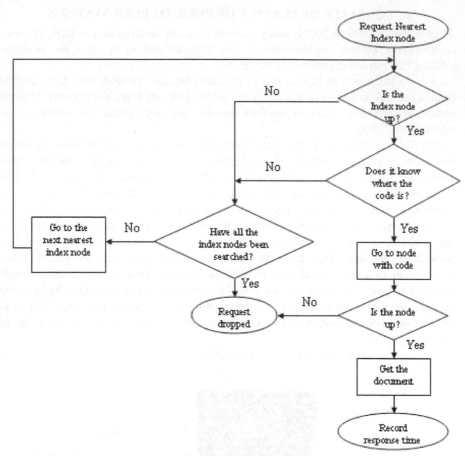

Figure 10.11. Flowchart of request-response process.

This section derives analytical expressions for the *average delay*, *jitter* (standard deviation of delay), and *loss probability* of requests in a P2P network. These expressions are in terms of the network parameters (the number of nodes in the network, average arc degree, the link and node speeds, and the storage capacity of the network) and the mean and variance of the number of hops. In the next section, we use analytical expressions for performance measures in an optimization model to determine the optimal number of indexes and time-out value based on this distribution.

Figure 10.10 illustrates the problem we present. Parameters on the left side of the black box are inputs over which we have no control. The set of nodes and arc distribution are fixed prior to determining system parameters. Although we do not explicitly state link and computing (i.e., node) speeds as inputs, we assume their values are known. Inputs at the top of the box are controllable variables; we choose the number of indexes and time-out values to optimize performance. The arc exiting the box represents the objective function (weighted sum of QoS and dependability measures) to be optimized. We assume nodes fail randomly and independently. Nodes fail for several reasons including Denial of Service attacks.

We divide the network into approximately equal-sized groups per index. Each index node has a database of the files available from nodes in its group. The source node requests a particular document from its index node and starts a timer. (An index node can also be a source node, in which case the travel time to the first index node is zero.) If the index node knows the location of the requested document (i.e., the document and source node are in the same group), it informs the source node of the location of the node containing the document (destination node). Otherwise, the index node sends the location of the next nearest index node to the source node. The source node queries index nodes for the document until all indexes have been searched. If the destination node is identified, the source node requests the document from it. If a transfer is completed before the timer expires, then it is a success; otherwise the request is lost. A request is also lost if an index node with document information is down or the destination node is down. In case of a loss, the source node does not retry the same request. The request-response process is shown in Figure 10.11.

A source node makes a request to its index node. If the index node does not know the location of the required code, the source node forwards the request to the next nearest index node until the required mobile code package is downloaded. The time for this process consists of the round trip time from the source node to the index node, the time to search the index node, round trip time from the source node to the destination node and the time to search the destination node. The notations used are: number of nodes n, average arc degree k_{ave}, communication speed (link speeds) l, processing (computing or node) speed d, number of different documents or code modules mo, probability that an index node is up p, average query size q, code size B, number of documents replicas co, mean number of hops to index i (as a function of n, k, and s) $\mu_i(n,k,s)$, standard deviation of number of hops to index i (as a function of n, k, and s) $\sigma_i(n,k,s)$. Starting from the closest index (index 1) the mean number of hops to eventually reach index i (as a function of n, k, and s) is $\alpha_i(n,k,s)$, and, starting from index 1 the standard deviation of number of hops to reach index i (as a function of n, k and s) is $\beta_i(n,k,s)$.

Since the number of indexes (I) and the time-out values are design variables, we would like to select them optimally. To do so, we first build analytical models relating performance measures to the design parameters. We initially assume an infinite time-out and infrequent request arrival so there is no resource contention (i.e., queuing) among requests. Later we use a model that includes queuing and time-outs, respectively. The analytical models are then compared with the simulation results. All the numerical results were performed for only 1 copy (i.e., $co = 1$) of each mobile code package. However, the expressions we derive can be used for any number of copies.

A. ANALYTICAL EXPRESSION FOR DELAY

Let T be the time to receive a response to a request.

Theorem: The expected delay is given by:

$$E(T) = \left(\frac{1}{1-(1-p)^{co}}\right)\left(\frac{2*q}{l} * \sum_{i=1}^{I} \mu_i(n,k_{ave},s)*p_i + \frac{p*d*mo*co}{I}\sum_{i=1}^{I} p_i(i-1)\right.$$

$$\left. +0.5*d*mo*co(\frac{1}{n}+\frac{1}{I})\sum_{i=1}^{I} p_i + (\frac{q}{l}+\frac{E(B)}{l})\sum_{i=1}^{I}\alpha_i(n,k_{ave},s)p_i\right) \tag{60}$$

where,

$$p_i = P \text{ (Code location is found in index } i) \qquad \text{For i = 1, 2, ...I}$$

$$= \sum_{r=1}^{i} \frac{{}^{(i-1)}C_{(r-1)} *{}^{(I-co)}C_{(r-1)}}{{}^{(I)}C_{(r-1)}} * p^r * (1-p)^{i-r} * \min\left[\frac{co}{I-r+1},1\right]$$

(with the understanding that ${}^{i}C_r = 0$ if $i < r$) and

$$p_0 = \text{ Probability that all the indexes with the code are down}$$

$$= 1 - \sum_{j=1}^{I} p_j = 1-(1-p)^{co}$$

Proof. The analytical expression for delay, E(T), is determined by conditioning on where the document is, using the information in index nodes, and computing the time to reach the document and retrieving it. The expected delay would be:

$$E(T) = \sum_{i=1}^{I} E(T \mid \text{document available in index i})* P \text{ (document available in index i)}.$$

$$= \frac{1}{(1-(1-p)^{co})} \sum_{i=1}^{I} \{2E(\text{Time to travel from source to index i}) +$$

$$E(\text{time to search (i-1) indexes, some possibly down}) + E(\text{Time to find code in i}^{th} \text{ index})\}\, p_i +$$

$$\frac{1}{(1-(1-p)^{co})} \sum_{i=1}^{I} \{E(\text{Time required to reach destination node in region i}) +$$

$$E(\text{Time to search node in region i}) + E(\text{Time to respond})\}\, p_i.$$

The expected time to travel from source to index i is

$$\frac{\text{Number of hops to index node} * \text{Average query size}}{\text{Link speed}},$$

The time to search (i-1) index nodes without the code is

$$\frac{(i-1)*\text{Time to search one document}*\#\text{ of different documents}\#\text{ of copies of a document}}{\#\text{ of index nodes}},$$

The expected time to find code in i^{th} index node is

$$\frac{0.5*\text{Time to search one document}*\#\text{ of different documents}*\#\text{ of copies of a document}}{\#\text{ of index nodes}},$$

Time required to reach destination node is

$$\frac{\text{Number of hops to destination node} * \text{Average query size}}{\text{Link speed}},$$

The expected time to search destination node is

$$\frac{0.5 * \text{Time to search one document} * \text{\# of different documents} * \text{\# of copies of a document}}{\text{\# of nodes in the network}}$$

and the expected time to respond is

$$\frac{\text{Number of hops to destination node} * \text{Average code size}}{\text{Link speed}}$$

Therefore, the delay will be

$$E(T) = \frac{1}{(1-(1-p)^{co})} \left(\sum_{i=1}^{I} \frac{2 * \mu_i(n,k_{ave},s) * q}{l} * p_i + p(i-1) * \frac{d * mo * co}{I} * p_i \right.$$

$$+ \frac{0.5 * d * mo * co}{I} * p_i + \frac{\alpha_i(n,k_{ave},s) * q}{l} * p_i + \frac{0/5 * d * mo * co}{n} p_i$$

$$\left. + \frac{\alpha_i(n,k_{ave},s) * E(B)}{l} * p_i \right)$$

Summing yields the result

$$E(T) = \left(\frac{1}{1-(1-p)^{co}} \right) \left(\frac{2 * q}{l} * \sum_{i=1}^{I} \mu_i(n,k_{ave},s) * p_i + \frac{p * d * mo * co}{I} \sum_{i=1}^{I} p_i(i-1) \right.$$

$$\left. + 0.5 * d * mo * co(\frac{1}{n} + \frac{1}{I}) \sum_{i=1}^{I} p_i + (\frac{q}{l} + \frac{E(B)}{l}) \sum_{i=1}^{I} \alpha_i(n,k_{ave},s) p_i \right)$$

Note that $\alpha_1(n,k_{ave},s)$ = Average number of hops from a node to i^{th} farthest index (or a node in that region) when there are n nodes, k_{ave} arcs on an average, and s standard deviation of arcs in the network. This is obtained from the analytical hop count model.

B.   ANALYTICAL EXPRESSION FOR JITTER

The jitter of the response time is

$$Jitter = \sqrt{Var(T)} \tag{61}$$

To compute $Var(T)$, we use the relation $Var(T) = E(T^2) - [E(T)]^2$ with $E(T)$ from (60). To obtain $E[T^2]$, we define T_i as the random variable denoting the time to retrieve the document conditioned upon the document indexed in index i; therefore, we have the following theorem.

Theorem: The expressions for $E(T^2)$, $Var(T_i)$ and $E(T_i)$ are

$$E(T^2) = \frac{1}{(1-(1-p)^{co})} \sum_{i=1}^{I} \{Var(T_i) + [E(T_i)]^2\} p_i$$

$$Var(T_i) = \frac{4*\sigma_i^2(n,k_{ave},s)*q^2}{l^2} + \left(\frac{d*mo*co}{I}\right)^2 (i-1)*p*(1-p) +$$

$$\frac{1}{12}*\left(\frac{d*mo*co}{I}\right)^2 + \frac{\beta_i^2(n,k_{ave},s)*q^2}{l^2} + \left(\frac{0.5*d*mo*co}{n}\right)^2 +$$

$$\frac{1}{l^2}\{Var(B)\ \beta_i^2(n,k_{ave},s) + Var(B)*\ \alpha_i^2(n,k_{ave},s) +$$

$$E(B)^2 * \beta_i^2(n,k_{ave},s)\}$$

and

$$E(T_i)=\left(\frac{2*q*\mu_i(n,k_{ave},s)}{l}+p(i-1)\frac{d*mo*co}{I}+\frac{0.5*d*mo*co}{I}+\frac{\alpha_i(n,k_{ave},s)*q}{l}\right.$$

$$\left.+\frac{0.5*d*mo*co}{n}+\frac{\alpha_i(n,k_{ave},s)*E(B)}{l}\right)$$

Proof.

$$E(T^2) = \frac{1}{(1-(1-p)^{co})} \sum_{i=1}^{l} E(T^2 \mid \text{document available in the vicinity of index i)} \ p_i$$

$E(T^2 \mid$ document available in the group of index i)

$= \text{Variance}(T \mid \text{document available in the vicinity of index i}) +$

$E(T \mid \text{document available in the vicinity of index i})^2 E(T \mid \text{document available in vicinity of index i})$

$$= \left(\frac{2*q*\mu_i(n,k_{ave},s)}{l}+p(i-1)\frac{d*mo*co}{I}+\frac{0.5*d*mo*co}{I}+\frac{\alpha_i(n,k_{ave},s)*q}{l}\right.$$

$$\left.+\frac{0.5*d*mo*co}{n}+\frac{\alpha_i(n,k_{ave},s)*E(B)}{l}\right)$$

$= E(T_i)$

where

$\dfrac{2*q*\mu_i(n,k_{ave},s)}{l}$ = the round trip time from the source node to the index node

$\dfrac{d*mo*co}{I}$ = time to search an index node without code information

$p(i-1)$ = expected time of Binomial distribution with parameters (i-1) and p

$\dfrac{0.5*d*mo*co}{I}$ = time to search the index node with the code given that it is up (expected value of uniform

distribution with parameters 0 and $\dfrac{d*mo*co}{I}$)

$\dfrac{\alpha_i(n,k_{ave},s)*q}{l}$ = time to go to the destination node

$\dfrac{0.5*d*mo*co}{n}$ = time to search the destination node and

$$\frac{\alpha_i(n,k_{ave},s)*E(B)}{l} = \text{time to transfer the code from the destination node to the source node}$$

$Var(T_i) = \text{Variance(T | document available in the vicinity of index i)}$

In order to complete the derivation, we need some notations. Let h_i be the number of hops to a node in region i.

$$E(h_i) = \alpha_i(n,k_{ave},s) \qquad\qquad Var(h_i) = \beta_i^{\ 2}(n,k_{ave},s)$$

Let $Y_i = h_1 + h_2 + h_3 + ... h_i$ Therefore,

$$E(Y_i) = \mu_i(n,k_{ave},s)$$

$$Variance(Y_i) = \sigma_i^{\ 2}(n,k_{ave},s) = \sum_{j=1}^{i} \beta_i^{\ 2}(n,k_{ave},s)$$

Variance(T_i) will be

$$Var(T_i) = \frac{4*\sigma_i^{\ 2}(n,k_{ave},s)*q^2}{l^2} + \left(\frac{d*mo*co}{I}\right)^2 (\text{i-1})*\text{p}*(\text{1-p}) +$$

$$\frac{1}{12}*\left(\frac{d*mo*co}{I}\right)^2 + \frac{\beta_i^{\ 2}(n,k_{ave},s)*q^2}{l^2} + \left(\frac{0.5*d*mo*co}{n}\right)^2 + \frac{1}{l^2}\ \{Var(B)$$

$$\beta_i^{\ 2}(n,k_{ave},s) + Var(B)*\ \alpha_i^{\ 2}(n,k_{ave},s)\ +E(B)^2 * \beta_i^{\ 2}(n,k_{ave},s)\ \}$$

where

$$\frac{4*\sigma_i^{\ 2}(n,k_{ave},s)*q^2}{l^2} = \text{variance of the time from source node to index node}$$

$$\left(\frac{d*mo*co}{I}\right)^2 = \text{variance of the time to search an index node without code information}$$

(i-1)*p*(1-p) = variance of binomial distribution with parameters (i-1) and p

$$\frac{1}{12}*\left(\frac{d*mo*co}{I}\right)^2 = \text{variance of time to search the index node with code (variance of uniform}$$

distribution with parameters 0 and $\dfrac{d*mo*co}{I}$), and

$$\frac{1}{l^2}\ \{Var(B)\ \beta_i^{\ 2}(n,k_{ave},s) + Var(B)*\ \alpha_i^{\ 2}(n,k_{ave},s)\ +E(B)^2 * \beta_i^{\ 2}(n,k_{ave},s)\ \}$$

= variance of time to go to the destination node and come back with the code

{This is because Var(XY) = Var(X)Var(Y) + Var(X) $[E(Y)]^2$ + $[E(X)]^2$Var(Y)}.

C.   ANALYTICAL EXPRESSION FOR LOSS PROBABILITY

Since the time-out is infinite at this point of the analysis, requests will be lost only if the index node with mobile code information or the destination node is down. The proportion of requests lost or loss probability (L_S) will be

$$L_s = 1 - p_d[1-(1-p)^{co}] \tag{62}$$

where, $1-(1-p)^{co}$ is the probability of the index node with code information being down, and p_d is probability of destination node being up, a function of the number of index nodes.

D. QUEUING MODEL

So far we have considered a scenario where the nodes go up and down from time to time and requests arrive very infrequently so that there is no contention among requests for resources; this is especially the case at the index nodes and the destination nodes that could potentially receive a large number of requests. Now we consider the case where no nodes fail and there is resource contention so requests may have to be stored in a queue at the indexes and destination nodes. Queues at index nodes and destination nodes are approximated as M/G/1 queues with Poisson inter-arrivals, uniformly distributed service times and a single server. To ensure the stability of the M/G/1 system, we use a lower limit on the interarrival times given the average service time at index nodes.

Theorem: The expected delay with queues at the index nodes and destination nodes is given by (proof in [Kapur 2002a])

$$E(T) = \left(\frac{2q}{l} \sum_{i=1}^{i} \mu_i(n,k_{ave},s) + pE(W_I) + E(W_I) + E(W_n) + (\frac{q}{l} + \frac{E(B)}{l}) \sum_{i=1}^{I} \alpha_i(n,k_{ave},s) \right) \tag{63}$$

where $E(W_I)$ is the average waiting time a randomly arriving request spends in the index node queue plus the expected time to search the index node, and $E(W_n)$ is the average waiting time a randomly arriving request spends in destination node queue plus the expected time to search the destination node.

Theorem: The jitter with queues at index nodes and destination nodes is given by (proof in [Kapur 2002a])

$$Jitter = \sqrt{Var(T)} \quad \text{where} \quad Var(T) = E(T^2) - [E(T)]^2 \tag{64}$$

$E(T)$ is from Equation (63), $E(T^2) = Var(T) - [E(T)]^2$ with

$$Var(T_i) = \frac{4*\sigma_i^2(n,k_{ave},s)*q^2}{l^2} + \left(\frac{d*mo*co}{I}\right)^2 + \frac{1}{12}*\left(\frac{d*mo*co}{I}\right)^2$$

$$+ E(I)*Var(W_q) + \frac{\beta_i^2(n,k_{ave},s)*q^2}{l^2} + \left(\frac{0.5*d*mo*co}{n}\right)^2 +$$

$$\frac{1}{l^2}\{Var(B)\ \beta_i^2(n,k_{ave},s) + Var(B)*\alpha_i^2(n,k_{ave},s) + E(B)^2*\beta_i^2(n,k_{ave},s)\},$$

$$E(T_i) =$$

$$\frac{2q\mu_i(n,k_{ave},s)}{l} + E(W_I) + 0.5E(W_I) + \frac{\alpha_i(n,k_{ave},s)q}{l} + 0.5E(W_n) +$$

$$\frac{\alpha_i(n,k_{ave},s)*E(B)}{l}$$

Note: Any loss that will occur here is due to time-outs only as we assume all the nodes to be up always.

Up to now, we assumed that the time-out value is infinite. This means that a request is lost only if the index node or the destination node with the document is down. If the time-out value is finite, then requests will also be lost if the time to get a response exceeds the time-out value. Since the delay is a sum of a large number of independent random variables, we can approximate using the central limit theorem that $T \sim$ Normal [E(T), Var(T)]. Now the probability that time-out occurs even when the document is available will be $P(T > \theta) = 1 - P(T \le \theta)$ where, θ is the finite time-out value. The above expression can be written as:

$$P(T > \theta) = \varepsilon = 1 - \Phi\left[\frac{\theta - E(T)}{\sqrt{Var(T)}}\right] \tag{65}$$

where Φ can be obtained from z tables for the normal distribution. Then, the response time given that document is retrieved before time-out (E(T_θ)) becomes

$$E(T_\theta) = \frac{\int_{-\infty}^{\theta} xf(x)dx}{(1-\varepsilon)} \tag{66}$$

where $f(x)$ is the normal probability density function. The variance will be

$$Var(T_\theta) = \left\{\frac{(1-\varepsilon)\int_{-\infty}^{\theta} x^2 f(x)\ dx - \varepsilon(E(T_\theta))^2}{(1-\varepsilon)^2}\right\} \tag{67}$$

The loss probability will be

$$L_\theta = 1 - p_d[1-(1-p)^{co}](1-\varepsilon) \tag{68}$$

E. COMPARISON WITH SIMULATIONS

We now compare the results from the analytical models with simulations run using Matlab. First we compare systems with no queues, node failures, and finite time-out values. For 3 random graph structures, the number of nodes was taken as 100 (due to limitations for the simulations; however, the analytical models can handle much higher values), average arc degree as 3 and the number of indexes as 5. The link speeds were taken standard 56Kbps, the average query size as 60 bytes, the document size as normally distributed with a mean of 100 Kb and standard deviation of 10 Kb and the node speed was taken as 0.001 seconds per document. The time-out value was infinite and the probability of the index node being up was 0.952 and that of the destination node was 0.95. Ten replications were taken for all the simulation runs. There were no queues at any of the nodes. The results are summarized in Table 10.2. From the table it can be seen that results from analytical and simulation models are fairly close. The difference in the two results is due to the difference in the mean and the variance of the number of hops in the two models.

Table 10.2. Analytical and Simulation Results for Systems without Queues.

	Analytical			Simulation		
	Delay	Jitter	Loss Prob.	Delay	Jitter	Loss Prob.
Erdös-Rényi	20.2117	9.0909	0.0956	21.9535	10.118	0.0957
Small world	20.139	9.0767	0.0956	21.8319	8.1615	0.0957
Scale-free	16.9804	8.1009	0.0956	18.0994	9.8971	0.0952

We now consider the model with queues and perfectly reliable nodes. The *delay*, *jitter*, and *loss probability* for the three networks were determined using both the analytical model as well as the simulation model to verify the results for the queuing case with infinite and finite time-out value. For all the 3 graph structure examples, the number of nodes was taken as 100, average arc degree as 3, the number of indexes as 5 and the arrival rate of requests into the system was taken as Poisson with 1 request in 4 seconds. The link speeds were taken standard 56 Kbps, the average query size as 60 bytes, the document size as normally distributed with a mean of 100 Kb and standard deviation of 10 Kb and the node speed was taken as 0.001 seconds per document. Also 10 replications were taken for all the simulation runs. This simulation was done using a package called *Arena* as Arena simulates queuing models well. The results are summarized in Tables 10.3 (for infinite time-out value) and 10.4 (for time-out value of 50 seconds).

Table 10.3. Comparison of Analytical and Simulation Results for Infinite Time-out Value

	Analytical		Simulation	
	Delay	*Jitter*	*Delay*	*Jitter*
Erdös-Rényi	30.0351	12.7749	27.61	13.452
Small world	32.4967	13.3071	30.005	13.694
Scale-free	29.3821	12.8987	27.086	13.41

Table 10.4. Comparison of Analytical and Simulation Results for Time-out Value of 50 seconds

	Analytical			Simulation		
	Delay	*Jitter*	*Loss Prob.*	*Delay*	*Jitter*	*Loss Prob.*
Erdös-Rényi	28.8205	10.8854	0.06	25.317	10.882	0.06071
Small world	30.0634	10.9015	0.095	27.076	10.717	0.07884
Scale-free	27.8087	11.1569	0.0508	24.801	10.946	0.05645

From Tables 10.3 and 10.4 it can be seen that results from the analytical and simulation models are fairly close. The difference in the two results is due to a few approximations that we made in deriving the analytical models. One approximation is the Central Limit Theorem we used to incorporate finite time-out value. We also approximated the arrival process of requests at index nodes as Poisson with a certain mean. Since the index node gets requests from its group and also from its neighboring groups, the arrival process at the index nodes is not exactly Poisson.

7. CORRECT NUMBER OF INDEXES

In this section, we look at P2P QoS and network dependability issues. The application domain is a distributed servent network that uses mobile code to reconfigure itself dynamically. This network is a prototype highly survivable distributed network service.

Formally: Given a network of n nodes, how does the number of indexes affect global system dependability? QoS issues have been initially considered in [Kapur 2002]. Here we analyze the issue of network dependability. Specifically, we define dependability to be the probability that an arbitrary request can be completed.

Indexes serve subgraphs of approximately equal size created from the original graph. Determining where to place the indexes is equivalent to performing these two steps:

- Perform the k-way partition problem in graph theory, where a graph is partitioned into k (in this case i) partitions of equal size with a minimal number of connections between the partitions. The problem is NP-complete. Many heuristics have been developped to solve this problem for VLSI layout. Known approaches include self-organizing maps and the use of eigenvalues of the connectivity matrix.

- Place the index at the centroid of each partition.

Now we explain how to optimize the number of indexes and time-out value. The number of indexes can be varied from 1 to n (centralized index to completely distributed indexes) to determine the optimum number of indexes in a P2P network. Also the time-out value can be varied from infinite to a certain finite value. Our objective function is to find out the optimal number of indexes and time-out value by minimizing *delay* and *jitter*, keeping the *loss probability* to no more than a given value.

During simulations we used a request loss probability of 7%. In the simulations we found that the variation in jitter was less than the variation in delay with the variations in index nodes and the time-out values. Therefore, we normalized the delay and the jitter so that delay does not overshadow the jitter when solving the problem.

Delay was normalized by dividing the entire delay matrix by the maximum value of the matrix. Similarly the jitter was normalized by dividing the jitter matrix with the maximum value of the matrix. It is also possible that the decision maker might want to give some weights to the delay and the jitter depending upon how much influence he/she wants these two to have on the optimal solution. Therefore, if W_d and W_j are the weights assigned to delay and jitter, respectively, and D_m and J_m are the maximum value in the delay and jitter matrix, respectively, then the objective function can be written in terms of θ and I, (the decision variables) as, minimize:

$$\frac{1}{D_m}*(1-W_d)*(E(T_\theta))+\frac{1}{J_m}*(1-W_j)*\sqrt{Var(T_\theta)} \qquad (69)$$

with the constraints

$$L_\theta \leq 7\%, \ \theta < \infty, \text{ and } I \geq 1 \qquad (70)$$

where θ is time-out value, I is number of indexes, $E(T_\theta)$ is *delay* from, $Var(T_\theta)$ is *jitter*, L_θ is *loss probability* , W_d is the weight that a decision maker wants to give to *delay* (0.5 in our case), and W_j is the weight that a decision maker wants to give to *jitter* (0.5 in our case). ***Note:** The sum of the weights is 1 and we subtract each weight from 1 since the objective function is to minimize. We chose equal weights for both jitter and delay.*

For the scenario where there is no resource contention among requests and when nodes go up and down, the above optimization problem was solved for 25 nodes and 5.28 average arc degree using complete enumeration. The number of indexes was varied from 1 to 25 and the time-out value was varied from 20 seconds to 50 seconds. The complete enumeration yields the optimal number of indexes as 19 and the time-out value as 35 seconds. Figure 10.12 shows how the objective function and the loss probability vary with the number of indexes and the time-out value. From Figure 10.2 it can be seen that there is a tradeoff between loss probability and the objective function. The loss probability is minimum for 25 index nodes and time-out value of 50 seconds. For a loss probability less than 7%, the objective function is minimum for 19 index nodes and time-out value of 35 seconds, and that is what our mathematical program also reports as the optimal solution.

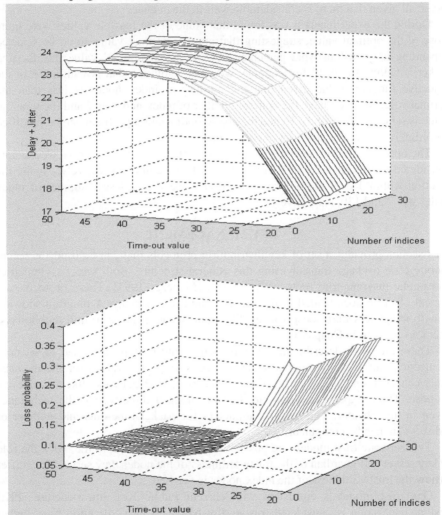

Figure 10.12. The optimal solution. (Top) Delay + jitter vs. number of indexes and time-out value. (Bottom) Loss probability vs. number of indexes and time-out value.

The performance parameters vs. number of index nodes and time-out value for traffic intensity of 0.8 at each index node for any number of index nodes was solved for a traffic intensity of 0.9. For this case as well, the number of nodes was 25 and average arc degree was 5.28.

It can be seen that, for a loss probability less than 7%, the objective function is minimum for 17 index nodes and time-out value of 75 seconds, and that is what our mathematical program also reports as the optimal solution. Seventeen indexes are better than having only one, as now there is not a single point of failure in the P2P network. It is also better than having all the nodes as indexes as the traffic along the network will not be high. The time-out value of 75 seconds is neither too large nor too small given that there is considerable wait in the queues.

During the experiments it was found that some of the feasible values were quite close to the optimal value, suggesting that another optimal value could be selected depending upon within what percentage of the actual optimal value the decision maker is willing to go. If, for example, we want a solution that is within 1% of the objective function value given that the number of index nodes is less than the optimal value, then we have the optimal number of index nodes as 7 and the time-out value is same as 75 seconds. Hence the above optimization problem can be modified accordingly to suit any given set of constraints.

The optimal solution for traffic intensity of 0.9 (notice that the previous example considered traffic intensity of 0.8) was 8 and 130 seconds respectively. Again, the solution within 1% of the objective function value with a lesser number of index nodes was 7 and 130, respectively.

8. KEY MANAGEMENT

This section provides a set of key distribution protocols that can be used for secure mobile code package transfer using this general structure. Both secret (symmetric) and public (asymmetric) protocols are given [Menezes 1997]. These protocols are typical of those documented in the literature and in use today. A diagram showing how to integrate secure sockets layer (SSL) and secure shell (ssh) into mobile code daemons is given in Chapter 6.

These protocols describe all the steps that would be typically used to set up a connection and exchange mobile code packages. Expected values for the message sizes can be found for any specific instance of a P2P network, like the one we propose. These expected values can then be plugged directly into the techniques given in this chapter. The design parameters for packet time-outs and number of indexes can then be computed.

Two separate trust models are possible. Both models assign to the index the role of key server and guardian of the trustworthiness of the nodes they serve. They differ in how the trustworthiness of the index nodes is verified.

One trust model is consistent with current Public Key Infrastructure (PKI) design. Each node is considered trustworthy based on its verification by a higher authority. In which case, trust propagation takes the form of a directed acyclic graph (DAG). The highest level of the hierarchy is an entity, that is assumed inviolate and always trustworthy. In our terminology, this entity is God.

The alternative topology does not assume the existence of an inviolate entity. It does assume that fewer than 1/3 of the currently active indexes can be corrupted at any point in time. In this case, indexes can be removed from the system by the other indexes using a Byzantine Generals approach [Brooks 1998].

The public key protocol is:

IU is public key of Index I
IR is private key of Index I
RU is public key of Node R
RR is private key of Node R
CU is public key of Node C
CR is private key of Node C
Message 1:

> **Node R sends a message asking Index I where mobile code package P**
> **is.**

> > **Request contains:**
> > > **1. Name of P (Encrypted)**
> > > **2. Nonce (Encrypted)**
> > > **3. Address of R's index if I is not R's index**
> > > **4. R's Address (Clear text)**
> > **Both 1 and 2 are encrypted with R's private key RR**
> > **The entire request is encrypted using Index I's public key IU.**

> > **The Nonce is undefined but may contain:**
> > > **1. Request sequence number**
> > > **2. Time stamp**
> > > **3. Random number**
> > **or some combination of the above**

Message 2:

> > **I decrypts the message with its private key. Verify whether R's**
> > **privileges have been revoked. If so, then drop the request.**

> > **If R is not a node normally served by I, checking for**
> > **revocation of R requires checking that the privileges of the**
> > **index given in 1 have not been revoked, and then checking**
> > **with that index that R has not been revoked. If either one fails,**
> > **drop the request.**

> > **R's public key - RU - is known by I if R is normally served**
> > **by I. Else RU is retrieved from R's index while checking for**
> > **revocation of R's privileges.**

> > **I decrypts the name of P using R's public key to verify that**
> > **the message is from R. Optionally check validity of the nonce**
> > **and drop the request if it is invalid. Find address of node C**
> > **containing package P. If package P cannot be found address of**
> > **C is NULL.**

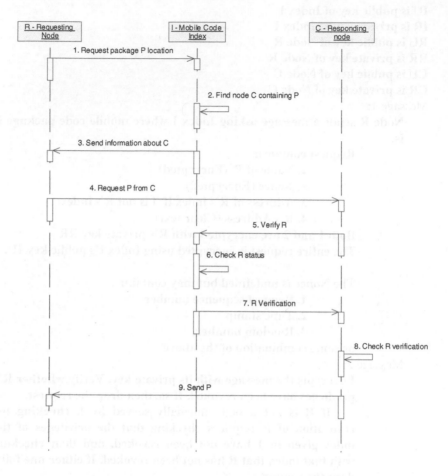

```
  R - Requesting              I - Mobile Code              C - Responding
       Node                        Index                        node
         |    1. Request package P location  |                    |
         |─────────────────────────────────>│                    |
         |                                   │                    |
         |                                   │ 2. Find node C containing P
         |                                   │◄─┐                 |
         |                                   │  │                 |
         |    3. Send information about C     │◄─┘                 |
         |◄──────────────────────────────────│                    |
         |                                   |                    |
         |              4. Request P from C                       |
         |──────────────────────────────────────────────────────>│
         |                                   |                    |
         |                         5. Verify R│                    |
         |◄──────────────────────────────────│                    |
         |                         6. Check R status              |
         |                                   │◄─┐                 |
         |                                   │  │                 |
         |              7. R Verification    │◄─┘                 |
         |───────────────────────────────────────────────────────>│
         |                                   |     8. Check R verification
         |                                   |                    │◄─┐
         |                                   |                    │  │
         |              9. Send P            |                    │◄─┘
         |◄───────────────────────────────────────────────────────│
         |                                   |                    |
```

Figure 10.13. Public key protocol.

    Message 3:

        I sends to R:

            1. Network address of node C containing package P

            2. Public key CU of node C

            3. Nonce from message 1

        This message is encrypted with private key of Index - IR and public key of R - RU.

            R decrypts the message. Verifies the source of the message and that the nonce matches the nonce in message 1. If the address of C is NULL, then the protocol recommences at the next index. R can also time-out while waiting for this message. If it does so and not all indexes have been checked, then the protocol recommences at the next index. If R times out and all indexes have been checked, then the request fails. If the

address of C is nonNULL and R has not timed out, then the protocol continues.

Message 4:

> **Node R requests package P from node C by sending:**
>> **1. Nonce from message 1**
>> **2. Address of R**
>> **3. RU in plaintext**
>> **4. Name of package P**
>> **5. Hash code of 1-4 encrypted with RR**
>
> **This message encrypted is with C's public key - CU. After decrypting with CR, C does hash of 1-4 and compares with 5 decrypted with RU. This verifies that R is the message source and that the message has not been modified.**

Message 5:

> **Message sent to Index I containing:**
>> **1. Address of R**
>> **2. R's public key - RU**
>> **3. Address of C**
>> **4. Nonce**
>
> **All are encrypted using IU.**

Message 6:

> **Decrypt using IR. Look to verify that node R's access has not been revoked. Since verification of nodes not served by R was done by message 2, no extra processing for that case is necessary here. (I retains the fact that R was valid for a limited time.) If R has been revoked set R verification to NULL. Else set R verification to True. If R verification is true, check as well that RU is in fact the public key of R.**

Message 7:

> **I sends message to C containing:**
>> **1. Nonce from 5**
>> **2. R verification**
>> **3. R's address**
>
> **Both are encrypted using IR and CU.**

Message 8:

> **Decrypt using CR. Then C verifies that 7 came from I using IU. Verify which package P is needed using nonce. If R is still part of the system prepare to send P. Else drop the processing.**

Message 9:

> **C sends message to R containing:**
>> **1. Nonce from step 4**
>> **2. P**
>> **3. Hash of 1 and 2 encrypted using CR**
>
> **The message is encrypted with RU. R may have timed out during the process. If all indexes have been tried and timed out**

then the request fails. If R times out and an index remains, the protocol recommences using the next index. If R receives message 9, it decrypts the message and does the following:

1. It uses the nonce to match this with the correct request.
2. R compares the hash of 1 and 2 with 3 decrypted using CU to verify the source and integrity of 9.
3. The request terminates.

We now present variations of three widely used symmetric key establishment protocols: Needham-Schroeder, Denning-Sacco, and Yaholom.

For all symmetric key protocols:
> KR is a symmetric key known only to R and I
> KC is a symmetric key known only to C and I
> Message 1:
> > Node R sends to I:
> > > 1. Address of R
> > > 2. Name of package P
> > > 3. Nonce
> > (In the classical Needham-Schroeder the requester sends the address of node C instead of package name).
> Message 2:
> > I sends to R:
> > Encrypted with KR{
> > > 1. Nonce from message 1.
> > > 2. Address of C
> > > 3. Name of P
> > > 4. Symmetric session key in clear text
> > > 5. Encrypted with KC{
> > > > 1. Session key in clear text
> > > > 2. Address of R
> > > }
> > }
> > (In the classic Needham-Schroeder protocol, item 3 is not needed.)

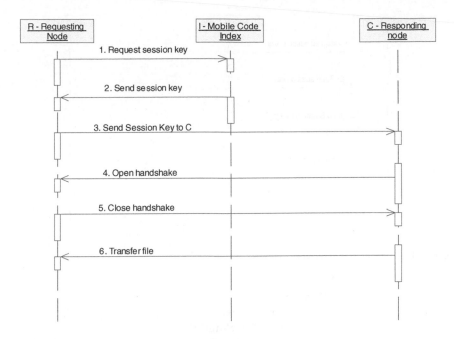

Figure 10.14. Needham-Schroeder secret key protocol.

Message 3:

> **R sends to C:**
> **Encrypted with KC{**
> > **1. Session key in clear text**
> > **2. Address of R**
>
> **}**

Message 4:

> **C sends a nonce to R encrypted with the symmetric key**

Message 5:

> **R sends to C:**
> **Encrypted with session key{**
> > **1. Nonce-1**
> > **2. Program module name**
>
> **}**

Message 6:

> **C sends to R:**
> **Encrypted with session key{**
> > **1. Mobile code module P**
> > **2. Nonce-2**
>
> **}**

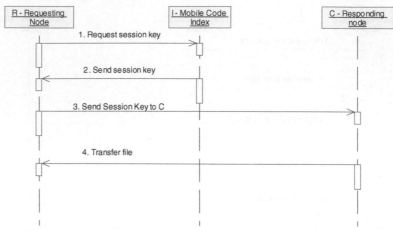

Figure 10.15. Denning Sacco secret key protocol.

Message 1:

> **Node R sends to I:**
> > **1. Address of R**
> > **2. Name of package P**
>
> **(In the classical Denning-Sacco the requester sends the address of node C instead of package name.)**

Message 2:

> **I sends to R:**
>
> **Encrypted with KR{**
> > **1. Time stamp**
> > **2. Address of C**
> > **3. Name of P**
> > **4. Symmetric session key in clear text**
> > **5. Encrypted with KC{**
> > > **1. Session key in clear text**
> > > **2. Address of R**
> > > **3. Time stamp**
> >
> > **}**
>
> **}**
>
> **(In the classic Needham-Schroeder protocol, item 3 is not needed.)**

Message 3:

> **R sends to C:**
> > **1. Encrypted with KC{**
> > > **1. Session key in clear text**
> > > **2. Address of R**
> > > **3. Time stamp**
> >
> > **}**

> **2. Program module name encrypted with session key**

Message 4:

> **C sends to R:**
> **Encrypted with session key{**
> > **1. Mobile code module P**
>
> **}**

We now present a variant of the Yaholom protocol.

Message 1:

> **Node R sends to I:**
> > **1. Address of R**
> > **2. Name of package P**
> > **3. Nonce**
>
> **(Not in classic Yahalom)**

Message 2:

> **I sends to R:**
> **Encrypted with KR{**
> > **1. Nonce from message 1.**
> > **2. Address of C**
>
> **}**
> **(Not in classic Yahalom)**

Message 3:

> **R sends to C:**
> > **1. Nonce R**
> > **2. Address of R**
>
> **(Start of Yahalom)**

Message 4:

> **C sends to I:**
> **1. Address of R**
> **2. Encrypted with KC{**
> > **1. Address of A**
> > **2. Nonce R**
> > **3. Nonce C**
>
> **}**

Message 5:

> **I sends to R:**
> **1. Encrypted with KR{**
> > **1. Address of C**
> > **2. Session key**
> > **3. Nonce R**
> > **4. Nonce C**
>
> **}**
> **2. Encrypted with KC{**
> > **1. Address of R**
> > **2. Session key**
>
> **}**

Message 6:
> **R sends to C:**
> **1. Encrypted with KC{**
> > **1. Address of A**
> > **2. Session key**
>
> **}**
> **2. Encrypted with session key{**
> > **1. Nonce C**
> > **2. Name of P**
>
> **}**

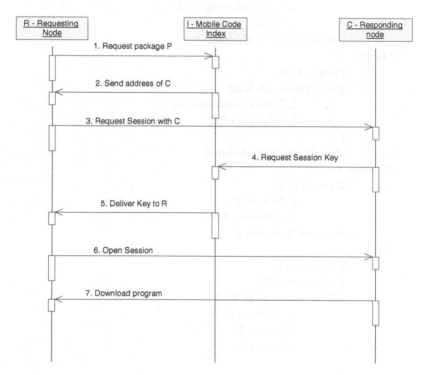

Figure 10.16. Yaholom protocol.

Message 7:
C sends to R:
Encrypted with session key{
> **1. Mobile code module P**

}

9. CONCLUSION

This chapter presented an in-depth analysis of P2P systems. Since the systems are chaotic, we did not assume a known fixed infrastructure. Rather, we use random graph formalisms to describe and analyze their behavior. We have shown how random graphs can be used to predict

- The expected number of hops between nodes
- The dependability of the global P2P system
- The vulnerability of the P2P network to attack

We also showed how to predict the delay and jitter in a P2P system and used that prediction to determine the proper number of indexes and time-out value to use.

Much work remains to be done. A particularly promising approach to future work is the design of P2P systems by defining the statistics each node needs to maintain. Our results to date indicate that by doing so it should be possible to maintain globally desirable attributes with no centralized control. Chapter 11 looks further into this concept.

10. EXERCISES

Exercise 10.1 Construct connectivity matrices for Erdös-Rényi graphs with the number of nodes varying from 50 to 200 (by 50) and p varying from 0.25 to 0.75 by 0.25.

Exercise 10.2 Construct connectivity matrices for scale-free networks of 100 nodes with the scaling parameter varying from 1.2 to 4.2 (by 1).

Exercise 10.3 Determine the vulnerability to attack of the graphs from Exercise 10.1 and 10.2.

Exercise 10.4 Create graphs using the probability matrices from Exercises 10.1 and 10.2. Discuss the implications of their topologies.

CHAPTER 11

Emergent Routing [1, 2]

This chapter extends some of the concepts presented in Chapter 10. A robust infrastructure has to be able to adapt quickly to disruptions. This chapter looks at approaches to wireless information routing and resource discovery. These ideas are complementary to the hierarchical index ideas presented in Chapter 10. Indexes, or individual nodes, can use these adaptive routing approaches for disseminating and searching for information. Their distributed nature makes them ideal for chaotic environments.

1. *AD HOC* DATA ROUTING BACKGROUND

There are two general classes of *ad hoc* routing algorithms: table driven and reactive. Table driven protocols maintain up-to-date routing tables between all pairs of nodes in the network. Topology changes propagate through the network to update the routing tables of each node. The storage requirement of routing tables and the transmission overhead of topology changes are the drawbacks of this approach. The following three approaches are variations of table driven routing. They differ mainly in the number of routing tables required and the way they propagate topology changes.

Destination sequenced distance vector routing (DSDV) is derived from the classical Bellman-Ford routing mechanism [Kurose 2003]. Each node maintains routing information to all other nodes and the corresponding hops value. Regular routing table updates incur a large communications overhead. Each routing table entry has the following fields:

- Next gives the next node hop for reaching the destination.
- Hops give the number of hops to the destination.

---

[1] Coauthored with Mengxia Zhu, Matthew Piretti, Christopher Griffin, and S. S. Iyengar.

[2] Portions reprinted, with permission, from:

R. R. Brooks, M. Piretti, M. Zhu, and S. S. Iyengar, "Adaptive routing using emergent protocols in wireless *ad hoc* sensor networks," *SPIE 48th Annual Meeting Symposium, Advanced Signal Processing Algorithms, Architectures, and Implementations,* pp. 155-163, pp. 197-208, August 2003

R. R. Brooks, M. Piretti, M. Zhu, and S. S. Iyengar, "Distributed adaptation methods for wireless sensor networks," *Globecom 2003*, vol. 5, pp. 2967-2971, December 2003.

- A sequence number from the destination with a timer. This allows mobile nodes to distinguish stale routes from new ones.
- Install time representing when the entry was established.
- A table containing information about route stability that can be used to dampen network fluctuations.

Routing table updates are done on a periodic basis. Two types of packets can be used to update the routing tables. Full dump packet carries all available routing information. Incremental packets only contain entries that have been changed since the last full dump. This decreases the amount of traffic generated. This protocol is simple and loops free through the usage of sequence number. Scalability is a big problem for this protocol.

The cluster head gateway switch routing protocol [Royer 1999] has a hierarchical structure. A cluster head controls a group of nodes within its radio transmission range. Three types of nodes exist in the network and they are node, gateway and cluster head. A gateway node serves as an intermediate between cluster heads. A distributed cluster head selection algorithm is utilized to select a node as the cluster head. However, frequent cluster head vote can degrade the performance since limited energy and other resources are consumed on cluster head vote instead of useful packet relay. Hence, a least cluster change (LCC) clustering algorithm comes in. In LCC, cluster head change occurs only if network change causes two cluster heads to fall into one cluster or one of the nodes moves out of the range of all the cluster heads. Each node keeps a cluster member table, which stores the destination cluster head for each node in the network. Each node periodically broadcasts its dynamic cluster head member table. Upon reception of the cluster head member table, nodes update their cluster head member tables. A routing table used to determine the next hop in order to reach the destination is also needed. When a packet arrives, a node uses the cluster member table and routing table to determine the nearest cluster head along the route to the destination. It knows the best suited to reach that cluster head and the packet is sent to that node.

The wireless routing protocol is a table-based protocol that maintains routing information among all nodes in the network [Royer 1999]. Each node maintains a routing, distance, link cost, and message retransmission list tables. Nodes send update messages to neighbors after receiving updates or detecting a link change. In the case of a link loss between two nodes, update messages are sent to all neighbors. The neighbors modify their distance table entries and try to find new possible paths through other valid nodes. New paths are relayed to the original link loss nodes to update their tables. Nodes become aware of their neighbors from acknowledgement receipts. If there is no routing table change, nodes send idle hello messages to ensure connectivity. Otherwise, the system assumes a link failure. This algorithm checks for consistency of all its neighbors every time it detects a change in link of any of its neighbors. Looping is eliminated and convergence is fast.

Reactive methods are on-demand routing protocols. Since they run only when a message is sent from a source node to a destination node, the control packet overhead is greatly reduced. These protocols start with a route discovery procedure followed by a route maintenance procedure until either the destination becomes inaccessible or the route is no longer desired.

Ad hoc on-demand distance vector routing (AODV) [Royer 1999] is an extension of the DSDV algorithm. Instead of maintaining a complete list of all potential routes, only nodes on communications paths maintain routing information and participate in routing table exchanges. The number of required broadcast is minimized as well. When a node seeks a path to a destination, it broadcasts a route request packet (RREQ) to its neighbors, which pass the request to their neighbors. The flood continues until either the destination or an intermediate node with an up-to-date route to the destination is reached. The broadcast ID and the IP address uniquely designate a RREQ. Each node receiving the message creates a reverse route to source based on the first copy of the broadcast packet received. The destination unicasts a route reply message back to the neighbor from which it first received the RREQ packet. As the RREQ is routed back to the source, nodes along the path create forward route entries. Thus, each node remembers only the next hop required to reach the destination, not the whole route. A route timer is associated with a route entry; if the route entry is not used for a specific lifetime, the route entry will be deleted as a stale route. This method requires periodic updates of routing information. AODV broadcasts periodic hello messages. Failure to receive a consecutive number of hello messages determines failure of a node. In that case source initiates a new route discovery.

Dynamic source routing protocol (DSR) is an on-demand routing protocol [Royer 1999]. Each node maintains a route cache recording the source routes that it is aware of. Route cache entries are being constantly updated once new routes are learned. When a node S requires a route to a destination D, it examines its route cache to see if a route to the destination already exists. If a fresh route is found, it will use the route in the cache. Otherwise, it initiates the route discovery phase by broadcasting the RREQ packet to its neighbors, which will do the same. Propagation stops if the destination node or an intermediate node with a route to the destination is located. Nodes receiving the RREQ packet first check their route cache for known paths to the destination. If none exist, it adds its own address to the route record and forwards the packet along its outgoing links. To limit the number of route requests propagated, a node processes a route request packet only if it has not already seen the packet and its address is not present in the route record of the packet. A route reply is generated by the destination or intermediate node. The destination node places the route record into the route reply. An intermediate node will append its cached route to the route record.

DSR utilizes route error packets and acknowledgements for route maintenance. Any topological change or fatal transmission error will be reflected in the route cache of nodes. If a node receives an error message due to fatal transmission error or failure link, it deletes the erroneous hop from all of its route cache entries and selects a new route. Wise usage of the route cache can greatly reduce the amount of control overhead.

The temporally ordered routing algorithm (TORA) [Royer 1999] is a highly adaptive distributed routing algorithm based on link reversal. TORA is source initiated and can discover multiple routes between any source and destination pairs. The key concept of TORA is the localization of messages exchange in case of topological change. A node needs to maintain the routing information about adjacent nodes. During the route establishment phases, nodes use a height metric to construct a directed acyclic graph (DAG) routed at the destination. Links are assigned a direction according to the relative height metric of neighboring nodes. In case of topological change, DAG is reestablished at the same destination.

A good analogy would be water flowing down the hill through pipes. The hilltop is the source, pipes are links, and pipe connections are nodes. TORA assigns level numbers to each node down the hill. Water will flow from high nodes to low nodes. This routing protocol is similar to the spin glass model that we discuss later in this chapter.

We now present a number of technologies for decentralized adaptive routing in networks built on the complex adaptive systems concepts presented in Chapter 4. These are three distributed adaptation methods we originally developed for use by wireless sensor networks (WSNs) in Military Operations in Urban Terrain (MOUT) scenarios. Urban scenarios are challenging since obstructions to radio communications may cause the shortest path between two points to not be a straight line. The chaotic nature of MOUT missions means paths are not reliable. Only transient paths may exist. In spite of this, timely communications are required. Our approaches use local decisions to adapt to a constantly changing substrate. The insights we gained by testing these adaptation methods are being used to design and implement wireless routing protocols. The methods we analyze are: (*i*) spin glass, (*ii*) multifractal, and (*iii*) pheromone. We then discuss these approaches using concepts from epidemic routing.

A WSN is a set of sensor nodes monitoring their environment and providing users with timely data describing the region under observation. Nodes have wireless communications. Centralized control of this type of network is undesirable and unrealistic due to reliability, survivability, and bandwidth considerations. Distributed control also has other advantages: (*i*) increased stability by avoiding single points of failure, (*ii*) simple node behaviors replace complicated global behaviors, and (*iii*) enhanced responsiveness to changing conditions since nodes react immediately to topological changes instead of waiting on central command. Our definition of a WSN does not preclude nodes being mobile.

Consider the WSN application in [Brooks 2003e] a surveillance network tracks multiple vehicles using a network of acoustic, seismic, and infrared sensors. For a MOUT application, it is essential that the user community have timely track information. Figure 11.1 shows an idealized MOUT terrain. Black squares are walls or buildings that block radio signals. White squares are open regions allowing signal transmission. Gray squares are either choke points for signals that are open (closed) or intermittent disturbances that occur at random throughout the sensor field. Random factors are inserted to emulate common disruptions for this genre of network. Each square capable of transmission contains a sensor node. This amounts to having a sensor field with a uniform density. This provides an abstract example scenario approximating situations likely to exist in a real MOUT situation. This allows us to examine multiple adaptation techniques without being distracted by implementation details. After evaluating adaptation at this abstract level, the insights gained can then be used to create more robust routing protocols.

WSN applications will typically require a large number of nodes to adequately determine the number, position, and trajectories of the objects under observation. To be affordable, individual nodes will be inexpensive and thus unreliable. Power consumption is an important issue. Our goal was to design a WSN that is fault tolerant, consumes minimal resources, supports secure message passing, and adapts well to environmental changes. These same concepts can be leveraged for constructing other survivable infrastructures.

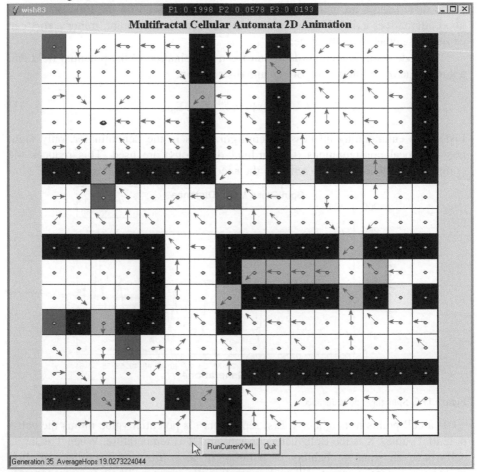

Figure 11.1. Idealized urban terrain. Oval is the data sink.

2.   SPIN GLASS ROUTING

The spin glass method is based on the Ising model in physics. Locally interacting magnets generate a macroscopic magnetic field. Field intensity depends on a kinetic factor. No macroscopic field exists when randomly pointing magnets cancel each other out. Magnets can align in metals like iron creating a perceptible magnetic field. We apply a similar concept to route data in an *ad hoc* sensor network.

Our simulations use a two-dimensional MOUT scenario like Figure 11.1. Each cell is a miniature magnet pointing in one of eight cardinal directions as its next hop on its way to the data sink. A potential energy field is established by data propagating hop by hop from the data sink, defining the minimum number of hops from each node to the data sink. One or more sinks can exist. Cells attempt to find optimal routes to the nearest data sink. Link failures update the potential field locally. This change diffuses through the system starting where the error occurs. Some disturbances are minor (e.g., no other nodes depend on the link, or equally good alternatives exist). If a link serves as a critical routing point, minor errors can cause phase changes in the system.

The node's spin direction (data route) is a combination of the potential field and a kinetic factor. It follows the Boltzmann distribution:

$$P[s] = e^{-E(s)/KT} / \Sigma_A e^{-E(A)/KT} \tag{71}$$

Instead of enumerating all possible configurations in the denominator, only eight possible local configurations (the cardinal directions) are used. This reduces the computation needed and also removes the need for global information.

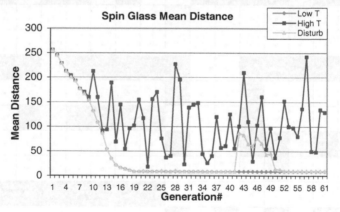

Figure 11.2. Spin glass mean distance

If a cell points to neighbor s, E(s) represents s's potential value minus the cell's potential value. K is the Boltzmann constant and T is temperature. When T is large, cells have an equal probability of pointing in any direction, regardless of their neighbors' potential energy. When T is small, cells are more likely to point towards low energy neighbors. If T is at or below the freezing point, the system is in a rigid state and does not respond to its environment. T is important, because the shortest path is not the only important factor. A large T may reduce the power drain on choke points by data taking longer routes. A low T can protect the system by reducing oscillations in the system. T can be specified on a per-region basis, allowing flexible control of the system.

To quantify system adaptation we measure the average distance from each node to the data sink. Figure 11.2 shows the mean number of hops vs. generation number (time step) for a low temperature system (Low T), high temperature system (High T), and a system with a topological disturbance (Disturb). Topological disturbances correspond to choke points in Figure 11.1 opening or closing. The system converges well when T is small, but not when T is large. Topological disturbances are accommodated after a number of fluctuating generations.

Figure 11.3 shows system power consumption. This is indicative of system scalability. Our analysis considers only communications overhead. To quantify the amount of energy consumed we compute the total number of messages sent and their size. Figure 11.3 shows communications cost with and without two topological disturbances.

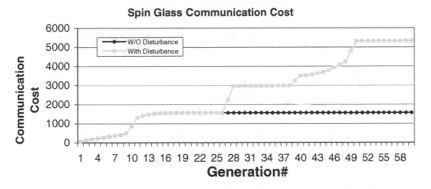

Figure 11.3. Spin glass communication cost.

Figure 11.4 further illustrates how mean distances are affected under various temperatures. We observe that there is an abrupt rise in mean hops if the temperature is raised above 500 Kelvin.

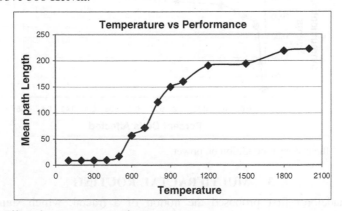

Figure 11.4. Effect of temperature on performance.

The number of messages sent during the route establishment phase was quantified to evaluate the scalability of our routing model. We also study how the spin glass model behaves under error conditions. Figure 11.5 illustrates how system performance in terms of mean hops is affected by error conditions. We have identified two different error conditions: (*i*) nodes randomly choose a spin direction instead of following the Boltzmann distribution function, and (*ii*) nodes send an incorrect potential value to neighbors. Notice that the system is very sensitive to these error conditions. Performance drastically deteriorates as errors begin to occur with a frequency beyond 1%. Figure 11.6 illustrates the communication cost vs. error conditions. As expected, the number of messages exchanged increases largely due to error message diffusion throughout the system. We conclude that although the spin glass model achieves high performance, power consumption is high and error tolerance is quite limited.

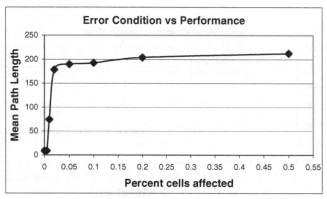

Figure 11.5. Effect of error condition on performance.

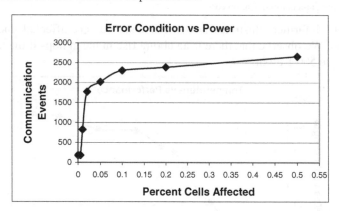

Figure 11.6. Effect of error condition on power.

3.   MULTIFRACTAL ROUTING

Benoit Mandelbrot first proposed the notion of a fractal, which stands for an irregular geometric object with an infinite nesting of structure at all scales. The classic irreversible fractal growth model for gas and fluid is called Diffusion Limited Aggregation (DLA), first introduced by Witten and Sander (WS) in the early 1980s. Beginning with one foreign seed or even a line segment, a random walk of gas or fluid particles becomes immobilized upon contact with the seeds if a certain crystallization condition is satisfied. Randomly diffusing particles keep sticking to each other and form an aggregate. The structure of this fractal is affected by many factors including crystallization growth inhibition exerted by the crystallization site, which limits adherence to the crystalline structure in a local area. Interfacial surface tension and latent heat diffusion effects can physically explain this inhibition [Gaylord 1996].

In our multifractal routing model, the data sink is set to be the single foreign seed. A routing tree starts growing from the seed. A sensor node can attach itself to the tree only if any tree nodes reach its neighborhood. Based on the number of neighboring immobilized tree nodes, a set of probabilities of joining the routing tree is specified. Cells are less likely to join in the routing tree as the number of neighboring tree nodes increases. Depending on different levels of the repulsion effect embedded in the crystallization inhibition parameters, the growth rate and the routing tree structure can be controlled. Generally a sparse tree with high region coverage that is grown in a reasonable amount of time steps is desirable. In order to select a probability set for a good routing tree, a fitness function is constructed to evaluate the quality of the routing trees. For tree i grown under a certain probability set, the fitness value is computed as

$$F_i = C_i / (T_i/b + N_i) \tag{72}$$

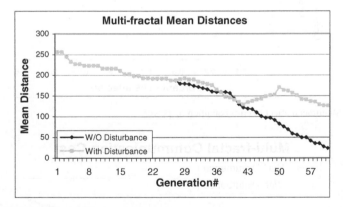

Figure 11.7. Multifractal mean distance convergence.

C_i is the percent coverage of the region, T_i is the number of discrete time steps, N_i is the number of tree nodes, and b is a constant used to normalize the time steps and number of tree nodes. The higher the fitness value is, the better the routing tree is. The constant b actually represents our tradeoff between scarcity and routing time.

Figure 11.7 shows the mean number of hops per generation number (time step) with and without topological disturbances. Communication cost as well as error tolerance are investigated as was done for the spin glass model. Malfunctioning nodes are no longer restrained by desired multifractal behavior. Two principle malfunctions have been modeled: (*i*) faulty nodes have the same probability of joining the tree or not, and (*ii*) faulty nodes randomly choose neighbor tree nodes to attach to.

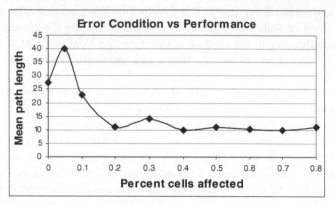

Figure 11.8. Multifractal effect of error condition on performance

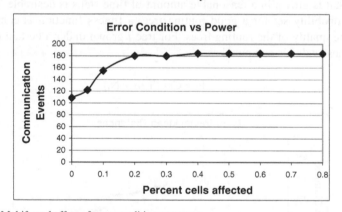

Figure 11.9. Multifractal effect of error condition on power

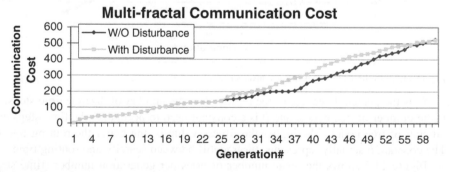

Figure 11.10. Multifractal communication cost

Figure 11.8 shows how error conditions affect the routing performance. Notice that there is a spike in the mean hops when the random errors occur, and then the mean hops begins to drop down by almost half and stays steady when the error percentage goes up to 20%. The shorter mean hops come with the cost of denser trees as can be seen in Figure 11.9. Increased incidence of errors incurs considerably more communication events, however, the extra communication cost is relatively less than that of spin glass model under the same circumstances. Recall that we want a sparse tree, which covers most of the region. However, the final tree consists of approximately 75% more tree nodes compared with the original error-free tree. The fitness of error conditioned tree is actually not ameliorated. Our results indicate that the multifractal model is more error resilient in terms of performance and power in comparison with spin glass. Figure 11.10 shows power consumption with and without a disturbance.

4. PHEROMONE ROUTING

The pheromone model used is based on how ants forage for food and related to the approach in [Dorigo 1996]. Data sources (sinks) are ant nests (food). Messages are ants. Ants attempt to find paths between the nests and food sources. They release two different pheromones: (*i*) search pheromone when they look for food and (*ii*) return pheromone when they have food and return to the nest.

The ants also follow a random walk, but they also search for the opposite pheromone of the one they currently release. Ants searching for food tend to follow the highest concentration of return pheromone. Ants returning to the nest tend to follow the highest concentration of search pheromone. This is modeled as a probability distribution where each ant is more likely to move following the pheromone gradient.

The approach in [Dorigo 1996] was designed for wired networks. Our scenario is more similar to an open field. In our initial implementation a pathology was noticed where ants moving to and from the data sink would form a cycle. To counteract this, we caused the ants to be repulsed by the pheromone they currently emit.   A parameter was created denoting the relative strength of repulsion and attraction. This compels ants not to stay in one area and solved the pathology.

To evaluate this algorithm we measure the number of hops an ant needs to make a round trip from its nest to a food source. Figure 11.11 plots this vs. the repulsion ratio. A ratio of approximately 80% works best.

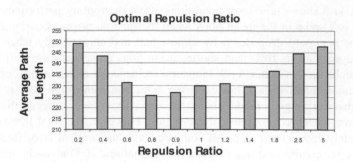

Figure 11.11. Effect of repulsion on performance.

To evaluate the algorithm's power consumption we have used the same metric as was used in previous sections, namely how often each cell changes its state. Figure 11.12 shows how varying the repulsion ratio affects the power consumption of the algorithm. Analysis of this graph indicates that increasing the repulsion ratio beyond 90% has a positive effect on power and that a ratio of 90% (which yields optimal performance) also yields the highest power consumption.

The rate at which a data source (ant nest) generates ants is controlled by a parameter setting that denotes the probability that a data source will spawn an ant in any particular generation. Figure 11.13 shows how varying this parameter affects performance; a spawn frequency at or above 25% yields good performance. We have also evaluated how spawn frequency affects power as is seen in Figure 11.14. Power increases quite rapidly for spawn frequencies below 25%. Beyond this point the rate that power increases becomes quite small.

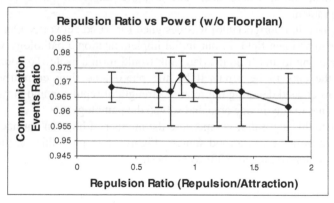

Figure 11.12. Effect of repulsion on power.

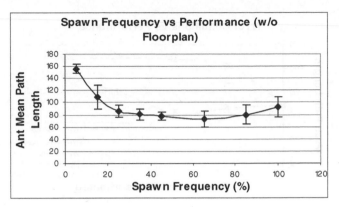

Figure 11.13. Effect of spawn frequency on performance.

We have evaluated this algorithm for several different error conditions to determine its robustness. These error conditions are (*i*) haywire random (a random selection of ants will move randomly for a random amount of time), (*ii*) haywire weighted (a random selection of ants will follow the opposite pheromone), and (*iii*) haywire cells (a random selection of cells will produce a random amount of pheromone). How these error conditions affect performance is illustrated in Figure 11.15. Notice how up to 50% of ants affected with haywire random increases performance. The effects of haywire cells and haywire weighted are similar, in that they reduce performance drastically up to about 25%, where further hits to performance begin to level off. In Figure 11.16 we show how these error conditions affect the power consumption of the algorithm. The power consumption for haywire cells is quite dramatic; anything beyond 25% is near maximum power consumption. The decrease in power consumption attributed to haywire weighted can be attributed to how this behavior tends to cause the ants to conglomerate into groups and not move, which has the side effect of reducing communication.

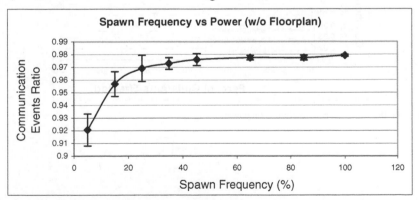

Figure 11.14. Effect of spawn frequency on power.

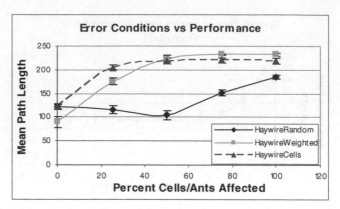

Figure 11.15. Effect of error conditions on performance.

It has been our experience that incorporating a random component into these algorithms usually results in improved performance. The manner in which we have included randomness into this algorithm is by having the ants occasionally move randomly instead of utilizing the pheromones. The performance impact of this method is presented in Figure 11.17. We have determined that a parameter value of about 25% is best for improving performance. We have also evaluated the random movement capability on power consumption. The results are provided in Figure 11.18. We have determined that power consumption and the random movement parameter are unrelated.

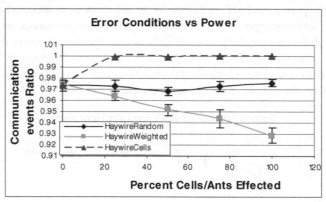

Figure 11.16. Effect of error conditions on power.

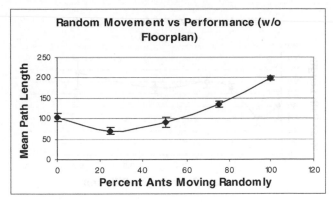

Figure 11.17. Effect of random ant movement on performance.

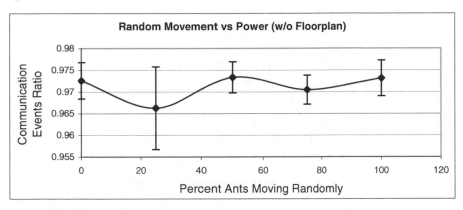

Figure 11.18. Effect of random ant movement on power.

A parameter known as diffusion rate has been concocted so that the algorithm can control how readily the pheromone in one cell spreads to its neighboring cells. This parameter's effect upon performance is provided in Figure 11.19. From our experience a setting of 0.1 works best. The effect of diffusion upon power is illustrated with Figure 11.20. This graph indicates that a diffusion rate of below 0.2 is preferred for low power.

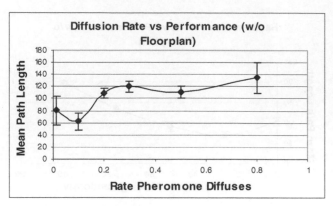

Figure 11.19. Effect of diffusion on performance.

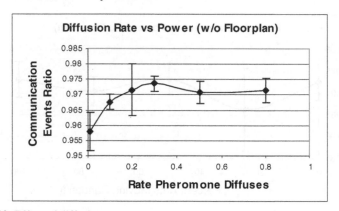

Figure 11.20. Effect of diffusion on power.

To reduce power we have included a parameter denoted as evaporation. In each generation of the algorithm a certain percentage of the ant pheromone evaporates (i.e., it disappears). As Figure 11.21 indicates evaporation beyond 0.05 begins to adversely affect performance. Interestingly enough parameter settings below 0.05 improves the algorithm's performance.

We have analyzed evaporation based on power as well, as Figure 11.22 indicates. Not surprisingly, increasing the value of this parameter helps to reduce the power of this algorithm. Unfortunately, any parameter setting that would result in significant power savings coincides with greatly decreased performance. As a result we find a setting of 0.01 to be optimal.

As a result of our analysis we have come to the conclusion that this algorithm has good performance and excellent error resistance when proper parameters have been specified.

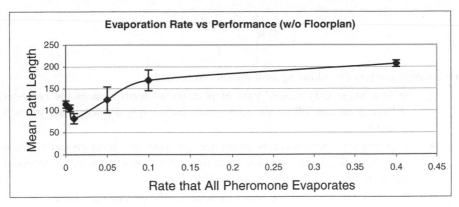

Figure 11.21. Effect of evaporation on performance.

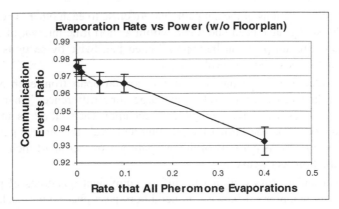

Figure 11.22. Effect of evaporation on power.

To understand the behavior of ant pheromone the following iterative equation was developed:

$$P_{x,y,t} = (1 - E)P_{x,y,t-1}(1 - \rho F) + L(x, y, t) + \sum_{i=1}^{\sqrt{N+1}} \sum_{j=1}^{\sqrt{N+1}} (1 - E)P_{i,j,t-1} \frac{F}{N} \rho * s(i, j) \qquad (73)$$

where

$P_{x,y,t}$ = Pheromone level at location (x,y) at time t
E = Evaporation rate in $[0,1]$
ρ = Gossip probability in $[0,1]$
F = Diffusion rate in $[0,1]$
$L(x,y,t)$ = Path of ant for time t
N = Size of neighborhood

$$s(i,j) \begin{cases} 0, \text{ if } i = j \\ \\ 1 \end{cases}$$

To simplify matters the following assumptions were made:

- An instantaneously formed path of pheromone approximates the behavior of having an ant follow the same path laying down pheromone in each generation.
- Perpendicular cross-sections along the ant path are independent of each other. Specifically, it is assumed that the pheromones in one cross-sectional region do not affect another cross-sectional area.
- The evaporation rate should not be allowed to be exceedingly large.

We justify these assumptions as follows:

- Consider sections of the ant path that are close to each other. These sections will usually have been laid down within a short time interval of each other. The entire ant path can be approximated piecewise by sections laid down instantaneously across local regions.
- Consider sections of the ant path that are far apart from each other. They were laid down with a relatively large time difference. Their respective pheromones will have negligible effect upon each other, as indicated by Equation (73). The further the pheromone travels the more it gets diffused. Consequently as portions of the ant path get further apart their pheromone interactions get weaker.
- A particular cross-section will diffuse equivalent quantities of pheromone into its neighbors. Likewise its neighbors pass pheromone back into it. If the cross-sectional area's pheromones are similar to that of its neighbors, it can be assumed that the pheromone leaving the region is similar to the pheromone coming in. Thus the cross-sectional areas can be considered to be independent of each other.
- For the second assumption to be valid the evaporation rate cannot be too high. Since this is entirely controlled by a parameter setting this can be readily done. Fortunately, a high evaporation rate is not particularly interesting, since most ant paths are reduced to nothing quite rapidly making pheromone routing largely ineffective.

Given (73), if one were to look at any point along the ant path during the instant that the ant laid down the pheromone one would see the following behavior:

- Initially all the pheromone would be located along the ant trail.
- As time progresses, Equation (73) dictates that the pheromone will spread. Specifically, the pheromone will move one hop further from the initial ant path each generation. It can be seen from Equation (73) that in each cross-sectional area the pheromone will resemble a curve. The peak of the curve shall always be located along the ant path. The further from the ant path a particular point is, the less its pheromone level will be.

- As time progresses, the curve of pheromone in a cross-section expands to new regions. The curve will flatten over time. This can be seen by examining (73) and seeing that large local differences in pheromone will smooth out with time.

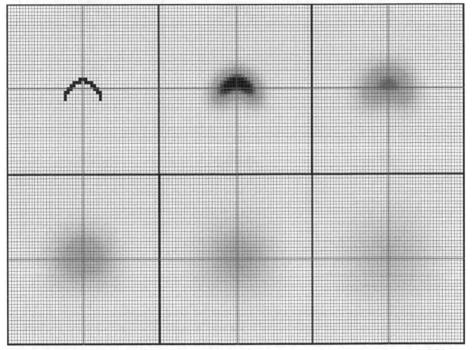

Figure 11.23. Pheromone diffusion at work. (Top left) shows an initial curve of pheromone is laid down at time 0. As time progresses the pheromone diffuses as shown by (top middle) at time 10, (top right) at time 20, (bottom left) at time 40, (bottom middle) at time 60, and (bottom right) at time 100.

The ant's path divides the region into two portions. On one portion, the cross-sectional areas will point towards the center of the curve (call these sections type a), while in the other portion the cross-sectional areas will point away from the center of the curve (call these sections type b). Given the symmetry of the pheromone model both of these regions will have the same amount of pheromone within them.

The type b cross-sectional region will diffuse into a larger area than the type a cross-sectional region. Therefore the individual pheromone levels in the type a cross-sectional region will be higher than the pheromone levels in the type b cross-sectional region. This will cause the ants to want to follow the pheromone in the type a region, which contains the optimal path (i.e., the straight line connecting the curve's endpoints).

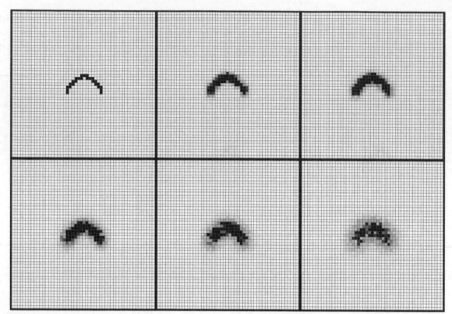

Figure 11.24. The effect of a gossip probability of 0.25. (Top left) shows an initial curve of pheromone is laid down at time 0. As time progresses, the pheromone diffuses as shown by (top middle) at time 10, (top right) at time 20, (bottom left) at time 40, (bottom middle) at time 60, (bottom right) at time 100.

Gossip is a communication method that can be used to replace message flooding. Consider the following example using flooding. A node in a sensor network wants to send a message to all other nodes in the network. So the node broadcasts the message to all of its neighbors. These neighbors in turn broadcast the message to their neighbors. Each time a node receives such a message for the first time it will broadcast. When a node receives a duplicate message it will not broadcast. Eventually the entire network receives the message at the expense of a huge volume of messages. With gossip instead of always routing a received message to all neighbors, there is a probability that the node will broadcast the message. This technique greatly reduces the number of messages required to contact all nodes in a region. With proper parameter settings this technique gets the message to all nodes with a near 1 probability, with far fewer messages than required with flooding. An excellent example of different types of gossip that shows the effect of varying parameter values is provided in [Haas 2002]. More in-depth analysis of gossip is in [Kempe 2001, Chandra 2001], and [Wokoma 2002].

The probabilistic message passing idea from gossip has been applied to how pheromone behaves in the ant pheromone algorithm. Diffusion of pheromone in particular was modified. Now a node will have a certain probability that it will diffuse its pheromone upon its neighbors. Examining (73) shows that including gossip slows diffusion of pheromone. It also makes the pheromone gradient more sporadic when pheromone information is shared less often.

To illustrate the effects of utilizing gossip, two separate examples similar to Figure 11.23 are provided. Again an initial curve shaped path of pheromone is laid down at time 0, and as time progresses the pheromone diffuses through the region. In Figure 11.23 example, every generation a cell would diffuse some of its pheromone to its neighbors. In Figure 11.24 there is a 0.25 probability that a cell diffuses its pheromone, and in Figure 11.25 there is a 0.75 probability that a cell diffuses its pheromone.

These examples show using gossip in the pheromone makes the gradient less smooth. Further, the lower the probability that a cell passes pheromone information, the longer it takes the pheromone region to expand.

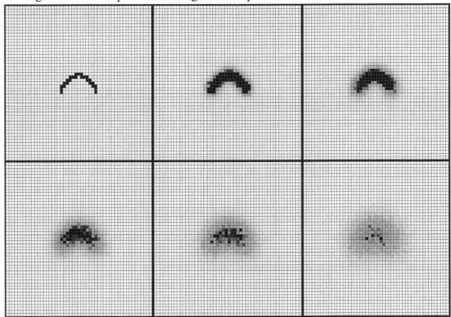

Figure 11.25. The effect of a gossip probability of 0.75. (Top left) shows an initial curve of pheromone is laid down at time 0. As time progresses the pheromone diffuses as shown by (top middle) at time 10, (top right) at time 20, (bottom left) at time 40, (bottom middle) at time 60, and (bottom right) at time 100.

5.   COMPARISON OF ROUTING ALGORITHMS

Many adaptive routing protocols have been proposed. The Link State (LS) routing algorithm requires global knowledge about the network. Global routing protocols suffer serious scalability problems as network size increases [Kurose 2003]. DSDV is an iterative, table-driven, and distributed routing scheme that stores the next hop and number of hops for each reachable node. The routing table storage requirement and periodic broadcasting are the two main drawbacks to this protocol.

In Dynamic Source Routing Protocol (DSR), a complete record of traversed cells is required to be carried by each data packet. Although no up-to-date routing information is maintained in the intermediate nodes' routing table, the complete cell record carried by each packet imposes storage and bandwidth problems.

AODV alleviates the overhead problem in DSR by dynamically establishing route table entries at intermediate nodes, but symmetric links are required by AODV. Cluster head gateway switch routing (CGSR) uses DSDV as the underlying routing scheme to hierarchically address the network.

Cluster head and gateway cells are subject to higher communication and computation burden and their failure can greatly deteriorate the system [Royer 1999]. Greedy perimeter stateless routing algorithm (GPSR) claims to be highly efficient in table storage and communication overhead. However, it heavily relies on the self-describing geographic position, which may not be available under most conditions. In addition, the greedy forwarding mechanism may prohibit a valid path to be discovered if some detouring is necessary [Karp 2000].

The spin glass and multifractal models are related to the table-driven routing protocols by establishing routes from every cell to data sink(s). These protocols ensure timely data transmission on demand without searching for the route each time. The ant pheromone model is related to the packet-driven protocols. Ants can be viewed as packets traversing from data sources to data sinks. All of the models we presented are decentralized, using only local knowledge at each node. They dynamically adapt to topological disturbances (path loss). Storage requirements for the routing table of spin glass and multifractal are low compared with most other protocols, while the ant pheromone's storage requirements are even lower than these two.

The temporally ordered routing algorithm (TORA) is a source initiated and distributed routing scheme that shares some properties with the spin glass model. It establishes an acyclic graph using height metric relative to the data sink and also has local reaction to topological disturbances [Royer 1999].

The kinetic factor in our spin glass model and the frequency of ant generation in the ant pheromone model provides the system with flexibility in controlling routing behaviors under various conditions. Route maintenance overhead is moderately high for the spin glass model.

The multifractal approach, as a probabilistic space-filling curve, has very light computation and communication load, and overhead is saved in route discovery and maintenance. This is at the cost of a higher distance to the data sink(s). Route maintenance overhead for the pheromones is low due to the reduced number of nodes involved in each path. Since the multifractal model strives to cover the sensor field by using as few cells as possible, the sparse routing tree sparse conserves energy. The shortest routes to the data sink are not found using the multifractal model.

On the other hand, spin glass model is more sensitive to internal errors since any possible error may diffuse throughout the network. The multifractal and ant pheromone models are very resistant to internal errors. The time required for the ant pheromone algorithm to converge to a steady state is much longer than required by the other two adaptations. For applications requiring short data paths, the spin glass model is preferred.   For overhead sensitive applications that require quick deployment, the multifractal model is a better candidate. If error resilience and low overhead are the principle requirements, then the ant pheromone model is appropriate. Hybrid methods or switching between methods at different phases may be useful.

6. EPIDEMIC RESOURCE DISCOVERY

In both wireless networks with uncoordinated node placement and peer-to-peer systems without centralized coordination, it is necessary for nodes to partially or fully discover the topology of the network to locate resources in the network. Resource discovery algorithms dynamically set up and maintain paths to network resources as needed. These algorithms are analyzed in terms of the probability that they find a given resource, their latency to find the resource, and the resources consumed during their search.

Resource discovery has received significant attention in the research community. We found that the algorithms considered can be discussed in terms of a spectrum of algorithms: from flooding, through gossip, to random walk. Resource discovery algorithms are usually variations or hybrid versions of these three techniques. The spectrum can be seen as

← Flooding	Gossip	Random Walk →
Least Latency (optimal)		Highest Latency
Most Message Passing		Least Message Passing

As this figure indicates flooding has the least latency and most overhead, random walk has the highest latency and least overhead; gossip lies between these extremes.

Flooding algorithms rely on massive replication of information to convey a single message to any number of destinations. In the examples, we present a network organized in a two-dimensional grid. The examples also show a source node interested in reaching one particular destination with all nodes able to communicate with their neighbors directly. This is a specific instance of the problem for illustration. These approaches can easily be expanded to any tessellation or graph structure.

In flooding, a node creates a message and sends a copy to each of its neighbors (as indicated by the node labeled 1 in Figure 11.26). When a node B receives a message from a node A it will forwards the message to each neighbor except A. This flooding process is terminated by a maximum time to live (TTL) parameter. Each time a message is replicated its TTL is decremented by 1. Once the TTL parameter becomes 0 the message is not propagated further. The TTL must be large enough to guarantee that the destination is within TTL hops of the source. The message reaches its destination in the minimum number of hops. The shortcoming of this technique is the huge amount of messages generated. The number of messages generated at each hop L by flooding is given by

$$T_F = \begin{cases} 1, & L=1 \\ 4*(L-1), & L \neq 1 \end{cases} \tag{74}$$

This equation is derived by observing that the perimeter of the "diamond" created by flooding increases by 4 nodes each iteration (e.g., in the fourth iteration the perimeter has 12 nodes). The total number of messages generated can be determined by summing the previous equation over the TTL:

$$N_f = \sum_{l=1}^{TTL}\left(4(l-1)*2+4\right) = 4TTL+8\sum_{l=1}^{TTL}(l-1)$$

$$= 4TTL+8\frac{TTL}{2}(TTL-1+0) = 4TTL^2 \tag{75}$$

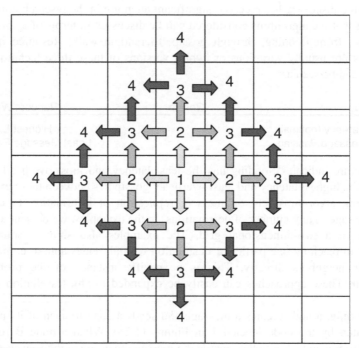

Figure 11.26. In flooding, each node forwards a message to all neighbors that may not have a copy of the message.

Gossip algorithms are a variant of flooding. They are part of a class of epidemic algorithms that probabilistically propagate messages. When a node receives a message, it forwards the message to each of its neighbors with probability p (flooding is gossip with p set to 1). The number of messages generated is drastically reduced. When p is properly chosen, the algorithm latency approaches that of flooding. Figure 11.27 shows an example of a gossip algorithm. Notice how nodes marked with underlines do not propagate the message to their neighbors.

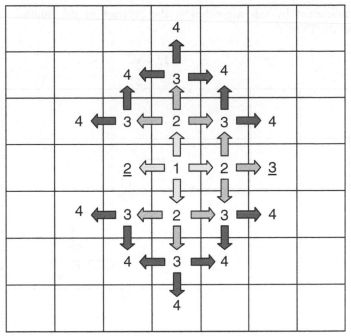

Figure 11.27. With gossip, each node forwards the message to each neighbor with probability p.

In gossip, when the value for p is large enough, the message reaches its destination with a very high probability. The latency is close to that of flooding. Noting that the number of messages in a gossip iteration is related to the number generated in the flooding algorithm by the parameter p gives

$$T_G = \begin{cases} 1, & L = 1 \\ 4*(L-1)p, & L \neq 1 \end{cases} \tag{76}$$

The total number of messages generated by flooding is

$$N_g = 4pL^2 \tag{77}$$

Random walk algorithms have the message source initially generate a preset number of message copies. These messages wander the network until they successfully find their destination or exceed the TTL parameter and are dropped. Figure 11.28 shows a node generating one random walker. The important distinction between random walk and the other techniques is that it generates an initial quantity of messages. Messages are not replicated during the algorithm. Random walk approaches reach their destination with less probability and higher latency than the other techniques, but with far fewer messages generated. The maximum number of packets transmitted by this algorithm is the product of the number of random walkers and the TTL:

$$N_r = TTL \times N \tag{78}$$

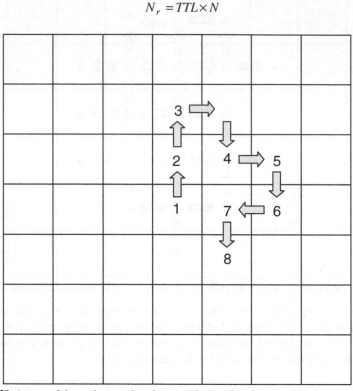

Figure 11.28. A copy of the packer wanders the network at random for up to TTL hops or until the destination is reached.

To determine when each approach is appropriate, we evaluated them on the basis of probability of message reaching destination, the latency required for a message to reach its destination, and the total number of packets transmitted. For comparison we used a network topology that was a two-dimensional grid of infinite size.

The number of packets transmitted by each algorithm uses Equations (75), (77), and (78). Several trends are evident from Figure 11.29. First, flooding produces the most messages. Gossip produces the second highest amount of messages. The number of messages generated increases linearly with the value of p. We also see that the number of random walkers generated increases the number of message hops in a linear manner. It is clear that in terms of message overhead random walk becomes increasingly more attractive as the TTL parameter increases.

To compute the probability that a random walker finds its destination and the expected latency, we model the network as a Markov chain. This requires finding a transition probability matrix that models how each node communicates with its neighbors. As an example, Figure 11.30 shows a Markov chain modeling a 5-by-5 array of nodes. The corresponding transition probability matrix has a row and column for each of the 25 nodes. Matrix element [*i,j*] is the probability of a random walker going from point *i* to point *j*. The matrix will be very sparse as a random walker only moves to the neighbors of the node it currently occupies.

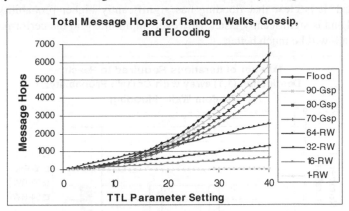

Figure 11.29. Comparison of the overhead incurred by epidemic propagation approaches vs. TTL.

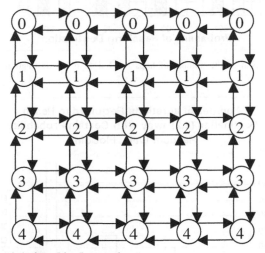

Figure 11.30. Markov chain for a 5-by-5 network.

The probability that a flooding message reaches its destination is straightforward. If the TTL is smaller than the number of hops to the destination, the probability the message reaches its destination is 0. If the TTL is large enough, the probability the message reaches its destination is 1.

$$P_f = \begin{cases} 0, & L < d \\ 1, & L \geq d \end{cases} \tag{79}$$

For flooding if the TTL is large enough, the number of hops required to reach the destination is optimal.

Figures 11.31 and 11.32 illustrate how random walks with 16, 32, and 64 random walkers compare to flooding when the destination is two and four hops away in an infinite grid. It is clear that flooding has significantly higher probability of being successful and is significantly faster. However, in a finite grid the performance of the random walk will be much better.

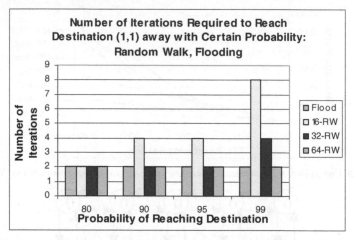

Figure 11.31. Comparison of the number of hops needed to reach destination (1,1) with a high probability.

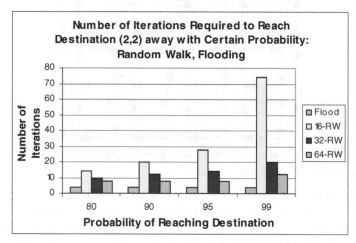

Figure 11.32. Comparison of the number of hops needed to reach destination (2,2) with a high probability.

Now consider a random walker moving through a more difficult region, one similar to a maze (i.e., there are various obstacles in the network breaking up the regular structure). More formally let $G=(V,E)$ be a (nondirected) graph and let v_0 and

v_f be two vertices in G. Suppose that we are given a path π_0 from v_0 to v_f. Consider the following questions:

- Assuming we can only "see" within one hop, is it possible to determine an algorithm to improve π_0?

- What is the convergence rate of the algorithm? Can it be improved?

We propose an algorithm that incrementally improves the structure of the path. Suppose that we are able to see at most n hops away and we have left a set of markers on the path π_0 so that we know whether we are n hops from π_0 by being able to see the marker. Further, suppose that each vertex $v \in V$ can provide a number d_v that it believes is its distance from v_0 in the absence of network failure. This number may be false. Let $N(v)$ be the neighbors of vertex v. For each v in π_0, we evaluate the vertices of $N(v)$ for the following criteria:

- The alleged distance from $u \in N(v)$ to v_0 is less than the distance from v to v_0.

- The neighbors of u are within distance n of π_0.

From $N(v)$ we choose the y satisfying these criteria and minimizing the perceived distance to v_0. Suppose that by time t we have reached vertex v_t. It may be the case that vertex v_t was wrong about its distance to v_0 and all its neighbors are farther away from v_0, then we backtrack to vertex v_{t-1} and repeat choose a new vertex with the new knowledge we have been given about v_t.

This process is summarized in the following algorithm:

Algorithm 1 IMPROVEPATH

Input: Graph G, Position $v \in V(G)$, Destination $v_0 \in V(G)$, Seed Path $P : \mathbb{N} \to V(G)$, Distance Function $d : V(G) \times V(G) \to \mathbb{N}$, Sight Distance n, Current Path P', Step k;
Output BOOLEAN
if $v' = v_0$ **then**
    return TRUE;
end if
$P'(k) = v$; {Extend P'}
$N(v) \leftarrow \{x : (x, v) \in E\}$; {Define valid neighbors}
$\leq_v \leftarrow \{(x, y) \in N(v) \times N(v) : d(x, v_0) \neq \infty \wedge d(y, v_0) \neq \infty \wedge d(x, v_0) \leq d(y, v_0)\}$
{Define a partial order on the neighbors}
repeat
    $v' \leftarrow$ least v in $(N(v), <_v)$; {Try the vertex closest to the goal}
    $d_{\min} \leftarrow d(v', v_0)$;
    if $d_{\min} = \infty \vee (d(v_0, v) < d(v_0, v')) \vee (|P'| + d_{\min} > |P|)$ **then**
        break;
    else if IMPROVEPATH$(G, v', v_0, P, d, n, P', k + 1) =$ FALSE **then**
        $N(v) = N(v) - \{v'\}$ {That vertex didn't work. Try something else.}
        $d(v_0, v') \leftarrow \infty$;
        $<_v \leftarrow \{(x, y) \in N(v) \times N(v) : d(x, v_0) \neq \infty \wedge d(y, v_0) \neq \infty \wedge d(x, v_0) < d(y, v_0)\}$
    else
        return TRUE {There is a path to the goal along that vertex}
    end if
until $N(v) = \emptyset$
$P'(k) \leftarrow$ NULL; {Go back, this vertex doesn't work}
return FALSE;

The following things can be shown for this process:

- A path from v_f to v_0 will be produced.
- If there is a shorter path π_1 from v_f to v_0 within distance n of π_0, then this process will find the shorter path.
- The rate of convergence to the shortest such path is dependent on the structure of G.
- Suppose that the degree of every vertex in V is bounded above by D. Then the number of steps to reach v_0 from v_f following this procedure is at worst $(D-1)^n |\pi_0|$.

Proving these facts is easy. For the first statement, at the very worst, we will simply walk along π_0; hence a path will be found, since we know that π_0 exists. To prove the third statement, consider the first step away from v_f. We may take 1 step away from v_f and then there may be from D-1 choices to make. Repeat this again to take a second step away and there are now at most D-1 choices. If we repeat this process for n steps and each branch ends in a failure, then we've taken $(D-1)^n$ wrong steps to make the first successful step of the trip from v_f to v_0. Lastly, to prove the second statement, it suffices to observe that if there is a path that is shorter and within distance n of π_0, then our algorithm will find it by a greedy heuristic. This process can then be iterated.

We now provide several examples of this algorithm in use. Consider a random walker on $\Lambda = R^2$. Suppose that this walker has a path from a point $x_0 \in \Lambda$ to some other point $x_f \in \Lambda$ and that this path is not optimal. We show several examples of the performance of the algorithm we have posed above.

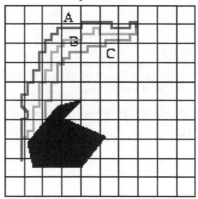

Figure 11.33. A successful use of the algorithm to avoid a nonconvex obstacle.

Figure 11.33 shows the operation of the algorithm when the path connecting points v_0 and v_f is almost optimal. At each stage of execution, the algorithm will improve on the existing path by finding a new path that is "in sight" of the original path but contains locations with a shorter total distance to the target.

Figure 11.34 shows a run of the algorithm when there is a large nonconvex hole in the lattice. The algorithm will construct a path that hits the hole in the graph and then returns to the previously known shortest path.

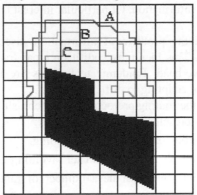

Figure 11.34. A mostly successful use of the algorithm. When the new path hits the obstacle, it will return to the known path and the algorithm will stop.

Figure 11.35 shows one of the natural limitations of this approach. The algorithm will make improvements to the existing path, but is unable to find the true shortest path because it cannot move too far away from a node working path between v_0 and v_f.

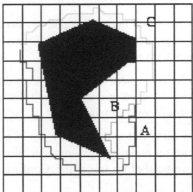

Figure 11.35. The natural limitation of this approach.

7.   CONCLUSION

This chapter has extended the P2P design concepts from Chapter 10. Once a P2P structure is set up, the issues become

- How to transmit information within an uncoordinated infrastructure
- How to find the location of resources in a constantly changing environment

Practical methods need to make minimal assumptions about the topology and stability of the environment.

We started this chapter by presenting the current state of *ad hoc* routing protocols, since the environment they consider is closest to the one we are interested in. We then discussed new techniques that we developed specifically to adapt to disturbances using local information. Of particular interest is the resources consumed by these approaches.

We then considered the problem of information discovery and established a hierarchy of techniques. This hierarchy codifies a clear trade off between message latency and protocol overhead. Epidemic techniques are useful because they are simple and yet capable of adapting to difficult terrains.

Closer inspection of the routing protocols we present, show them to be hybrids of the epidemic approaches presented later in the chapter:

- Spin glass is a protocol built on local flooding.
- Multifractal protocols are built from self-avoiding random walks.
- Pheromone techniques combine a number of random walkers with local flooding of information.

In many ways, the robustness of these techniques is a direct consequence of their epidemic substrate.

8.   EXERCISES

Exercise 11.1 Use the epidemic analysis techniques to confirm the routing robustness results and contrast the routing techniques presented.

Exercise 11.2 For a simple, given network topology, predict the number of time steps needed by the epidemic information discovery techniques to find the destination. Confirm this with simulations.

Exercise 11.3 For a simple, given network topology, predict the number of packet transmissions needed by the epidemic information discovery techniques to find the destination. Confirm this with simulations.

Exercise 11.4 For a given network topology and random failure model, choose one of the routing techniques for maintaining communications in the network. Predict the performance and overhead of the technique. Confirm with simulations.

CHAPTER 12

Denial of Service Countermeasures[1, 2]

This chapter looks in detail at Denial of Service (DoS) attacks. We are particularly interested in Distributed Denial of Service (DDoS) attacks, where multiple attackers work together to disable a system. Either individual nodes or communications channels can be disabled to stage these attacks. Recently DoS attacks have been attempted against the Internet domain name system (DNS) infrastructure, Microsoft, the White House, and Amazon.com.

Few countermeasures for these attacks exist. They take advantage of the open nature of our computing infrastructure. In this chapter, we describe these attacks in detail and then propose a technique for early detection of DoS events. As we will see, this problem is very challenging and provides insights into the nature of Internet traffic. We then perform a game theoretic analysis of the DoS problem. We will find a way of quantifying the vulnerability of the network to attack.

We will verify our approaches using network simulations and operational traffic when possible. An important conclusion of the research presented here is the importance of testing concepts on operational systems. Unfortunately, this is often difficult or impossible.

1. DENIAL OF SERVICE (DoS) BACKGROUND

A DoS attack is an explicit attempt by attackers to prevent legitimate users of a service from using a service. There are two principal classes of DoS attacks:

- DoS attacks that exploit product defects to cause the system to crash or degrade its performance. They can cause operating systems to lock or reboot. Examples include the "bonk" and the "Ping of Death" attacks. These attacks are product specific and can often be prevented by upgrading faulty software [Strother 2000].

- DoS attacks that exploit vagueness in protocol specifications. Depending on the packet types used by attackers, these DoS attacks can be categorized

---

[1] Coauthored with Glenn Carl, Michael Young, Jason Schwier, Christopher Griffin, and Dr. S. Rai.

[2] Portions reprinted with the permission of The Institute of Industrial Engineers, 3577 Parkway Lane, Suite 200, Norcross, GA, from:

R. R. Brooks and C. Griffin, "Fugitive search strategy and network survivability," *2003 Industrial Engineering Research Conference*, invited paper, May 2003.

into transmission control protocol (TCP) SYN flooding, user datagram protocol (UDP) packet storm, Internet control message protocol (ICMP) ping flooding, etc [CERT 2001]. These attacks are more serious. They affect all implementations of the protocol [Kevin 2001]. Throughout this chapter we discuss this class of DoS attacks unless otherwise stated.

Note that resources such as network bandwidth, processing ability, and memory are always limited. Attackers can launch a DoS attack and deplete the resources available to legitimate users. Early detection of DoS attacks would be very useful. A number of commercial products are available. [Newman 2002] compared eight commercial products using false alarm criteria and observed, "One thing that can be said with certainty about network-based intrusion-detection systems is that they're guaranteed to detect and consume all your available bandwidth. ... Because no product distinguished itself, we are not naming a winner." They considered intrusion detection problems using signature and anomaly detection strategies.

There exist a number of other studies on DoS attacks. Most work is concerned with holes in protocols or products. Little attention has been paid to DoS attack traffic patterns. [Brooks 2002a] used cellular automata models of the network flow dynamics to detect intrusion. [Marin 2002] uses the idea that traffic distributions change and leverages changes in the Hurst parameter using variance-time plot to detect attacks. Their approach relies on two basic notions:

- The traffic before attack remains self-similar.
- DoS attack detection is an offline phenomenon.

It has been shown that the network traffic is multifractal over time scales [Riedi 1999]. This means that traffic is not self-similar at fine scales. This is not consistent with the first notion. An online DoS attack detection procedure, if possible, is desirable and needed for triggering attack countermeasures.

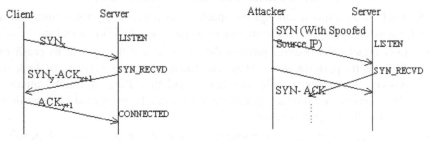

Figure 12.1. (Left) TCP three-way handshake. (Right) SYN flood attack.

Specific network-based DoS attacks include

- TCP SYN flooding: TCP SYN flooding is the most commonly used DoS attack. It is reported that more than 90% of DoS attacks are of this type [Moore 2001a]. When a client attempts to establish a TCP connection to a server providing a service, the client initiates the connection by sending a SYN message to the listening server. The server then acknowledges the connection by sending SYN-ACK message back to the client. The client then finishes establishing the connection by responding with an ACK message. The connection between the client and the server is then open and the service-specific data can be exchanged between the client and the server. This connection establishment process is called the three-way handshake (Figure 12.1). A potential problem of the three-way handshake process comes at the point when the connection is half-open, i.e., the server has sent a SYN-ACK message to the client, but has not yet received the ACK message from the client. At this state, the server has to keep the half-open connection in a backlog queue that is of limited length until the ACK message is received, or until a connection establishment timer expires (for most TCP implementations, the timer expiration time is set to 75 seconds). Since the Internet Protocol (IP) does not require the source address of a packet to be correct, attackers take advantage of this built-in vagueness of IP to launch the TCP SYN flooding attack by sending the SYN packets with spoofed source IP address to the server. When the server acknowledges the SYN packets with SYN-ACK, it can never reach the client (attacker) and the server has to keep the half-open connection in the backlog queue until the connection establishment timer expires (see Figure 12.1). If attackers send SYN packets with spoofed source IP addresses to the server at a very high rate, the backlog queue can be kept full all the time. In this case, no legitimate users can set up a connection with the server. Any system with TCP/IP can be used to launch a TCP SYN flooding attack. Since the TCP SYN packet is small in size, attackers only need a small bandwidth to execute this attack and can cause a very fast network to be paralyzed [CERT 1996].

* *UDP packet storm*: Attackers can also launch DoS attacks by creating a "UDP packet storm" [CERT 1996a]. In this, attackers use forged UDP packets to connect a service on one machine to another service on another (or the same) machine. For example, attackers can connect to the echo service on another (or the same) machine. This can produce a very large number of packets that can consume all available network bandwidth between them and can lead to a denial of service on the machine(s) where the services are offered.

* *ICMP ping flooding*: Attackers may also be able to consume all the available bandwidth on a network by generating a large number of packets directed to that network. Normally ICMP Ping/Echo packets are used. This type attack is thus known as ICMP ping flooding attack [CERT 2001].

Besides the above-mentioned three types of packets employed in DoS attacks, other packets, such as TCP RST, TCP FIN, etc., are also used to launch a DoS attack. However, the rationale of all these DoS attacks is the same, i.e., to deplete the limited resources available to legitimate users.

2. TRAFFIC FLOW MEASURES

Wavelet analysis is important in many areas, including Internet traffic modeling, network performance analysis, and change point detection in time series. We will use wavelets to analyze Internet traffic.

Consider a family of functions:

$$\psi_{j,k}(t) = 2^{j/2}\psi\left(2^j t - k\right) \quad k, j \in Z \tag{80}$$

where j is the scale index and k the position index. The discrete wavelet transform (DWT) of a function $f \in L^2$ can be defined as

$$DWT_f\left(j,k\right) = d_{j,k} = < f, \psi_{j,k}(t) > \tag{81}$$

where $< \cdot, \cdot >$ is the inner product. Note that $d_{j,k}$ is the discrete wavelet coefficient of function f at position k and scale j.

In practice, we only have a sampled version of function f, denoted as $\{f(k)\}$. If $\{f(k)\}$ has length 2^M, then the scale index j has upper-bound M. In which case, the DWT can be computed in $O(2^M)$ by Mallat's pyramid algorithm [Daubechies 1992]. In the following we use $J=M-j$ for the scaling index, so that scale $J=0$ refers to the original time series.

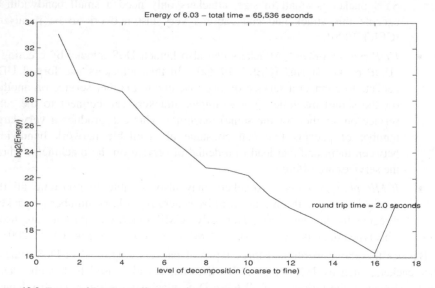

Figure 12.2. Energy of Internet traffic vs. scaling parameter.

Let time series $X(k)$, $k=0,1,2,\ldots$ be the number of packets per unit time received at a node in the Internet. Let $\{d_X(J,k)\}$, $k, J \in Z$ be the discrete wavelet coefficients of $X(k)$. Consider the energy function

$$E_J = \frac{1}{N_J} \sum_k |d_X(J,k)|^2 \tag{82}$$

where N_J is the number of coefficients at scale J. If we plot $\log(E_J)$ as a function of scale J, Figure 12.2 presents a typical curve [Feldmann 1999]. Observe that over a large range of scales, the curve has an asymptotically constant negative first-order derivative. This phenomenon reflects the self-similarity of Internet traffic in large time scales (>2 seconds). At finer scales ($J > 2$s), the curve changes, related to the round-trip time (RTT) of packets. The slope of the curve relates to the Hurst fractal dimension of the network traffic. The fact that the slope varies with scale is the basis for network traffic being considered multifractal.

As we show later, a DoS attack is characterized by a sudden change in network traffic patterns. When packet-flooding attacks occur, there is a substantial increase in the number of packets received by the victim.

For SYN flood attacks, the natural network traffic metric is the number of half-open connections at the server. A sudden spike in the number of half-open connections probably indicates a TCP SYN flooding attack. Other metrics are possible. [Wang 2002] suggests using the difference between the number of SYN packets and FIN packets to detect a TCP SYN flood.

We use the number of packets per unit time received at the server to detect DoS attacks. This measure is $N_{pt}(k)$, the number of packets of type pt received during the kth time interval.

3. ATTACK DETECTION

DoS traffic affects the statistical properties (mean, variance) of the arrival traffic, but with unknown magnitude and temporal variation. Target proximity, number of zombies, and attack coordination are factors. Monitoring of traffic statistics can be used to identify the onset of a DoS attack.

Any network link or end-system node can be monitored for DoS attack traffic. Let $N_{pt}(k)$ denote a time series representing the number of recorded packets of type pt during discrete time interval k. The nonoverlapping time intervals are of uniform length I; therefore $N_{pt}(k)$ can be considered the arrival packet rate during interval k. Interval length I is experimentally chosen such that the time series is not smeared nor contains large fluctuations.

If a DoS attack begins at time λ, the packet time series $N_{pt}(k)$ will be characterized by a significant increase for $k \geq \lambda$. Let $N_{pt}(k)$ be the superposition of normal traffic $N_{pt}^0(k)$ and attack traffic $N_{pt}^1(k)$.

$$N_{pt}(k) = \begin{cases} N_{pt}^0(k) & ;0 < k < \lambda \\ N_{pt}^0(k) + N_{pt}^1(k) ; & k \geq \lambda \end{cases} \tag{83}$$

Assuming $N_{pt}^0(k)$ and $N_{pt}^1(k)$ are independent, then the average rate $m(k)$ of $N_{pt}(k)$ is the summation of the individual traffic means $m^0(k)$ and $m^1(k)$:

$$m\ (k) = \begin{cases} m^0\ (k) & ; & 0 < k < \lambda \\ m^0\ (k) + m^1\ (k) & ; & k \geq \lambda \end{cases} \qquad (84)$$

Due to the DoS attack, the average arrival rate $m(k)$ will increase for $k \geq \lambda$. To identify this increase, change point detection based on a cumulative sum (CUSUM) statistic is used.

The CUSUM algorithm can be described as repeated testing of the null and alternative hypotheses [Basseville 1993] through the use of a sequential probability ratio test (SPRT). For time series $N_{pt}(k)$, let $P_0(N_{pt}(k))$ and $P_1(N_{pt}(k))$ denote the probability of no change and change, respectively. The SPRT process is then

$$S(k) = \left(S(k-1) + \log \frac{P_1(N_{pt}(k))}{P_0(N_{pt}(k))} \right)^+ ; \ S(0) = 0 \qquad (85)$$

where $(x)^+ = \max(0, x)$. The decision rule accepts the null hypothesis (no change) when $S(k) \leq h$, where h is a positive number. Conversely, when $S(k) > h$, the alternative hypothesis (change) is accepted. The optimal threshold h is given by

$$P_0(S(k) > h) = \gamma \qquad (86)$$

where γ is a given false alarm rate.

The CUSUM algorithm in (85) is optimal when the time series $N_{pt}(k)$'s pre-change and post-change distributions are independent and identically distributed. Since no model of the arriving process $N_{pt}(k)$ is available, the i.i.d. assumption of (83) does not hold. The pre-attack and post-attack distribution, $P_0(N_{pt}(k))$ and $P_1(N_{pt}(k))$, respectively, cannot be determined. The CUSUM of (85) cannot be applied directly to time series $N_{pt}(k)$ to detect a DoS attack. [Blazek 2001] addressed this issue by proposing the following nonparametric CUSUM-based method:

$$S(k) = \left(S(k-1) + N_{pt}(k) - m(k) \right)^+ ; \ S(0) = 0 \qquad (87)$$

where $m(k)$ is the estimated average packet rate.

The estimated average packet rate at time k is given by the recursion for $0 \leq \varepsilon < 1$

$$m(k) = \varepsilon * m(k-1) + (1-\varepsilon) * N_{pt}(k); \quad m(0) = 0 \qquad (88)$$

$S(k)$ is sensitive to changes in input $N_{pt}(k)$. Before a change, $S(k)$ is a zero mean process with bounded variance. After a change, $S(k)$ will have a larger variance due to addition of attack traffic and will become a positive process with growing variance.

At each k, $S(k)$ is the cumulative sum of the difference between current and (estimated) average packet rates. $S(k)$ increases (decreases) when the packet rate increases (decreases) more quickly than the average rate. The nonlinear operator $(.)^+$ limits $S(k)$ to positive values since decreasing arrival rates are of no significance in detecting a DoS attack.

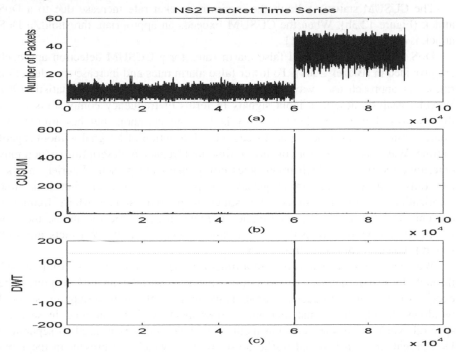

Figure 12.3. (a) ns-2 packet time series with a DoS attack starting at $k = 6 \times 10^4$; (b) CUSUM statistic $S(k)$; (c) 6th level wavelet decomposition coefficient ($d_{6,0}$) of the CUSUM statistic $S(k)$

To reduce high frequency noise in the arrival process, $N_{pt}(k)$ is low-pass filtered using a windowed averaging technique

$$\tilde{N}_{pt}(k) = \alpha * N_{pt}(k) + (1-\alpha) * \tilde{N}_{pt}(k-1) ; \tilde{N}_{pt}(0) = 0 \qquad (89)$$

where $0 < \alpha \leq 1$. Substituting (89) for $N_{pt}(k)$ in $S(k)$, along with small correction factor c, leads to a modified CUSUM algorithm

$$\tilde{S}(k) = (\tilde{S}(k-1) + \tilde{N}_{pt}(k) - m(k) - c)^+ ; \tilde{S}(0) = 0 \qquad (90)$$

where $\tilde{N}_{pt}(k)$ is a windowed average of $N_{pt}(k)$ and $c = c_e * m(k)$ is a correction factor.

Parameter c reduces the variance of slowly varying traffic by removing its contribution to the CUSUM. Also, c decays $S(k)$ back toward zero during periods of constant traffic activity. Parameters ε and $(1-\alpha)$ determine the amount of past history captured in $N_{pt}(k)$ and $m(k)$, respectively. Large values of ε and $(1-\alpha)$ imply long memory dependence.

The CUSUM statistic follows the incoming packet rate increase due to a DoS attack (Figure 12.3b). When the CUSUM exceeds an appropriate threshold, a DoS attack is detected [Blazek 2001].

DoS threshold settings and false alarm rates for a CUSUM detection approach are provided in [Blazek 2001]. To lower false alarm rates and increase true detection rates, our approach uses wavelet analysis of the modified CUSUM statistic (90). Wavelet analysis describes input signals in terms of frequency components rather than statistical measures. Fourier analysis is more common, but has limitations. Fourier transforms provide a global frequency description of a signal without regard to time. Wavelets provide for concurrent time and frequency description, which may determine the time at which frequencies components are present. Fourier analysis can only indicate if certain frequency components are present, but lack time localization. Fourier analysis is better suited to periodic signals whose frequency content is stationary. Packet time series contain many traffic dynamics, most of which are nonperiodic or periodic over time-varying intervals. Wavelets are well suited for analysis of packet time series.

Wavelet analysis can separate out a time-varying signal of interest from "noise" through localized filtering. At each time instance, wavelet analysis captures the energy of the active frequency components in multiple, nonoverlapping spectral windows. Ideally, the signal and noise components will be captured in separate spectral windows. In the detection method, wavelet analysis is used to separate a DoS signal from background traffic noise, both of which are present in the input time series $N_{pt}(k)$.

Wavelets are oscillating functions defined over small intervals of time. The family of discrete (orthogonal) wavelets functions used for analysis is

$$\psi_{j,l} = 2^{-j/2}\Psi(2^j k - 1); \quad l, j \in Z \tag{91}$$

where j is the scaling index, l is the time translation index, k is the time interval, and ψ is the mother wavelet. The Haar mother wavelet was used for its simplicity. Scale j is bounded by $2^j \leq M$, where M is the number of signal samples available at k. Wavelet $\psi_{j,l}(k)$ is zero-mean bandpass function of scale j, localized at time interval k. The effect of j is to compress the time window over which the mother wavelet ψ is defined. In the frequency domain, time compression is equivalent to stretching the wavelet spectrum and shifting by 2^{-j} [Jaffard 2001]. Scaling j is the wavelet decomposition level (WDL). The higher the value of j, the smaller the widths of the bandpass filters, resulting in finer frequency analysis. Adjustment of parameters j and l determine the spectral range of the wavelet filter $\psi_{j,l}(k)$.

Wavelet analysis is performed through the discrete wavelet transform (DWT). For a signal $X(k)$, the DWT is defined through the inner product of the signal and a wavelet:

$$DWT_X(j,l) = d_{j,l}(k) = \langle X(k), \psi_{j,l}(k) \rangle \tag{92}$$

The values $d_{j,l}(k)$ are the discrete wavelet coefficients of $X(k)$ at time position l and scale j, where $l = 0, \ldots, 2^j - 1$ and $j = 0, \ldots, 2^j - 1$. The wavelet coefficients at interval k, $d_{j,l}(k)$ capture the localized energy present in the wavelet's bandpass range. If the coefficients contain "enough" energy in a spectral range of interest, then a signal composed of these frequency components is declared as being present.

The use of the Haar wavelets for ψ allows for an intuitive interpretation. Haar wavelets calculate their coefficients iteratively through averaging and differencing of two data values. Depending on the scale j, the data values are either from the input signal ($j = 1$) or previously obtained wavelet coefficient values ($j > 1$). From these two operations, low-pass (average) and high-pass (difference) signal characteristics are stored in the Haar wavelet coefficients [Nievergelt 1999]. As an example, high-pass filter coefficient $d_{j,0}$ is the difference between the two coefficients containing the average signal value over $[k, (k+2^j)/2]$ and $[(k+2^j)/2, (k+2^j)]$, respectively. Coefficient $d_{j,0}$ represents the amount of signal change over the time window of 2^j samples.

The DoS signal is an abrupt, positive increasing signal. Detection of this event is equivalent to change point detection. Wavelets have been successfully applied to change point detection in time series [Antoniadis 1997, Wang 1999, Wang 1995, and Lavielle 1999], and generally outperform traditional statistical methods. By appropriate selection of scale j, the change point's signal energy is concentrated in a few coefficients.

For packet time series $N_{pt}(k)$, DoS attack detection by wavelets may be susceptible to high failure rates. Abrupt changes contain most of their energy in high-frequency components. If $N_{pt}(k)$'s high-frequency noise is nontrivial, the (DoS) signal may not be detectable through the coefficients, due to a low signal-to-noise ratio [Wang 1995]. Analysis of the coefficients' values may lead to high false rates or missed detections. To improve detection efficiency, wavelet analysis of the modified CUSUM statistic, $S(k)$, is performed. In $S(k)$, $N_{pt}(k)$'s arrival noise is filtered through parameters α and c, enhancing the DoS signal. Subsequent analysis uses wavelet to identify $S(k)$'s change point due to a DoS attack. With a vanishing moment of one, the Haar wavelet coefficients $d_{j,l}$ capture abrupt and linear increases of the CUSUM.

DoS attacks cause a sharp increase in the CUSUM statistic $\tilde{S}(k)$, followed by a linear increase. When $d_{j,l}$ is larger than a threshold value, a DoS attack is detected. In Figure 12.3c, the wavelet coefficient $(d_{6,0})$ of the CUSUM is shown. $d_{6,0}$ significantly increases at the CUSUM change, which is due to a DoS attack at interval $k = 6 \times 10^4$.

4. VERIFICATION OF DETECTOR

As explained, DoS attacks result in an increased mean and variance of the arriving number of packets. Given this increase, the CUSUM algorithm should also show a substantial and sudden increase. At the 6th level of wavelet decomposition, this change is made apparent via coefficients on the order of 4 times larger than under normal traffic conditions. Figure 12.4 uses data from an ns-2 simulation to detect DoS attacks resulting in detections at an average of 1.13 sec after attack (versus 7.6 sec for the CUSUM-only method). The DoS detection approach monitors the number and type of incoming IP packets over time. To verify the robustness of our approach, we apply it to the following:

- Network simulators (which frequently do not have the ability to break apart the TCP handshake)
- Recorded real-world data
- Online testing in our laboratory
- Operational data collected on a live network

Figure 12.6 shows results from applying the DoS detection technique to the network packet stream in Figure 12.5, which was generated using ns-2. The ns-2 simulations support our belief that the method is a valid indicator for packet flooding attacks. However, NS and some simulation tools do not scale well to larger, more complicated network layouts. This was one of the driving forces behind our development of our CANTOR cellular automata model [Brooks 2002].

Network simulation tools are not adequate tests for network monitoring applications. The simulations may not always be accurate for dealing with large or complex topologies. Some factors influencing network behavior may be missing from the simulation software. Recorded data of DoS attacks is not easily available. Security and privacy issues prevent large institutions and ISPs from releasing information about their network. The definition of an "attack" also varies among those with recorded DoS attacks. Some have data from several years ago when networking systems were not nearly as robust.

We examined MIT Lincoln Laboratory's Intrusion Detection Data Sets [MITLL 2002] to find a flood attack that we could use to test our method. A time series from that dataset is given in Figure 12.10. An issue with the data in [MITLL 2002] is that it is from a "virtual network." Parts of the network used were physical machines. Other portions of the network were partly virtual, designed to create the illusion that the network was larger than it was in reality. This introduces the possibility of experimental artifacts being introduced into the data. Our initial evaluations also indicated that the baseline traffic of the system, network traffic when no attacks were present, was unrealistically low. Although the testing in [MITLL 2002] is a step in the right direction, it is unfortunately not adequate for testing against the current batch of DoS attacks.

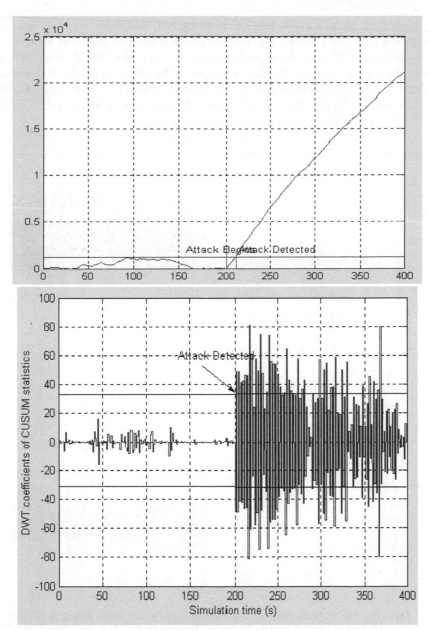

Figure 12.4. DoS attack detection using a CUSUM-only method on ns-2 data (top). When detecting the attack using the wavelet decomposition of the CUSUM (bottom) the delay is smaller.

We simulated attacks in our controlled lab environment. We developed a realistic network model of a small network. The detection program we use collects packets using the Packet Capture Library "pcap" [PCAP 2004]. As each new packet is collected, its time stamp is compared to collect 0.01 sec of packets at a time. Then, the number of packets per time slice is computed, and those numbers are sent through the CUSUM statistic. The wavelet decomposition requires 64 elements of data to perform a 6th level decomposition, and so every 64 CUSUM data points are sent to the wavelet analysis function. Each set of 64 elements results in 2 wavelet coefficients: a negative component and a positive component. When the absolute value of the coefficient exceeds 2.5 times the previous maximal value of any coefficient, the program signals that a DoS is occurring.

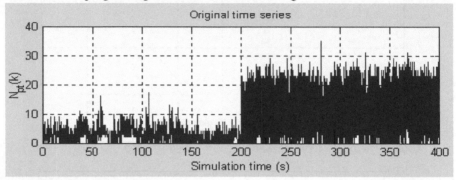

Figure 12.5. An arriving network packet stream. DoS starts at 200 sec.

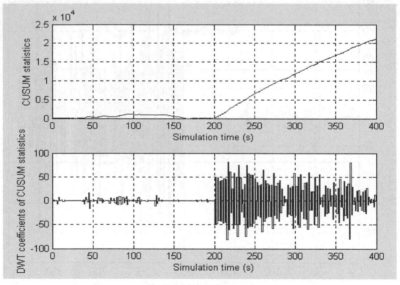

Figure 12.6. (Top) The CUSUM statistics of ns-2 simulation of a DoS attack starting at 200 sec; (Bottom) The wavelet coefficients at the 6th level of decomposition.

We generated a random distribution of sporadic data from several machines on our test network. The amount of data per "sporadic" burst was adjusted per each node to simulate certain nodes being more highly connected than others. Then to simulate the attack, we had two machines generate much larger bursts over much smaller time delays. We connected these machines so that one was behind a router and the other was not, so that network latency would also play a part. The network traffic from this generated attack is shown in Figure 12.7. The similarity of these results to the ns-2 simulation data (Figure 12.5) is striking.

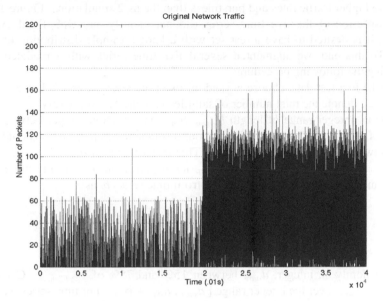

Figure 12.7. Network traffic from a lab generated DoS attack.

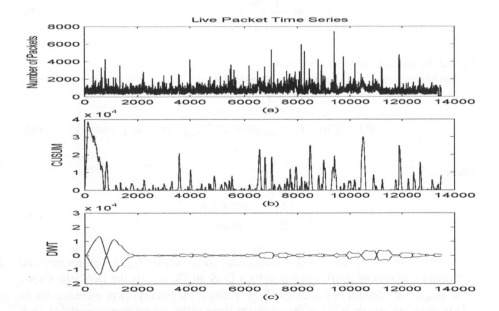

Figure 12.8. (a) Live packet time series; (b) CUSUM statistic; (c) Wavelet decomposition coefficient $d_{6,0}$

The final test dataset we consider is operational data. Test data was collected from a university site for 2 weeks yielding 119 packet time series. Our "live" time series have higher traffic rates and burstiness than the ns-2 simulations (Figure 12.3). Visual inspection of the live time series did not identify any DoS flood events. However, it is desired to have a test set with a known sample distribution of DoS attacks. To this end, we augmented several live time series with a modeled DoS attack using the following procedure:

From the live test data, choose at random two time series, a and b. Let a_{total_length} and b_{total_length} denote the total number of samples in a and b, respectively.

Define an integer range of length b_{length}. b_{length} is a random integer between 5% and 15% of a_{total_length}. The range's lower bound is denoted as b_{start}. b_{start} is randomly chosen between 5% and 20% of b_{total_length}. This integer range, [b_{start} , $b_{start} + b_{length}$], spans b_{length} consecutive samples of time series b starting at b_{start}. Using this range, define a time series b_{sub}, with data samples from time series b, as

$$b_{sub}(k) = \begin{cases} b(k+b_{start}) & ; \quad 0 \le k \le b_{length} \\ 0 & ; \quad \text{otherwise} \end{cases} \tag{93}$$

Choose randomly an integer, a_{start}, between 15% and 75% of a_{total_length}. Calculate the average, a_{mean}, over the integer range [a_{start} , $a_{start} + b_{length}$] of time series a as

$$a_{mean} = \frac{1}{b_{length}} \sum_{k=a_{start}}^{a_{start}+b_{length}} a(k) \tag{94}$$

Define the positive constant $scale > 0$.

Form time series a' by adding b_{sub}, constant $scale * a_{mean}$, and original time series a as

$$a'(k) = \sum_{k} [b_{sub}(k - a_{start}) + scale * a_{mean} * u(k - a_{start}) + a(k)] \tag{95}$$

where

$$u(k) = \begin{cases} 1 & ; \quad 0 \le k \le b_{length} \\ 0 & ; \quad \text{otherwise} \end{cases} \tag{96}$$

In the context of DoS attack modeling, time series $b_{sub}(k)$ represents the additional background traffic generated by a DoS attack. a_{start} is the DoS attack start time. b_{length} is the length of the attack. *Scale* reflects the packet count increase due to a DoS flooding attack. $a'(k)$ is the resultant time series containing a modeled DoS attack superimposed on realistic background traffic dynamics. No efforts were made to model possible packet loss due to congestion.

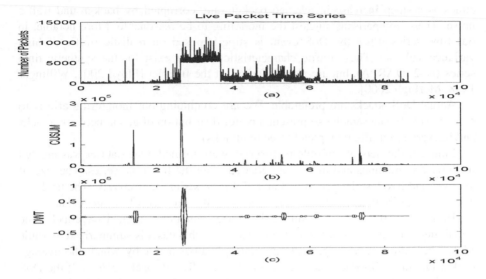

Figure 12.9. Live time series with a modeled DoS attack. (Top) Time series; (Middle) CUSUM statistic; (Bottom) wavelet coefficient $d_{10,0}$.

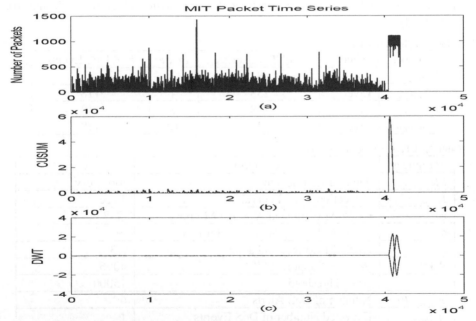

Figure 12.10. DARPA/MIT synthetic time series.

Figure 12.9 shows a live time series $a'(k)$ containing a model DoS attack of *scale* 7. Our DoS event is qualitatively similar to that modeled by ns-2 (Figure 12.3) and DARPA (Figure 12.10, [MITLL 2002]) simulations. In all three cases, the DoS attack is a steep increase in average packet rate, corrupted by background traffic noise. These comparisons suggest the modeling to be reasonable. More notable, in our time series $a'(k)$, the DoS event is superimposed on realistic traffic of high variance and rate. These traffic characteristics do not exist for the synthetic time series (ns-2, DARPA), but are representative of the Internet [Floyd 2001, Willinger 1998, McHugh 2000].

Actual DoS attacks are preferable. We are continuing our monitoring efforts to collect enough data samples to present a better distribution of actual network attacks and background traffic (completely free of attacks).

Four test datasets of multiple time series were formed. One dataset was created from ns-2 simulations and three were created from the live time series. The size of the ns-2 and live test datasets was 8 and 238 time series, respectively. The ns-2 test dataset was of limited size due to concerns about the veracity of synthetic data.

Half of the time series within each dataset contain a single DoS attack. The remaining time series contain zero DoS attacks. Each dataset is summarized in Table 12.1. The column *scale* represents the multiplicative factor by which the average packet rate increases due to a DoS attack. For the S_{ns-2} dataset, *scale* is 3; the DoS attack by twenty zombies produces traffic (30 packets/sec) that is triple that of the background rate (10 packets/sec). In the live datasets, the average traffic rate increase caused by a DoS attack is determined by the parameter *scale*. Datasets S_{LIVE4}, S_{LIVE7}, and S_{LIVE10} were constructed using *scale* values of 4, 7, and 10, respectively.

Table 12.1. Test Data Sets

Label	Source	# of Time series	*Scale*	# of DoS Events
S_{ns-2}	ns-2	8	3	4
S_{LIVE4}	Live	238	4	118
S_{LIVE7}	Live	238	7	118
S_{LIVE10}	Live	238	10	118

Table 12.2. Packet Time Series Report

Parameter	Description	Value
file	Time series Filename	foo_e.csv
I	Collection Time Interval	1 sec
ε	CUSUM Estimated Average Memory	.988
α	CUSUM Local Averaging Memory	.97
c_e	CUSUM Correction Factor	.13
WDL	Wavelet Support (2^{WDL})	4096
T	Alert Threshold	15000
$n_{alerts}^{s}(P)$	Number of DoS Alerts	6
$n_{expected}^{s}$	Expected Number of DoS Events	1
$n_{false}^{s}(P)$	Number of False Detects	5
$n_{true}^{s}(P)$	Number of Correct Detects	1

Each time series s within dataset S_i, where $i \in \{$ns-2, LIVE4, LIVE7, LIVE10$\}$, was evaluated by the two-stage detection method. The algorithm is adjusted by a set of operating parameters P. The elements of set P include

- Wavelet decomposition level (WDL)
- Wavelet coefficient threshold (T)
- CUSUM estimated packet rate memory (ε)
- CUSUM local averaging memory (α)
- CUSUM noise correction factor (c_e)

The detection method outputs the number of DoS events detected within time series s under test. This is equivalent to the number of times the wavelet decomposition coefficients exceed the threshold T. The wavelet decomposition level and threshold is defined in P.

An analysis report was generated for each test iteration of time series s (Table 12.2). Rows two through six reflect the operating parameters from set P. $n^s_{alerts}(P)$ is the number of DoS events identified during detection analysis. $n^s_{expected}$ is the expected number of DoS attacks. If the time series contains a DoS event, $n^s_{expected}$ is equal to one, zero otherwise. During construction of the test dataset, each time series s was identified as containing a single DoS attack or not. The number of true and false detections is the basis for determining the detection rate. For time series s, under operating parameters P, the number of true detects, n^s_{true}, is defined as

$$n^s_{true}(P) = \begin{cases} 1 & ; \ if \ n^s_{alerts}(P) \geq n^s_{expected} \\ 0 & ; \ otherwise \end{cases} \tag{97}$$

$n^s_{true} \in \{0,1\}$ as each time series was constructed to have at the most a single DoS attack event. The number of false detects, n^s_{false}, is given by

$$n^s_{false}(P) = \max(n^s_{alerts}(P) - n^s_{true}(P), 0) \tag{98}$$

The empirical detection rate is achieved from the entire dataset. For the ns-2 dataset, S_{ns-2}, the total number of true and false detects is given by

$$N^{NS2}_{true}(P) = \sum_{s \in S_{NS2}} n^s_{true}(P) \tag{99}$$

$$N^{NS2}_{false}(P) = \sum_{s \in S_{NS2}} n^s_{false}(P) \tag{100}$$

The average true detection and false positive percentages, $p^{NS2}_{true}(P)$ and $p^{NS2}_{false}(P)$, respectively, are determined from the total number of detection alerts as

$$p_{true}^{NS2}(P) = \frac{N_{true}^{NS2}(P)}{\sum_{\forall s \in S_{NS2}} n_{alerts}^{s}(P)} * 100 \tag{101}$$

$$p_{false}^{NS2}(P) = \frac{N_{false}^{NS2}(P)}{\sum_{\forall s \in S_{NS2}} n_{alerts}^{s}(P)} * 100 \tag{102}$$

The live test datasets, S_{LIVE4}, S_{LIVE7}, S_{LIVE10}, have a larger sample population. Empirical average detection percentage was derived across smaller sets $S_{i,j}^* \subset S_i$, where $i \in \{LIVE4, LIVE7, LIVE10\}$ and $j = 0,\ldots,75$. Each set $S_{i,j}^*$ contains 70 time series randomly chosen from the parent test set S_i.

Let $g_{i,j,k}$ represent the kth time series of set $S_{i,j}^*$, where $k = 1,\ldots,70$. The total number of true and false detects within set $S_{i,j}^*$ is given by

$$N_{true}^{S_{i,j}^*}(P) = \sum_{k=1}^{70} n_{true}^{g_{i,j,k}}(P) \tag{103}$$

$$N_{false}^{S_{i,j}^*}(P) = \sum_{k=1}^{70} n_{false}^{g_{i,j,k}}(P) \tag{104}$$

The true detection and false positive percentage for set $S_{i,j}^*$ is

$$p_{true}^{S_{i,j}^*}(P) = \frac{N_{true}^{S_{i,j}^*}(P)}{\sum_{k=1}^{70} n_{alerts}^{g_{i,j,k}}(P)} \tag{105}$$

$$p_{false}^{S_{i,j}^*}(P) = \frac{N_{false}^{S_{i,j}^*}(P)}{\sum_{k=1}^{70} n_{alerts}^{g_{i,j,k}}(P)} \tag{106}$$

The average detection percentage of the dataset S_i, $i \in \{LIVE4, LIVE7, LIVE10\}$, is given by

$$p_{true}^{S_i}(P) = \frac{1}{75} \sum_{j=0}^{75} p_{true}^{S_{i,j}^*}(P) \tag{107}$$

$$p_{false}^{S_i}(P) = \frac{1}{75} \sum_{j=0}^{75} p_{false}^{S_{i,j}^*}(P) \tag{108}$$

The standard error of $p_{true}^{S_i}(P)$ and $p_{false}^{S_i}(P)$, respectively, is given as

$$e_{true}^{S_i}(P) = \frac{1.96}{\sqrt{75}} \sqrt{\frac{\sum_{j=0}^{75}(p_{true}^{S_{i,j}*}(P) - p_{true}^{S_i}(P))^2}{(75-1)}} \qquad (109)$$

$$e_{false}^{S_i}(P) = \frac{1.96}{\sqrt{75}} \sqrt{\frac{\sum_{i=0}^{75}(p_{false}^{S_{i,j}*}(P) - p_{false}^{S_i}(P))^2}{(75-1)}} \qquad (110)$$

Equations (109) and (110) represent the interval over which the average detection percentage is reported with 95% confidence.

DoS analysis of the datasets was performed over multiple sets of P. In each testing iteration of time series s, only one element of P was varied while the others remained constant. The range of the single parameter variation was determined through experimentation.

For any test dataset S_i, optimum detection rate is achieved under those conditions that jointly maximize the true detection percentage $p_{true}^{S_i}(P)$ and minimize the false positive percentage $p_{false}^{S_i}(P)$. The set $P = P*$ under which $p_{true}^{S_i}(P)$ is maximized and $p_{false}^{S_i}(P)$ is minimized is the detector's optimum operating point. The values $p_{true}^{S_i}(P*)$ and $p_{false}^{S_i}(P*)$ represent the detector's best average performance.

Receiver Operating Curves (ROC) are provided to communicate testing results. In an ROC, the detection method's false positive ($p_{false}^{S_i}(P)$) vs. true detection ($p_{true}^{S_i}(P)$) percentage is plotted against a varying parameter. The ROC illustrates the performance gain between detection methods, the effects of parameter variations, and the best possible detection efficiency.

Each ROC is built from values of the dyadic set ($p_{false}^{S_i}(P)$, $p_{true}^{S_i}(P)$). Each data point represents the likelihood of detecting a true DoS attack ($p_{true}^{S_i}(P)$), or a false positive ($p_{false}^{S_i}(P)$). The values were determined by testing all samples of a dataset with a common parameter set P. The data point with minimum distance to the upper left point (0,1) represents the best detection efficiency.

Each test iteration varied one parameter value from P. At the most efficient value of ($p_{false}^{S_i}(P)$, $p_{true}^{S_i}(P)$), the varying element from P is determined. This parameter is best possible and becomes an element of the set $P*$. For subsequent parameter variation testing of the same dataset, parameters defined in $P*$ are used in P. After all parameters of P have been exercised, the optimum set $P*$ is found. Set $P*$ determines the detection's method operating parameters, which produce the maximum true and minimum false positive rate that can be jointly obtained.

For ns-2 datasets, detection efficiency was ideal (Figure 12.11). All DoS attacks within the dataset were true detected with zero false positives. This is visually evident as each ROC plot has a data point at (0, 1), representing $p^{NS2}{}_{false}(P) = 0\%$, $p^{NS2}{}_{true}(P) = 100\%$. The set P corresponding to this data point is the best possible parameter set $P*$.

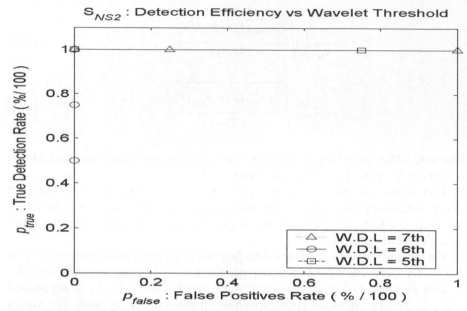

Figure 12.11. Efficiency vs. wavelet threshold for ns-2 Simulations. Varying parameters: wavelet threshold (*T*) and wavelet decomposition level (WDL); static parameters: CUSUM estimate average memory (ε) = 0.97, CUSUM local average memory (α) = 0.99, CUSUM correction factor (c_e) = 0.20.

In Figure 12.11, an individual ROC trace is built from data points with a varying wavelet threshold (*T*). Each ROC trace uses a unique setting for the WDL. CUSUM parameters variations (ε, α, *c*) were not investigated, as no increase from ideal detection performance would be gained.

For the ns-2 dataset, the optimal parameters set *P** is stated in Table 12.3. Detection efficiency under set *P** is ideal. The ideal performance is suggested to be an artifact of inadequate ns-2 traffic modeling. These issues have been discussed in earlier sections.

Table 12.3. ns-2 Parameter Set P*

Parameter	Setting
Wavelet Decomposition Level (WDL)	[5,6,7]
Wavelet Coefficient Threshold (*T*)	[30,130]
CUSUM Estimated Average Memory (ε)	0.97
CUSUM Local Averaging Memory (α)	0.99
CUSUM Correction Factor (c_e)	0.20

Testing results from the live datasets are more representative of the detection method's field performance. Affected by realistic background traffic, the detector's ability is more challenged. True and false positive detection percentages are seen to be less than ideal.

Wavelet analysis of the CUSUM statistic is proposed to obtain higher detection performance. To support this claim, live datasets were analyzed under both CUSUM and wavelet thresholding. For CUSUM thresholding, DoS detection is equivalent to $\tilde{S}(k)$ exceeding a threshold T_{CUSUM}, which is the basis for detection in [Blazek 2001]. Wavelet thresholding evaluates the coefficients $d_{j,l}(k)$ against wavelet threshold T. $d_{j,l}(k)$ is obtained from wavelet analysis of $\tilde{S}(k)$.

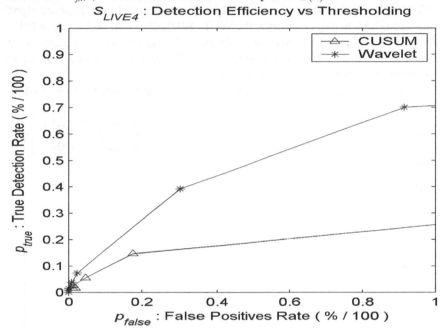

Figure 12.12 Efficiency vs. CUSUM/wavelet thresholding. Varying parameters: wavelet threshold (T), CUSUM threshold; static parameters: wavelet decomposition level (WDL) = 6th, CUSUM estimated average memory (ε) = 0.988, CUSUM local averaging memory (α) = 0.97, CUSUM correction factor (c_e) = 0.20.

Table12.4 Wavelet vs. CUSUM Best Detection Rate

Analysis	True Detect Rate	FalsePos. Rate	Detection Ratio
CUSUM only	15%	18%	.83
CUSUM with Wavelet	40%	30%	1.3
Detection Ratio Increase			56%

Figure 12.12 is a ROC with two traces. The lower trace provides detection likelihoods under CUSUM threshold variations, while the upper trace denotes wavelet threshold variations. Datapoints on the curves are measures of average detection efficiency. An increase in either threshold T or T_{CUSUM} can lower both the true detection and false detection percentages. The distance between the two curves is of interest. The dataset was S_{LIVE4}.

Datapoints for the wavelet thresholding trace lie closer to ideal point $(0, 1)$. Higher detection efficiency is achieved from the additional wavelet processing of the CUSUM. Extracted from the ROC of Figure 12.4, Table 12.4 shows the maximum average detection rates for each analysis method. The ratio of true detections vs. false positives percentages for the wavelet analysis is 56% more efficient than CUSUM processing alone. Wavelet analysis also has equal or greater average true detection rates for a given false positive rate. This was also seen for datasets S_{LIVE7} and S_{LIVE10} (not shown).

Wavelet analysis of the CUSUM statistic provides better detection efficiency than CUSUM analysis alone. Wavelet analysis is also capable of enhanced signal filtering through its scaling parameter, the WDL. WDL equals the value of j in (91).

Figure 12.13 shows the detection analysis of S_{LIVE4} dataset over variation of WDL and threshold (T). Each point represents a different wavelet threshold value, whereas each curve represents a different WDL.

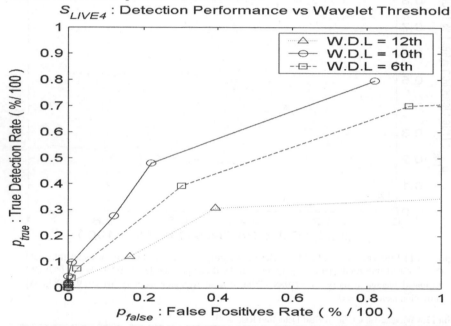

Figure 12.13 Efficiency vs. wavelet decomposition. Varying parameters: wavelet threshold (T) and wavelet decomposition level (WDL). Static parameters: CUSUM estimated average memory (ε) = 0.988, CUSUM local averaging memory (α) = 0.97, CUSUM correction factor (c_e) = 0.20.

The 6th level of decomposition is the baseline, since it was determined earlier to be better than CUSUM thresholding. Increases in WDL produces data points closer to (0,1), and thus better detection ratios. A maximum is reached at WDL = 10th. Further WDL increases have an adverse effect, producing data points that lie below the 6th level. Higher WDLs perform poorly in low signal-to-noise environments [Wang 1995]. Table 12.5 summaries the true detection and false positive rates for WDL = 6th, 10th, and 12th.

The uncertainty in average detection rates is defined by (109) and (110) with 95% confidence. This is shown by the errors bars superimposed on the ROC data points of Figure 12.14. For low threshold values, the error bars show about a 10%

spread around the data point. The horizontal error bars representing false positive uncertainty increase as the threshold is lowered. At lower values of wavelet thresholding, noise is more likely to causes a false positive, leading to more spread in detection uncertainty.

Table 12.5. WDL Variation on Detection Percentages

WDL	Threshold	True Detection Rate	False Positive Rate	Ratio
6th	43000	39%	30%	1.3
10th	30000	47%	21%	2.2
12th	6000	30%	39%	0.7

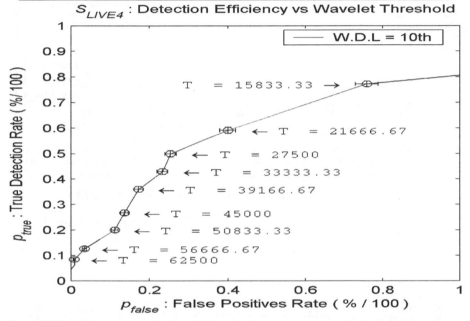

Figure 12.14. Efficiency vs. wavelet thresholding. Varying parameters: wavelet threshold (T); static parameters: CUSUM estimated average memory (ε) = 0.988, CUSUM local averaging memory (α) = 0.97, CUSUM correction factor (c_e) = 0.20.

The detection method was evaluated against multiple DoS scales. DoS scale is a measure of traffic increase incurred during an attack. The higher the scale, the stronger the attack is. Dataset S_{LIVE4}, S_{LIVE7}, S_{LIVE10} were constructed with DoS *scale* factors of 4, 7, and 10, respectively.

Figure 12.15 shows detection results for WDL = 10th across the 3 live test datasets (S_{LIVE4}, S_{LIVE7}, S_{LIVE10}). As expected, when the DoS scale is increased, the ROC traces approach the upper left corner, indicating better detection efficiency. The kink in trace of S_{LIVE10} and overlap of S_{LIVE4} and S_{LIVE7} require further investigation. Table 12.6 indicates the maximum detection efficiency per DoS scale variation.

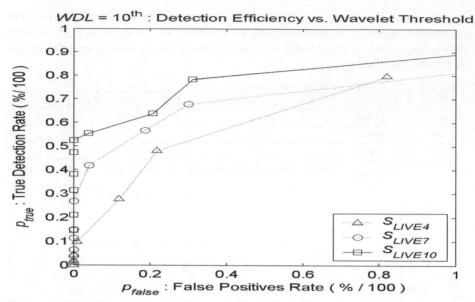

Figure 12.15. Efficiency vs. DoS scaling. Varying parameters: wavelet threshold (T); static parameters: wavelet decomposition level (WDL) = 10th, CUSUM estimated average memory (ε) = 0.988, CUSUM local averaging memory (α) = 0.97, CUSUM correction factor (c_e) = 0.20.

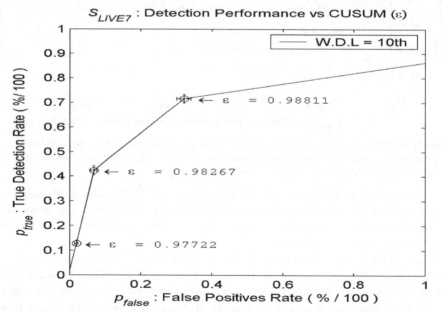

Figure 12.16. Efficiency vs. ε variation. Varying parameter: CUSUM estimated average memory (ε). Static parameters: wavelet decomposition level (WDL) = 10th; wavelet threshold (T) = 30000, CUSUM local averaging memory (α) = 0.97, CUSUM correction factor (c_e) = 0.20.

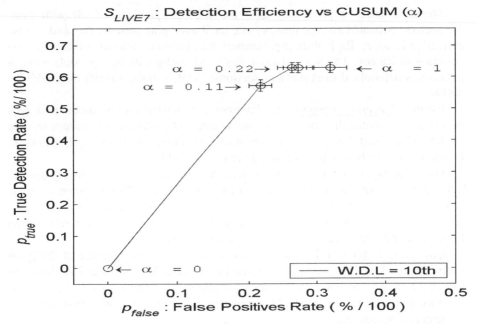

Figure 12.17. Efficiency vs. α Varying parameters: CUSUM local averaging memory (α); Static parameters: wavelet decomposition level (WDL) = 10th, wavelet threshold (T) = 30000, DoS scale = 7, CUSUM estimate average memory (ε) = 0.988, CUSUM correction factor (c_e) = 0.20

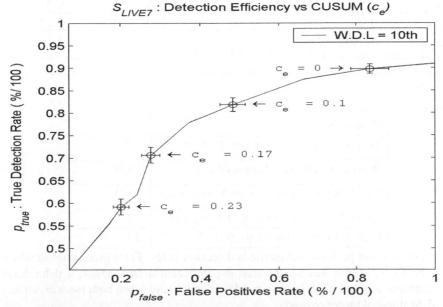

Figure 12.18. Efficiency vs. CUSUM correction c_e. Varying parameter: CUSUM correction factor (ce); Static parameters: wavelet decomposition level (WDL) = 10th, wavelet threshold (T) = 30000, DoS scale = 7, CUSUM estimated average memory (ε) = 0.988, CUSUM local averaging memory (α) = 0.22.

The first stage of processing used the CUSUM statistic of (8) with three parameters: estimated average memory (ε), local averaging memory (α), and a noise correction factor c_e. Each of these parameters was varied to determine their effect on detection efficiency. The S_{LIVE7} dataset was used, along with best possible wavelet parameters determined from previous sections: WDL = 10th, wavelet threshold T = 30000.

Estimated average memory (ε): Parameter ε determines the amount of past history used in estimating the average packet rate $m(k)$, which is a dominant term in the CUSUM statistic $\tilde{S}(k)$. The variation of ε on detection efficiency is shown in Figure 12.16. The best setting for parameter ε is 0.98811.

Local Averaging (α): Parameter α determines the amount of past history used to filter arrival noise within input packet time series $N_{pt}(k)$. The variation of α on detection efficiency is shown in Figure 12.17. Below 0.11, the true detections and false positive rates linearly approach 0. Little variation in true detection rate is seen for α values between 0.22 and 1. The best value for α is 0.22.

Correction factor (c_e): Parameter $c = c_e*m(k)$ reduces the variance of the input traffic on the CUSUM statistic. Its variation on detection efficiency is shown in Figure 12.18. The optimum setting for c_e is about 0.13. The removal of noise and variance from the arrival process by parameter c is seen as having a positive effect on detection percentages.

Table 12.6. DoS Scale Performance

DoS Scale	DataSet	True Detection Rate	False Pos. Rate	Ratio
4	S_{LIVE4}	46%	21%	2.1
7	S_{LIVE7}	68%	24%	2.8
10	S_{LIVE10}	78%	25%	3.1

All parameters for the statistical (CUSUM) and wavelet analysis have been evaluated. Table 12.7 states the resulting parameter set P* acquired from our live test datasets.

Table 12.7. Set P* for S_{LIVE7} Datasets

Parameter	Setting
Wavelet Decomposition Level (WDL)	10th
Wavelet Coefficient Threshold (T)	30000
CUSUM Estimated Average Memory (ε)	.98811
CUSUM Local Averaging Memory (α)	.22
CUSUM Correction Factor (c_e)	.13

Another useful performance metric is detection delay. For a time series in which both the CUSUM and wavelet thresholding indicated a DoS attack, a delta delay measurement was recorded. Detection delay is only valid when both the wavelet and CUSUM threshold were crossed.

Let k_1 and k_2 indicate the time interval at which the wavelet and CUSUM processing, respectively, have first declared a DoS attack.

$$k_1 = \arg \begin{cases} d_{j,0}(k_1 - z) < T & 1 \le z < k_1, \ z \in Z^+ \\ d_{j,0}(k_1) \ge T \end{cases} \quad (111)$$

$$k_2 = \arg \begin{cases} \tilde{S}(k_2 - z) < T_{CUSUM} & 1 \le z < k_2, \ z \in Z^+ \\ \tilde{S}(k_2) \ge T_{CUSUM} \end{cases} \quad (112)$$

where j equals the wavelet decomposition level.

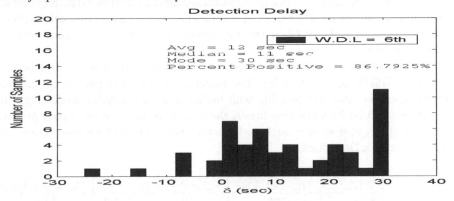

Figure 12.19. Detection delay distribution. Static parameters: wavelet decomposition level (WDL) = 6th; wavelet threshold (T) = 30000, CUSUM threshold = 140000, CUSUM estimated average memory (ε) = 0.988, CUSUM local averaging memory (α) = 0.22, CUSUM correction factor (c_e) = 0.13.

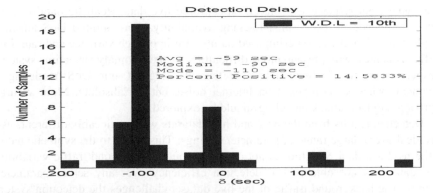

Figure 12.20. Detection delay distribution. Static parameters: wavelet decomposition level (WDL) = 10th; wavelet threshold (T) = 30000, CUSUM threshold = 140000, CUSUM estimated average memory (ε) = 0.988, CUSUM local averaging memory (α) = 0.22, CUSUM correction factor (c_e) = 0.13.

The delta delay measurement is defined as $\delta = k_2 - k_1$. A positive δ indicates how much earlier the wavelet analysis detected the DoS event relative to the CUSUM only processing.

The set of δ measurements were captured from the S_{LIVE4} dataset. The number of samples was limited (<60), due to low CUSUM detection rates (<25% in Figure 12.12). For WDL = 6th, the histogram of Figure 12.19 shows the distribution of δ delays. The median δ delay gain is 11 sec with a granularity of the sampling interval (1 sec). 86% of the DoS attacks were detected in a shorter amount of time by the wavelet analysis.

For WDL = 10th, the wavelet analysis results in poorer detection delay (Figure 12.20). The median δ delay "loss" is 90 sec, with only 14% of samples showing a positive delay gain. Increasing the WDL level increases the wavelet analysis's detection time. The latency is due to the increased amount of signal data required for calculation of higher levels of wavelet coefficients. Table 12.8 outlines the tradeoff between increasing the WDL level for detection efficiency and corresponding detection delays.

Wavelet analysis of the CUSUM has better detection efficiency of DoS attacks than the CUSUM approach alone. The increase in detection ratio is 56%. Even higher detection ratios are possible with higher levels of wavelet processing. The first stage of CUSUM processing lowers the amount of noise of the arrival process, while the subsequent wavelet analysis finds the change point of the time series. The change point is a DoS attack.

Table 12.8. Detection Delay vs. WDL

WDL	True Det. Rate	False Pos. Rate	Det.	Delta Det. Delay
6th	39%	30%	1.3	11 sec
10th	47%	21%	2.2	-90 sec
CUSUM	15%	18%	.83	-

Different sources of test data were used. Various synthetic data sources were investigated, but reliance was placed on captured live data. Realistic data provides better confidence in test results. Lacking availability of a captured DoS attack, a simple attack model was superimposed on live traffic of high variance and rate. Live traffic dynamics will present more difficulties to the anomaly detection systems, irrespective of the DoS model. Therefore we suggest our DoS modeling is reasonable when superimposed on Internet noise, but not absolute. More accurate approaches to DoS attack modeling should be explored.

Detection results from the ns-2 and live datasets were noticeably different. ns-2 was ideal over a large range of parameter settings. This is due to the synthetic nature of the ns-2 test data, which does not contain enough background traffic variability. Live data does not obtain ideal detection efficiency over any set of parameters settings. The background traffic of the live dataset challenges the detection system, thus reducing its true detection rate and providing a nonzero false positives rate. Tradeoffs in detection efficiency are possible through parameter "tuning" as indicated in the ROC graphs. Each has an effect of removing various amounts of arrival process noise or burstiness from the network time series. This increases the signal-to-noise ratio, allowing wavelet analysis to detect the abrupt change due to the DoS attack. Detection delay is dependent on amount of wavelet processing. Low WDLs provide better detection delay than a purely CUSUM approach, but at higher levels of wavelet analysis, the delay may increase. A tradeoff exists between increasing the WDL for detection efficiency gains and possible detection delays losses (Table 12.8). Further iterative testing on independently created datasets should be performed to ensure consistency of tuning parameters.

For a live dataset, 78% true detections and 37% false positives, for a detection ratio of 2.1 was determined. Over the 239 time series, each of which on average is 8 hours in duration, the false positive rate equates to 1.11 per day. Although high, approximately five false positives per week are due to our network's regular events described above. For a deployable solution, future improvements are needed, but they should be flexible, as detection of these normal events may be of some interest.

5. GAME THEORY ANALYSIS

Network flooding attacks clog a network with spurious packets, usually produced by rapid pinging of multiple hosts. Normal network traffic is replaced by ping packets that saturate the network, rendering it useless. In most DDoS attacks, malicious packets are produced by zombies residing within the network. Zombies are programs that target network nodes and disable them by flooding with TCP SYN packets, ping requests, or UDP packets.

Defending against DDoS attacks is challenging. Most defenses are reactive, involving identifying the attacking sources and deactivating them [Kevin 2001]. This is complicated by an attacker's ability to spoof IP addresses and distribute zombies across a network.

We model a network as a graph $G = (V, E)$, where V is a set of vertices (or nodes) and $E \subseteq V \times V$ is a set of edges (or links). The structure of the edge set E describes the connections that exist between nodes in the network. A distributed program P, consisting of programs $\{p_1, \cdots, p_k\}$ running in the network described by G, can be represented by assigning each program of P to a vertex of G via an assignment function $c : P \to V$. Each distributed application has a certain set of connectivity requirements that the network must satisfy in order for the distributed program P to execute successfully. For example, suppose that P is a distributed client-server system. Then each client must be able to connect to the server; however it may not be necessary for the clients to be able to connect to each other. We formalize this notion by saying that a program p_i is connected to a program p_j if there is a path connecting the vertex containing p_i with the vertex containing p_j. This sentiment may be formalized by a sentence π_{ij}, written in the first order graph predicate language. We shall denote by Π the set of all communications requirements for the distributed application P. When a network G and an assignment c satisfy all the requirements of a distributed application P, we shall write $(G, c) \models \Pi$, where it is understood that Π is the set of requirements of P.

Let $G = (V, E)$ be a graph describing a network, P be a distributed application, $c : P \to V$ be an assignment of programs to vertices and Π be a set of requirements such that $(G, c) \models \Pi$. A successful DDoS transforms the graph G into a new graph G' such that $(G', c) \not\models \Pi$. DDoS attacks work by introducing zombie programs into the nodes of G. These programs produce spurious packets, which either cause traffic congestion within the network itself or render a node in the network unavailable to receive legitimate traffic by bombarding it with illegitimate connection requests. To model the susceptibility of vertices and edges to zombie traffic, we defined a function $\tau_V : V \to \mathbb{N}$ ($\tau_E : E \to \mathbb{N}$) giving the number of simultaneous zombie attacks a given vertex (edge) could sustain before being rendered operationally ineffective by the attacker. In this model, we assumed that all zombies produce malevolent traffic at an equal rate and strength. This is not necessarily true, since a zombie's ability to produce traffic is related to the properties of the computer it is using. However, for our purposes, it is safe to assume that all nodes are created equally in terms of their ability to produce malevolent traffic when housing a zombie.

We studied the following problems related to this idealized view of DDoS attacks:

- What is the minimum number and configuration of zombies necessary for red to disrupt a requirement $\pi \in \Pi$?

- What is the maximum number of requirements that can be disrupted by the attacker?

- What is the minimum number and configuration of zombies necessary for red to disrupt the greatest number of requirements in Π?

The main result of our investigation was the following theorem, which completely determines the security of a distributed application running in an idealized computer network.

Let G be a network and P be a distributed application and let $c : P \to V(G)$ be the position of the programs in the network. Furthermore, let π be a requirement in Π saying that v_1^π must be connected to v_2^π. Then there is an algorithm with low order polynomial running time that determines whether π can be perpetually disabled; i.e., whether there is an attack such that for all counter strategies the resulting graph $G' \not\models \pi$.

To prove this result, we defined the minimum security edge cut and minimum security vertex cut of the graph G. Removing the edges and vertices in these sets will disconnect a graph. However, unlike the minimum edge (vertex) cut, which has the least number of edges (vertices), the minimum security edge (vertex) cut requires the smallest number of zombies of any other edge (vertex) cut to disable the edges (vertices) in the cut. Using this formalism, we were able to reduce the problem of determining the minimum security edge (vertex) cut to a max-flow/min-cut problem. Having shown this, we derived an algorithm to disable a single edge or vertex in the network using the smallest number of zombies. We proved this algorithm was minimal in its zombie use by applying a second min-cut argument. Taken together, these two results yield the theorem. The running time of the algorithm is at worst square in the edges and vertices of the graph, since this is an upper bound on the running time of the preflow push algorithm used to determine min-cuts in networks.

We can immediately use this result to help us determine optimal node placement in *ad hoc* mobile networks and optimal software placement in mobile code networks. Consider the later problem, when we are given mobile programs $P = \{p_1, \ldots, p_n\}$ and must determine an optimal placement for these programs under changing network conditions. In particular, suppose we are given a set of new criteria Φ, consisting of sentences $\phi_1, \ldots, \phi_k$, each stating that some program p_i must be placed in the same subgraph H of G. The next result follows immediately from above.

> *Let G be a network and P be a distributed mobile application. Let Π be a set of connectivity requirements for the programs of P and let Φ be a set of positioning requirements. Then there is a function $c : P \to V(G)$ that will minimize the maximum number of requirements of Π that can be perpetually disabled by DDoS attack. Furthermore, this function can be computed in $O(|P|^G)$ steps.*

This optimal placement function can be computed by using the results from the proof of theorem, were we to compute minimum security edge and vertex cuts for the entire graph. Since this placement is an absolute minimum, it is clear that it will not vary in the presence of optimal attacks; i.e., there will be no reason to recompute c, assuming that an attacker is playing optimally.

It is not clear whether it is possible to recover c using a polynomial algorithm. However, it may be possible to use a genetic algorithm with the fitness function being the security of the network and the population being placement functions of the nodes. More research must be done on this question to determine the best way to find the placement function c in the presence of a dynamically changing network.

Our results can be extended to mobile *ad hoc* network security questions as well. In Chapter 10, we derived a formulation for the expected structure of a random graph, given the probability distribution governing its structure. The algorithm runs in polynomial time. Hence, we may apply our theorems in the case of the expected value to find the expected vulnerability of a given graph to attack. The following theorem follows immediately:

> *Let $\mathcal{G}$ be a random graph family with a fixed number of nodes and let P be a distributed mobile application. Let Π be a set of connectivity requirements for the programs of P and let Φ be a set of positioning requirements. Then there is an expected function $c : P \to V(G)$ that will minimize the maximum number of requirements of Π that can be perpetually disabled by DDoS attack. Furthermore c can be computed in at worst $O(|P|^G)$.*

6.   NETWORK STRUCTURE VULNERABILITIES

We studied DDoS attacks using the *ns* network simulator. An ns-2 simulation script was written to generate pseudo-random traffic between connected nodes. Link speeds and delays were determined by finding the degrees of the connected nodes. Both the speeds and propagation delays of the links were scaled down to unrealistic speeds of arbitrary determination due to the infeasibility of simulating the thousands of nodes needed to generate realistic network traffic along links at actual Internet speeds. The link speeds and propagation delays ranged from 10 Mbps to 233 Mbps and 10 ms to 40 ms, respectively. The reason for choosing increasing speeds and delay times with increasing degree was based on the assumption that the number of connections from a node is proportional to the importance and rarity of the device.

The topology that was chosen for the simulations emulated a medium-scale network. Forty-one nodes were available to host zombies and fifteen nodes to be victims. In testing, only nodes with a single link could host zombies, while victims were restricted to core nodes not directly connected to a zombie node. The maximum hop distance, assuming that no cycles occurred, was nine hops. All connections were established as point-to-point to simplify the analysis of the packet flows. Any leaf node was assumed to be a point at the edge of an internal LAN and thus was modeled appropriately with our link speed and propagation delay definitions. The multipath option for ns was enabled for the topologies to allow packets to take multiple routes through the core nodes to reach the destination.

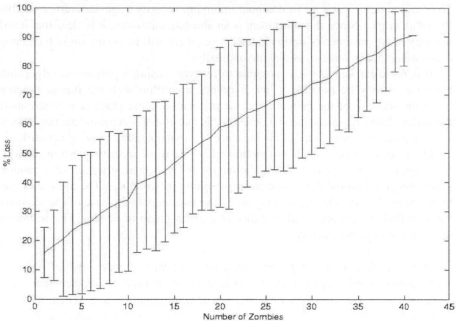

Figure 12.21. Legitimate packet loss % vs. zombie count (node 44 Pareto).

All background traffic used TCP since it is the *de facto* standard of the transport layer on the Internet. For burstier, nonuniform traffic, a Pareto random variable was used to approximate background Internet traffic because of its heavy tail and infinite variance. Conversely, for a more consistent pattern of traffic, the constant bit rate (CBR) generator was used. For both patterns, the TCP Reno agent was selected for the sender. The selective ACK sink was used to decrease the number of ACK packets the receiver must generate to alert the sender of a successful transmission.

To choose the sender and receiver pairs for the background traffic, a time-seeded uniform random variable was created to generate the integers representing the nodes. For our topology, the senders were restricted to the nodes between 0 and 40, while the receiver could be any node in the network. One hundred random pairs were generated with the guarantee that at least four connections would be created between four random senders and the victim. Except for tests involving background traffic structure, the one hundred sender and receiver pairs were kept the same for all simulations.

The DDoS attack was a link flooding attack generated by zombies placed at specific nodes in the network. A UDP agent was attached to a zombie with a CBR traffic generator. UDP was chosen for the zombie packets because of its connectionless characteristics. The CBR generator was configured to send a 404 byte packet every 0.5 ms. Note that the zombie packets are significantly smaller and sent more frequently than legitimate packets, as expected with a DoS attack.

To generate the order in which to add zombies, another time-seeded uniform random variable was created. This list was generated before the simulations and held constant through all simulations except for the zombie placement tests.

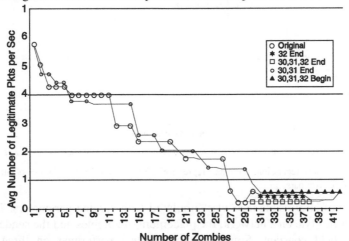

Figure 12.22. Legitimate packet loss % vs. zombie count (node 44 movement).

To track the success or failure of the DDoS attack, multiple methods were used dependent on the scope of the analysis. When considering the entire network, queue traces were placed on links connected to "sending" nodes. This allowed us to calculate the total number of legitimate packets sent for all leaf nodes. Queue traces were also placed on all of the receiver's links, allowing for a count of the number of received legitimate packets. The traces were configured to record all link activities. After completing each simulation, the traces were parsed to calculate the number of legitimate packets sent and received as the DDoS attack increased in strength.

To analyze the success of the DDoS attack on a specific node, traces were placed on links connected to nodes with a session to the victim. Additionally, all links connected to the victim were monitored. The packet ID fields in the ns-2 traces were parsed and compared to determine if the packet arrived at the victim successfully. Note that this does not take into account any packets that are routed through the victim, which would be contained within the first method of analysis.

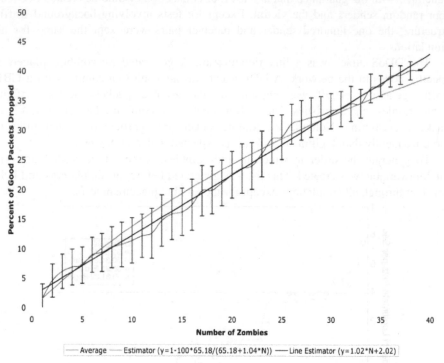

Figure 12.23. A linear regression, nonlinear regression and the average of a dataset of attacks on node 44 with error bars.

A subset of all possible tests was simulated with varying parameters. To test the effect of traffic style on a network, the placement of zombies and the sender/receiver pairs were held constant. Simulations were then performed on three different zombies with both types of traffic, CBR and Pareto. The number of zombies was then varied from 1 to 41. The same experiments could then be varied by changing the zombie locations and background traffic pairs. It should be noted that the numerical values of the packets and network were not our focus in this research, only the general patterns associated with performing a DoS attack upon a test topology that would resemble an actual network.

In the first simulations, we analyzed the combination of the traffic flows in the network. The data indicates that when not under a DDoS attack, the flows behave consistently and do not suffer much, if any, loss. This loss can be reasoned with TCP window size and congestion control effects. We assume that the ns-2 implementation of TCP follows the behavior of the "real world." As more individual sessions generate traffic, TCP window size will increase until the network is congested. This will cause a small packet loss if the simulated routers' queues are full. At this time, our data indicates that the congestion control algorithms of TCP are used to decrease the window sizes. On average, our simulation setup experienced a 0.04% loss rate due to only background traffic.

When a DDoS attack was overlaid on the background traffic, similar packet loss occurred but at a much larger scale. A total of 22 tests were performed per victim with different patterns of background traffic and zombie addition. For each case, the number of zombies was increased by one and the loss recorded from the addition of the extra zombie. Zombie positions were chosen from a uniform distribution in the range [0..40]. Simply placing zombies into the network did not always increase the loss experienced by the flows. In some cases, the resulting loss would either be zero or negative; the network loss rate decreased. This indicates that the addition of that particular zombie created a less optimal network state, with respect to the zombies. The traffic generated by the added zombie interfered slightly with the preexisting background and zombie traffic.

In Figure 12.22, the addition of zombies 30 through 32 caused the loss rate to decrease. When these particular zombies were moved to the end of the addition list (they were the last to activate), the loss rate did not experience the drop it had when the moved zombies were activated earlier in the sequence. If the zombies were moved to the beginning of the addition list (they were the first to activate), the network did not experience the maximum loss percentage that the original sequence underwent.

Suppose that when operating at maximum network efficiency, the victim can receive $r(t)$ packets when no zombies are present. We will attempt to construct an expression for the *measure* of the DDoS attack from $r(t)$. Let $\gamma(t)$ be the number of legitimate packets generated by time t and suppose that n is the number of zombies placed in the network. If each zombie generated $\zeta(t)$ packets by time t, then we can estimate the number of legitimate $y(t)$ packets received at the victim by time t as

$$y(t) = \frac{r(t)\gamma(t)}{\gamma(t) + n\zeta(t)}.$$

$$(113)$$

Computing the ratio of legitimate packets received to legitimate packets generated, we have

$$s_D(n) = \frac{r(t)}{\gamma(t) + n\zeta(t)},$$

$$(114)$$

where $s_D(n)$ is the success rate of the DDoS attack, when we assume that $\gamma(t)$, $r(t)$ and $\zeta(t)$ are linear in t.

Figure 12.23 shows the mean s_D value over 23 runs using node 44 as the victim, our estimator of $s_D = 65.182/(65.182 + 1.004n)$ and also a linear regression on the dataset $s_D = 0.010n + 0.020$ used to produce the mean. While the linear regression was more accurate, with an SSR (sum of squares of residuals) value of 5.41, our predicted regression has an SSR value of 5.61 and is more reasonable as a model. Furthermore, the variance of the data was high as is shown by the standard error computed around the mean.

7. CONCLUSION

This chapter presented an in-depth analysis of DoS attacks. These attacks are extremely difficult to avoid and counteract, since they leverage the distributed nature of the Internet. We considered issues relating to traffic flow and network structure.

The first part of this chapter presented results supporting our hypothesis that DoS traffic has different statistical properties than normal traffic. We presented multiple traffic sets that support this thesis. One technique for detecting DoS attacks was presented. As with any Intrusion Detection System (IDS), it is important to establish the false positive rate. We feel that the in-depth analysis we performed here provides the tools needed for verifying the utility of an approach. Similar approaches may be possible for detecting worm and virus traffic. A major problem with verifying IDSs is the inability to find representative datasets describing network intrusions. The chaotic nature of Internet traffic makes designing IDSs challenging.

The game theoretic work presented here provides useful insights into the DoS threat. It supports the intuitive notion that a firewall can filter disruptive external traffic to save a network from internal disruption. The minimum number of zombies required to disrupt the network is a useful metric for determining a network's vulnerability to DoS. It should be possible to extend this work to creating dynamic strategies. Our network simulation analysis supports these conclusions.

8. EXERCISES

Exercise 12.1 Given an example network, find the min-cut set and a zombie placement that disables the network. Determine whether or not the zombie placement is minimal.

Exercise 12.2 Why would a simple threshold on the number of packets received by a node not be a useful DoS detection device?

Exercise 12.3 Would a distributed approach that compares traffic arrival rates across nodes be a reasonable approach? Why or why not?

Exercise 12.4 Which class of network topologies presented in Chapter 5 would be least susceptible to DoS attacks? Provide quantitative support.

Exercise 12.5 Would it be possible to tailor a DoS implementation to avoid the DoS detection approach given? If so, how?

CHAPTER 13
Conclusion

This book presented a number of new technologies for network and computer security. We intentionally concentrated on the security problems that have not been sufficiently addressed to date. Of particular interest were security aspects of new, emerging, "disruptive" technologies. The disruptive technologies presented were:

- Mobile code
- Peer-to-peer (P2P) networks
- Field Programmable Gate Arrays (FPGAs)
- Complex adaptive systems

Advances in all of these realms contribute to creating a more distributed, adaptive infrastructure. Research has dealt primarily with the negative security aspects of these technologies. As we have shown, positive security aspects exist as well.

Chapters 2 and 3 presented a current overview of security threats and solutions. The most widely publicized threats are worms, viruses, and Denial of Service (DoS) attacks. A major reason why these attacks are difficult to deter is their intelligent use of the distributed infrastructure. More subtle and frightening attacks are possible using the same tools. Advances are being made in creating security solutions, but the majority of development is concerned with securing isolated machines.

Chapter 4 gave an overview of the disruptive technologies we consider. The utility of these technologies guarantees that they will have a growing presence in the marketplace. In addition to this, saturation of the desktop market means that other application domains will evolve. It is likely that these domains will be built using networks of embedded systems. We presented two application areas that we are most familiar with: sensor networks and embedded building control systems.

Chapter 5 gave an overview of networking technology. Of particular relevance to this book were issues concerning network topology and traffic statistics. Physics-based studies of both issues have found statistical measures that describe the global system. These results support one of our basic tenets, that networks are now examples of complex adaptive systems. There is little, if any, centralized control. The global behavior of the system is a consequence of local interactions among many independent, but interrelated, components.

Chapter 6 presented an in-depth study of mobile code. There are many interesting effects due to code migrating from node to node. In effect, we now have a system that can autonomously redesign itself in response to internal and external interactions. We presented an abstract model that expresses this and showed that it can be used to model real-world systems. It provides approximations of network behavior and scales better than other approaches. We then developed a taxonomy of mobile code paradigms and mapped them to network security issues. The chapter concluded with an in-depth discussion of a mobile code system implementation.

Chapter 7 concentrated on protecting mobile code from malicious hosts. We discussed control flow techniques for obfuscating code and then presented methods for obfuscating Java programs by modifying bytecode mappings. The Java technique was also extended to create a form of program steganography, where programs can be transmitted hidden inside host programs. Secure hardware is another way of protecting mobile code from hostile hosts.

In Chapter 8 we considered the inverse problem, how to protect a host that executes code. This is the more thoroughly studied problem. The technologies we presented were designed specifically for defense in-depth of information systems. We started with security analysis of two application domains that require hosts to be situated in unprotected environments:

- Smart cards
- BACnet building control systems

A new approach to implementing cryptography engines for embedded systems was given. Parallel cryptography implementations provide throughput comparable to pipelined implementations, but require less space on the processor and have more flexible key handling. We then considered power analysis threats in detail. A solution was given based on the implementation of a secure instruction set. This approach is an elegant way of integrating security into hardware ad software.

Chapter 9 showed how to maintain trust in distributed networks. The approach given requires a minimal trusted computing base and was accompanied by thorough proofs of correctness. The proofs had clearly stated assumptions.

Chapter 10 moved our focus to the design of P2P networks. Random graphs are useful tools for analyzing these decentralized systems. Techniques were given for predicting network dependability, vulnerability to attack, connectivity, and Quality of Service given statistical descriptions of the network topology. We showed how to use this to determine the index structure that maximizes the Quality of Service desired for the P2P network. We also showed how key management can enforce trust in a P2P network. The tools given here, in combination with the results from Chapter 6, hint at a new design technique for distributed systems. By locally enforcing statistical properties, it should be possible to maintain desirable global system attributes with little or no centralized control.

Chapter 11 looked at routing and information in P2P systems. Once again, the approach concentrated on decentralized implementations. All the approaches used were based on partly stochastic interactions among multiple components. These concepts are related to other current *ad hoc* routing systems. They are also strongly tied to recent studies of gossip protocols. We finished the chapter by showing a hierarchy of epidemic routing techniques from flooding through gossip to random walk. The original approaches were found to be hybrid techniques built on these epidemic concepts. Tools for predicting system performance were provided.

The final chapter looked in-depth at DoS attacks. These are particularly difficult attacks for current technologies to counteract. We first analyzed how DoS traffic differs from legitimate traffic. Legitimate traffic is very difficult to characterize, mainly because of its multifractal nature. Multifractal statistics often describe complex adaptive systems. We derived an attack detection approach and showed in-depth how to validate intrusion detection systems. After that, we used game theory to find vulnerabilities in network topologies. Simulations verified our conclusions.

Most security measures fortify potential targets of attacks. While this is important and necessary, consider the larger picture. Many e-mail viruses do not perform actions that are forbidden by a sandbox. Worms primarily exploit software implementation errors. It is unlikely that software design will advance in the near future, if ever, to the point where we automatically foresee the abuses of software features or consistently produce bug-free systems.

Our network infrastructure enables distributed attacks. Increasingly fortifying individual machines on the network does not fortify the network. A metaphor can be made between worms/viruses and *blitzkrieg*. The advent of *blitzkrieg* made fortification of individual positions insufficient. In much the same way, fortifying individual processors is no longer sufficient. Distributed attacks have become widespread. Distributed countermeasures are needed to defend against them. Concentrating on fortifying individual processors is like building a stronger Maginot Line after World War II. Let's not make that mistake again.

References

[Abadi 1999] M. Abadi and A. D. Gordon, "A calculus for cryptographic protocols: the spi calculus," *Information and Computation*, Report 149, 1999.

[Abelson 1999] H. Abelson, et al, *Amorphous Computing*, AI Memo 1666, Massachusetts Institute of Technology, Cambridge, MA, August 1999, http://www.swiss.ai.mit.edu/projects/amorphous/paperlisting.html

[Adleman 1988] L. M. Adleman, "An Abstract Theory of Computer Viruses," *Advances in Cryptology – Crypto'88*, Lecture Notes in Computer Science, vol. 403, pp. 354-374, Springer-Verlag, Berlin, 1988.

[Aesop 2000] Aesop, *Aesop's Fables*, Seastar Books, NY, 2000.

[AH 1992] *American Heritage Dictionary of the English Language*, Electronic Version, Microsoft Corporation, Redmond, WA, 1992.

[Aho 1974] A. V. Aho, J. E. Hopcroft, and J. D. Ullman, *The Design and Analysis of Computer Algorithms*, Addison-Wesley, Reading, MA, 1974.

[Aho 1986] A. V. Aho, R. Sethi, and J. D. Ullman, *Compilers: Principles, Techniques, and Tools*, Addison-Wesley, Reading, MA, 1986.

[Ahuja 1993] R. K. Ahuja, T. L. Magnanti, and J. B. Orlin, *Network Flows: Theory, Algorithms, and Applications*, Prentice Hall, Upper Saddle River, NJ, 1993.

[Alam 2002] M. Alam, W. Badawy, and G. Jullienn, "A Novel Pipelined Threads Architecture for AES Encryption Algorithm," *Proceedings of the IEEE International Conference on Application-Specific Systems, Architectures, and Processors*, 2002.

[Albert 2000] R. Albert, H. Jeong, and A. -L. Barabási , "Error and attack tolerance of complex networks," *Nature*, vol. 406, pp.378-382, July 27, 2000

[Albert 2001] R. Albert and A.-L. Barabási, "Statistical Mechanics of Complex Networks," arXiv:cond-mat/0106096v1, June 2001.

[Algesheimer 2001] J. Algesheimer, C. Cachin, J. Camenisch, and G. Karjoth, "Cryptographic security for mobile code," *Proceedings of IEEE Security & Privacy*, 2001.

[Alj 1990] A. Alj and R. Faure. *Guide de la Recherche Operationelle*. vol. 2, pp. 206-208. Masson, Paris. 1990.

[Alligood 1996] K. T. Alligood, T. D. Sauer, J. A. Yorke, *Chaos: An Introduction to Dynamical Systems*, Springer Verlag, New York, 1996.

[Amme 2001] W. Amme, P. S. Housel, N. Dalton, J. von Ronne, P. H. Frohlich, C. H. Stork, V. Haldar, S. Zhenochin, and M. Franz, "Project transPROSE: Reconciling Mobile-Code Security with Execution Efficiency," *DARPA Information Survivability Conference and Exhibition*, pp. II.196-II.210, June 2001, http://citeseer.ist.psu.edu/558350.html

[Anderson 1999] R. H. Anderson, P. M. Feldman, S. Gerwehr, B. K. Houghton, R. Mesic, J. Pinder, J. Rothenberg, J. R. Chiesa, *Securing the U.S. Defense Information Infrastructure: A Proposed Approach*, Rand Corporation, Santa Monica, CA, 1999, http://www.rand.org/publications/MR/MR993/

[Anderson 2001] R. Anderson, "Why information security is hard – an economic perspective," *17th Annual Computer Security Applications Conference (ACSAC)*, New Orleans, LA, Dec. 2001.

[Antoniadis 1997] A. Antoniadis, I. Gijbels, "Detecting abrupt changes by wavelet methods", Technical Report, Laboratoire LMC-IMAG, Universite Joseph Fourier, France, 1997.

[ARL 1999] *Adaptive C2 Coalitions Air Campaign Model*, Penn State ARL Technical Report delivered to DARPA JFACC Program office and AFRL, December 1999.

[Atkins 2003] D. Atkins and R. Austein, "Threat Analysis of the Domain Name System," http://www.ietf.org/shadow.html, Nov. 2003

[Austin 1995] K. Austin, "Data security arrangements for semiconductor programmable devices," U.S. Pat. No. 5,388,157, Feb. 7, 1995.

[Axelsson 2000] S. Axelsson, "Intrusion Detection Systems: A Survey and Taxonomy," Chalmers University of Technology, www.ce.chalmers.se/staff/sax/taxonomy.ps, March 2000.

[Baase 1988] S. Baase, *Computer Algorithms: Introduction to Design and Analysis*. Addison-Wesley, Menlo Park. 1988.

[Balfanz 1997] D. Balfanz and E. W. Felten, *A Java Filter*, Technical Report 97-567, Department of Computer Science, Princeton University, 1997.

[Barabási 1999] A-.L. Barabási and R. Albert, "Emergence of scaling in random networks," Science, vol. 286, pp. 509-512, 15 October 1999.

[Barabási 2002] A-.L. Barabsi, *Linked*, Perseus, Cambridge, MA, 2002

[Barborak 1993] M. Barborak, M. Malek, and A. Dahbura, "The Consensus Problem in Fault-Tolerant Computing," vol. 25, no. 2, pp. 171-220, June 1993.

[Basseville 1993] M. Basseville, I.V. Nikiforov, *Detection of Abrupt Changes: Theory and Applications,* Prentice Hall, Englewood Cliffs, New Jersey, 1993.

[Bauer 2002] L. Bauer, J. Liggati, and D. Walker, "More Enforceable Security Policies," *Princeton University Computer Science Technical Report TR-649-02*, June 2002.

[Berghel 2003] H. Berghel, "Malware Month," *Communications of the ACM*, vol. 46, no. 12, pp. 15-19, 2003.

[Biham 1991] E. Biham, A. Shamir, "Differential Cryptanalysis of DES-like Cryptosystems", *Journal of Cryptography*, vol. 4, no. 1, pp. 3-72, 1991

[Biham 1999] E. Biham, A. Shamir. Power Analysis of The Key Scheduling of The AES Candidates. *Proceedings of the second AES Candidate Conference*, March 1999, pp. 115-121.

[Bilmes 1998] J. Bilmes, K. Asanovic, C.-W. Chin, and J. Demmel, *The PHiPAC v1.0 Matrix-Multiply Distribution*. Technical Report TR-98-35, International Computer Science Institute, Berkeley, CA, October 1998.

[Blazek 2001] R. B. Blazek, H. Kim, B. Rozovskii, A Tartakovsky, "A novel approach to detection of 'denial-of-service' attacks via adaptive sequential and batch-sequential change-point detection methods," IEEE System, Man, and Cybernetics Information Assurance Workshop, June 2001.

[Blunden 2002] B. Blunden, *Virtual Machine Design and Implementation in C/C++*, Wordware Publishing, Plano, TX, 2002.

[Bollobás 2001] B. Bollobás, *"Random Graphs"*, Cambridge University Press, Cambridge, UK, 2001.

[Bonabeau 1999] E. Bonabeau, M. Dorigo, and G. Theraulaz, *Swarm Intelligence: From Natural to Artificial Systems*. Oxford University Press, New York 1999.

[Bonds 2000] T. Bonds, et al, *Employing Commercial Satellite Communications: Wideband Investment Options for DoD*. Rand Corporation, Santa Monica, CA, 2000. http://www.rand.org/publications/MR/MR1192/

[Bontchev 1989] V. Bontchev, "The Bulgarian and Soviet Virus Factories," http://citeseer.nj.nec.com/41264.html

[Boriello 2000] G. Borriello and R. Want, "Embedded Computation Meets the World Wide Web," *Communications of the ACM*, vol. 43, no. 5, pp. 59-66, May 2000.

[Breugst 1998] M. Breugst and T. Magedanz, "Mobile Agents – Enabling technology for Active Intelligent Network Implementation," *IEEE Network*, pp. 53-60, May/June 1998.

[Brogan 1991] W. L. Brogan, *Modern Control Theory*, Prentice Hall, Upper Saddle River, NJ. 1991.

[Brooks 1996] R. R. Brooks and S. S. Iyengar, "Robust Distributed Computing and Sensing Algorithm", *IEEE Computer*, vol. 29 No. 6, pp. 53-60, June 1996.

[Brooks 1998] R. R. Brooks and S. S. Iyengar, *Multisensor Fusion:Fundamentals and Applications with Software*, Prentice Hall PTR, Upper Saddle River, NJ, 1998.

[Brooks 1999] R. R. Brooks, S. Phoha, and E. Peluso. "Stability and Controllability Analysis of Fuzzy Petri Net JFACC Models," *DARPA-JFACC Symp. on Advances in Enterprise Control*, San Diego, CA, Nov. 15-16, 1999.

[Brooks 2000] R. R. Brooks, E. Grele, W. Kliemkiwicz, J. Moore, C. Griffin, B. Kovak, and J. Koch "Reactive Sensor Networks: Mobile Code Support for Autonomous Sensor Networks," *Distributed Autonomous Robotic Systems DARS 2000*, Pp. 471-472. Springer Verlag, Tokyo, October 2000.

[Brooks 2000a] R. R. Brooks, "Stigmergy – An Intelligence Metric for Emergent Distributed Behaviors," *NIST Workshop on Performance Metrics for Intelligent Systems,* pp. 1-7, Gaithersburg, MD. August 2000.

[Brooks 2000b] R. R. Brooks, *Distributed Dynamic Linking*. Penn State Invention Declaration, May 2000.

[Brooks 2001] R. R. Brooks, L. Grewe, and S. S. Iyengar. "Recognition in the Wavelet Domain: A Survey," *Journal of Electronic Imaging*, vol. 10, no 3, pp. 757-784, July 2001

[Brooks 2002] R. R. Brooks, and N. Orr, "A Model for Mobile Code using Interacting Automata," *IEEE Transactions on Mobile Computing*, vol. 1, no. 4, pp. 313-326, October-December 2002.

[Brooks 2002a] R. R. Brooks, C. Griffin, J. Zachary, and N. Orr, "An Interacting Automata Model for Network Protection," Invited Paper, *Fusion 2002*, July 2002.

[Brooks 2002b] R. R. Brooks, S. A. Racunas, N. Gautam, and S. Rai, "On Path Dependability in Graph Models for P2P Networks," *IEEE Transactions on Dependability and Reliability*, Submitted for review, September, 2002.

[Brooks 2002c] R. Brooks, C. Griffin, and D. S. Friedlander, "Self-Organized distributed sensor network entity tracking," *International Journal of High Performance Computer Applications*, special issue on Sensor Networks, vol. 16, no. 3, pp. 207-220, Fall 2002

[Brooks 2003] R. R. Brooks and C. Griffin, "Fugitive Search Strategy and Network Survivability," *2003 Industrial Engineering Research Conference*, invited Paper, May 2003.

[Brooks 2003a] R. R. Brooks, J. Lamb, M. Zhu, M. Piretti, and S. S. Iyengar, "Emergent Control of Surveillance Networks," *Second International Workshop on Multi-Robot Systems*, NATO ASI Workshop, March 17-19, 2003, Naval Research Laboratory, Washington, DC, March 2003.

[Brooks 2003b] R. R. Brooks, S. A. Racunas, and S. Rai, "Mobile Network Analysis using Probabilistic Connectivity Matrices," *IEEE Transactions on Mobile Computing*, submitted for review, March 2003.

[Brooks 2003c] R. R. Brooks, M. Piretti, M. Zhu, and S. S. Iyengar, "Emergent routing protocols for wireless Ad Hoc Sensor Networks," *SPIE 48th Annual Meeting Symposium*, Accepted for publication, April 2003

[Brooks 2003d] R. R. Brooks, M. Piretti, M. Zhu, and S. S. Iyengar, "Distributed Adaptation Methods for Wireless Sensor Networks," *Globecom 2003*, submitted for review, March 2003.

[Brooks 2003e] R. R. Brooks, P. Ramanathan, and A. Sayeed, "Distributed Target Tracking and Classification in Sensor Networks," *Proceedings of the IEEE*, Invited Paper, vol. 91, no. 8, pp. 1163-1171, August 2003.

[Brooks 2004] R. R. Brooks, D. Friedlander, J. Koch, and S. Phoha, "Tracking Multiple Targets with Self-Organizing Distributed Ground Sensors," *Journal of Parallel and Distributed Computing* Special Issue on Sensor Networks, In Press, Jan. 2004.

[Brown 1996] S. Brown and J. Rose, "Architecture of FGPAs and CPLDs: A Tutorial," *IEEE Design and Test of Computers,* vol. 13, no. 2, pp. 42-57, 1996.

[Brunner 1975] J. Brunner, *The Shockwave Rider,* Ballantine Books, NY, 1975.

[Bukkapatnam 2000] S. T. S. Bukkapatnam, S. R. T. Kumara and A. Lakhtakia, "Fractal estimation of flank wear in machining," *ASME Transactions on Dynamic Systems Measurement and Control,* Vol. 122, pp. 89-94, 2000.

[Burgess 2000] M. Burgess, "Thermal, Non-Equilibrium Phase Space for Networked Computers," *Physical Review E,* Vol. 62, p. 1738, 2000.

[CAIDA 2001] *The Spread of the Code-Red Worm CRV2,* http://www.caida.org/analysis/security/code-red/coderedv2_analysis.xml

[CC 1999] *Common Criteria for Information Technology Security Evaluation,* v. 2.1, Aug. 1999.

[CERT 1996] "TCP SYN Flooding and IP Spoofing Attacks," CERT Advisory CA-1996-21, 1996.

[CERT 1996a] "UDP Port Denial-of-Service Attack," CERT Advisory CA-1996-01, 1996.

[CERT 2001] "Denial of Service Attack," CERT Coordination Center, 2001.

[Chander 2001] A. Chander, J. Mitchell, I. Shin, "Mobile code security by Java bytecode instrumentation," *DISCEX II,* 2001

[Chandra 2001] R. Chandra, V. Ramasubramanian, and K. Birman, "Anonymous gossip: Improving multicast reliability in mobile ad-hoc networks," *Proc. 21st Int. Conf. on Distributed Computing Systems,* pages 275-283, 2001.

[Chang 1999] M.-H. Chang, and J. E. Harrington, "Centralization vs. Decentralization in a Multi-Unit Organization: a Computational Model of a Retail Chain as a Multi-Agent Adaptive System," *Working Papers of the Santa Fe Institute, 1999*

[Chinoda 2000] T. P. Chinoda, *Protecting Java Applications Against Decompilation via Control Flow Obfuscation,* Masters Thesis, Department of Computer Science and Engineering, The Pennsylvania State University, December, 2000.

[Chodowiec 2001] P. Chodowiec, P. Khuon, and K. Gaj, "Fast Implementations of Secret-Key Block Ciphers Using Mixed Inner- and Outer-Round Pipelining," *Proceedings of the 2001 ACM/SIGDA Ninth International Symposium on Field Programmable Gate Arrays,* Pages 94-102.

[Christensen 1997] C. M. Christensen, *The Innovator's Dilemma,* Harvard Business School Press, Cambridge, MA, 1997.

[CNN 1996] CNN Online "'Domino Effect' Zapped Power in West," August 11, 1996 http://www.cnn.com/TECH/9608/11/power.outage/index.html

[CNN 2003] CNN Online, "Computer worm grounds flights, blocks ATMs," Jan. 26, 2003, http://www.cnn.com/2003/TECH/internet/01/25/internet.attack/

[Cohen 1986] F. Cohen, *Computer Viruses,* Ph.D. Dissertation, Electrical Engineering, University of Southern California, 1986.

[Cohen 1987] F. Cohen, "Computer Viruses – Theory and Experiments," *Computers and Security,* vol. 6, pp. 22-35, 1987. http://www.all.net/books/virus/index.html

[Collberg 1997] C. Collberg, C. Thomborson, and D. Low, *A Taxonomy of Obfuscating Transformations,* Technical Report #148, Department of Computer Science, University of Auckland, July 1997.

[Collberg 1998] C. Collberg, C. Thomborson and D. Low., "Manufacturing cheap, resilient, and stealthy opaque constructs". Department of Computer Science, University of Auckland, New Zealand, January, 1998.

[Com 2003] http://www.commerce-database.com

[Compton 2002] K. Compton and S. Hauck, "Reconfigurable Computing: A Survey of Systems and Software," *ACM Computing Surveys*, vol. 34, no. 2, pp. 171-210, June 2002.

[Computer 2000] "Love Hurts: New E-mail Worm Afflicts Millions," *Computer*, vol. 33, No. 6, p.22, June 2000.

[Coore 1999] D. Coore, *Botanical Computing: A Developmental Approach to Generating Interconnect Topologies in an Amorphous Computer*, PhD thesis, MIT Dept. of Electrical Engr. and Computer Science, Feb. 1999.

[Coron 1999] J. Coron. Resistance Against Differential Power Analysis for Elliptic Curve Cryptosystems. *Ç.K Koç and C. Paar, Eds., Cryptographic Hardware and Embedded Systems*, vol. 1717 of *Lecture Notes in Computer Science*, pp. 292-302, Springer-Verlag, 1999.

[Cowan 1994] G. A. Cowan, D. Pines, and D. Meltzer, ed.s *Complexity: Metaphors, Models and Reality*, Addison-Wesley, Reading, MA, 1994.

[Cowie 2001] J. Cowie, A. Ogelski, B. J. Premore, and Y. Yuan, "Global Routing Instabilities during Code Red II and Nimda Worm Propagation," Sep 19 2001, http://www.renesys.com/projects/bgp_instability/

[Crary 1999] K. Crary, R. Harper, P. Lee and F. Pfennig, "Automated Techniques for Provably Safe Mobile Code," DARPA Information Survivability Conference and Exposition, 2000. DISCEX '00. Proceedings ,Volume: 1 , 1999 , pp.: 406 -419, vol.1, 1999.

[Crovella 1997] M. E. Crovella and A. Bestavros, "Self-Similarity in World Wide Web Traffic: Evidence and Possible Causes," *IEEE/ACM Trans. on Networking*, vol. 5, no. 6, pp. 835-46, Dec. 1997.

[CVDQ 1992] *Computer Virus Developments Quarterly*, American Eagle Press, Tucson, AZ, vol. 1, no.1, 1992

[Cvetkovic 79] D. M. Cvetkovic, M. Doob, and H. Sachs, *Spectra of Graphs*, Academic Press, NY, 1979.

[CW 2002] "Steganography: Hidden Data," *Computerworld*, June 10, 2002, http://www.computerworld.com/securitytopics/security/story/0,10801,71726,00.html

[Czerwinski 1998] Czerwinski, T. (1998) *Coping with the Bounds: Speculations on Nonlinearity in Military Affairs*. National Defense University, Washington, DC.

[Dabek 2001] Dabek F., E. Brunskill, M. F. Kaashoek, D. Karger, R. Morris, I. Stoica, H. Balakrishnan *"Building Peer-to-Peer Systems with Chord, a Distributed Lookup Service"*, In the Proceedings of the *8th Workshop on Hot Topics in Operating Systems (HotOS-VIII)*, Schloss Elmau, Germany, May 2001. http://www.pdos.lcs.mit.edu/papers/chord:hotos01/

[Daemen 2000] J. Daemen, V. Rijmen, "The Block Cipher Rijndael," *Smart Card Research and Applications, LNCS 1820*, J.-J. Quisquater and B. Schneier, Eds., Springer-Verlag, 2000, pp. 288-296.

[Daubechies 1992] I. Daubechies, "Ten Lectures on Wavelets," SIAM, 1992.

[David 1989] R. David and H. Alla, *Du Grafcet aux reseaux de Petri*. pp. 212-226. Hermes, Paris. 1989.

[Delorme 1999] Delorme, M., "An introduction to cellular automata," *Cellular Automata: a Parallel Model*. M. Delorme and J. Mazoyer (eds). pp. 5-50. Kluwer Academic Publishers, Dordrecht. 1999.

[DES 1993] Data Encryption Standard (DES). Federal Information Processing Standards Publication 46-2. 1993 December 30.

[Devadas 2003] S. Devadas, *Physical Unclonable Functions and Applications*, *http://theory.lcs.mit.edu/classes/6.857/handouts/6857-puf-6up.pdf*

[Dhem 2001] J.- F. Dhem and N. Feyt, "Hardware and software symbiosis helps smartcard evolution," *IEEE Micro*, vol. 21, No. 6, pp. 14-25, Nov-Dec., 2001.

[Diestel 2000] R. Diestel, *Graph Theory*, Graduate Texts inMathematics, Springer Verlag, NY, 2000.

[DoA 1990] *Basic Cryptanalysis*, Department of the Army, Field Manual No-34-40-2. September 13rd, 1990.

[Dolev 1982] D. Dolev. "The Byzantine Generals Strike Again," *J.Alg.* 3, pp. 14-30. 1982.

[Donald 2001] S. D. Donald and R. V. McMillen, *Therminator-2: Developing a real-time thermodynamic based patternless intrusion detection system*, Naval Postgraduate School Thesis, Sept. 2001

[Dorigo 1996]] Marco Dorigo, Vittorio Maniezzo, Alberto Colorni, "The Ant System: Optimization by a colony of cooperating agents," *IEEE Transactions on Systems, Man, and Cybernetics Part B.* 26(1):29-41, 1996

[EFF 1998] Electronic Frontiers Foundation, *Cracking DES: secrets of encryption research, wiretap politics & chip design,* O'Reilly, Sebastopol, CA, 1998.

[Ellison 2003] C. Ellison and S. Dohrmann, "Public-Key Support for Group Collaboration," *ACM Transactions on Information and system Security*, vol. 6, no. 4, pp. 547-565, Nov. 2003.

[Encarta 1998] *Encarta Encyclopedia*, Microsoft Corporation, Redmond, WA, 1998.

[Enriquez 2003] F. Rodriguez-Henriquez, N.A. Saqib, and A. Diaz-Perez, "A 4.2 Gbit/s Single-Chip FPGA Implementation of AES Algorithm," *Electronics Letters*, July 2003, Pages 1115-1116.

[Erramilli 1994]] A. Erramilli, W. Willinger, and P. Pruthi, "Fractal Traffic Flows in High-speed Communications Networks," *Fractals*, vol. 2, no. 3, pp. 409-12, 1994.

[Erramilli 2000] A. Erramilli, O. Narayan, A.Neidhardt, abd I. Sanice, "Performance impacts of multiscaling in wide area TCP/IP traffic," in *Proceedings of IEEE Infocomm'2000*, Tel Aviv, Isreal, 2000, pp. 253-359.

[EU 2003] European Union, *Data Protection*, http://europa.eu.int/comm/internal_market/privacy/index_en.htm

[Farley 2003] T. Farley and P. McDaniel, " A Surevy of BGP Security Issues and Solutions," Technical Report TD-5UGJ33, AT&T Labs-Research, http://www.patrickmcdaniel.org/pubs/td-5ugj33.pdf, Dec. 2003.

[Fedoroff 1984] N. Fedoroff, "Transposable genetic elements in maize." *Scientific* American, pp. 65-74, June 1984.

[Feldmann 1998] A. Feldmann, A. C. Gilbert, and W. Willinger, "Data networks as cascades: Investigating the multifractal nature of Internet WAN traffic," in *Proceedings of the ACM/SIGCOMM'98*, pages 25--38, Vancouver, B.C., 1998.

[Feldmann 1999] A. Feldmann, A. C. Gilbert, P.Huang, W. Willinger, Dynamics of IP traffic: A study of the role of variability and the impact of control, in *Proc. of the ACM/SIGCOMM'99*, pp. 301--313, Boston, MA, 1999.

[Fisher 1982] M. Fisher and N. Lynch. "A Lower Bound for the Time to Insure Interactive Consistency," *Inf. Process. Lett.* 14, 4(June), pp. 183-186. 1982.

[Fisher 1999] D. A. Fisher and H. F. Lipson, "Emergent Algorithms: A New Method for Enhancing Survivability in Unbounded Systems," *Proceedings of the Hawaii International Conference on System Sciences,* 1999, http://www.cert.org/archive/html/emergent-algor.html

[Fletchner 1984] H.-J. Fletchner, *Grundbegriffe der Kybernetik*, dtv Wissenschaft, Munich, 1984.

[Floyd 2001 S.Floyd and V. Paxson, "Difficulties in Simulating the Internet", *IEEE/ACM Transactions on Networking*, Vol.9, No.4, pp. 392-403, August 2001.

[Forrest 1997] S. Forrest, A. Somayaji, and D. Ackley, "Building Diverse Computer Systems," *Proceedings of the Sixth Workshop on Hot Topics in Operating Systems*, pp. 67-72.

[Forrest 2000] S. Forrest and S. A. Hofmeyr, "Immunology as Information Processing," *Design Principles for Immune Systems & Other Distributed Autonomous Systems*, L. A. Segel and I. R. Cohen, ed.s, Oxford University Press, Oxford, UK, pp. 361-387, 2000.

[Freenet 2000] http://freenet.sourceforge.net/

[Friedman 1980] W. F. Friedman, *Miltary Cryptanalysis vol. I-IV*, Aegean Park Press, Laguna Hills, CA, 1980.

[Fuggetta 1998]A. Fuggetta, G. P. Picco, and G. Vigna, "Understanding Code Mobility," *IEEE Transactions on Software Engineering*, vol. 24, no. 5, pp. 342-361, May 1998.

[Gaertner 1999] F. C. Gaertner, "Fundamentals of Fault-Tolerant Distributed Computing in Asynchronous Environments," *ACM Computing Surveys*, vol. 31, no.1, pp. 1-26, March 1999.

[Gaertner 2001] F. C. Gaertner, *Formale Grundlagen der Fehlertoleranz in verteilten Systemen*, Ph. D. Dissertation, Informatik Dept. Technischen Universitaet Darmstadt, 2001.

[Garber 2000] L. Garber, "Denial of Service Attacks Rip the Internet," *Computer*, vol. 33, no.4, pp. 12-17,Apr.2000.

[Gassend 2002] B. Gassend, D. Clarke, M. van Dijk, and S. Devadas, "Silicon Physical Random Functions", *Proceedings of the Computer and Communication Security Conference*, November 2002.

[Gassend 2003] B. Gassend, D. Clarke, D. Lim, M. van Dijk, and S. Devadas, "Identification and Authentication of Integrated Circuits," *Concurrency and Computation: Practice and Experience*, vol. 3, pp. 1-20, 2003.

[Gautam 1997] N. Gautam, *Quality of Service for Multi-Class Traffic in High-speed Networking*, Ph. D. dissertation in Operations Research, University of North Carolina, Chapel Hill, 1997.

[Gaylord 1996] R. J. Gaylord K. Nishidate *Modeling Nature Cellular Automata Simulations with Mathematica*, Telos, 1996

[Gerrold 1972] D. Gerrold, *When H.A.R.L.I.E. was One*, Ballantine Books, 1972.

[Gilbert 1998] A. C. Gilbert, W. Willinger, A. Feldmann, Visualizing multifractal scaling behavior: A simple coloring heuristic, in *Proc. of the 32nd Asilomar conference on signals, systems, and computers*, Pacific Grove, CA, Nov. 1998.

[Gilbert 1999] A. C. Gilbert, W. Willinger, A. Feldmann, Scaling analysis of random cascades, with applications to network traffic, *IEEE Trans. of Info. Theory*, vol. 45, no. 3, pp.971--991, 1999.

[GNUtella 2000] http://gnutella.wego.com

[Goubin 1999] L. Goubin, J. Patarin. DES and Differential Power Analysis The "Duplication" Method. *Proceeding of CHES'99, Springer, Lecture Notes in Computer Science, Vol. 1717, August 1999.*

[Govindavajhala 2003] S. Govindavajhala and A. W. Appel, "Using Memory Errors to Attack a Virtual Machine," *2003 IEEE Symposium on Security ad Privacy,*

[Griffin 2003] C. Griffin, R. R. Brooks, and A. Payne, "A Comparison of Network Simulations," *Complexity,* submitted for review, March 2003.

[GRIP 2002]*GRIP (Gigabit Rate IP Security)*,2002, http://www.east.isi.edu/projects/GRIP/

[Grossglauer 1999] M. Grossglauer and J.-C. Blot, "On the Relevance of Long-Range Dependence in Network Traffic," *IEEE/ACM Transactions on Networking*, vol. 7, no. 5, pp. 629-640, Oct. 1999.

[GS 2003] GlobalSecurity.Org, "Solar Sunrise," http://www.globalsecurity.org/military/ops/solar-sunrise.htm

[Guan 2001] Y. Guan, X. Fu, D. Xuan, P. U. Shenoy, R. Bettati, and W. Zhao, "NetCamo: Camouflaging Network Traffic for QoS-Guaranteed Mission Critical Applications," *IEEE Transactions on Systems, Man, and Cybernetics – Part A*, vol. 31, no. 4, pp. 253-265, July, 2001.

[Gudonov 2001] V. Gudonov and J. Johnson, *Network as a Complex System: Information Flow Analysis*, oai:arXiv.org:nlin/0110008 (2003-05-28)

[Gutowitz 1991] H. Gutowitz, "Introduction," *Cellular Automata: Theory and Experiment*, pp. vii-xiv, MIT Press, Cambridge, MA, 1991.

[Haas 2002] Z. Haas, J. Halpern, and L. Li, "Gossip-based ad hoc routing," *Proceedings of the IEEE INFOCOM*, 2002.

[Haberman 1998] R. Haberman, Mathematical Models: Population Dynamics, and Traffic Flow, SIAM, Philadelphia, 1998.

[Hagen 1990] H. Hagen and A. Wunderlin, "Application of Synergetics to Pattern Formation and Pattern Recognition," *Self-Organization, Emerging Properties and Learning*, NATO ASI Series B: vol. 260, pp. 21-30, Plenum Press, NY, 1991.

[Haines 2001] J.W.Haines, et al, *1999 DARPA Intrusion Detection Evaluation Design and Procedures*, Technical Report 1062, MIT Lincoln Laboratories

[Haken 1978] H. Haken, *Synergetics: An Introduction*, Springer-Verlag, Berlin, 1978.

[Haldar 2002] V. Haldar, C. H. Stork, M. Franz, "The source is the proof," *Proceedings of the 2002 New Security Paradigms Workshop*, pp. 69-73, 2002.

[Halls 1997] D. A. Halls, *Applying Mobile Code to Distributed Systems*. Ph.D. Dissertation, Cambridge.

[Harchol-Balten 1997] M. Harchol-Balten, and A. B. Downey, "Exploiting Process Lifetime Distributions for Dynamic Load Balancing," *ACM Transactions on Computer Systems*, vol. 15, no. 3, pp. 253-285, August 1997.

[He 2002] J. He, S. Rai, Z. Yu, and R. R. Brooks, "Wavelet-Based Approach for Detecting Denial-of-Service Attacks in the Internet," *Computer Communication Review*, Submitted for review, October 2002.

[Hofmeyr 2000] S. Hofmeyr and S. Forrest, "Architecture for an Artificial Immune System." *Evolutionary Computation 7(1)*, Morgan-Kaufmann, San Francisco, CA, pp. 1289-1296 (2000).

[Hohl 1997] F. Hohl, *An Approach to Solve the Problem of Malicious Hosts*, Universitaet Stuttgart Fakultaet Informatik, Bericht Nr. 1997/03, 1997.

[Hong 2001] T. Hong, "*Chapter 14: Performance*", in *Peer-to-Peer Harnessing the Power of Disruptive Technologies*, A. Oram, ed. pp. 203-241, O'Reilly, Beijing, 2001.

[Hopcroft 1979] J. E. Hopcroft and J. D. Ullman, *Introduction to Automata Theory, Languages and Computation*, Addison Wesley, Reading, MA, 1979.

[Hordijk 1999] W. Hordijk, *Dynamics, Emergent Computation, and Evolution in Cellular Automata*, Ph.D. Dissertation, Computer Science, University of New Mexico, December 1999.

[Horwitz 1990] S. Horwitz, T. Reps, and D. Binkley. Interprocedural Slicing Using Dependence Graphs. *ACM Transactions on Programming Languages and Systems 12*, 1 (January 1990), 26-60.

[Householder 2002] A. Householder, B. King, and K. Silva, *Securing and Internet Name Server*, CERT Coordination Center, http://www.cert.org/archive/pdf/dns.pdf, Aug. 2002.

[Housely 1999] R. Housely, W. Ford, W. Polk, and D. Solo, *Internet X.509 Public Key Infrastructure Certificate and CRL Profile*, Request For Comments 2459, January 1999, http://www.ietf.org/rfc/rfc2459.txt

[Howard 1998] J. D. Howard, T. A. Longstaff, *A Common Language for Computer Security Incidents*, Sandia Report, SAND98-8867.

[Howard 2003] M. Howard and D. LeBlanc, *Writing Secure Code*, Microsoft Press, Redmond, WA, 2003.

[Hwang 1993] K. Hwang, Advanced Computer Architecture: Parallelism, Scalability, Programmability, McGraw-Hill, New York, 1993.

[IDS 2001] "Internet Domain Survey," January, 2001, http://www.isc.org/ds/WWW-200101/index.html

[Intanagonwiwat 2000] C. Intanagonwiwat, R. Govindan and D. Estrin, "Directed diffusion:A scalable and robust communication paradigm for sensor networks," *Proceedings of Mobicom '00*, 2000.

[IOCCC 2004] International Obfuscated C Code Contest. http://www.ioccc.org/

[Iren 1999] S. Iren, P.D. Amer, and P. T. Conrad, "The Transport Layer: Tutorial and Survey," *ACM Computing Surveys*, vol. 31, no. 4, pp. 361-405, December, 1999.

[Irvine 2000] C. Irvine and T. Levin, "Quality of Security Service," *New Security Paradigms Workshop 2000*, pp. 91-99, 2001.

[Iyengar 2004] S. S. Iyengar and R. R. Brooks, ed.'s, *Frontiers in Distributed Sensor Networks*, CRC Press, Boca Raton, FLA, in press, publication Fall 2003.

[Jacob 2001] C. Jacob, *Illustrating Evolutionary Computation with Mathematca*, Morgan Kaufmann, San Francisco, CA, 2001.

[Jaffard 2001] S. Jaffard, "Wavelets. Tools for Science and Technologies", Philadelphia Society for Industrial and Applied Mathematics, pp. 72-75. 2001.

[Jalote 1994] P. Jalote, *Fault Tolerance in Distributed Systems,* Prentice Hall, Englewood Cliffs, NJ, 1994.

[Jansen 1999] W. Jansen and T. Karygiannis, *Mobile Agent Security*, NIST Special Publication 800-19, http://csrc.nist.gov/mobileagents/publication/sp800-19.pdf, August 1999.

[Jarvinen 2003] K. Jarvinen, M. Tommiska, and J. Skytta, "A Fully Pipelined Memoryless 17.8 Gbps AES-128 Encryptor," *Proceedings of the 2003 ACM/SIGDA Eleventh International Symposium on Field Programmable Gate Arrays,* Pages 207-215.

[Jensen 1998] H. J. Jensen, *Self-Organized Criticality*, Cambridge University Press, Cambridge, UK 1998.

[Jensen 2000] S. Jensen, T. Luczak, A. Rucinski, *Random Graphs*, John Wiley & Sons, New York, 2000.

[Jerkins 1997] J. L. Jerkins and J. L. Wang, "A Measurement of ATM Cell-Level Aggregate Traffic," *Proc. IEEE Globecom*, Nov. 1997, pp. 1589-95.

[Jha 2002] S. Jha, O. Scheyner, and J. M. Wing, *Minimization and Reliability Analysis of Attack Graphs*, Technical Report, CMU-CS-02-109, Carnegie Mellon University, February 2002.

[JhaSW 2002] S. Jah, O. Sheyner, and J. M. Wing, "Two Formal Analyses of Attack Graphs," *Proceedings of the 15th IEEE Computer Security Foundations Workshop (CSFW'02)*, 2002.

[Kan 2001] G. Kan, *"Chapter 8: GNUtella"*, in *Peer-to-Peer Harnessing the Power of Disruptive Technologies*, A. Oram, ed. pp. 94-122, O'Reilly, Beijing, 2001.

[Kapur 2002] A. Kapur, N. Gautam, R. R. Brooks, and S. Rai, "Design, Performance and Dependability of a Peer-to-Peer Network Supporting QoS for Mobile Code Applications," *Proceedings of the Tenth International Conference on telecommunications systems,* pp. 395-419, Sept. 2002.

[Kapur 2002a] A. Kapur, *Quality of Service QoS Analysis of Peer-to-Peer Networks with File-sharing Applications*, M. S. Thesis, Industrial and Manufacturing Engineering, M.S., Penn State, Fall 2002.

[Karp 2000] Brad Karp and H.T.K Ung Greedy Perimeter Stateless Routing for Wireless Networks *Proc. of the 6th Annual ACM/IEEE International Conference*, 2000.

[Kauffman 1993] S. A. Kauffman, *The Origins of Order: Self-Organization and Selection in Evolution*, Oxford University Press, New York. 1993.

[Keiser 2004] T. Keiser, and R. R. Brooks, "Implementation of Mobile Code Daemons for a Wired and Wireless Network of Embedded Systems," *IEEE Internet Computing*, July 2004.

[Kempe 2001] D. Kempe, J. M. Kleinberg, and A. J. Demers, "Spatial gossip and resource location protocols," *Proceedings of 33rd Annual ACM Symposium on Theory of Computing*, pages 163-172, 2001.

[Kennel 1992] M. B. Kennel, R. Brown, and H. D. I. Abarbanel, "Determining embedding dimension for phase-space reconstruction using a geometrical construction," *Physical Review A*, Vol. 45, no. 6, pp. 3403-3411, 15 March 1992.

[Kephart 1993] J. O. Kephart, S. R. White, D. M. Chess, "Computers and Epidemiology," *IEEE Spectrum*, Vol. 30, No. 5, pp. 20-26, May 1993.

[Kevin 2001] J. Kevin, G. M. Weaver, N. Long, and R. Thomas, "Trends in Denial of Service Attack Technology," Tech. Report, CERT Coordination Center, Carnegie Mellon University, October, 2001.

[Knight 1998] J. C. Knight, "Is Information Security an Oxymoron?" *IEEE AES Magazine,* pp. 6-7, Feb 1998.

[Kocher 1996] P. Kocher. Timing Attacks on Implementations of Diffie-Hellman, RSA, DSS and other Systems, *Advances in Cryptology, Proceedings of Crypto'96*, LNCS 1109, N.Koblitz, Ed., Springer-Verlag, 1996, pp.104-113.

[Kocher 1998] P. Kocher, J. Jaffe, and B. Jun. Introduction to Differential Power Analysis and Related Attacks. *http://www.cryptography.com/dpa/technical,1998*.

[Kocher 1999] P. Kocher, J. Jaffe, and B. Jun, "Differential Power Analysis," *CYPTO '99*, pp. 388-397, 1999.

[Kolesnikov 2002] O. Kolesnikov, and B. Hatch, *Building Linux Virtual Private Networks (VPNs)*, New Riders publishing, Indianapolis, 2002.

[Komerling 1999] O. Kommerling and M. G. Kuhn. Design Principles for Tamper-Resistant Smart card Processors. *USENIX Workshop on Smart card Technology*, Chicago, IL, May 10 – May 11 1999.

[Kott 1999] A. Kott and B. Krogh, "Toward a Catalog of Pathological Behaviors in Complex Enterprize Control Systems,"*Proceedings from November 1999 DARPA-JFACC Symposium on Advances in Enterprize Control*, pp. 1-6, San Diego, CA, Nov 15-16, 1999. (http://www.darpa.mil/iso/jfacc/symposium/sess2-1.doc)

[Krishnamachari 2001] Bhaskar Krishnamachari, Stephen B. Wicker, and Ramon Bejar, "Phase Transition Phenomena in Wireless Ad-Hoc Networks," *Symposium on Ad-Hoc Wireless Networks, GlobeCom2001*, San Antonio, Texas, November 2001. http://www.krishnamachari.net/papers/phaseTransitionWirelessNetworks.pdf

[Krol 1986] T. Krol. "(N,K) Concept Fault Tolerance," *IEEE Transactions on Computers*. Vol. C-35, No 4(April), 339-349. 1986.

[Krol 1991] T. Krol. *A generalization of fault-tolerance based on masking*. PhD. Dissertation. Eindhoven Univ. of Technology, Eindhoven, the Netherlands. 1991.

[Kurose 2003] James F. Kurose and Keith W. Ross, *Computer Networking a Top-Down Approach Featuring the Internet*, AW Higher Education Group 2003

[Lamport 1982] L. Lamport, R. Shostak, and M. Pease. "The Byzantine Generals Problem," *ACM Trans. Program. Lang. Syst.* 4, 3(July), pp. 382-401. 1982.

[Lampson 1973] B. W. Lampson, "A Note on the Confinement Problem," *Communications of the ACM*, vol. 16, no. 10, pp. 613-615, October, 1973.

[Landwehr 1993] C. E. Landwehr, A. R. Bull, J. P. McDermott, and W. S. Choi, *A Taxonomy of Computer Program Security Flaws, with Examples*, NRL/FR.5542—93—9591, Naval Research Laboratory, Nov. 19, 1993.

[Langley 2001] A. Langley, *"Freenet"*, pp. 123 – 132b, Orielly 'Peer-to-Peer'.

[Lavielle 1999] Lavielle, "Detection of multiple changes in a sequence of dependent variables," *Stoch. Porc. and Appl.*, Vol. 83, pp. 79-102, 1999.

[Lazarevic 2002] A. Lazarevic, J. Srivastava, and V. Kumar, "Cyber threat analysis – a key enabling technology for the objective force (a case study in network intrusion detection).," *Army Science Conference*, 2002, http://www.asc2002.com/manuscripts/O/OO-05.PDF

[Leinwand 1996] A. Leinwand, K. F. Conroy, *Network Management: A Practical Perspective*, Addison-Wesley, Reading, MA, 1996.

[Leland 1994] W. E. Leland, M. S. Taqqu, W. Willinger, and D. V. Wilson, "On the Self-Similar Nature of Ethernet Traffic (Extended Version)" *IEEE/ACM Transactions on Networking*, vol. 2, no. 1, pp. 1-15, Feb. 1994.

[Leyden 2004] J. Leyden, "Virus writers in malicious code hide-and-seek," *The Register*, Mar. 5, 2004, http://www.securityfocus.com/news/8196

[Limnios 2000] Limnios, *Arbres de Defaillance*, Hermes Editions, Paris, 2000.

[Lipmaa 2004] H. Lipmaa, "AES Candidates: A Survey of Implementations," http://www.tcs.hut.fi/~helger/aes/.

[Loughry 2002] J. Loughry and D. A. Umphress, "Information leakage from optical emanations," *ACM Transactions on Information and System Security (TISSEC)*, vol. 5, no. 3, pp. 262-289, 2002.

[Loureiro 2000] S. Loureiro, R. Molva, "Mobile Code Protection with Smartcards," *6th ECOOP Workshop on Mobile Object Systems*, http://citeseer.nj.nec.com/408410.html, June, 2000.

[Loureiro 2001] S. Loureiro, *Mobile Code Protection*, Ph. D. Dissertation, Institut Eurecom, 2001.

[Loureiro 2002] S. Loureiro, L. Bussard, and Y. Roudier, "Extending tamperproof hardware security to untrusted execution environments," *5th Smart Card Research and Advanced Application Conference (CARDIS '02)*, Nov 2002.

[Low 1998] D. Low . *Java Control Flow Obfuscation*, Thesis, Department of Computer Science, University of Auckland, New Zealand, June 1998

[Lucas 1997] M. T. Lucas, D. E. Wrege, B. J. Dempsey, and A. C. Weaver, "Statistical Characterization of Wide-Area IP Traffic," *Proc. 6th IEEE Intl. Computer Communications and Networks Conf.*, Sept. 1997, pp. 442-7.

[Ludwig 1991] M. A. Ludwig, *The Little Black Book of Computer Viruses,* American Eagle Press, Tucson, AZ, 1991.

[Ludwig 1995] M. A. Ludwig, *The Giant Black Book of Computer Viruses*, American Eagle Press, Show Low, AZ, 1995.

[Ludwig 2002] M. A. Ludwig, *The Little Black Book of E-mail Viruses*, American Eagle Press, Show Low, AZ, 2002.

[Lynch 1996] N. A. Lynch, *Distributed Algorithms*, Morgan Kaufmann Publishers, San Francisco, CA, 1996.

[Madnick 1978] S. E. Madnick and J. J. Donovan, *Operating Systems*, McGraw-Hill International, Auckland, 1978.

[Mandelbrot 1997] B. Mandelbrot, *Fractales, Hasard, et Finance*, Flammarion, Paris, 1997.

[Mano 1997] M. M. Mano, and C. R. Kime, *Logic and Computer Design Fundamentals,* Prentice Hall, Upper Saddle River, NJ, 1997.

[Marin 2002] G. A. Marin, W. Allen, and S. Luo, "Network monitoring for computer intrusion detection," preprint.

[Marker 2002] D. Marker, *Model Theory: An Introduction*, Springer Verlag, NY, 2002.

[Matsui 1994] M. Matsui, "Linear Cryptanalysis Method of DES Cipher", *Advances in Cryptography – EUROCRYPT '93 (Lecture Notes in Computer Science no. 765)*, Springer-Verlag, pp. 386-397, 1994.

[McDowell 1998] C. E. McDowell, B. R. Montague, M. R. Allen, E. A. Baldwin, and M. E. Montoreano, "JAVACAM: Trimming Java Down to Size," *IEEE Internet Computing*, vol. 2 3, pp. 53-59, http://computer.org/internet/, May-June, 1998.

[McGhan 1998] H. McGhan, M. O'Conner, PicoJava: A Direct Execution Engine for Java Bytecode, *IEEE Computer*, pp. 22-30, 1998.

[Mc Hugh 2000] J. McHugh, "Testing Intrusion Detection Systems: A Critique of the 1998 and 1999 DARPA Intrusion Detection System Evaluations as Performed by Lincoln Laboratory", *ACM transactions on Information and System Security*, Vol. 3, No. 4, pp. 262-294, Nov. 2000

[Meir 1991] K. S. Meier-Hellstern, P. E. Wirth, Yi-Ling Yan, and D. A. Hoeflin, "Traffic Models for ISDN Data Users: Office Automation Application," *Proc. 13th Intl. Teletraffic Congress*, June 1991, pp. 167-72.

[Menezes 1997]. A. J. Menezes, P. C. van Oorschot, S. A. Vanstone, *Handbook of Applied Cryptography*, CRC Press, Boca Raton, FL, 1997.

[Microsoft 1997] *Microsoft Bookshelf Computer and Internet Dictionary*, Microsoft Corp., Redmond, WA, 1997.

[Milojicic 1999] D. Milojicic, F. Douglis, and R. Wheeler, ed.s, *Mobility: Processes Computers, and Agents*, Addison-Wesley, Reading, MA, 1999.

[MITLL 2002] http://www.ll.mit.edu/IST/ideval/index.html

[Mitnick 2002] K. D. Mitnick and W. L. Simon, *The Art of Deception*, Wiley, Indianapolis, Indiana, 2002.

[Molander 1996] R. C. Molander, A. S. Riddile, and P. A. Wilson, *Strategic Information Warfare: a New Face of War*, Rand Corporation, Santa Monica, CA, 1996, http://www.rand.org/publications/MR/MR661/MR661.html

[Moore 2001] A. P. Moore, R. J. Ellison, and R. C. Linger, *Attack Modeling for Informaion Security and Survivability,* Technical Note, CMU/SEI-2001-TN-001, 2001.

[Moore 2001a] D. Moore, "Inferring Internet Denial-of-Service Activity," *Proceedings of the 2001 USENIX Security Symposium*.

[Moore 2002] S. Moore, R. Anderson, and M. Kuhn. Improving Smart card Security Using Self-Timed Circuit Technology. *The Eight IEEE International Symposium on Asynchronous Circuit And Systems, Manchester, UK*, April 8 – April 11 2002.

[Moore 2003] J. Moore, T. Keiser, R. R. Brooks, S. Phoha, D. Friedlander, J. Koch, A. Reggio, and N. Jacobson, "Tracking Targets with Self-Organizing Distributed Ground Sensors," *2003 IEEE Aerospace Conference*, Invited Paper, March 2003.

[Moore 2003a] D. Moore, V. Paxson, S. Savage, C. Shannon, S. Staniford, and N. Weaver, "Inside the Slammer Worm," *IEEE Security & Privacy*, vol. 1, no. 4, http://www.computer.org/security/v1n4/j4wea.htm

[Nagel 1998] K. Nagel, "From Particle Hopping Models to Traffic Flow Theory," *Traffic Flow Theory Simulation Models, Macroscopic Flow Relationships, and Flow Estimation and Prediction: Transportation Research Record No. 1644*, pp. 1-9, Transportation Research Voard National Research Council, National Academy Press, Wash. DC, 1998.

[Necula 1998] G. C. Necula and P. Lee, "Safe, Untrusted Agents using Proof-Carrying Code," *Mobile Agents and Security*, Lecture Notes in Computer Science, vol. 1419, pp. 61-91, 1998.

[Necula 2002] G. C. Necula and R. R. Schneck, "Proof-Carrying Code with Untrusted Proof Rules," *Proc. of International Software Security Symposium*, pp. 283-298, 2002.

[Nelson 1988] Nelson, Welch, Ousterhout, "Caching in the Sprite Network File System", ACM TOCS, 6(1), Feb. 1988.

[Newmann 2001] M. E. J. Newmann, S. H. Strogatz, and D. J. Watts, "Random Graphs with arbitrary degree distributions and their applications", *arXiv: cond-mat/007235*, May 7, 2001.

[Newmann 2001a] M. E. J. Newmann, *"Ego-centered networks and the ripple effect or Why all your friends are weird"*, *Working Papers, Santa Fe Institute*, Santa Fe, NM, http://www.santafe.edu/sfi/publications/workingpapers/01-11-066.pdf.

[Newman 2002] D. Newman, J. Snyder, R. Thayer, "Crying Wolf: False alarms hide attacks," http://www.nwfusion.com/techinsider/2002/0624security1/html

[NF 1985] "Network Forth," http://www.sandelman.ottawa.on.ca/People/Michael_richardson/network-forth.html

[Nichols 2002] R. K. Nichols and P. C. Lekkas, *Wireless Security: models, threats, and solutions*, McGraw-Hill, NY, 2002.

[Nicolis 1977] G. Nicolis, I. Prigogine, *Self-organization in Non-equilibrium Systems*, Wiley & Sons, NY, 1977.

[Nievergelt 1999] Y. Nievergelt, *Wavelets Made Easy*, Boston: Birkhauser, pp. 3-35, 1999.

[Nolan 1998] G. Nolan, *Decompiling Java*, McGraw-Hill, NY, 1998.

[NYTimes 2000] "Powerful Music Software Has Industry Worried," *New York Times*, New York, March 7, 2000. http://nytimes.com/library/tech/00/03/biztech/articles/07net.html

[OED 2003] *Oxford English Dictionary*, http:www.oed.com

[Oldfield 1995] J.V. Oldfield and R.C. Dorf, *Field Programmable Gate Arrays: Reconfigurable Logic for Rapid Prototyping and Implementation of Digital Systems*. John Wiley & Sons, 1995.

[Oram 2001] A. Oram, ed. "Peer-to-Peer Harnessing the Power of Disruptive Technologies", O'Reilly, Beijing, 2001.

[Orr 2002] N. Orr Nathan Orr, Computer Science and Engineering M.S. thesis Penn State, *A Message-Based Taxonomy of Mobile Code for Quantifying Network Communication*, Summer 2002.

[Park 1996] K. Park, G. Kim, and M. Crovella, "On the Relationship Between File Sizes, Transport Protocols, and Self-Similar Network Traffic," Proc. IEEE Intl. Conf. on Network Protocols, Oct. 1996, pp.171-80.

[Pattersson 2000] C. Patterson, "High Performance DES Encryption in Virtex FPGAs using Jbits," *IEEE Symposium on Field-Programmable Custom Computing Machines*, 2000, Pages 113-121.

[Paxson 1995] V. Paxson and S. Floyd, "Wide Area Traffic: The Failure of Poisson Modeling," IEEE/ACM Trans. on Networking, vol. 3, no. 3, pp. 226-44, June 1995.

[PBS 1996] Online Newshour, "Blackout," July 3, 1996 http://www.pbs.org/newshour/bb/science/blackout_7-3.html

[PBS 2003] Frontline, "Cyber War!" http://www.pbs.org/wgbh/pages/frontline/shows/cyberwar/warnings/

[PCAP 2004] http://www.tcpdump.org/

[Peha 1997] J. M. Peha, "Retransmission Mechanisms and Self-Similar Traffic Models," Proc. IEEE/ACM/SCS Communication Networks and Distributed Systems Modeling and Simulation Conf., Jan. 1997, pp. 47-52.

[Perrig 2001] A. Perrig, R. Szewczyk, V. Wen, D. Culler, and D. Tygar: SPINS: Security Protocols for Sensor Networks, *Proceedings of Mobicom* 2001.

[Phoha 1999] S. Phoha, R. R. Brooks and E. Peluso. "A Constructivist Theory for Distributed Intelligent Control of Complex Dynamic Systems," *DARPA JFACC Symposium on Advances in Enterprise Control*. Nov. 1999.

[Phoha 2001] V. Phoha, *Internet Security Dictionary*, Springer Verlag, 2001.

[Portugali 2000] J. Portugali, *Self-Organization and the City*, Springer Verlag, Berlin, 2000.

[Pottie 1998] G. J. Pottie "Hierarchical information processing in distributed sensor networks." *Proceedings 1998 IEEE International Symposium on Information Theory*, p. 163, Aug. 1998.

[Press 1992] W. Press, S. Teukolsky, W. Vetterling, and B. Flannery. *Numerical Recipes in Fortran,* 2nd edition. Cambridge University Press, Cambridge. 1992.

[Qi 2001] H. Qi, S. S. Iyengar, K. Chakrabarty, "Multi-resolution data integration using mobile agents in distributed sensor networks," *IEEE Transactions on Systems, Man, and Cybernetics Part C: Applications and Reviews*, vol. 31, no. 3, pp383-391, August, 2001.

[Radhakrishnan 1999] R. Radhakrishnan, J. Rubio and L. John: Characterization of Java Applications at Bytecode and Ultra-SPARC Machine Code Levels, *In Proceedings of IEEE International Conference on Computer Design*, pages 281-284, 1999

[Rai 1990] S. Rai and D. P. Agrawal. *Distributed Computing Network Reliability*. IEEE Computer Society Press, Los Alamitos. 1990.

[Rai 1990a] S. Rai and D. P. Agrawal, ed.s *Advances in Distributed System Reliability*, IEEE Computer Society Press, Los Alamitos, CA, 1990.

[Ratnasamy 2001] Sylvia Ratnasamy, Paul Francis, Mark Handley, Richard Karp, Scott Shenker, *"A Scalable Content-Addressable Network"*, ACM, 2001
http://www.acm.org/sigcomm/sigcomm2001/p13-ratnasamy.pdf

[Riedi 1999] R. H. Riedi, M. S. Crouse, V. J. Ribeiro, and R. G. Baraniuk, "A Multifractal Wavelet Model with Application to Network Traffic," *IEEE Transactions on Information Theory*, Vol. 45, No. 4, pp. 992-1018, 1999.

[Ritter 2001] J. Ritter, *"Why GNUtella Can't Scale. No, Really"*
http://www.darkridge.com/~jpr5/doc/gnutella.html

[Rivest 1992] R. Rivest, "The MD5 Message Digest Algorithm." *RFC 1321*. MIT Laboratory for Computer Science, April 1992.

[Roseaux 1987] Roseaux. *Exercises et Problemes Resolus de Recherches Operationelle*. pp. 137-176. Masson, Paris. 1987.

[Rothe 2002] J. Rothe: Some facets of complexity theory and cryptography: a five-lecture tutorial, *ACM Computing Surveys*, vol. 34, no. 4, pp. 504-549, December 2002.

[Rowstron 2001] A. Rowstron and P. Druschel, *"Pastry: Scalable, distributed object location and routing for large-scale peer-to-peer systems"*. IFIP/ACM International Conference on Distributed Systems Platforms (Middleware), Heidelberg, Germany, pages 329-350, November 2001.

[Royer 1999] Elizabeth M. Royer. A Review of Current Routing Protocols for Ad Hoc Mobile Wireless Networks *IEEE Personal Communication* April 1999

[Rubin 1998] A. D. Rubin, and D. E. Geer, "Mobile Code Security," *IEEE Internet Computing*, pp. 30-34, Nov-Dec 1998.

[Russell 2003] R. Russell, et al, *Stealing the Network: How to Own the Box*, Syngress, Rickland, MA, 2003.

[Ryan 2001] P. Ryan and S. Schneider, *Modeling and Analysis of Security Protocols*, Addison-Wesley, Harlow, UK, 2001.

[Sabelfield 2003] A. Sabelfield and A. C. Myers, "Language-Based Information-Flow Security," *IEEE Journal on Selected Areas in Communications,* vol. 21, no. 1, pp. 5-19, Jan. 2003.

[Sahner 1987] R. Sahner and K. Trivedi. "Performance and Reliability Analysis Using Directed Acyclic Graphs," *IEEE Transactions on Software Engineering.* SE-13, 10(Oct), pp.1105-1114. 1987.

[Sander 1998] T. Sander and C. F. Tschudin, "Towards Mobile Cryptography," *Proceedings of the 1998 IEEE Symposium on Security and Privacy*, pp. 215-224, 1998.

[Sapaty 1999] P. Sapaty, Mobile Processing in Distributed and Open Environments, Wiley, New York, 1999.

[Saputra 2003] H. Saputra, N. Vijaykrishnan, M. Kandemir, M. J. Irwin, R. Brooks, S. Kim, and W. Zhang. Masking the energy behavior of DES encryption, *Proc. the 6th Design Automation and Test in Europe Conference (DATE'03)*, Munich, Germany, March 2003. nominated for best paper award.

[Saputra 2003a] H. Saputra, R. R. Brooks, N. Vijaykrishnan, M. Kandemir, and M. J. Irwin, "Code protection for resource-constrained embedded devices," *Third International Symposium for Embedded Systems Software*, Submitted for Review, April 2003.

[Saputra 2003b] H. Saputra, N. Vijaykrishnan, M. Kandemir, M. J. Irwin, R. R. Brooks, S. Kim, and W. Zhang, "Masking the Energy Behavior of DES Encryption," submitted for review, May 2003.

[Saputra 2004] H. Saputra, G. Chen, R. Brooks, N. Vijaykrishnan, M. Kandemir, and M. J. Irwin. "Code protection for resource-constrained embedded devices." *ACM SIGPLAN /SIGBED 2004 Conference on Languages, Compilers, and Tools for Embedded Systems* (LCTES'04), Washington, DC, June 2004.

[Sarkar 2000] P. Sarkar, "A Brief History of Cellular Automata," *ACM Computing Surveys,* vol. 32, No.1, pp, 80-107, March 2000.

[Schneider 1993] M. Schneider, "Self-Stabilization," *ACM Computing Surveys*, vol. 25, no. 1, pp. 45-67, March 1993.

[Schneider 2000] F. Schneider, "Enforceable Security Policies," *ACM Transactions on Information and System Security (TISSEC)*, vol. 3, no. 1, pp. 30-50.

[Schneider 2004] F. B. Schneider, *Introduction to Cryptography*, Lecture notes, Computer Science, Cornell University.

[Schneier 1996] B. Schneier, *Applied Cryptography*, Wiley, Indianapolis, IN, 1996.

[Schulman 2003] B. Schulman, "Finding the Right Processing Architecture for AES Encryption," http://www.eetimes.com/story/OEG20030618S0012.

[Science 1999] "'Self-Tuning' Software Adapts to its Environment," *Science*, vol. 286, p. 35, October 1, 1999.

[Sekar 2001] R. sekar, C. R. Ramakrishnan, I. V. Ramakrishnan, and A. A. Smolka, "Model-Carrying Code (MCC): A New Paradigm for Mobile-Code Security," *New Security Paradigms Workshop*, Sept. 2001

[Shin 1998] I. Shin and J. C. Mitchell, *Java Bytecode Modification and Applet Security*, Technical Report, Computer Science Department, Stanford Univversity, 1998, http://www.cis.upenn.edu/~ishin/papers/java-bytecode-mod.pdf

[Siewiorek 1982] D. P. Siewiorek and R. S. Swarz. *The Theory and Practice of Reliable System Design*. Digital Press, Maynard, MA.1982.

[Simmons 1998] G. J. Simmons, "The History of Subliminal Channels," *IEEE Journal on Selected Areas in Communication*, vol. 16, no. 4, May 1998.

[Smulders 1991] S. A. Smulders, *Control of freeway traffic flow,* CWI Tract, Amterdam, 1991.

[Snort 2003] http://www.snort.org

[Sole 2000] R. Sole and B. Goodwin, *Signs of Life*, Basic Books, New York, 2000.

[Son 2000] S. H. Son, R. Mukkamala, and R. David, "Integrating Security and Real-Time Requirements Using Covert Channel Capacity," *IEEE Transactions on Knowledge and Data Engineering*, vol. 12, no. 6, pp. 865-879, Nov./Dec. 2000.

[SPI 2003] "Internet worm infects state's big businesses," *Seattle Post-Intelligencer*, January 28, 2003, http://seattlepi.nwsource.com/business/106129_worm28.shtml

[Stallings 1995] W. Stallings, *Network and Internetwork Security*, Prentice Hall, Upper Saddle River, NJ, 1995.

[Staniford 2002] S. Staniford, V. Paxson, and N. Weaver, "How to own the Internet in your spare time," *USENIX Security Symposium*, pp. 149-167, Aug. 2002.

[Stauffer 1992] D. Stauffer, and A. Aharony, *Introduction to Percolation Theory*, Taylor & Francis, London, 1992.

[Stevens 1993] W. R. Stevens, *Advanced Programming in the UNIX Environment*, Addison-Wesley, Reading, MA, 1993.

[Stevens 1994] R. W. Stevens, *TCP/IP Illustrated*, Vol.s 1, 2, and 3, Addison-Wesley, Reading, MA, 1994.

[Storras 2001] R. Pastor-Storras and A. Vespignani, "Epidemic Spreading in Scale-Free Networks," Physical Review Letters, vol. 86, no. 14, pp. 3200-3203, 2 April 2001.

[Strother 2000] E. Strother, "Denial of service protection - the Nozzle," *Proceedings of the 16th Annual Computer Security Applications Conference* (ACSAC'00), pp. 32-41, 2000.

[Sun 1999] *Jini Technology Helper Utilities and Services Specification*, Sun Microsystems, Palo Alto, CA, 1999.

[Swaminathan 2000] V. Swaminathan and K. Chakrabarty, "Real-time task scheduling for energy-aware embedded systems", accepted for publication in *IEEE Real-Time Systems Symposium,* Orlando, FL, November 2000.

[Swankoski 2004] E. Swankoski, *Encryption and Security in SRAM FPGAs*, M. S. Thesis, Computer Science and Engineering Dept., The Pennsylvania State University, Spring 2004.

[Tanenbaum 1996] A. S. Tanenbaum, *Computer Networks*, Prentice Hall PTR, Upper Saddle River NJ, 1996.

[Tanenbaum 1997] A. S. Tanenbaum and A. S. Woodhull, *Operating Systems: Design and Implementation*, Prentice Hall, Upper Saddle River, NJ, 1997.

[Tennenhouse 1997] D. L. Tennenhouse, et al, "A Survey of Active Network Research," *IEEE Communications Magazine*, vol. 35, no. 1, pp. 80-86, Jan. 1997.

[Thompson 1984] K. Thompon, "Reflections on trusting trust," *Communications of the ACM*, vol. 27, no. 8, pp. 761-763.

[Thompson 2003] M. R. Thompson, A. Essiaria, and S. Mudumbai, "Certificate-based Authorization Policy in a PKI Environment," *ACM Transactions on Information and System Security*, vol. 6, No. 4, pp. 566-588, Nov. 2003.

[Tipton 2003] H. F. Tipton and M. Krause, ed.s *Information Security Management Handbook*, CRC Press, Boca Raton, FL, 2003.

[Toxen 2003] B. Toxen, *Real World Linux Security*, Prentice Hall PTR, Upper Saddle River, NJ, 2003.

[Tsai 1990] C-. R. Tsai, V. D. Gligor, C. S. Chandersekaran, "On the Identification of Covert Storage Channels in Secure Systems," *IEEE Transactions on Software Engineering*, vol. 16, no. 6, pp. 569-580, June 1990.

[Tschudin 1993] C.-F. Tschudin de Bâle-ville, *On the Structuring of Computer Communications*, Ph.D. Dissertation, Informatique, Université de Genève, 1993.

[van Creveld 1980] M. L. Van Creveld, *Supplying War: Logistics from Wallenstein to Patton*, Cambridge University Press, Cambridge, UK, 1980.

[van Creveld 1986] van Creveld, M. L., *Command in War,* Harvard University Press, Cambridge, MA, 1986.

[Vijaykrishnan 1998] N. Vijaykrishnan, N. Ranganathan and R. Gadekarla. *Object-oriented architectural support for a Java processor*. In Lecture Notes in Computer Science, Vol. 1445, pp. 330-354, Springer Verlag, July 1998.

[Volchenkov 2002] D. Volchenkov and Ph. Blanchard, "An algorithm generating scale free graphs," arXiv:cond-mat:/0204126v1, Apr 2002.

[von Neumann 1966] J. von Neumann, *Theory of self-reproducing automata,* A. W. Burks, ed., University of Illinois Press, Urbana, IL, 1966.

[VINT 2002] *Virtual InterNetwork Testbed*, 2002. http://www/isi.edu/nsnam/VINT

[Wang 1995] Y. Wang, "Jump and sharp cusp detection by wavelets," Biomertika, Vol. 82, No. 2, pp. 385-397, 1995.

[Wang 1999] Y. Wang, "Change-points via wavelets for indirect data," *Statistica Sinica,* Vol. 9, No. 1, pp. 103-117, 1999.

[Wang 2002] H. Wang, D. Zhang, and K. G. Shin, "Detecting SYN Flooding Attacks," Proceedings of IEEE-Infocom 2002.

[Ware 1996] W. H. Ware, *the Cyber-Posture of the National Information Infrastructure*, Rand Corporation, Santa Monica, CA, 1996. http://www.rand.org/publications/MR/MR976/mr976.html

[Watts 1999] D. J. Watts, *Small Worlds*, Princeton University Press, Princeton, NJ, 1999

[Watts 2001] D. J. Watts, S. H. Strogatz, and M. E. J. Newman, Personal correspondence.

[Weiser 1991] M. Weiser, "The Computer for the 21st Century," *Scientific American*, pp. 94-100, Sept. 1991.

[Weiss 2000] A. Weiss, "Out of thin air," *Networker*, vol.4, no.4, pp. 18-23, December 2000.

[Weisstein 1999] E. W. Weisstein, *CRC Concise Encyclopedia of Mathematics*, Chapman & Hall / CRC Press, Boca Raton, FL, 1999.

[Willinger 1997] W. Willinger, M. S. Taqqu, R. Sherman, and D. V. Wilson, "Self-Similarity Through High- Variability: Statistical Analysis of Ethernet LAN Traffic at the Source Level," *IEEE/ACM Trans. on Networking*, vol. 5, no. 1, pp. 71-86, Feb. 1997.

[Willinger 1998] W. Willinger, and V. Paxson, "Where Mathematics Meets the Ineternet," *Notices of the American Mathematical Society*, vol. 45, no. 8, pp. 961-971, Sept. 1998.

[Wired 2001] "Scary hybrid Internet worm loose," Sept. 18 2001, http://www.wired.com/news/technology/0,1282,46944,00.html

[Wired 2001a] "Bin Laden: Steganography Master?" Feb. 7, 2001, http://www.wired.com/news/politics/0,1283,41658,00.html?tw=wn_story_page_prev2

[Wokoma 2002] I. Wokoma, I. Liabotis, O. Prnjat, L. Sacks, I. Marshall, "A Weakly Coupled Adaptive Gossip Protocol for Application Level Active Networks," *IEEE 3rd International Workshop on Policies for Distributed Systems and Networks*, 2002.

[Wolf 2001] Wayne Wolf, *Computer as components: The art of Embedded System Programming*, Morgan Kaufmann, San Francisco, 2001.

[Wolfram 1994] S. Wolfram, *Cellular Automata and Complexity*. Addison-Wesley, Reading, MA, 1994.

[Wu 1999] D. Wu, D. Agrawal, and A. Abbadi, "StratOSphere: Unification of Code, Data, Location, Scope and Mobility," *Proc. of the International Symposium on Distributed Objects and Applications*, pp. 12-23, 1999.

[Wu 2003] Q. Wu, *Control of Trasport Dynamics in Overlay Networks*, Ph.D. Dissertation, Dept. of Computer Science, Louisiana State University, 2003.

[Xiao 2002] H. Xiao, "BGP Security Issues and Countermeasures," http://cs.gmu.edu/~hxiao/BGP%20security.pdf, 2002.

[Ye 2000] W. Ye, N. Vijaykrishnan, M. Kandemir, and M. J. Irwin, "The Design and Use of SimplePower: A Cycle-Accurate Energy Estimation Tool". *Design Automation Conference,* June 2000.

[Yee 1994] B. Yee, *Using Secure Coprocessors*, Ph.D. Dissertation, Computer Science, Carnegie Mellon University, 1994.

[Yip 2000] K. W. Yip and T. S. Ng, "Partial-Encryption Technique for Intellectual Property Protection of FPGA-Based Prodcuts," *IEEE Transactions on Consumer Electronics,* pp. 183-190, Feb. 2000.

[Young 2003] M. Young, R. R. Brooks, and S. Rai, "Testing Denial of Service (DoS) Detetection Methods," *Internet Computing,* submitted for review, March 2003.

[Zachary 2002] J. Zachary, R. R. Brooks, and D. Thompson, "Secure Integration of Building Networks into the Global Internet," *NIST GCR 02-837, National Institute of Standards and Technology*, US Dept. of Commerce, Gaithersburg, MD, Oct. 2002.

[Zachary 2003] J. M. Zachary and R. R. Brooks, "Bidirectional Mobile Code Trust Management Using Tamper Resistant Hardware," *Mobile Networks and Applications*, 8, pp. 137-143, 2003.

[Zavas 1987] E. Zayas, "Attacking the Process Migration Bottleneck," *Proceedings of the 11th ACM Symposium on Operating Systems Principles,* pp. 13-24, Nov. 1987.

[Zhou 1996] K. Zhou, J. C. Doyle, and K. Glover, *Robust and Optimal Control,* Prentice Hall, Upper Saddle River, NJ, 1996.

[Zhu 2004] M. Zhu, R. R. Brooks, J. Lamb, and S. S. Iyengar, "Aspect oriented design of sensor networks," *Journal of Parallel and Distributed Computing* Special Issue on Sensor Networks, In Press, Jan. 2004.

[Zimmerli 1984] E. Zimmerli and K. Liebl, *Computermissbrauch Computersicherheit: Faelle-Abwehr-Abdechung*, Peter Hohl Verlag, Zurich, 1984.

[Zou 2002] C. C. Zou, W. Gong, and D. Towsley, "Code Red Worm Propagation Modeling and Analysis," *CCS'02*, Washington DC, Nov 18-22, 2002.

Index

T - #0082 - 101024 - C0 - 234/156/21 [23] - CB - 9780849322723 - Gloss Lamination